CHILDHOOD REVISITED

CHILDHOOD REVISITED

EDITED BY

Joel I. Milgram

Dorothy June Sciarra

University of Cincinnati

Foreword by James L. Hymes, Jr.

MACMILLAN PUBLISHING CO., INC.
New York

Macmillan Publishing Co., Inc.
866 Third Avenue, New York, New York 10022

Collier-Macmillan Canada, Ltd., Toronto, Ontario

Library of Congress Cataloging in Publication Data

Milgram, Joel I.   comp.
   Childhood revisited.

   1. Autobiographies. I. Sciarra, Dorothy June, joint comp. II. Title.
CT120.M54   920   73–1038
ISBN 0–02–381120–X

Printing: 1 2 3 4 5 6 7 8   Year: 4 5 6 7 8 9 80

ACKNOWLEDGMENTS

JOAN BAEZ
From *Daybreak* by Joan Baez. Copyright © 1966, 1968 by Joan Baez. Reprinted by permission of the publisher, The Dial Press.

CHRISTIAAN BARNARD
Reprinted with permission of Macmillan Publishing Co., Inc. from *One Life* by Christiaan Barnard and Curtis Bill Pepper. Copyright © 1969 by Christiaan Neethling Barnard.

BERNARD BARUCH
From *Baruch—My Own Story* by Bernard M. Baruch. Copyright © 1957 by Bernard M. Baruch. Reprinted by permission of Holt, Rinehart and Winston, Inc..

GERTRUDE EDELSTEIN BERG
From *Molly and Me* by Gertrude Berg. Copyright © 1961. Reprinted by permission of Lewis Berg.

GERALD BRENAN
Reprinted with the permission of Farrar, Straus & Giroux, Inc. and Hamish Hamilton, London from *A Life of One's Own* by Gerald Brenan, copyright © 1962 by Gerald Brenan.

CHARLES SPENCER CHAPLIN
From *My Autobiography* by Charles Chaplin copyright © 1964 by Charles Chaplin. Reprinted by permission of The Bodley Head, Ltd., London.

JAMES CONANT
From pp. 9–16 *My Several Lives* by James Conant. Copyright © 1970 by James B. Conant. By permission of Harper & Row, Publishers, Inc.

DWIGHT DAVID EISENHOWER
From *At Ease: Stories I Tell to Friends* by Dwight D. Eisenhower. Copyright © 1967 by Dwight D. Eisenhower. Reprinted by permission of Doubleday & Company, Inc.

DICK GREGORY
From the book *nigger: An Autobiography* by Dick Gregory with Robert Lipsyte. Copyright © 1964 by Dick Gregory Enterprises, Inc. Published by E. P. Dutton & Co., Inc. and used with their permission.

JOHN HOLLOWAY
Reprinted by permission of Charles Scribner's Sons from *A London Childhood* by John Holloway. Copyright 1966 John Holloway.

CHET HUNTLEY
Condensed from pages 31–95 of *The Generous Years* by Chet Huntley. Copyright © 1968 by Chet Huntley. Reprinted by permission of Random House, Inc.

CHRISTINE JORGENSEN
From *Christine Jorgensen: A Personal Autobiography*. Copyright © 1967 by Christine Jorgensen. Reprinted by permission of Paul S. Eriksson, Inc., Publisher.

HELEN KELLER
From *The Story of My Life* by Helen Keller. Reprinted by permission of Doubleday & Company, Inc.

ARTHUR KOESTLER
Reprinted with permission from Macmillan Publishing Co., Inc. from *Arrow in the Blue* by Arthur Koestler. Copyright © Arthur Koestler 1952, 1969. Reprinted by permission of A. D. Peters & Company.

ELMER VERNER MCCOLLUM
From *From Kansas Farm Boy to Scientist: The Autobiography of Elmer Verner McCollum*. Copyright 1964 © by Elmer Verner McCollum. Reprinted by permission of the University of Kansas Press, Lawrence, Kansas.

ACKNOWLEDGEMENTS

JOHN D. MCKEE
From *Two Legs to Stand On* by John D. McKee. Copyright © 1955 by John D. McKee. Reprinted by permission of Hawthorn Books, Inc.

ROBERT MERRILL
Reprinted with permission from Macmillan Publishing Co., Inc. from *Once More from the Beginning* by Robert Merrill with Sandford Dody. Copyright © Robert Merrill and Sandford Dody, 1965.

ANNE MOODY
From *Coming of Age in Mississippi* by Anne Moody. Copyright © 1968 by Anne Moody. Reprinted by permission of the publisher, The Dial Press.

KWAME NKRUMAH
From *Ghana: Autobiography of Kwame Nkrumah*, first published in London in 1957. Panaf Books Limited, 243 Regent Street, London W1R 8PN, UK.

GEORGE ORWELL
From *Such, Such Were the Joys* by George Orwell, copyright 1945, 1952, 1953 by Sonia Brownell Orwell. Reprinted by permission of Harcourt Brace Jovanovich, Inc. and Mrs. Sonia Brownell Orwell and Secker & Warburg.

SATCHEL PAIGE
From *Maybe I'll Pitch Forever* by Satchel Paige as told to David Lipman. Copyright © 1962 by David Lipman. Copyright © 1961 by Curtis Publishing Company. Reprinted by permission of Doubleday and Company, Inc.

ELEANOR ROOSEVELT
Abridged from pp. 5–17 *The Autobiography of Eleanor Roosevelt*. Copyright © 1937 by Anna Eleanor Roosevelt. By permission of Harper & Row, Publishers.

LILLIAN ROTH
From *I'll Cry Tomorrow* by Lillian Roth. Copyright © 1954 by Lillian Roth. Reprinted by permission of the publisher, Frederick Fell, Inc.

JEAN-PAUL SARTRE
George Braziller, Inc.—from *The Words* by Jean-Paul Sartre; translated from the French by Bernard Frechtman; reprinted with the permission of the publisher. English translation copyright © 1964 by George Braziller, Inc.

HELEN SEKAQUAPTEWA
Reprinted by permission from *Me and Mine: The Life Story of Helen Sekaquaptewa, As Told to Louise Udall*, Tucson: University of Arizona Press, copyright 1969.

UPTON SINCLAIR
From *The Autobiography of Upton Sinclair*. Copyright © 1962 by Upton Sinclair. Reprinted by permission of Bertha Klausner International Literary Agency, Inc.

LINCOLN STEFFENS
From *The Autobiography of Lincoln Steffens*, copyright, 1931, by Harcourt Brace Jovanovich, Inc.; renewed, 1959, by Peter Steffens. Reprinted by permission of the publishers.

DYLAN THOMAS
Dylan Thomas, *Quite Early One Morning*. Copyright 1954 by New Directions Publishing Corporation. Reprinted by permission of New Directions Publishing Corporation. Reprinted in Canada by permission of J. M. Dent & Sons, Ltd., Publishers and the Trustees for the Copyrights of the late Dylan Thomas.

MARK VAN DOREN
Reprinted with permission of the author from *The Autobiography of Mark Van Doren* by Mark Van Doren. Copyright © 1958 by Mark Van Doren. Republished by Greenwood Press, 1968.

WILLIAM ALLEN WHITE
Reprinted with permission of Macmillan Publishing Co., Inc. from *The Autobiography of William Allen White* by William Allen White. Copyright 1946 by Macmillan Publishing Co., Inc.

To Ivo, Mary, Leslie, Toni, Ian, and Jason
and to our many supportive students and colleagues

FOREWORD

For many long years our society acted as if nothing happened "down there" in the years of childhood. Life—rightly spelled with a capital L—presumably began at some later time. This is no longer most people's understanding. Most *know*—an intellectual feat—that the childhood years are of great importance.

Two areas of incompleteness persist, however. We are intellectually aware of childhood but are not yet emotionally involved in it. Our knowledge does not move us into any massive action on behalf of children. What little we do is well publicized, but this obscures how little it is that we do: in health, in recreation, in psychological services, in education, in preventive efforts, in enrichment efforts, and in curative efforts.

More important, perhaps, is the confusion about the real importance of the childhood years. The tendency is to assume that the years are important because we now realize they are available to *us*— to adults. We have "discovered" childhood—discovered that we can manipulate and move and manage children for ends *we* think are important.

There is too little willingness to believe that the childhood years of life are important to the *child*—to the human living them. Too little willingness to believe that the childhood years of life are important *at the time*—to the human living them.

This provocative, intriguing, so-human collection of memories can be a means of helping to put the matter to rights: The importance of these years is to the human experiencing them, not to the outsider who so often becomes the exploiter. And I must add that I can't think of a more painless way . . . . That says it too mildly. I can't think of a more pleasant way . . . . That says it too blandly. I can't think of a more *absorbing* way of seeing that children hurt and they hate. They fear, and they are frustrated. They have their hopes. They are disappointed, they are elated . . . . They are human.

James L. Hymes, Jr.

Carmel Valley, California

viii

CONTENTS

CROSS-REFERENCE CHART

INTRODUCTION

"After several such skirmishes, Uncle Luther decided that something had to be done. He took an old broom and cut off all the straw, leaving a short, hard knob. He showed me how to swing the weapon, then took me out and announced that I was on my own. More frightened at the moment of my uncle's possible scolding than of the gander's aggression, I took what was meant to be a firm, but was really a trembling, stand next time the fowl came close. Then I let out a yell and rushed toward him, swinging the club. He turned and I gave him a satisfying smack right on the fanny. He let out a squawk and ran off. From then on I was the proud boss of the backyard. I had learned never to negotiate with an adversary except from a position of strength."

"The teacher thought I was stupid. Couldn't spell, couldn't read, couldn't do arithmetic. Just stupid. Teachers were never interested in finding out that you couldn't concentrate because you were so hungry, because you hadn't had any breakfast. All you could think about was noontime, would it ever come? Maybe you could sneak into the cloakroom and steal a bite of some kid's lunch out of a coat pocket. A bite of something. Paste. You can't really make a meal of paste, or put it on bread for a sandwich, but sometimes I'd scoop a few spoonfuls out of the big paste jar in the back of the room. Pregnant people get strange tastes. I was pregnant with poverty. Pregnant with dirt and pregnant with smells that made people turn away, pregnant with cold and pregnant with shoes that were never bought for me, pregnant with five other people in my bed and no Daddy in the next room, and pregnant with hunger. Paste doesn't taste too bad when you're hungry."

"The major part of my childhood was spent in fighting off terror of things which don't exist, and I don't think my father ever understood that kind of fear. The overriding and most terrifying bogeyman of my life, which has been with me since my earliest memories, and remains faithfully with me though now it seldom puts me out of commision, has been a fear of vomiting."

THE stuff that memories are made of—memories of childhood. Disturbing? Frightening? Fascinating? If we tell you that the foregoing are glimpses into the early lives of well-known personalities, can you find the Eisenhower, the Dick Gregory, and the Joan Baez in these quotes? Each one is there. How did each become the person we know? How important were these early experiences in his life? Did your early experiences determine who you are? Who *are* you?

You are an adult now, independent in your thinking and aware of your surroundings. You proceed through life adjusting and adapting and constantly seeking and reaching for a vague, elusive happiness in a sometimes not-so-happy world. Although you often experience difficulty in seeking an identity, you need not be an expert to know why you are you. In many ways you are your parents, for they were your first and often your strongest influences. You are your brothers and sisters, your grandparents and your neighborhoods. You are you because of your second-grade teacher's comments about your poor posture and the traffic policeman's smile as you crossed the busy street. You are you because your father had a mustache that tickled when he kissed you goodnight, and you are you because Winnie-the-Pooh was your friend and a cap pistol was kept under your pillow to fight off whatever creatures lurked in your room. We are our past, and our past can be dramatically revealing. That is how this book came to be written.

The book is a collection of excerpts from autobiographies of individuals who have attempted to explore and describe their pasts— their beginnings. In effect, each individual discloses why he is what he is.

Autobiographies can be a rich field of exploration for those interested in the study of child development and its related fields, as they provide a vehicle for the study of the forces at work in childhood that shape and influence the personality. As teachers, we feel this approach can be used in the study of child development, early childhood education, guidance of behavior, psychology, and home and family life. When we have used it, students' reactions to this method have been overwhelmingly favorable. What better reason for putting this book together and passing it on to you?

CRITERIA FOR SELECTION OF EXCERPTS

Readability as well as diversity were among the several criteria used to select the excerpts included in this volume. We have chosen writers whose styles not only are exciting but also show some depth of introspection into life's experiences. We have attempted to represent as many of the facets of childhood as possible: thus you will find lives described in rural as well as urban settings—in ghettos as well as lavish estates. Some of the individuals were brought up within the context of the extended family, whereas others were forced to manage with one or no parent. They lived in various countries and cultures, many claiming happy childhoods—others recalling only misery.

Death, jealousy, trust, sibling rivalry, and sexual encounters are among the many experiences described by the authors. Although these general themes can be noted, the reader will also find each selection uniquely different.

The individuals represented in this book are men and women of this century; therefore, our approach is not a historical one. However, one can still see trends in child-rearing during the past 75 years as older writers describe their Victorian upbringings and contrast these with their observations of the modern family.

Finally, we have elected to use childhood experiences up to, but not including, the developmental stage of adolescence. This decision was an arbitrary one and is in no way meant to demean the importance of the adolescent experience on the developing personality.

LIMITATIONS OF THIS APPROACH

This approach, like others, has limitations that should be borne in mind. An autobiographer's subjective interpretation of his own childhood necessarily places restrictions on the validity of those interpretations. Furthermore, subjective views written for the public are subject to both the bias and the constraints of conscious recall; each individual gives his personal perception of his own childhood. However, the subjectivity of these insights is also their strength, because it is what the individual chose to tell and the very act of choosing that is significant.

This collection of readings provides supplementary material for the study of young children and, therefore, is not regarded by the editors as a substitute for a standard text. It includes many dimensions of childhood but is not all-inclusive. The subject areas that are dealt with here can be studied in greater depth by using other resource materials.

ORGANIZATIONAL FEATURES OF THE BOOK

The autobiographical excerpts appear in alphabetical order by author; however, this organizational feature of the book does not dictate that it be read in that sequence. Indeed, for the reader who is interested in a particular aspect of child development, the Cross-Reference Chart (p. xiv), which immediately follows the Contents, will be more useful. It is possible, through this chart, to quickly identify those selections that have common themes.

A short biographical sketch appears at the beginning of each excerpt. Although many of the authors are well-known personalities, some of them may require an introduction. Knowing something about the achievement of the person in adult life will help the reader appreciate more fully the influences of childhood experiences.

The discussion and inquiry section at the end of each excerpt is a guide for discussion and further study. The richness of each selection precluded complete discussion coverage of all the influential features of childhood for each personality; however, in each case, many salient features of the childhood experience have been culled from the excerpts. The questions posed are not necessarily answered within the selections but, rather, are meant to provide a basis for a discussion of general issues. It is through the understanding of these broader issues that the reader will gain insights into the field of child development.

SUGGESTED ACTIVITIES

There are a variety of ways in which this book can be used. The ideas presented here are necessarily limited to the imagination of the editors. However, those who use the book can lend their own creative talents to its uses.

For many of you, there will be a natural inclination to read the complete autobiography of some of the personalities. We encourage you to do so, for in most cases the description of an author's life as an adult will further emphasize the influence of his childhood experiences.

Working with the selections in this book of readings may also kindle an interest in your writing the biography of a parent or sibling, or trying your hand at writing an autobiography. This might indeed be the most exciting and creative activity to come out of working with the book. Delve into your own past and attempt to evaluate your feelings about it while relating those feelings to the self you experience today. This conscious effort at recalling and relating those feelings can be both provocative and satisfying to someone interested in understanding human behavior.

J. I. M.
D. J. S.

Joan Baez

BIOGRAPHICAL SKETCH

Joan Baez, best known as a folksinger who is committed to nonviolence, is the daughter of Mexican-Irish parents. Born in 1941, she lived with her family in a number of foreign countries as well as in New York, California, and Boston. She started singing and playing the guitar when she was a teen-ager, although folk music did not interest her until the late 50s, when she began making public appearances. She married David Harris in 1968; he was later sent to jail for resisting the draft. The two of them used their talents to express their political concerns. Joan founded the Institute for the Study of Nonviolence in Palo Alto, California, in 1965.

SELECTIONS FROM

DAYBREAK

MOTHER tells me that I came back from the first day of kindergarten and told her I was in love. I remember a Japanese boy who looked after me and wouldn't let anybody knock me around. When they gave us beans to eat in the morning I told him they'd make me sick, and he buried them under the table for me.

A Saint Bernard tried to play with me one afternoon and he rolled me down the hill. I was so terrified that I wet my pants.

There was a boy who drank milk with me. He picked flowers a lot, and I always wanted to pat his head. The kids called him a she-she boy.

I usually ran home in the morning with a stomach ache and got in bed and listened to Babar or Uncle Don's Nursery Rhymes. Once when I was sick Arthur Foster Bevelockway fell off the banister and knocked his front teeth out. I fell in love with him.

We moved.

I hated first grade. I hated "Red Rover, Red Rover, Let Joanie Come

1

Over," because it was easy to get hurt, and because I hated to be on a losing side, so I'd do anything, even cheat, to win.

One morning in second grade I ran to the girls' room and hung my head over the toilet to be sick; the teacher held my head but nothing happened. I think that was during arithmetic. The next time it happened I know it was during arithmetic. Pretty soon it was worked out that I could go to the teacher's room whenever I felt sick. I loved that. I could fall asleep. It was next best to being home.

One day I found a treasure. It was a silver key-chain, about one foot long. The kind you close by pushing the last little ball at each end into a silver latch. I stayed after school by myself and threw the chain up in the air over and over, watching it flash and glisten in the sun. I lay down in the deserted schoolyard and dropped the chain into my mouth and pulled it out all wet, whirling it around over my head until it was freezing cold and then lowering it onto my forehead in loop designs . . . Ecstasy. The afternoon ended in tragedy when I threw the chain in the air and it landed on the school roof. I was too stunned even to cry. And when I went to get my sweater there was a bumblebee on it and I was afraid to pick it up. I tried to reason with the bee, and then tried to shoo it away from a safe distance of three feet and finally, in a state of perfect terror and guilt, I stepped on it and ground my foot into the sweater to be sure the bee was dead.

About that time my career with men began to get really active. I remember chasing a Japanese boy around the entire schoolyard—under jungle-gyms and around swings. When I finally caught up to him he had stopped running and seemed to be staggering in slow motion. He was holding the top of his head and blood was mixed with the dust on his hands. He had cracked his head open on the metal merry-go-round. He was absent for a few days, and came back to school with a round spot shaved in the middle of his thick black hair and some dark stitches showing on a very white scalp. I felt guilty about him.

I found a snake one day and decided to stuff it the way they do in museums, so I got all the proper equipment: scissors, a bucket of water to keep things clean, some cotton for the stuffing and a needle and thread to sew it up. I become discouraged after his innards were all floating around in the bucket, and I figured he'd never look too good anyway, since his head had been run over to begin with, so I gave up and ripped a dead gopher apart with the neighbor boy. He took the head and I took the tail and we pulled. I did it to show how tough I could be, and to make my sister sick. She got sick and we put the gopher remains in a paper bag and left it behind the house.

I was the fastest runner in second grade. I knew how to draw a cow with huge udders and a tepee and a rooster standing on the right-hand side of the page with "Cock-a-doodle-doo" coming out of his beak from right to left in mirror writing. I envied everything about my older sister, Pauline, including the patch she had to wear over one eye, and I didn't care if my little sister, Mimi, lived or died. I had a beautiful dress that was red velvet on top and plaid satin on the bottom, which Mother finally let me wear to school, and I was the first person in the whole school to come down with pink eye. I loved the Sons of the Pioneers and Tex Ritter and "Last night I heard the wild goose cry" by Frankie Laine. I was crazy for fast vibratos. My mother passed by me in the kitchen one time and smoothed my forehead and said, "You look as if you were carrying the whole world on your shoulders." Once in the middle of the night I heard "The Star Spangled Banner," and I stood up in bed in my nightie and saluted until it was finished because I thought that's what you were supposed to do.

We moved.

Third grade was in the East. I got straight A's. A boy named Michael and I were the smartest ones in our class, and the time I got straight A's he got one A minus. He took it hard. Winter was a big thing for us kids. It snowed on Christmas Eve. We hung onto car bumpers after dinner when it was dark and slid on the ice for blocks. We used to sneak across the street and watch television through the neighbor's window —Kooklafrananolly. It was a small-minded little town, and one night the neighbors ran a wire from tree to tree around the entire house. As we were running across the yard to the bushes, I got it in the neck. The wire knocked me down and I lost my wind and hurt my head.

Another neighbor didn't like niggers or Mexicans or professors or kids, and I wasn't allowed on his lawn. Pauline was, because she was light.

The old lady next door lived with an old man who wasn't her husband and who didn't ever wear his teeth. The old lady's son was a criminal, and she kept his daughter. One night he came to town to claim his little girl. He was drunk and he had a knife and he backed the old lady, his mother, against the kitchen wall and said he was going to slit her open from here to here. She got out of it by telling him she had to go to the bathroom. One night Pauline and Mimi and the old lady's granddaughter and I were out in the old man's pigpen dumping things on the pig's head and getting nervous that we'd be caught, and in the middle of our whispering and hysterical giggles came a blinding flash of lightning followed almost immediately by a crack of thunder, which sounded as if it had come right from the pigpen. We didn't stop to look at each other. Home had never been so many paces away.

An evangelist came to town one spring. Mother took us kids to see him. He sang:

> Get the new look from the old book,
> Get the new look from the Bible.

All the women in town went to his meetings. I liked him—until he pointed at me and told me to pray out loud. I couldn't do it.

I was the school veterinarian, and the kids brought me all their animals when they were sick or even dead. I would draw pictures of the dead ones first and then bury them. One Friday I left a Baltimore oriole in my school desk, and on Monday the teacher walked into class and nearly fainted from the smell. I didn't know what the smell was until I opened my desk. It was pretty terrible. I'd never seen maggots before and I felt bad about the bird. I drew pictures of all of Disney's characters and sold them to the kids for two cents apiece. I lined the pennies up in the groove which was cut out for pencils.

I had a great friend named Lily. She was some weird religion, and her parents wouldn't let her cut her hair. She lived on a farm across from a pea cannery, and Lily and I slept up in her hayloft. She could yodel and she said her S's so clearly that they almost whistled, and her chin moved in a way that I could watch for hours. At the end of fourth grade she gave me a going-away present. It was a chopped-off chicken leg with the tendons all sticking out so that you could pull them and make the claws move separately. I kept it until it rotted.

There was a very poor and raggedy girl who lived just out of town, almost on top of the railroad tracks. She was thin and shy and unhealthy-looking and wore all hand-me-downs. She had no friends at all, and I used to go and play with her baby pigs. At the end of the year I went around to all the kids and their parents to collect money. I got thirteen dollars and Mother helped me get her a dress and some shoes and socks and a hair ribbon. She didn't know what was happening when the class presented her with the presents. I think she cried.

We moved.

In fifth grade we were in Southern California. There was a big black boy who looked after me. He was the first person to come up and say hello on the playground. He told me if there was anything I needed just let him know. A bunch of Mexican girls said they were going to beat me up on the way home from school, so I told David, and he walked me home every day until it was safe. There were three Nancys and two Carols in my class. I wasn't very popular because I was a new kid again and because I was a Mexican. I was skinny and very brown. I had a crush on Andy Crane, but he had a crush on my best friend, Sharon, and they used to kiss in the coat room after school and I would stand there and count for them. Count how long the kiss was.

I loved my teacher. He was the best elementary school teacher I ever had. His name was MacIntosh and we called him Mr. Mac. I think he liked me. One day in the schoolyard I called someone a son of a bitch at the top of my lungs and Mr. Mac called me in. He said, "I suppose you know what I have to talk to you about?" and I said, "If it's about what I said at recess, we both know that a bitch is a she-dog and there's nothing wrong with saying it," and he smiled. He made me feel as though we could understand, but the other kids couldn't, so I never said it again. He had a smooth forehead and pretty eyes.

I was still a fast runner, and when we had the big inter-school track meet, I would have won the footrace but this tall skinny super-athlete girl from another school entered at the last minute. Her teachers pushed her into the starting line at my place, which had little starting foot-blocks, and I had to take another place with no foot-blocks. I ran like the wind but could only come in second. She did the same thing at standing broad jump, and I got another red ribbon. She was a sixth-grader and not supposed to compete in our class. I could have killed her.

I thought I was kind of funny looking, but my mother and father said I had a million-dollar smile. For my tenth birthday they gave me a collie. It was too good to believe. He was just a puppy and we called him Professor Wooley. He had an especially long nose when he grew up, and a way of talking to me from his throat. I don't think he was very smart, but it was like a wonderful movie having my own dog. And it ended the way all of those movies end. Goodbye, Professor Wooley. . . .

We moved.

This time we were going to Baghdad, Iraq. We stopped overnight in a hotel in Lebanon and the shower and sink and wall toilet were all in one closet. You could go to the bathroom and take a shower at the same time. We didn't sleep much because it was hot and the sounds were so foreign. My father and his flock had never smelled anything like those smells. The next day, on the way to the airport bus, I was running my hand along a park fence and all of a sudden there was bare flesh under my hand. It was the swollen tummy of a half-naked beggar boy. The airplane from Lebanon to Baghdad was flown by Middle Eastern Airways and it was hot in the front and freezing in the back, and filled with flies. The first thing we saw when we landed in Baghdad was an old beggar being beaten and poked at by the police. It put my soul in anguish. We stayed at the Semiramis Hotel and all got diarrhea. I watched Arab men in their pretty robes eat rice and lamb with their hands. They were very graceful with their hands, but their faces were coarse and ugly. We saw round boats floating down the Tigris. One time we saw a dead horse doing the same thing. He looked like a balloon made of hide. We stayed at the YMCA for a while and I ate rice cakes and dates and threw up. We were all pretty sick. Pauline lived in the bathroom for about three days and we finally had to call a doctor. The doctor was a big mannish woman who said we must eat lebon, which was yogurt, but I wouldn't touch it and I think we eventually stayed alive on mashed bananas. I had jaundice too. They took me to the hospital three times and I finally showed the doctor my palms and the soles of my feet and explained that the reason they were yellow was because I had jaundice and he said, "Oh, you think so?" I was getting sicker and sicker and the last time we went they took blood from my arm and when I tried to get up and walk I fainted in a chair. They said, "Bring her back tomorrow and we'll see what the tests tell us." My mother said, "No. You get her a bed here. Now." They got me one. "Second floor, madam," said the doctor. "You carry her. She's not taking another step." Someone carried me and put me in a bed. Later that day I asked to be moved to the bed near the window and they moved me and made up the old bed without changing the sheets. I now looked out over the main street in town. Al Rashid Street. I could look down and see red double-decker English buses and skinny horses, and camels; there was an overwhelming smell of exhaust. Once I saw a man carrying a piano on his back. After two days in the hospital I asked them if they could give me a bath and two giggling Arab nurses came in and washed me, all but my private parts, which they kept covered with a towel. I got so angry I sent them out of the room and washed myself. Mother brought me home. I was very sick for a long time. When I was on my feet again I saw some amazing things. Women came to eat out of our garbage can. I wrapped up some cake once and put it in the garbage. I watched a woman open the package and frown. She didn't know what it was. I tried to motion to her to eat it, but she wouldn't. I guess she just didn't trust me.

Once I gave a crazy old beggar lady some coins. She put them in her mouth. I had no food on me so I gave her my Chiclets. She took them out of the box and put the box in her mouth.

There was a big wall around our house. In the next yard a family lived in a mud hut. The children had one robe apiece for clothing, and when one washed his robe, he went naked until it was dry.

My father was having a Quaker meeting in the house one day and I didn't want to interrupt it, but the neighbors on the left side of our house were beating a puppy to death in an upstairs window. They had him cornered in the screen, which was caving out, and they were stoning him. I screamed at them in Arabic to give me the dog and they thought that was a real joke. He died, probably of fright. I've seldom known such anguish. I looked after all the dogs in the neighborhood. The dog across the street was named Tarzan. He belonged to the servant girl. When she'd call him he'd run up, wagging his tail, then crouch to the ground and cower. She'd kick him in the head. I think he loved her anyway. It was all they knew. One day the master of the house called Tarzan over and when the dog crouched in front of him, the man shot him in the head and killed him. I was happy.

That same awful man brought us some pigeons for a gift. He said they'd make good pets, only you had to cut their wings. We said, oh no, we liked them better with their wings on, but he was suspicious, and he sat right there, talking and clipping their wings in front of us. Pauline and Mimi and I looked at each other in sorrow and exasperation. We put the birds on the roof, where we planned to keep them until their wings grew back, and then let them go. But the big terrible Bull-bull birds attacked and killed one of the pigeons and pecked the other's eyes out. I saw it first and was almost hysterical with hate for the Bull-bulls and agony for the pigeons. We built a little house for the bird that was left, but in his blindness he wandered out into the sun and was also killed. Now I think that a child might be reading this and I won't tell any more painful things. Just that the dog I loved best, named Findick, knew that we were leaving Baghdad, and while Pauline packed all the trunks, because Mother was sick, Findick sat and watched us and quit wagging his tail. Every night as I was going to sleep on the flat roof of our house, I would pray to the Big Dipper that Findick would die so he couldn't suffer when we'd gone. . . . And now I know that he must be dead, because all of that happened seventeen years ago, and dogs over there have short lives, to say nothing of the people.

We left Baghdad.

We went to Switzerland for a month, where I drank too much milk because we hadn't had real milk in eight months. Wild strawberries grew around the chalet where we lived. We stayed for a while in a place where they didn't allow liquor. One day Pauline and Mimi and some friends we'd met and I ran off to play in the woods. We were playing Follow the Leader, and Pauline noticed a man watching us from behind a tree. . . . Every time we looked back at him he had moved a little closer, and it was getting very spooky. We were about to take off for home when I thought of a plan. We ran up to him and danced around him like Indians and then stopped and puffed on a big stick and handed it to him saying, "Smokum peace pipe." He went away.

We visited Rome for two days and went on a bus tour to the Vatican and some museums. I was so tired that I held Mother's hand and walked along with my eyes closed and asked her to tell me if there was anything especially pretty and I would look. I woke up for the Sistine Chapel.

We moved back to Southern California. The big black boy was still there to look after me. And the problem with the Mexicans was still there. I became best friends with a girl who was Mexican but refused to speak Spanish. She did everything that she could to be like the popular kids. I was jealous of her because she had fifteen stick-out slips, and I had three, which I wore every day and ironed with wax paper at night to make them stiff again.

I wore undershirts until the girls, trying to be nice, asked me when I would start wearing a bra. I was completely flat-chested but bought the tiniest bra made and stuffed it with all sorts of things to pad it up . . . Kleenex and bits of material. I worried constantly about the rings under my eyes, and some days I wouldn't go to school because I thought I looked so awful. My socks belled at the top and I had a forehead full of pimples. My parents went on saying that I had a million-dollar smile. I thought that it was all I had. Mother always told me I was much better than pretty but my father didn't understand that I needed to hear something aside from the fact that I had a million-dollar smile.

Eighth grade was the same as seventh. We had a nice girls' principal. She was fat and kind and let me go home when I was too down to stand it. Some of the popular kids were kind to me. They all *liked* me, but it was a risk for them to treat me as anything aside from sort of a witty court jester when we were in public.

I was the best artist in school and when school elections came around I made posters for everyone I knew. I even made them for both the guys who were running for president. That's how badly I wanted to have friends, and that's how much I cared about class officers.

In the middle of all that hell there was a man who threw me a lifeline. He was our family doctor. He told me I could come to his office whenever I wanted. Just walk in. One time I left class and walked to his office. I hadn't eaten anything solid for about three days. I was living on a sick, hot and cold energy. He told me I was not ill, and he gave me a pill which he said would help me relax. He said just to rest there as long as I wanted and if I needed him, to call. Then he went off to see his other patients.

Half an hour later I was starving hungry, and about that time he walked in with a milkshake and a hamburger and took time to talk to me. He told me that I was not ordinary pretty, but beautiful. He said that the girls at school whom I envied so much were burning themselves out. Just when they had burned themselves completely out, I would be starting to show that I was something special. I said yeah, but what about the rings under my eyes, and he said they were very fashionable, that women paid money to make their eyes dark like that. He said I was beautiful. And that was the beginning of the end of my childhood and the beginning of the end of the sorrow that came with

8

seeing myself as a skinny brown friendly knock-kneed flat-chested artistic bold black-haired outcast with a million-dollar smile.

. . .

The major part of my childhood was spent in fighting off terror of things which don't exist, and I don't think my father ever understood that kind of fear. The overriding and most terrifying bogeyman of my life, which has been with me since my earliest memories, and remains faithfully with me though now it seldom puts me out of commission, has been a fear of vomiting. It has used up and wasted and blackened many hours of my life. But my father never had a notion of what I was talking about when I cried and shook and said, "You know . . . It's that thing again. . . ." While I was in junior high school and even high school, I was still going to my parents' bedroom, sometimes five nights a week, and climbing in their bed, all hot and cold and shaking, pleading for Mother to say the key sentences which would begin to send the fear away. Always I felt dreadfully ill. Always I wanted to hear only one thing: "You won't be sick." Always I kept my food down, though the nausea was so extreme that anyone in his right mind would have stuck his fingers down his throat and been done with it. My father would follow Mother and me to the bathroom in the middle of the night, and as I sat on the toilet clutching their hands, he would pat my head and say things to Mother like, "Did she eat something funny?" or "S'pose she's got a little bug?" and Mother would shake her head and signal him that he was saying the wrong thing again. Once, as I was crawling into bed crying, and Mother was moving over to give me room, mumbling to me that everything would be all right, my father half woke up and said to Mother in a soft voice which had shades of annoyance, "What's the matter with her? Is it her stomach?" I think I said, "No, it's my head," and the degree to which my anger rose equaled the degree to which the nausea sank. One time my mother was out of the house, and I had a bad attack of whatever you would call that terror, and I had no one to call but my father. I was crying, and I told him what to say. "Just tell me I won't throw up. You know I won't, so just tell me I don't have to."

"What's so bad about throwing up?" he asked. Those perfectly reasonable words threw me into a fresh panic and I let go of his arm and covered my ears and sobbed and said, "No, no, don't say that, you can't say that. . . ."

"Look," he said, "right now there must be a hundred sick Arabs throwing up this very minute. It's nothing. You just, blughh, and it's over, and then you feel great. . . ." That was advice I was in no way ready to hear, and I simply hated him for it. He has to admit now that the doctors I've seen over the past ten years have been a great help to me. But his general feeling is that psychiatry is for the rich, and one

9

could rise above time-consuming phobias (which, I'm convinced, are as foreign to him as the joy of physics is to me) and carry on in a healthy manner if one only had enough to do. In a sense I agree with him.

DISCUSSION AND INQUIRY

It is clear from this selection that the Baez family moved frequently and lived in various parts of the world. Such an experience for the child under 12 must have certainly provided a great deal of stimulus and general knowledge of other cultures. Joan's memory of Iraq seemed mostly filled with impressions of poverty. Do you think that exposure to other cultures will influence the degree of ethnocentrism and prejudice among children?

Joan expresses several fears and anxieties; fear of the bee in her sweater, fear of getting hurt playing "Red Rover" in the first grade, fear of vomiting. Childhood fears are common, but some are more characteristic at certain ages and stages. There are those childhood fears that stay with us into adulthood. What interpretation can you give to Joan's fear of vomiting, which apparently has stayed with her to some degree? Can you identify childhood fears you still have and interpret them? Are childhood fears related to the sex of the individual?

Joan's "million-dollar smile" was not enough to vanquish her poor feelings about her physical appearance. The doctor's explanation to Joan about becoming something special just as the other pretty girls were burning themselves out was clearly an attempt to improve her self-image. Do you think his explanation was a psychologically sound one? Baez's sensitivity as a child to the underdog (both human and canine) comes through. Does her present activity in politics reflect this same sensitivity?

Christiaan Barnard

~~~~~~

BIOGRAPHICAL SKETCH

Christiaan Barnard is the surgeon who performed the first heart transplant. He grew up in South Africa; and it was there that he started his medical practice. He came to America to study open heart surgery, and performed the original heart transplant in 1967. His contributions to medicine are many. Among them are treatments for a number of formerly fatal children's diseases. Presently, he is a member of the Groote Schurr hospital staff in Capetown, South Africa, and is an associate professor at the University of Capetown Medical School.

~~~~~~

SELECTIONS FROM

ONE LIFE

PERHAPS the first time I doubted God could handle all the accidents of mankind occurred while attending a church service on New Year's Eve in Beaufort West, South Africa, where I grew up as a boy.

My mother was there to play the organ and I stood next to her. She was slightly deaf and a quick nudge was needed to start her off at the correct moment. I was expected also to fill the bellows of the organ, keeping the air pressure at a level marked by a little weight on a cord. This was done by pumping a hand lever, and often all my force—I was twelve then—was needed to keep the weight at its proper level.

Success depended largely upon what music was played. Light trills and runs did not affect the weight much. But deep notes and chords—especially in numbers such as "Many a Brave Heart Is Asleep in the Deep"—sent it soaring upward toward disaster. When this occurred, I pumped wildly to catch up, desperately aware that I could never provide sufficient wind for everyone to shout their love of the Lord—at least not long enough for it to count much or be heard very far.

Yet this evening had not gone too badly. Dominie Rabie, the minister, had dropped one hymn to pick up extra time for his New

11

Year's sermon, saving me a lot of work. So I imagined the service would end with the weight down low and my spirits on high.

The minister began by standing erect and wordless in his circular pulpit, until the congregation fell into obedient silence. Once I had entered the church at night and seen the devil in that same pulpit. He had long donkey ears, a tail crawling about like a snake, and a pitchfork long enough to skewer anybody, even in the back row. Now in the same spot stood Dominie Rabie—his little gray beard jumping up and down over the Bible as though it, too, was pointing the way—while behind him, beyond the organ pipes, lay dark shadows. The devil could be lurking there, hiding from the bright light which fell on a cloth draped over the lectern, bearing the golden words *Die Waarheid*— meaning in Afrikaans, The Truth.

Perhaps it was this and the late hour—the bells were soon to toll midnight—that caused me to remember this entire night so vividly, including the minister's first startling words.

"Add up all your sins for this past year and put them in a pile before you! [pause] Which one of us, I repeat which one of *you* can lift up his awful load? [pause] Or who among us can walk out of here without his back bent under his own terrible burden?"

I tried to figure out how big was my burden and if I could pick it up. But it was no use and I soon gave up. For how was it possible to put into one pile such differing events as cheating the city on dead mice, eating stolen candy, killing a cat, robbing an orchard, or touching a girl's leg under a wild apple bush? Besides, all of these happenings involved other people—some of them grownups. So whose pile did they belong in?

Take the mice, for example. The city paid one penny for every mouse. We caught them in traps and then, mouse in hand, ran down to the health department to receive a piece of paper worth one penny when presented at the City Hall. In order to get the paper, it was necessary to show the mouse to Tom, the caretaker, then raise the lid off a big drum full of corrosive Jeyes Fluid and drop it in.

That was theoretically the end of the mouse—but not always. If old Tom was not looking, we would drop the mouse behind the drum, bang down the lid, and take the receipt. Afterward, we would sneak back, grab the mouse and stuff it into a pocket—showing up again later in the day with the same old mouse for another penny.

Fanie Bekker claimed the largest mouse tally of four pence, but I came close to him with a little brown number that brought me a tickey, or three pennies, before its tail broke off. You had to work fast on them before something like that happened, or they got suspiciously stiff and too dangerous to handle.

12

Even so, I suspected Tom knew what was going on and was either kind to us or perhaps figured that a little extra money for one mouse would only drive us into catching many more in the long run. So he was either a partner in our crime or simply moved by good Christian charity. Whatever it was, the mice did not all belong in my pile.

Most certainly, Conradie, the fat policeman, was as guilty as we were in stealing fruit. This was really fun and always a success. It began by sneaking into the orchards on the south side of town, to gather pomegranates, apricots, quince, and lemons—big, thick ones you could eat without sugar. We would pick for a while, until Conradie came—announcing himself from a distance by shouting. This gave us a good headstart, which we needed since he had a bicycle and we were running it barefoot, our shirts bulging with fruit.

The usual escape route was through a blue gum grove, then past Goldenboom's shop, and so down to the river bank. Conradie followed, huffing and puffing and yelling at us—but always at a safe distance. Once at the riverside, we would sit down to eat the fruit and give Conradie his share when he eventually caught up with us, crying, "Naughty boys!"—laughing until he choked on fruit pits.

That sin certainly belonged more in his pile than in my own or in that of Fanie Bekker or Michel Rossouw or Piet Theron.

From the pulpit on high, Dominie Rabie was now reading Psalm 141:

> Set a watch, O Lord, before my mouth;
> Keep the door of my lips.
> Incline not my heart to any evil thing,
> To practice wicked words with men
> That work iniquity:
> And let me not eat of their dainties.

By not eating dainties did he mean the food we stole from Mortimer & Hill? Michel Rossouw did it and he was always very successful since his father was general manager. He simply walked in and helped himself to sardines, condensed milk, Vienna sausages, peppermint crisps, and chocolates. Loaded with these delights, we would ride on his bike out to the dam at the edge of town. Or we would go next door to my backyard and climb up into the little house in the walnut tree. This feast was a regular weekly event.

> Let the righteous smite me; it shall be a kindness ...

Nobody was smiting Michel for all that food. Nor were they after us for stealing the feed sacks. These were kept in a rear shed by old Jaap, the storekeeper, who used them for sugar and corn meal. Empty sacks were worth two pennies each. Translated into more practical

13

terms, a sack was thus worth one Billy Bunter magazine for boys and one red Nestlé chocolate from the slot machine at the railway station. Or five sacks were equal to a movie ticket. Michel used to crawl into the shed on Wednesday afternoon, when the store was closed, and throw them over the fence into my backyard. He worked fast and hard, and the sacks would come sailing over like kites, settling on the woodpile, on top of the outhouse, and even in the pear tree.

Later we would sell them back to old Jaap, who said, *"Ja, ja"* and paid us twopence each without any questions asked.

> When their judges are overthrown in stony places,
> They shall hear my words;
> For they are sweet.

So were the words of Michel, for he was very kindhearted and would share everything he had with me. If I lacked money for a movie, he would obtain enough for both of us. If he had a sweet, half of it would be mine. It went like that in all things. I could not remember how he entered my life or how I met him. He was just there. He came in the afternoons and he had a special call, a sort of yodel. Then I knew Michel was there and we would go out together.

His family was rich and they lived up on a hill in a house named *"Petra"*—rock. They had a radio set, a Frigidaire and a pantry filled with food. In the backyard they had an extra large reservoir for rainwater—used especially for ladies to wash their hair—where we swam naked at night when everyone was in bed. I slept there sometimes, ate there often, and I loved Michel and his family.

His father was always very neat and well dressed, even when we went hunting springbok. I called him Mister Rossouw and liked the way he threw back his head and laughed at a good joke. His wife, Aunt Connie, was short and fat, but a very lovable sort of woman. I don't think she ever beat Michel or his brother, Laurie.

I felt secure and safe in their house—as though I was on a vacation. The return to my own home late at night, or the next morning if my father allowed me to sleep over, was the end of fun and laughter—a return to household chores, school work, and to the mystery of my own self before my three brothers, my mother—and my father.

> Our bones are scattered at the grave's mouth,
> As when one cutteth and cleaveth wood upon the earth.

Yes, I killed the cat—but that cat killed six little bantam chicks. They were my chicks and they had just been hatched. I could see them from my window where I was studying—moving about in the sunlight. After a bit, I went into the kitchen for a drink of water and suddenly heard the mother bantam making a big racket. I ran outside, but it was too late. Yellow feathers and tiny heads lay scattered over the gravel, separate from four motionless chicks. Two of them had been carried away or just gobbled up.

Back in my room, I tried to study. Then I saw the cat sitting on top of the wall cleaning itself in the sun. That did it for me. I took down my eighteen-gauge and killed it with one shot through the window. When I told my father about it he was sad—but he saw my grief and did not scold me.

> Keep me from the snares which they
> Have laid for me . . .

Jessie Grimbeeck did not put out a snare for me, nor did I lay one for her. It just happened without any plans at all during a game at the school social when we both hid under a kei-apple bush. I was there first when she popped in after me. There were flowers on the bush like yellow stars and when she wiggled close to hide better, her leg touched my hand. I did nothing at all except stay there, but afterwards I felt unclean and sorry because she was such a nice girl. I knew it was wicked and something I should not do again. Yet merely thinking about it made me excited and very worried about what would happen if Jessie and I ever ended up under another bush.

Dominie Rabie closed his service with a benediction for everyone. All that remained was for my mother to play a hymn while the congregation filed out. She sat there, her rich auburn hair up in a bun, her head tilted toward the ceiling as though waiting for a sign from on high. I gave it to her from nearer at hand, using two fingers to indicate people walking from the church. She got the message and plunged into a spirited "Onward Christian Soldiers"—obviously convinced this had the proper spirit to send everyone with his bundle of sin from the House of the Lord into the waiting New Year.

Earlier, I had looked for Jessie but not seen her. Now I looked again —with a mixed sense of joy and guilt—only to discover that a group of people had gathered around the front pew where a woman had fainted. She was old and dressed in black, and they had stretched her out on the bench as though she were dead and ready for Dominie Rabie to make a funeral oration.

Oh Lord, I thought, if that happens I'll never be able to pump the whole thing—unless there is very little music.

Gradually everyone left, except the small group gathered around the old lady on the front bench. One woman removed her shoes and began massaging her feet. Another put a hymnbook under her head, causing a yellow, pie-shaped hat to spring away like a departing halo.

15

I leaned forward, wondering how this could happen in church. You could faint in a closed car or in a crowd, or you could even go to sleep and never wake up. But while singing the praises of the Lord—wasn't this the safest, most glorious moment of the whole week? Had the old woman been so wicked she could not pick up her bundle? If so, then church was a dangerous place for those suffering from great sin. It did not seem right, and I decided to ask my father about it.

In the excitement, I forgot to tell my mother to stop playing. As a result, her music urging Christian soldiers onward boomed out over an empty church, bouncing off the vaulting brown ceiling and onto the little group huddled below.

Finally, one of the elders called up to me, "Son, every Christian soldier who can do so has gone home. So your mother can let up now, thank you."

On the way out, the church door was flung against us by a man who seemed very frightened. He was out of breath and he rushed down the aisle toward the old lady. I wanted to follow for a closer look—maybe the woman was really dead—but my mother was in a hurry. It was after midnight and we had to be up at 4 A.M. to begin the drive to the seacoast for our summer vacation.

"I still have to get the food ready," she said.

"I'll be along in a minute."

"No—you come now."

On the sidewalk, a little girl ran toward us. I had never seen her before but obviously she was in trouble. Her blond hair was a mess from running, and she was sobbing so much she could hardly run anymore. I watched her turn into the church and decided she was the daughter of the man we had seen. Her father had gone ahead, leaving her to follow, all alone and frightened. This made me quite sad and I wanted more than ever to go back into the church.

"Please, Mother, I'll come soon."

"No."

Once, many years ago, that had happened to me. I must have been six at the time—about the same age as that little blond girl—and it was linked to the first memories of my father. I was lying with him in bed, as a young boy lies with his father, when a doctor came to examine him. Upon seeing us, the doctor said: "My boy, your father is too ill for you to lie with him in the bed."

They took him to the hospital with double pneumonia and my mother began to send me across the town each day with something for him to eat—a little soup, or some jelly or custard in a bowl.

One night they sent word my father was dying and my mother hurried to the hospital. After some time, she came home and made

16

some hot soup—telling me to take it to my father. It might, she said, help save his life.

I ran alone through the dark streets, afraid I would not get there in time. As I ran, the soup spilled on my legs, burning them. It began to rain and I was frightened, realizing for the first time that someday I would be alone in the world.

I remember the red polished cement floor of the hospital, the smell of disinfectants and medicines—and then my father. He had almost suffocated from parotitis, until the doctors slit his throat. When I arrived, the throat was bandaged, yet blood continued to seep through and my father was gasping for air. He seemed to be dying and I could only think of how often he had spoken of God and the angels—and now he was going to see them in Heaven.

Sometime later, I returned to find him in the garden, walking between two nursing sisters with long white veils. They appeared beautiful—luminous and white, with the sun shining through their veils. My father was walking for the first time, his arms around their shoulders, and both sisters were smiling as though they shared with him a secret too deep to tell anyone.

"It looks as if your father hasn't finished yet," said my mother.

We had walked across Church Street, passed the Town Hall, and were standing in front of a smaller church—my father's. It had not yet let out, which was unusual since both churches generally finished at the same time. Yet from inside we could hear my father was still engaged with his sermon. After that was over, he normally met with the church elders. My mother was concerned that this might keep him too long.

"Go in and let him know after he's finished that he's needed to help us get ready for the trip."

I nodded and ducked into the church—glad not to be sent to bed.

> And Jesus said unto him;
> "Foxes have holes,
> And birds of the air have nests—
> But the son of man hath not where to lay his head . . ."

It was my father in the pulpit. He had white hair and a white mustache and hazel-green eyes, and, standing in the box above us, he looked like an old eagle peering from his nest into a distant valley. Over the pulpit hung a white plaster canopy and from below it was supported by curving arms of wrought iron. The Bible lay open on a flatboard and below it in front hung a black velvet cloth with golden tassels and five golden words: THE HOUSE OF THE LORD. My father stood as always, his arms extended, hands grasping the rim of the pulpit as though he continued to peer into the valley and relate what happened

17

to Jesus on his way to Jerusalem—how it happened that a man came up and said he would also go along, but first needed to go home and say good-bye to everyone. Jesus, however, did not want that:

> No man, having put his hand to the plow,
> And then looking back,
> Is fit for the kingdom of God.

The assembly nodded approval, and I wondered if this applied to my mother. She wanted my father home to help pack as soon as he finished the sermon, while he was in the pulpit saying anyone who took his hand off the Lord's plow was not fit for the kingdom of God. That certainly meant talking to the elders for as long as they needed him. It was an impossible situation, and I tried to decide what to do. Finally I gave up and began to look around the church. One of the Morkels saw me and nodded. Every member of that family could sing beautifully, and I hoped my father would finish soon so that we could hear them sing the final hymn. This was a different church than the other one. I felt more at home here. It was my father's church, of course, but there was something else which I came to recognize when I grew older.

The other church, the *Boerekerk*, or Farmer's Church, had a great white steeple that rose up over the town—so high that when you looked at it from Donkin Street it seemed to be taller than the Nuweveld Mountains. It shot up into the sky in a most startling manner, helped along the way by thrusting gothic arches and stone ramparts. In its race to heaven, the tower paused briefly at a black-faced clock with white, bold Roman numerals. Then it shot upward into a white steeple, topped by a black weather-vane rooster that turned about haughtily— often refusing to move unless the wind shook every tree in town.

Our church, on the other hand, had a plain red roof like a big barn and no steeple in the sky. There was a black one, shaped as though made for a church in Russia, on top of the Town Hall next door. It was this white mansion topped by a Russian steeple that stood between us and the great Farmer's Church—two houses of worship separated by the seat of civic power. Nor did we have a church bell. The bell which hung on a frame in the yard of the big church also summoned us.

The two churches were also different inside. Being of Dutch Reformed faith and thus of Calvinist descent, they were both severe and lacked any art suggesting the children of God could sweat and love and—alas—sin. Yet they differed in the substance of their simplicity. The other church had a vast interior, made of natural wood that pleased the eye with beautiful planes and joints. They rose with the

18

ease of a soaring hymn into a vaulted ceiling that surely touched a corner of heaven. Our church more clearly touched a corner of the earth where man had come to sing and pray. It was made of broad beam planks and painted blue and white. It had little gothic arches shaped from pine wood and patches of red and blue glass in its windows. Less than a reach for heaven, it resembled more a shelter on earth and was as warm and comfortable as a manger.

Yet something else separated the two churches—beyond their different appearance or the walls of the Town Hall. The barrier was immediately evident in the faces of men and women, as they often sang the same hymn at the same moment under separate roofs. For the people of the big church were white, and those who came to my father were colored.

The main difference was there—in the color of the skin. For just as they shared the same God, the two people also shared a common ancestry more recent than the parenthood of Adam and Eve. The whites were a mixture of Dutch, French Huguenot, German, and British —and called themselves Europeans. The nonwhites were a mixture of European, Malayan and Hottentot—an indigenous, pre-Negroid South African people, today almost extinct. As such, they were called non-Europeans, or, more commonly, "coloreds."

So the two people shared some common ancestors, yet sat in different, untouching churches. Similarly, the two ministers shared a common faith, yet stood in separate, untouching pulpits. Both were ordained pastors of the Dutch Reformed Church. Yet their different assignments in the same town gave them different titles. Mr. Rabie was a Dominie, or minister to the Europeans. My father was Eerwaarde, or Reverend, and a missionary to the coloreds. There were 7,000 of them, against 3,400 whites, living in primitive conditions—suffering from sickness, hunger, and all the inherited ills of social outcasts. My father's mission was therefore immensely more difficult. For this, and for occasionally standing in as minister to the Europeans, he received each month twenty pounds, or about fifty dollars—one third of the sum paid to Dominie Rabie. Besides this, the minister of the European church socially had little to do with my father, his brother in Christ.

To help relieve our poverty—on Christmas morning my brothers and I would find our hung stockings empty, except for a few pitiful pieces of toffee candy—my mother played the organ in the European church when they had no one else. My father also got one pound ten shillings, or about four dollars, a month for preaching to prisoners in the jail. Every Sunday he would rise early and walk two miles through town to be at the jail by seven o'clock.

He wore a black suit and waistcoat, with a white strikkie, or bowstring tie. He carried his Bible and hymn book and people in town seeing him would say: *"Goeie môre, Meneer,"*—Good morning, sir. There were some, however, who said little more than that and avoided further contact with him because of his close association with coloreds. Years later, at Beaufort West, a lawyer confessed to me: "I am ashamed to say this, but I avoided shaking your father's hand whenever possible. I knew he shook the hand of thirty or more coloreds every day and I didn't want any of it to rub off on me."

As a boy, however, I was not acutely aware of this. I played freely with other children my age and was accepted in their homes—including that of Eric Louw who later became Minister of Foreign Affairs. Yet I was set apart in many ways which could not be hidden. There were no presents on Christmas morning. At the yearly sports show I ran the mile in my bare feet. There was no steeple with a fat cock on my father's church. The people who prayed with him were colored. And when the day came for me to be confirmed in the Dutch Reformed Church, I would make my vows to God before a minister in a pulpit who would be Dominie Rabie—and not my father whom I loved and admired above all other men.

> Behold I give unto you power
> To tread on serpents and scorpions,
> And over all the power of the enemy;
> And nothing shall by any means hurt you.

My father had given me that—and more. He had shown me scorpions under rocks. He had taught me the names of the trees, the wildflowers, and the succulent plants. He had brought me to the birds, to the animals, and even to the lizards—especially the rare, blue-headed koggelmander which stares to the north when rain is on the way.

But above all else, he taught me to hunt on the Great Karoo—the vast and wonderful plain of semidesert where we lived. He was a good shot and an excellent hunter, and walking in the veld he seemed more than ever to have the eyes of an eagle, often seeing game long before anyone else.

We hunted an antelope called springbok and the desert hare—hasie in Afrikaans. Most of the time we went after hare, my father and I with three of his friends, walking in a row fifty yards apart until we jumped one. The men used twelve-bore guns while I had a smaller eighteen-gauge one.

We used to make a fire in the veld at midday, roasting chops and sausages, then washing it down with hot, black coffee. After that, we would put the bags again on our backs and continue to hunt until evening. I learned to love the Karoo then—the flat plains with distant

20

mountains, blue in the morning, pink and purple and gold at sunset. Sometimes on the way home the sun would be a red ball sinking over the horizon. But often it was after nightfall and in the darkness the day's companionship would be gone, leaving me with a deep, almost painful loneliness.

> All things are delivered to me of my father
> And no man knoweth who the son is, but the father:
> And who the father is, but the son . . .

Whenever we were ill, my father got up at night to doctor us. My brothers and I went constantly barefoot and often during the winter our feet would toughen up and crack open. This was quite painful, especially when we washed them at night. Our father helped us to soften them by rubbing in a mixture of paraffin and candle wax. Besides this, I suffered from festering toenails that pained so much that I would cry in bed. My mother, who helped us greatly with schoolwork during the day, did not hear us calling at night. My father came instead, with a *wildeblare* home remedy, wrapping it around my toe in a bandage. He also used to draw out the fester with a poultice made of milk and bread crumbs, or Sunlight soap and sugar. And when I had a cold, he would rub my chest with Vicks and cover it with a red flannel cloth.

Sunday afternoons we walked together to the top of the hill by the dam. Once there, we would sit on a rock and look at the town below us, and across the valley at the distant Nuweveld Mountains. Sometimes one of my brothers came along, but usually it was only the two of us. Then I would tell my problems to my father, and he would speak of his to me.

One day I asked him to explain death and the soul leaving the body. I did not know how important this would be to me some day, and I asked it as would any boy of his father.

"How do you know it happens? You can't see it."

"Do you see that train?"

Far across the valley, a freight train pulled around Lemoenfontein Mountain. We watched it approach the bridge and saw a white puff of steam come from the whistle. Ten seconds later, its sound came to us on the hilltop—who! whooo!

"You saw the steam?"

"Yes."

"And the sound?"

"The steam and sound—they became separated."

"How do you know—did you see it happen?"

Another time I wanted to know about dancing with girls. Was it all right—or was it wrong?

21

"By dancing do you mean placing your two bodies in contact with one another and vibrating to music?"

"Yes."

I had not yet begun to take out girls, and did not even know how to dance. Yet, other older boys were doing it, and I knew the main purpose was to do just that—vibrate together in harmony with music.

"I don't think it's wise to be that close to a girl," said my father. "You're throwing yourself into the arms of temptation."

I said nothing. We were cracking almonds on a rock and eating them with raisins.

"On the other hand," he said, "Paul says we can trust God to always provide us with an escape from temptation. And Peter says to be joyful when tempted, since you are blessed when you resist it."

"You can trust me," I replied, with the confidence of a boy who had never held a girl.

So my father helped me. He did not, however, have easy answers for all his own problems—especially financial ones. We owed five hundred pounds on our house at the seaside, and there were other expenses too. My eldest brother, Johannes, whom we called Barney, had failed twice at the university. Besides this, there were three other sons to put through school.

One day on the hilltop he revealed his secret solution for all our troubles: a lottery ticket. I stared at it in amazement. The church was opposed to gambling and I could not believe what I saw.

"It's a lottery ticket," he said.

I nodded. A strong wind was blowing and it whipped the ticket in his hand. It also tugged at his mustache and it flapped our pants about our legs.

"If I win first prize," he said, "it will pay a fortune."

"And take care of the mortgage on the house," I said, trying to be helpful.

"And Johannes' university bills," he said. "Then a thousand for your schooling, plus two more for Dodsley and Marius. We can even get an electrical hearing aid for your mother so she can hear something in church."

With a stick he wrote our names on the ground and next to them he put how much was needed. Obviously, this was not gambling. It was more in the nature of a family investment—even a municipal one.

"We'll have enough left over," he said finally, "to build an extension on the colored school and maybe even dig a well for them.

> He answered, saying:
> Thou shalt love the Lord thy God,
> With all thy heart,

And with all thy soul,
And with all thy strength,
And with all thy mind;
And thy neighbor as thyself.

In the pulpit, my father paused. The congregation waited in silence. Finally he spoke:

"That is the great commandment. I did not say two commandments because it is not two. It is one, since you cannot love God unless you love man. And you cannot love man unless you love God. It's all one piece—like an open-ended pipe. . . ."

"AAAAA-MENNNNN!"

I looked at the men and women before me, packed between the blue and white walls and crammed onto the balcony where some had carved their names into the wooden benches.

I remember now the ladies' hats—was it actually that night or was it years later or maybe really a composite of all my boyhood? They were of many colors, each tilted differently as though a great wind had blown through a flower garden. It was these, the hats, which suggested the women were the brightest and most intense. Yet their eyes told you otherwise, shifting eventually to their men who sat there, each one very much alone, with gnarled hands on old, dog-eared psalm books, hands beaten and shaped like worn tools. Above all else, there was something in the triangle of jaw, mouth, and eyes that seemed to ask: "How can *you* explain it?"

At that age I did not know what "it" was, although I sensed there was an unexplored area, an untouched field where they stood alone, waiting for someone to come and write their names with ours on the earth.

So the unasked question was always there, becoming most intense after the service when there was contact with them, their hands pressed into my father's—and so into mine—before they took leave to go back to the Location, their ghetto on the edge of town where their dogs bit white men, and children behind walls made of mud asked their parents the unasked question.

It went that way this same night, with the deacons and elders pressing around my father. After wishing him well on the New Year, and safe return from his vacation, they spoke their fears. There was a move underway to deconsecrate our church and so force the coloreds to worship in a church away from the center of town. Would it happen while my father was away?

"It will never happen while I am alive," he replied.

"May God spare you until you die," said one.

"Reverend, don't go too far out into the sea," said another.

23

I whispered my mother's message to come as soon as possible and left, going through the vestry that was attached to our home. On the way I found my father's office open, with a lamp lit. Normally no lights were allowed after nine o'clock. Electricity was too expensive, and late studies had to be done by oil lamp or candlelight. Yet this was New Year's Eve, the family was packing, the lights were on—and my father's study was open.

I sat down at his big roll-top desk where often he let me study. I knew every drawer, including the one on the upper left, which I pulled out to discover, as always, the little tin candy box. Inside the box was an old envelope, tied with a red ribbon, which I opened quickly to find my father's two most precious treasures: a little brown Marie biscuit and a sharpened matchstick—all that remained of the touch of my dead brother.

One corner of the biscuit had been bitten off, leaving marks of little teeth, and the matchstick was bent slightly at its sharpened point. I touched them both gently, wondering what he would be like if he had lived. They had called him Abraham, but he had not lived long enough to hear it with pride. Perhaps he did not even know it belonged to him. He could speak, they said, but he died before he was four—dying of a heart disease while my father sat beside his bed, trying to be of help, giving him a little biscuit to eat, then cleaning his tiny fingernails with the matchstick.

It was not the first death in the family. Barney had come with a twin sister, but she had died at birth—too soon to have a name or to be kissed or to leave her mark on a biscuit or a matchstick. I looked at them again, wondering if Abraham would have been a good friend like Michel. My brothers were too old or too young to be close to me. Barney was ten years ahead of me, Dodsley was five, and Marius was four years younger.

In later years, I learned Abraham had a congenital defect of the heart that modern surgery could have corrected. But as a boy, I did not know this and could only wonder why there was no way to stop death, to somehow send it away. Why did it come so suddenly—snatching little boys from the bedside of their fathers, grabbing old ladies while praying in church, yet leaving others to sit and stare at a biscuit, a matchstick, or an old photograph?

There was a photo of him in the living room, hanging on the wall. It showed a baby sitting in a chair on a velvet cushion staring out at the world with mixed wonder and fright. Yet this was more a record of grief than joy, for next to it hung another one of my mother, dressed in black with a white handkerchief in her hand, standing beside a fresh grave with a jar of flowers tilted against a white cross. A third photo in the line-up was of a little angel in a cloud, its hand raised as though waving good-bye.

I had never seen my mother cry, or even with tears in her eyes. But once Barney had found her weeping before these photos, my father standing beside her with his arm around her waist, saying her name over and over—her true name and not just Mommy—"Maria, Maria. . . ."

"Christiaan!"

It was my mother in the doorway holding a wrinkled mosquito net and an old pair of Dodsley's pants. Her hair had come loose and hung down over one ear.

"What are you doing here?"

"Waiting for Daddy."

I rose quickly, hoping she would not see the opened candy box. She could get very angry. When we did something terribly wrong, she would even beat us with a hairbrush.

"Did you tell him to hurry up?"

"Yes, I did that, Mother."

I nodded as I spoke to make certain she understood. Without her earhorn, she did not always hear everything. Sometimes this led to misunderstanding and trouble.

"Come to bed immediately. I want you to try on these pants for the summer."

"I have to go outside first."

"What?"

"I have to go to the toilet!"

"Be quick about it," she said, turning down the corridor.

I closed the tin and put it back into the top drawer. Then I went out into the back garden where the toilet was in a corrugated iron shed, separate from the house. I always dreaded making this trip at night, fearing ghosts would leap upon me. Everybody in Beaufort West knew about the man who went into the graveyard one night, only to be jumped by a spook who slapped him in the face, leaving a hideous burn caused by five flaming fingers.

Worse than that was the dreaded *oog*, or eye, a fiery and awful will-o'-the-wisp, larger than a new moon. Most often it was seen moving up and down the river bank—the demented spirit of a woman with a lantern looking for her drowned daughter. Everyone had seen it. Even horses began to sweat and panic as it approached, vanishing at the last minute—but not always. Once, a man charged at it with a carriage and became a raving lunatic. After that, everyone stayed away. Michel and I had seen it when driving with his father to Jeffrey's Bay. It came along the top of a little hill and suddenly headed toward us.

25

We raced away in the car as Michel was screaming, "Daddy, the *oog*, the OOG IS COMING AT US!"

The black form of the outhouse loomed before me, and with it came the familiar feel of the door handle. At that moment, there was a clank-clanking, coming through the garden gate. Hearing it, I leaped inside the privy and slammed the door shut—just in time, for the clanking came nearer and nearer, until it struck the back of the outhouse with a terrible groan. Trembling with fear, I leaned against the door and held my head, certain I was about to be seized by the throat.

Then I heard the latrine bucket under the toilet seat being pulled out through a back trap door, with another one slid into its place. No ghosts, these were the coloreds on their nightly round to empty latrines. I waited for them to leave, then hastened to finish and hurry back toward the safety of lights in our home.

In the kitchen there was the odor of freshly baked *soetkoekies*. It made me immediately hungry and I began to sniff around looking for some. My mother was a wonderful cook. When she won prizes at the annual domestic show, we went around proudly looking at the red cards on her cakes and cookies. Our wood stove had no thermometer, but she could judge the heat by simply putting her hand into the oven. On these special baking days we were not even allowed to tiptoe through the kitchen, for fear the cake would fall. Our reward came afterward, when we helped beat the egg whites for frosting and could lick the pan.

In the kitchen, the longer I looked for the cookies the hungrier I became. There was nothing in the cupboard or the pantry. Everything had been put away and packed for the trip. Finally, in the breakfast room I found a picnic basket. The cookies were in it—and within two seconds I had one in my mouth and a spare in my pocket.

The family trunk and some other bags were in the hall, ready to be loaded into the car. The linoleum floor had lost its polish, but I could forget about that for a month or until we came home. Then it would begin again—the weekly chore of polishing the hall floor that ran through the center of the house. It had an orange and green pattern and my mother wanted it to shine like a mirror. To achieve this, I had to go over it three times on my knees, first with wax and a rag, then with a brush and another rag, and finally with a clean rag to obtain a bright finish. The hall ran from the front door, past the living room and the room we rented out to boarders—for many years, a beloved teacher, Miss Dodsley-Flamstead—continuing alongside other bedrooms to the dining room we never used except for special dinners, ending finally at the cramped breakfast room where we ate all the time.

After that, I would polish the furniture, or stamp the washing with my feet, or haul firewood by wheelbarrow from the front to the rear of the house. Sometimes I also helped make soap in the big iron pot filled with sheep fat, caustic soda, and a lye obtained from a special bush growing in the veld. The round of chores was always the same, but the long hall was worst of all. It collected dust from the street all week long and no matter how hard I tried, I could never please my mother. She would always find a corner or a little spot that did not shine like the rest, saying, "You haven't done this properly."

This hurt because I had tried so hard, only to have her knock everything down. She was a strongly determined woman—insisting everything be perfect, that we boys be first in school, and that we never admit defeat. I was afraid of my mother, of displeasing her, and of making her angry.

Marius and I shared a bedroom next to my parents with a door in between. When I entered he was already asleep. Dodsley's pants were laid out on my bed, and I tried them on. They were the usual khaki shorts we all wore, but a little big around the waist.

"You'll fill it out during the summer," said my mother in her room when I showed them to her. She was in her nightgown, and knelt on the floor to inspect the fit.

"If you made them a little tighter, they wouldn't fall off when I run—like this."

I sucked in my stomach and wiggled and the pants fell to the floor around my ankles.

"All right," she said, giving me a pat on the rear, "I think you're going to be skinny all your life, just like your father."

My father was sitting on the bed, taking off his shoes. They were high ones, above the ankles, and he was opening the laces.

"Daddy, a woman fainted tonight in the church while she was praying."

"A woman what?"

"Fainted, in the big church."

"Who was she?"

I looked toward my mother who was now seated before her dressing mirror, letting down her hair.

"Mommy, the woman who fainted—who was she?"

"It looked like one of the Stroebel relatives."

"Which one?" asked my father.

"I don't know."

"The cousin from Knysna?"

"I don't know—why must you feel responsible for everybody?"

My father peeled off his socks and said nothing.

"Everybody," said my mother, "everybody from everywhere and all colors—he worries about them."

Daddy wiggled his toes and winked at me.

"Yes?"

"What I wanted to know is how can it happen there, I mean in church, while you're praying?"

"Son, if people believed they could not die while praying in church, we'd never be able to close our doors. The Lord knows this and asks only that we keep ready to go at any time—even while praying to him, which is rather beautiful when you think about it."

It did not seem beautiful at all. In fact, it made me decide to say my prayers as fast as possible. As though aware of this, my father pulled a big watch from his waistcoat pocket and flipped open the lid.

"It's after one o'clock, Chris. You'd better go to bed."

"Yes, Daddy."

The watch was silver and it had a silver chain. Leaving the lid open, he always put it on the stand next to the bed. Then he took off his waistcoat and began unbuttoning his shirt. On the other side of the bed my mother was brushing her hair. She had never cut it and it came down to her waist. Against the pink nightgown it was like a dark waterfall and was lovely to look at. She combed it with the same brush with which she beat me, pulling it slowly. In the oval mirror, her face was framed by the dark hair, her brown eyes were soft and sleepy, and I thought she looked beautiful.

My father had asked her to marry him one day when they were walking together. He had picked a pomegranate from a tree and had broken it apart, saying: "Maria, so is my heart open to you."

We all knew these blushing words of love, given with the two red halves of the fruit in his long, delicate hands. But none of us ever knew how Maria Elizabeth de Swart, the young school teacher from George, said her first "yes" to our father. I had my own version of her reaction to his romantic proposal: She took one half of the split pomegranate, and then nodded—her eyes downcast.

Even when older, I never imagined either of them kissing with their eyes open or actually making love, other than in the dark. In fact, I had never seen them kiss with the heat of lovers. They were for us two ends of a house, fixed and untouching as different doors—one with an arch, the other with pillars, one who came to you at night, the other who drove you on by day with a hairbrush. One whom you loved, the other whom you loved and feared.

I looked at the double bed where they slept every night together—its black iron frame topped by bright bronze balls and a bronze headpiece. Everything had happened there—or most everything. I was born in that bed, and so were all my brothers, except Barney. He was nearby, however, the night of my birth—apparently dying of double pneumonia in an adjacent room where my father knelt praying at his bedside while

I came into the world, November 8, 1922. At the same moment, Barney passed his crisis—to live and not to die as had Abraham before him.

All of that, and more, had happened in the bed of bright bronze. It was there my mother and father said their *huisgodsdiens*, or prayers, each day before rising. Often I awakened to hear my father already underway, in soft, peaceful prayer. Then my mother would pray. She was more excited about it and more definite in what she asked from God. After that they would sing together in bed. They did not do this in bed at night because we always said *huisgodsdiens* at the evening dinner table, kneeling by our chairs after my father read from the family Bible, then all singing together. Most often, it was my father's favorite, "Rock of Ages."

Before retiring, however, my parents always knelt at the side of their bed, doing it separately as soon as one or the other got into night clothes. My father wore pajamas that consisted of pants and shirt with a white vest, and he prayed in silence on his knees. My mother did not always pray in silence, because of her deafness, and you could often hear what she said.

". . . and please dear Lord help us on the road tomorrow, preserve us against accidents or trouble with those awful tires, and keep our loved ones forever in your care, Amen."

Back in my bedroom I recalled my father as saying we should be ready to be snatched away by God's hand, especially during prayer. So I raced through mine in record time. Then I hopped into bed and tried to sleep. The trip to the seaside was always exciting and many things happened along the way.

There was the far-off cry of a train going across the Karoo plain. I thought of my father in the pulpit, saying only a father could know his son, and only a son would know his father, I remembered once seeing him in the garden trimming roses. Thorns pricked his hands, and as he came toward me in the evening light I saw blood on them, and I feared for him.

DISCUSSION AND INQUIRY

Christiaan Barnard spent his boyhood in South Africa in a deeply religious environment. His concerns about sinning and the accompanying guilt he felt about childhood pranks such as fruit stealing or touching a girl's leg were partly an outgrowth of his religious teachings. Can these feelings of guilt affect a child's self-concept?

How? Religious teachings are but one source of guilt in children. What are some of the other sources of guilt? What are the possible effects of guilt on personality development?

The boy admired his father and developed deep concern for others, probably as a result of his identification with his father's beliefs and values. His chosen profession certainly reflects his concern for others. Christiaan was confused about the inconsistency between his father's preachings to the "coloreds" about the equality of all God's children and the reality that he observed, namely, the social position of these folks. They emptied latrines and were forced to worship in the church with no steeple or church bell. Conflict between what adults say and what children experience as reality is quite common in childhood. What effect may this have on a child's attitudes toward adults? How may it affect the child's feelings about the issue involved, which, in this case, was racial prejudice?

When Christiaan was 6 years old, he was told that his father might die—the father he loved and admired. He suddenly realized that he would someday be alone in the world. What might this mean to a 6-year old? Consider the other experiences Christiaan had with death, including the death of his brother and the possible death of the old lady in church. When do most children begin to come to grips with the reality of death and find themselves fearing for their own lives or those of their loved ones? What is the origin of these fears, according to Freud?

Bernard Baruch

BIOGRAPHICAL SKETCH

Born in 1870, Bernard Baruch devoted his life to finance and government. For many years he was a member of the New York Stock Exchange. President Wilson appointed him to the advisory committee of the Council of National Defense. His economic expertise was important to the country during the First World War; he directed Allied purchases and headed the War Industries Board. His services were also valuable during Roosevelt's administration. In 1946, Baruch represented the United States at the United Nations Atomic Energy Commission. He died in 1965.

SELECTIONS FROM

BARUCH—MY OWN STORY

THE two-story frame house in which I was born on August 19, 1870, stood on the main street of Camden, South Carolina. Still, living there was almost like living in the open country. Directly behind the house were a vegetable garden, stables, and barn. Beyond them stretched three acres of land which Father had turned into a kind of experimental "farm." One year I remember it was set out in sugar cane, on whose cultivation Father bestowed as much pains as if it were a plantation of money-making cotton.

Father used to spend time on his "farm" which Mother thought should have been devoted to his medical practice. Yet he was one of the most successful physicians in the state. He was only thirty-three when the South Carolina Medical Association elected him president. He also served as head of the State Board of Health and was active in the troubled and sometimes bloody politics of the Reconstruction.

Recently I was reading through one of his early case books. Those scribbled pages mirrored his role in the community. He treated Negroes and whites alike for all their ailments and accidents, from the lad who caught a fish-hook in his leg to the poor old Negro who, on the death of

31

his former master, refused to eat or drink for eighteen days and starved to death.

Father often took me along in his two-seater buggy when he made his rounds through the countryside. Sometimes I would hold the reins while he read or dozed. Once we stopped at a crude cabin. I waited in the buggy while Father went inside. Soon he came hurrying out. Taking an ax, he smashed in the wooden shutters, exclaiming, "That man is dying for lack of fresh air!"

Father's work on his experimental "farm" reflected an interest in bettering the community which he displayed through his whole life. When we moved to New York about six months after my tenth birthday, he pioneered in establishing public baths in overcrowded tenement districts. In South Carolina, when we lived there, the state had not yet set up its own agricultural service to experiment with better farming methods. But Father saw the need of such experimentation and, although he had no prior agricultural training, soon became expert at it.

Alongside the medical books in his office were heaped a stack of yellow-backed farm journals. He tested the theories he drew from them on his own three acres. His yields of cotton, corn, oats, and sugar cane took first prize at the County Fair.

He gave away seeds and was never too busy to help a farmer solve a problem. Once Father bought a few acres of lowland to show it could be drained with tile. This was, I believe, the first experiment of its kind in our part of the country.

Father was a man worth looking at—six feet tall, erect and military, with a dark beard and mild, unwavering blue eyes. His dress was rather formal. Never do I recall seeing him in his shirt sleeves. Yet he had a kindly manner, and a soft voice which had no trace of accent to suggest his foreign birth.

. . .

Up to the time of Sherman's raid, Mother's family had been so well off that she had never even dressed herself. But until Father's practice was firmly established, she taught piano and singing at twenty-five cents a lesson. She also sold milk and butter from the herd of Jersey cows which was one of Father's prides.

One habit of luxury Mother retained, however. She always had breakfast in bed. Each morning my three brothers and I would present ourselves before her for inspection. "Let me see your fingers. Let me see your ears. Did you clean your teeth?" Frequently these examinations meant another trip to the wash basin.

In those days, Camden was a town of about 2,000, with Negroes making up about half the population. During the Revolutionary War, Camden was occupied by Lord Cornwallis. One of Camden's tourist sights was the grave of a woman named Ellen Glasgow, who had followed her sweetheart, General Cornwallis, to America. When the waters of the nearby Wateree River flooded over, the Negroes used to say that Ellen's ghost had the power to stop the flood short of her grave.

Camden also took pride in the fact that it gave six generals to what then was called the Confederate War. The war brought economic hardship to Camden, as it did to all of the South. Still, I cannot recall that our family ever suffered real economic adversity.

We lived in a large, comfortable house and had about as much of material things as any of our neighbors. A good part of Father's income came in the form of goods and services—a cord of wood, a bale of cotton, a load of corn, chickens, a colt or calf, a day's work on his farm. We raised our own vegetables, fruit, and berries, which were dried or preserved for winter use. In our yard grew damson plums, walnuts, and a mulberry tree. When the mulberry tree didn't bear, Minerva, our Negro nurse, would tell us to beat it with a switch so that next year we would be sure to have mulberries.

We made our own sugar—I never knew sugar was any color but brown until we moved North. In the fall everyone gathered hickory nuts and walnuts. Candy, oranges, bananas, and raisins we received only on occasions like Christmas. Cloth, shoes, coffee, tea, salt, and spices were about all we bought regularly. Books, magazines, and the Charleston *News and Courier* were treasured articles to be passed from house to house.

Strawberry festivals and the visit of the circus were the big excitements. There was also a local dramatic organization which staged Shakespearean readings and plays at the Camden town hall. In one performance of *Kathleen Mavourneen*, by William Travers, Mother was playing the lead while Uncle Nathan Baruch had the part of the villain. In one climactic scene, the villain threatens the heroine with a knife. The sight of Mother cowering while Uncle Nathan brandished his dagger proved too much for me. I jumped from my seat crying. "Oh, Uncle Nathan, don't hurt Mama!" The players were thrown somewhat off their lines and I was hustled out of the theater.

As a child I was shy and sensitive, something of a mamma's boy. I always sat at Mother's right at the dinner table, and I remember how fiercely I fought for this privilege. When I married, I asked my wife to sit where my mother would have sat—with me to her right.

When Mother taught us elocution, my brother Hartwig, who was two years older than I, displayed considerable talent. Eventually, in fact, he became an actor. But for me, getting up to recite was an agonizing ordeal.

I never have forgotten one disastrous evening at Mannes Baum's house. Mother took me by the hand and, leading me to the center of the room, urged, "Now say something, dear."

I was scared to death but started off in a singsong voice. So deeply etched into my memory is the incident that I still can quote the opening lines of the piece I was trying to recite. They were from "Hohenlinden," by Thomas Campbell, a Scotch poet:

On Linden when the sun was low,
All bloodless lay the untrodden snow;
And dark as winter was the flow
Of Iser, rolling rapidly.

I got no further than that when Father lifted a finger to the side of his nose and made a mimicking noise that sounded like:

A-toodle-dah!

That finished me. I rushed from the room, ran back to our house through the night, of which I was afraid, and cried myself to sleep.

In later years Father often told me how much he regretted his little joke. That episode nearly destroyed any hope I ever had of mastering the art of public speaking. For years afterward I never could rise to my feet to say anything without remembering "A-toodle-dah!"

Once I told President Woodrow Wilson about this. At first he consoled me by saying, "There are too many men who like to speak and too few to do things. Most of them the world does not care to hear. I wouldn't advise even you to try to learn."

I couldn't agree. I believe it is almost as important for a man to be able to express his views as to have them.

Later President Wilson helped me improve my speech delivery. During the Peace Conference in Paris, he took enough time one evening to show me how to gesture graciously rather than abruptly. "Do it this way," he explained, gesturing slowly with his hand, "not this way," illustrating his point with an abrupt thrust.

Other friends also helped. I had a habit of speaking through almost clenched lips. Herbert Bayard Swope would often say, "For heaven's sake, open your mouth!" In 1939, I was asked to deliver a short radio tribute on the death of Pope Pius XI. As I talked, Swope stood in front of me making facial gestures to remind me to "open your mouth."

. . .

I was four or five years old when I started at a school kept by Mr. and

Mrs. William Wallace. It was about a mile from home, and Harty and I walked, carrying our lunches in a tin box with the food wrapped in a doily. In those days a "napkin" was something you put on babies, and for a long time I thought of it as not a nice word.

Mrs. Wallace conducted what would now be called kindergarten. The "classroom" was the kitchen of her house. I learned my letters lying on my stomach on the floor while she sat nursing her baby or preparing the noonday meal. Mr. Wallace presided over the upper grades, or the school proper, in another building equipped with long benches and crude desks which opened at the top.

Mr. Wallace was an excellent teacher, although some of his methods would hardly be tolerated today. Inattention brought a ruler down across the offender's knuckles or opened palm. Persistent negligence or other serious offenses meant a sound thrashing. In a corner of the room stood a number of switches ready for use. I do not remember that those switches ever were used on me, but it was at Wallace's school that I first felt the switch that is wielded by one's conscience.

One afternoon as class ended I saw a boy leave half of a red-and-white peppermint stick in his desk. Store candy was so rare a treat that I was tempted beyond my strength. With a crony I plotted to get that candy.

When the school was empty we stole back, crawled under the building, forced up a loose plank in the floor with our hands and squirmed through. We took the candy and went off under a tree and ate it.

A feeling of guilt came over me almost at once. The sweet peppermint taste in my mouth seemed bitter. Curiously, again and again in later life this trivial episode came back to me.

Once, when I was just starting in Wall Street, James R. Keene, one of the master speculators of his time, asked me to look into the underwriting of a new company, Brooklyn Gas. My investigation convinced me that it would be a good investment. Then a young man connected with the syndicate selling the securities offered me a $1,500 "commission" to turn in a favorable report.

Fifteen hundred dollars was a lot of money to me at the time. But the memory of that red-and-white peppermint stick rose before me and I couldn't take it. In fact, it made me fear that there might be something wrong with the stock so I went over my ground again. And in my report to Mr. Keene, I told him of the offer of the "commission."

The Wallace school ground was also a tough arena for testing one's character. You had to fight or be known as a coward. My brother Harty was a scrapper by instinct. But it took me a long time to learn to fight skillfully and with a cool head.

My main trouble was that I lost my temper too quickly. I was fat,

freckle-faced, and relatively short as a boy—"Bunch" was my nick-
name—and inevitably seemed to get licked in every scrap. The humiliation of being beaten did not improve either my self-confidence or my
temper.

Once when Harty took my fishing pole and started up the street
with it, I ran after him, picked up a stone and angrily threw it at him.
When I saw the stone was going to hit him I called out a warning.
Harty turned around just in time to get the stone on the mouth. It left
a scar on his lip which he bore to the end of his days.

On another occasion, while visiting Grandfather Wolfe, I flew into
a tantrum at the breakfast table. I got so angry over something—just
what I can't recall—that I lunged across the table, grabbed a piece of
meat and stuffed it down my throat. I did no harm to myself, but I
"caught it" from my grandmother.

The boys of Camden were divided into two gangs, an "uptown"
gang to which we belonged, and a "downtown" gang which was considered tougher than we were. Behind this division there may have
been some deeper social conflict of which I was unaware, since, as I
recall, we "uptown" boys had to wash our feet every night while the
"downtowners" seldom washed theirs.

The rivalry between the two groups was intense. The annual baseball game between the two sections of town was always an exciting
event. We played in a field behind the old jail. In one game I tried to
beat a throw to third base. I didn't make it but collided with the base-
man and he dropped the ball. That started a fight in which I got my
usual licking.

There was a Huckleberry Finn or Tom Sawyer quality in how we
lived. In fact, whenever I read Mark Twain or saw the cartoons of
Clare Briggs or H. T. Webster's "Life's Darkest Moment," I would feel
a sense of nostalgia for my boyhood.

Every spring the Wateree River would flood the Camden countryside. The floods were calamities to the grownups but we boys enjoyed
them. We built rafts to explore the inundated country for miles about.
We always regretted the fall of the waters.

The best place to fish and swim was Factory Pond, which furnished
the power for Malone's mill, a cotton compress and corn mill, and was
also used for baptisms. During the long summers we were in the water
every day. A shirt and a pair of pants were our only clothes and these
were unbuttoned on the run as we neared the pond. Without stopping,
we would jump out of our clothes and plunk into the water like so
many bull frogs.

Strung out across the pond were First Stump, Second Stump, Third
Stump, and Flat Stump. I remember what a thrill it was the first time I

swam to First Stump and back. Then I tackled Second Stump. I had worked up to Third Stump when our family left South Carolina.

Nearly all the boys in town would collect birds' eggs, which we would trade with each other. Harty was particularly good at shinning up trees, although Mother didn't take kindly to our robbing birds' nests. Harty and I also used to hunt small game in the woods with muzzle-loading shotguns.

. . .

Like all boys I had my childhood heroes. They seem to have been drawn less from books than from among my relatives and a few figures in the community.

I was brought up to believe that Robert E. Lee was the epitome of all virtues. Father often quoted a maxim of Lee's as a guide to my own conduct: "Do your duty in all things. You could not do more. You would not wish to do less."

Generals Beauregard, Stonewall Jackson, and Jeb Stuart were other shining figures, as were Marion, Sumter, and Picken from the Revolutionary War. Not even George Washington loomed as large in my mind as those soldiers of the swamp.

Beyond these soldierly figures, my favorites were Mannes Baum, my uncles Herman and Joe Baruch, and Fischel Cohen, my great-uncle.

Uncle Herman, who had gone to war because he could not stand the reproach in the eyes of the ladies, was a bon vivant and a free spender. After working for Mannes Baum, whose mercantile establishment had grown to be the largest in Camden, Herman opened his own store. He would regale us with tales of high times on buying trips to New York. But what interested us more was that he never returned without gifts for every member of the family.

Uncle Joe, Father's youngest brother, had served in a Uhlan cavalry regiment in Germany. He was "considerable of an athlete," as we used to say, and taught us to perform on the horizontal and parallel bars, which he put up in our back yard. My tomboy Aunt Sarah, Mother's youngest sister, who used to visit us from Winnsboro, would compete with us on the bars. I remember how shocked everyone was when she hung by her toes.

I adored my great-uncle Fischel Cohen, the only son of Rabbi Hartwig Cohen. He had been a telegraph operator on General Beauregard's staff and would tell, by the hour, humorous stories of his wartime experiences.

"Yes," he used to say, "I was a brave man in the war—always where the bullets were thickest—under the ammunition wagon."

Uncle Fischel played the banjo and had a whole line of songs. The refrain of one ran:

> I would rather be a home guard private,
> Than a brigadier brought home to die.

I recall many happy evenings with Fischel strumming his banjo. Mother at the piano, and a roomful of friends singing Southern songs. One which I have not heard for seventy-odd years ended every verse with the line: "And the bells went ringing for Sarah!"

Mother, being a talented amateur actress, was eager that her sons should play and sing. In this we uniformly disappointed her. Only Harty and Sailing learned any musical instrument and that was the banjo. I have never been able even to whistle a tune.

One local personality I admired, although secretly, was Boggan Cash of the celebrated dueling Cashes from Chesterfield County. His father, Colonel E. B. C. Cash, had commanded a regiment in Father's brigade. Young Boggan was not old enough for the Civil War, but he did all he could to make up for that lost opportunity to display his marksmanship.

Dueling was fairly common in the South Carolina of my childhood. Camden, in particular, seems to have been a center for it. I remember watching Boggan Cash at target practice, wheeling and firing at an iron man which had been set up on the bank of Factory Pond. Sometimes he would get one of the older boys to call, "Ready, fire!" for him.

One duel in which the Cashes were involved had a profound effect on my life in that it led to Father's leaving South Carolina.

The trouble began when a brother of Mrs. Cash assaulted another man in the course of a drunken orgy. To avoid a court judgment, Mrs. Cash's brother transferred some property to his sister's name. Colonel William M. Shannon, as an attorney for the man who had been assaulted, instituted an action against Mrs. Cash's brother on grounds of constructive fraud.

Declaring that this suit was an affront to Mrs. Cash, Colonel Cash and his son, Boggan, began a campaign of insult which Colonel Shannon, a man of peace, bore patiently for a year. The situation finally became intolerable and Colonel Shannon challenged Colonel Cash to a duel.

The Shannon family and ours were intimate. Shannon had been a leader in the revival of country fairs as a means of stimulating better farming methods. Mother often pointed him out to us as a model of courtesy.

The duel was arranged for July 5, 1880, at Du Bose's Bridge in Darlington County. Hoping to avert any shooting, Father, without

Shannon's knowledge, advised the sheriff of the hour and place of the meeting. The sheriff promised to be on hand in time to prevent hostilities.

First to reach the appointed spot was Colonel Shannon, attended by Dr. Burnett, his physician, a second, and a few friends, including Father. A few minutes later Colonel Cash arrived. There was no sign of the sheriff.

The seconds paced off the ground, decided by lot the choice of position and the giving of the signal. Still no sheriff.

The principals took their stations. At the word of command Shannon fired quickly. The bullet tore up the earth in front of Colonel Cash. Cash aimed deliberately and fired. Shannon fell. When he was reached he was beyond help.

A few minutes later the sheriff galloped up.

This was one of the last fatal duels in the United States. Its repercussions were many, for Camden had no more highly respected citizen than William M. Shannon. I remember a group of grim-looking men, armed with rifles and shotguns, riding up to our house to see Father. Among them I recognized a young fellow who was engaged to Colonel Shannon's daughter.

Father invited them into his office. Presently the men emerged, mounted their horses, and rode slowly away. Father had persuaded them not to take the law into their own hands and kill Cash. Public sentiment avenged Colonel Shannon's death. Cash, who had been a man of distinction in his community, was ostracized and left to a fate similar to Aaron Burr's.

This tragedy also resulted in legislation which outlawed duels in South Carolina and disqualified from public office anyone who had taken part in one. At the inauguration of James F. Byrnes as governor in 1951, I was amused to hear him take a solemn oath that he had never engaged in a duel.

For some time Mother had been urging Father to go North where opportunities would be greater. But Father held back until the Cash-Shannon duel, which he had tried to prevent and which was such a shock to him.

In the winter of 1880, Father sold his practice and the house with its little "farm." Together with his savings, the sale brought his total financial assets to $18,000, the fruit of sixteen years as a country doctor.

Father went on ahead to New York City. Mother followed with her four boys. The first leg of the journey was made in our old carriage to Winnsboro, where we took the train North. In the hamper of food we carried aboard the train were some of Grandmother Wolfe's cookies.

When the hamper was emptied we left the train to eat at the regular meal stops. Our best meal was in Richmond, and to this day that city suggests good food to me. We arrived on the New Jersey side of the Hudson River at dusk and took the ferry across the river.

~~~~~~

DISCUSSION AND INQUIRY

If one holds to the theory that a child's conscience is based on his identification with his parents, then it is easy to understand the development of Bernard Baruch's social conscience. His father's concern for the community, as well as for the individuals within it, certainly must have served as a model for young Baruch. The influence of the conscience is displayed with the incident of the peppermint stick. Baruch's immediate reaction to the theft was a feeling of guilt to the point where the sweet candy tasted sour to him, and the memory of the episode recurred even in adulthood. What would be a Freudian explanation of the development of moral judgment and conscience? How would the theories of Piaget and Erikson differ from this and each other? (See Jean-Paul Sartre, for further discussion of conscience development.)

Adult humor at the expense of a child can often create an emotional impact that will stay with the individual through his adult years. Such was the case when Baruch's father made fun of his recitation of a poem. Why do parents ask their children to perform for guests? Why would Baruch react to his father's jeering the way he did? Do you agree with this statement by Upton Sinclair, "Grown-up people do not realize how intensely children feel, and what enduring impressions are made upon their tender minds"? (See the selection by Upton Sinclair.)

The author describes himself as a "mamma's boy," shy and sensitive. Yet, he also states that he participated in fighting, gangs, and various physical feats to gain status among his peers. How hard is it for the nonathletic child to gain acceptance? (See the selection by Gerald Brenan.)

Young Baruch's heroes were military men of the Civil War. Many parents become concerned when their children play war games and worship military figures. Why are children attracted to war games? Are parents' concerns justified? At what stage of development does hero worship begin, and what need does it fulfill?

Gertrude Edelstein Berg

BIOGRAPHICAL SKETCH

Gertrude Edelstein Berg, known affectionately as Molly Goldberg, was born in 1899, educated in New York, and married Lewis Berg in 1918. Her professional start was on radio. She wrote and starred in a show called "The Goldbergs." Her face became as popular as her voice when "The Goldbergs" and "Mrs. G. Goes to College" became favorite television shows in the late '40's and in the '50's. She was given the Sara Siddon award for her performance in the Broadway production of Majority of One, *and received the Antoinette Perry award for the original play she and James Yaffe wrote,* Dear Me the Sky Is Falling. *She died in New York, in 1966, at the age of sixty-seven.*

SELECTIONS FROM

MOLLY AND ME

I SHOULD probably say that I liked school—it sounds better. But the whole truth is, I didn't. I wasn't interested and there was always something I would rather be doing than sitting in a classroom, like, for instance, sitting at home. Besides, I was scared. It wasn't psychological, it was just the way the school looked.

The school was known by a number. P.S. (for Public School) 103. It was built out of depressing reddish blocks that my father insisted were probably made by the brother of some city official. The building was big and ugly. When I first went to it at the age of six it was new, but it looked old and somebody had carefully designed it to look like a prison. The windows on the first floor were all barred and I thought that was to keep the students from escaping. When I went into the building I was sure I was right. There were two entrances, one for boys and one for girls. When I got inside I saw I wasn't the only one being accused. Both sexes were lined up by class and marched off to their rooms.

Marching through the halls at nine in the morning was like tramping through a cloudy day. I learned things, though, like the physical law that says the smaller a light bulb is, the less light it gives. The walls were painted gray except where the blackboards broke the monotony and the whole effect was of a place in which no one was going to smile, not even me. Not even when it finally came my turn to have what I thought was one of the best jobs in the class, using the long pole to open and shut the big classroom windows. Whenever I was in charge of the windows I suddenly became very careful about drafts. Five minutes after I had opened the windows I was up and out of my seat closing them. Then, of course, the room got too hot, so I had to get up again and open them just a little bit. I really made use of my turn when it came around about once every twenty-five days. On the other days I wasn't too eager to be a schoolgirl.

Every morning when I woke up I would hope for rain or snow or maybe a flood because if the weather was bad enough I could always talk my mother into letting me stay home. She was afraid of colds. I was a healthy child but as soon as I saw a cloud in the sky I began to talk through my nose. I became very good at sniffling.

The school wasn't too far from home, a few blocks, and as I walked I would see people doing all sorts of things that looked like more fun than what I was going to be doing. The grocer would be in front of his store carrying in supplies of milk and fruit; there would be a van in front of the butcher's and the driver would be lugging in a huge side of beef; the hardware-store man would be unlocking his store—the whole world looked busy and I was the only one who didn't have anything to do but go to school.

I could always talk to my parents about almost any problem but school was one exception. There were two reasons: First, I knew I was being foolish and it wasn't such a terrible problem; I could put up with it. Second, my parents had ambitions for me; they wanted me to go to school and I didn't feel I could disappoint them. At least not right away.

My attitude about school had something to do with the few friends I made. I didn't like children who liked school and it seemed to me that I was in a class of teacher's pets. But there was one girl, Claire, who shared my sour attitude about going to school. Claire and I met, became friends when we were 10, and have been friends ever since.

The first thing that showed me that Claire and I were soulmates was her love of being a monitor. To me being a monitor was the best part of going to school. Maybe I was born to boss because I enjoyed that first little taste of authority.

I felt very responsible in that job and I shushed my classmates for the sheer joy of shushing. And so did Claire. From the minute I saw her bossing her side of the room I knew we would be friends.

43

The second thing that attracted me to Claire was her clothes. She always wore knee-length gingham dresses, patent leather shoes that buttoned up the side, and a corset. It was the corset that did it. Claire was a big girl for her age and you don't find a ten-year-old girl with the figure of a woman every day. I always tried to get close to Claire so that I could see what made her go in here and out there. Poor Claire must have suffered agonies, because those were the days when the flat-chested figure was the rage and she just wasn't the type, even in the fourth grade.

There was one more thing that made Claire my friend: I was very bad at arithmetic but good at English; Claire was very bad at English and very good at arithmetic. So the solution was obvious: Claire did my numbers and I did her compositions, and together we managed a B average.

One day Claire just happened to take a composition of mine home with her. She showed it to her father, who was a doctor and a very scientific man. He wouldn't believe that anyone in Claire's class could have written it. Claire argued with him so loud and long that, to prove he was right, he told Claire to bring me home.

I should have been flattered but I was nervous. To me a doctor was next to God and before you called one the house was cleaned, the linen was changed and not only in the sick-room, the furniture was dusted, and the bathroom shone like an operating room. Being sick was just a side issue. Diagnostically speaking, a clean house meant that the patient wasn't so badly off.

When I got to Claire's house—a handsome private brownstone in the very fashionable neighborhood of Madison Avenue and 119th Street—I was good and scared. I was introduced to the doctor, who didn't say much but asked me to go into his office and told Claire to wait outside. That didn't exactly put me at my ease. He asked me, in very medical tones, if I had written the composition. He had it on his desk and he waved it in front of me. I told him that I had written it. He looked at me as though I had a loathesome disease. The diagnosis was clear. I was a liar. He handed me a paper and pencil and told me to write something.

I wrote. I don't remember what I wrote but it must have satisfied his scientific soul because he let me out of the office and told me I could play with Claire—upstairs in her room where we wouldn't disturb the patients.

The house that Claire lived in was the most beautiful I had even seen and it was the first private house in New York City that I had ever been in. It reminded me of a furniture store—every floor was a showplace. The kitchen was in the basement and it was big enough to hold two apartments like the one I lived in. The front room, on the first floor, was decorated with red damask and the furniture was all of heavy carved wood, the kind with lion's heads and taloned feet. The rugs were thick and it felt so good to walk on them that I was sure it was the wrong thing to do. The second floor was a parlor and the furniture there was all gold and petit point; there were Oriental rugs on the floor and oil paintings on the walls, all with little lights attached to make sure you could see they were the real thing.

The higher we climbed the more ornate things became. Claire's room was on the third floor and I expected to be taken into a princess' fairyland. Claire opened the door of her room—to a white iron bed, a chest of drawers, a throw rug on the floor. Not even one picture broke up the eggshell walls. I had expected flounces and frills, dolls and toys, lace curtains and bright pictures. What I saw was a child's Siberia—a room that could have been part of an orphanage or a hospital. It no more belonged to Claire than I belonged in her house.

The finishing touch to my visit was Claire's grandmother. Right out of a Russian novel she was—tall, stately, white-haired, and absolutely confirmed in her opinion that she was a member of the intelligentsia. She spoke correctly, in measured tones, and acted as though the Tsar was waiting for her in the next room. She popped into Claire's room— one minute she wasn't there, the next minute there she was. I was raised to be polite so I stood up. She didn't pay any attention to me but walked over to Claire, felt her forehead, and decided that *her* granddaughter had a fever. "Clairitchke," she said, "you have a temperature. I think you had better send your friend home." She did notice me after all. She uttered her ukase and left the room—she popped out. I never forgot that moment. After all, I was in the room too. She could have insulted me to my face.

I went home. I could hardly wait to get there and to hug my mother and kiss my father. Here was one place in the world that I was wanted. It wasn't such a fancy home but what we lacked in furniture we made up in love. I looked around my home and I saw the Grand Rapids couch, the checkered tablecloth in the kitchen, the pencil sketch of who knew what relative on the wall. I walked on a rug that wasn't Persian or Oriental but plain New England and worn in places, and I looked at my room—the nicest room, the room that had the most attention—and saw what I should have seen at Claire's—a brass bed, white curtains, dolls and toys, pictures on the walls, a room that showed the affection and warmth of those who planned it for me. I looked at what had been given me with new eyes and I saw that somebody loved me.

. . .

When I was in the country I was very glad that my father ran a hotel, but in the city I used to tell all my friends that my father owned a summer estate—it sounded better than a hotel—with fifty rooms and thirty in help. That wasn't entirely a lie; at least the figures were accurate.

I felt free to say whatever I wanted to say while I was in the city because I was sure that none of my friends would ever come up to the country to see. I was so sure that I even added a swimming pool. I was going to put in a stable and horses, but even I thought that would be going too far. I settled for a Duesenberg instead, and if anyone wanted to know why my father wasn't driving it in the city I could always say it was too long to park on Lexington Avenue.

Claire was my favorite confidante to whom I spoke about the country estate. Her father was a well-to-do doctor and she understood all about percale sheets, silver service, and how to speak to chambermaids. If the sort of estate I dreamed of existed today, the taxes would be so impossibly high that my father would have to donate it to the state for a public park—the government would be the only organization capable or keeping it.

One day, one summer, naturally, my sins came home to roost. I was in the village, when I saw Claire, her grandmother, and an aunt riding down the main street on horseback. They just happened to be staying up in the hills somewhere on a farm, and because I'm the kind of person whose sins always come full circle to smite me, they just happened to be riding through the village when I was there.

Claire was overjoyed to see me. I would have been happy to see her except for memories of what I had told her about the estate. I was in too deep to invite Claire and her grandmother to the hotel—and because Claire was my dearest friend, how could I not invite her? At first I tried to avoid all questions that I could see were going to lead to the "estate." The first thing I just mentioned, in passing, was that the house, all fifty rooms, were being painted and that the immediate family, my mother, my father, and myself, were occupying the guest cottage, a small shack with only three rooms. As soon as the house was all painted, they simply *must* come up for a visit, and as soon as I made the invitation I knew it would take all summer to finish the painting I had just started.

Claire's grandmother was one of those district-attorney ladies who, if you said it was a nice day, cross-examined you on exactly what you meant by that highly controversial statement. She wanted to know, room by room, what color everything was going to be. By the time I got to the second floor I ran out of colors.

Actually Claire helped me out by reminding me of all the things I had told her about the "estate" during the winter, little imaginary details I was forgetting under the glare of her grandmother. It occurred to me in a flash of insight—and I should have known it months ago— that Claire knew there was no such thing as an estate. After all, I had

46

written her English compositions at school and she was familiar with my style of living. But Claire was that kind of friend. She understood being caught in a lie and having to live with it. She knew, in those early days, what it took me years to find out: the difference between the real world and the world you make up in the mood of the minute. You can, if you want to, be an orphan when you're talking to your mother and father, the Queen of England on the Staten Island ferry, or, if you have a good friend, you can live on an estate instead of a hotel.

Imagination plays games that have no rules, and mine always makes trouble for me. I can feel sorry for myself in a second or I can feel just wonderful in the same amount of time. Also I can relive embarrassing moments as though they were happening in front of me. I have total recall for terrible things and the worst thing about it is that I can't tell myself to stop. It goes right on and I can't walk away. Even a book in the window of a store can remind me of the time when I was a nine-year-old criminal.

Fleischmanns [a small village in the Catskills] had a library, a small, white house donated to the town by the Skenes, a wealthy family that had an estate in the hills above the village. From the outside the library looked like any other private house, but inside it was the real thing, complete with the special smell that comes from bookbindings, a little dust, and library paste. The librarian was a lady who looked like a librarian, tall, thin, with eyeglasses and a bun on the back of her head. She was the only person in town who could move across the wooden floor without squeaking a board. Whenever I came in to borrow a book she was ready with suggestions and advice. So my crime was not only against society, but also against that very nice lady.

I happened to borrow *The Deerslayer*, a very long book, believe me, and even at that age I felt I had to finish any book I started, if not for myself, then out of respect for the author. I kept the book for a long time, so long that it became overdue. At first the fine was two cents, then four, then eight. It was approaching fifty cents when I became panicky. I was reluctant to tell my mother and disappoint her, and I didn't dare to face my father. Every time I walked through the village I crossed the street to avoid the library. I walked up back streets and through alleys until I was sure that I had passed it. I was positive that everyone in the town knew of my terrible crime, and at home, when the doorbell rang, I shuddered: it might be the sheriff or the librarian or the mayor coming to take me and the book away.

A child can be desperate. I know now that if I had told my parents I would have got a little lecture and the fifty cents to pay the fine, but that was then, and who knew?

I felt that there really wasn't anyone I could turn to, not even my closest friend, Kenneth Avery, who, at the age of eight, was a financier.

47

There are some children who cast shadows of themselves as adults and Kenneth's shadow was rich. He grew sweet peas in his father's back yard and sold them at The New Switzerland Hotel. (The New Switzerland was Kenneth's territory, he explained, since it was the closest hotel to his house.) His price, depending on the size of the bouquet and the attitude of the customers, was five or ten cents a bunch. During the sweet-pea season Kenneth might average three to four hundred dollars. But that wasn't the end of it: he would lend the money to his father at six per cent interest. He was the wealthiest self-made eight-year-old I ever met.

I didn't want to ask Kenneth for the money because I was too ashamed to tell him, but his mother was a different story. Finey Avery was a comfortable woman, a lady who understood children and always had cookies in the oven and a ready ear for children's problems. I don't know why I felt that Mrs. Avery would be more understanding than my own parents except that she looked the part, and besides, she was familiar with high finance through her son. I decided to confess to her.

Committing a terrible deed is simple compared to confessing it. I approached Mrs. Avery's house four times before I had the nerve to go in. Of course she welcomed me as though I were an innocent child. She didn't know yet. How she would feel about me in another minute was something I didn't want to think about. Maybe she'd never let me see Kenny again; after all, a self-confessed criminal wasn't a good companion for a young tycoon. I built up my nerve by eating the cookies she placed on the table. When I finished the last one I went into a long explanation about what I was going to tell her. First, I wanted her to promise not to say a word to my mother or my father, and, second, I wanted it understood that what I was suggesting was a purely business proposition. As the mother of my wealthiest friend she could understand that. I finally told her about the overdue book. Mrs. Avery looked very serious. I thought she was going to say no, so I reassured her that I would pay her back at the rate of one cent a week for fifty weeks, plus six per cent interest. She nodded and said that she would extend the credit. She handed me two quarters—and suddenly the world seemed to be a brighter place; it began to look as though I really had a future. My heart stopped pounding and my hands stopped shaking. I tried to thank her but the words didn't seem to come out right.

I ran home. I got the book and marched up the main street to the library. I went inside like an honest woman, paid the fine, and walked out—free!

I paid Mrs. Avery one cent a week every week, secure in the knowledge that no one knew about my debt except the two of us. I should have known better, but I didn't until many years had passed. Of course Mrs. Avery told my mother, and they had a good laugh. Can you imagine? They laughed at my suffering, and years later my agony became one of my mother's favorite stories. Even when I was married and the mother of two children I still felt the hot flush of shame whenever my mother started to tell the story. In some ways a person is always a child and whenever I think about the library and the book I'm 9 years old again and I have no place to turn.

The other sufferer in this affair was Mr. James Fenimore Cooper. I never could read him again.

DISCUSSION AND INQUIRY

The elementary school that is "big and ugly . . . designed to look like a prison" is still an apt description of many inner-city schools. Gertrude Berg reacted to it by wanting to be anywhere else but in it. Recall your own elementary school building. How would you change it to make it become a more joyful place, with an atmosphere that might be more conducive to learning?

The author gives us a description of her friend Claire's parents and home. She was moved by the starkness of Claire's room in contrast to the rest of the house. Can you speculate as to the reasons Claire was such a good friend to Gertrude, besides the reasons offered by the author? Do children sense how much they are valued in the home by the way the family attends to their needs within the family setting?

Being a monitor had its appeal for Gertrude as it does for many children. Some would say that the desire to have power or control over others is natural to man. Others would argue that such desires are learned. What do you think? Many teachers would claim that being a monitor allows a child to take on responsibilities and that, therefore, he learns to become a good citizen. Think about the times that you were given a position of authority in your early school days. How did you regard your role? (See the selection by Anne Moody, in which the issue of children having authority over other children is considered.)

Compare Gertrude Berg's bragging about her father's country home with the selection by Dylan Thomas. Why do children brag? Are their purposes different from those of bragging adults?

The money that was borrowed from a friend's mother to pay for a library fine became a humorous story between that woman and Gertrude's mother. Why does the author recall this with agony, even though many years have passed? The breaking of a trust is not often forgotten by child or adult. Most of us can easily recall those incidents where we felt a confidence was violated by one we trusted. How might this affect the relationship between the two individuals?

Gerald Brenan

BIOGRAPHICAL SKETCH

The author, Gerald Brenan, was raised in a Victorian world, a life-style he struggled to escape. He was born in Malta, in 1894. He ran away from home at the age of 16, only to return after being defeated by the winter in Serbia and Montenegro. After serving in the First World War, Brenan moved to Spain, where he found the inspiration for much of his writing. The Face of Spain *and* A Holiday by the Sea *are among his many books.*

SELECTIONS FROM

A LIFE OF ONE'S OWN

WHEN I try to recall my early life at my prep school, the things that come before me most obstinately are the faces of my masters and school-fellows. They float to the surface of my mind, as fresh and as vivid as when I first saw them, and nearly every one of them resembles an animal. I seem to be living in a zoo, each inmate of which is slightly repellent, while taken all together they are terrifying because, like the figures in dreams, I have no control over them. Nor can this impression be entirely subjective, because many of the boys and masters had animal nicknames.

But I had better begin at the beginning and put down my recollections in their proper order. My parents took me to my school and left me there—if I may trust my mother's diary—in a state of excitement and self-confidence. I was tired of my solitary, governess-ruled life, I longed to have other boys as companions and had no doubts that I should get on with them and win their approval. And indeed my first acts appear to show that I felt sure of myself. Within a couple of days of being at school I had put my hand to two characteristic exploits: explored a deep sewer that ran under the main road, and led a party of new boys from my dormitory onto the roof of the house. The first yielded some flint nodules containing blue crystals: the second was discovered and led to my being scolded. Then, a day or two later, I walked off after breakfast and did not return until the evening. "We call him the Radical Reformer," my headmaster remarked playfully to my parents, "because he has no respect for any of the rules." I imagine that the school had begun to pall on me and that I was trying to repeat the trick that had worked so well at Montreux.

Anyone who took his information about English schools from boys' adventure books might suppose that this brief show of truancy made me popular. But schoolboys, though they love to attribute to themselves all sorts of heroic roles in their daydreams, are in reality the most convention-bound creatures in the world. The right to any show of individuality among them has to be won by a long period of apprenticeship supplemented by skill in the approved kinds of games. Till then their tribal law demands complete uniformity. Now, as it happened, I found myself sinning from the start against the first canon of this law —that which relates to dress. My mother, in her ignorance of school etiquette, had provided me with house shoes that fastened by a strap and button instead of with that more manly kind which have elastic sides. When this was discovered I was surrounded by a hostile mob, staring and pointing at the disgraceful appendages. "New boy. New boy. He's got buttons on his shoes. He's got buttons on his shoes. He's got buttons on his shoes," the chorus repeated. In a moment my self-confidence, which had never been subjected to a strain of this sort before, vanished.

Thus, by a fatality deriving from a pair of buttoned shoes, I was sent spinning down a slope into the abyss of unpopularity. And this was terrible. In the dense herd life of a schoolboy in a junior form nothing matters except whether he is popular or not, and I was on the bottom rung of the ladder. So abject was my state that I remember wondering to myself at the end of my first term whether the most unpopular boy in the school was a certain Gresley or myself. This Gresley was a pathetic little creature, aged not much above eight, with a baby face, curly hair and a look of having been smeared in butter: on the least provocation he burst into tears. I despised him because, being entirely crushed in my own self-esteem, I had adopted the tribal standards of the other boys; yet out of loneliness I was compelled to consort with him.

The story of every schoolboy's life being simply that of his gradual rise to popularity, I shall not bore the reader by plotting the stages of mine. I will only say that my progress was particularly slow. The usual procedure of boys who, like myself, were not good at games was to link themselves to others more favoured than they were and hope to be carried along with them. But I found this a disheartening business. As a rule I had no difficulty in making friends with a more successful

or athletic boy of my own age whenever I happened to be thrown together with him because there were subjects like riding and stamp- and
egg-collecting that we shared in common. But then, just as we were
beginning to get on, the stigma of my unpopularity would descend.
This was a blank, impersonal label, like that of being a Jew in Germany, which attached itself for no particular reason and continued out
of habit. It was so much a part of one that one could not dispute it or
argue with it. Thus, when my new friend came up against some sudden
expression of hostile opinion about me, he would cold-shoulder me
and then drop me, while if I struggled against this it would be said that
I was sucking-up to him. "Sucking-up" was a crushing term. We were
like the courtiers of Elizabethan times, living all of us by flattery and
toad-eating, yet damned as Rosencrantzes if our flattery was noticed.

The sense of being beyond the pale set up a train of morbid states of
mind. Thus from my first and second years I preserve a group of
memories that all share the same depressing tone. I was still a miserable, deeply unpopular little boy, but among the other miserable, unpopular little boys I had found a few companions. Our pursuits were
secretive and macabre. For example, I remember how with another boy
(whose face comes down to me as an enormous red pear with a few
rat-like teeth projecting from it) I used to creep into an empty lot of
building-land that lay next to the railway cutting and which, because
it was overgrown with bushes and strictly out of bounds, we called
No-man's-land. We had made a tunnel through the dense undergrowth
of privet and snowball and along this we used to creep fearfully on our
hands and knees. At the end of this tunnel, in a little grassy space,
stood a willow tree, gnarled and decaying, and in the hollow of its
trunk, under a stone, there lived a toad. We pretended to ourselves that
a skull was buried under this tree and that the toad was in some way
connected with it. Then occasionally we would dare one another to
take it up in our hands. I remember the state of suspense and almost
agony I used to be in when I thought that my companion might on a
sudden impulse throw it to the ground or squash it under the stone,
and I suspect that subconsciously I was tempted to do this myself. Yet
had I come on it in my parents' garden I should not have had to resist
this sadistic temptation because there I felt secure and happy.

The attraction of this shrubbery came, of course, from its being out
of bounds. One escaped when one crept on all fours down its green
tunnel and at the same time one entered a disturbing, uncanny precinct.
Dead men's bones lay mouldering under the earth, trains rushed by
leaving after them a strange silence, a murderer might perhaps be
lurking there. One day I came across a dead rat of enormous size lying
belly upwards on the ground and was so disgusted that I kept away

for a whole term. Rats, toads, dead men's skulls, shrieks of trains and owls, white-sheeted ghosts, the glaring eyes and corpse-like hands of murderers—that is what some little schoolboys' dreams are made of.

Another sinister spot was a small grass-grown mound that stood on the edge of the drive by the front door. We invented a story that our maths master, Mr. Wood, known to his pupils as "The Sheep," had murdered a man and secretly buried him here. Our only reason for this suspicion lay in the fact that The Sheep wore his hair close-cropped and so of course must have spent some part of his life in a convict prison—until, by means of the usual file and two knotted sheets, he had contrived to escape. We worked up this story with such fervor that for a time we actually believed it to be true and determined, as good citizens ought, to expose him. One moonlight night, we swore, when everyone else was sleeping, we would creep out of the fourth-form window, dig up the grassy grave and publish The Sheep's infamy. But when it came to the point either our courage or our faith in our story failed us.

When many years later I began to read books on primitive societies, these early years at my prep school flooded back into my mind. Yes, I knew what it was to be an Arunta of Central Australia or a Dobu Islander of Melanesia or a devil worshipper in an African jungle. In his genteel boarding-school, between the ages of nine and twelve, a modern Englishman goes through a state which is not unlike that in which the more benighted among the primitive races still live.

It must, I think, have been in the Easter term of 1905—that is, when I was nearly twelve—that both my misery and the neurosis that was associated with it reached their critical point. I had taken to reading with all the zest and fury with which one takes to it at that age. Books were my opium and I could hardly bear to have one out of my hand. Boys' adventure stories, especially when they led into remote regions of the world, were my first taste and from them I went on to melo-dramas written for adults. These sometimes affected me powerfully. During the holidays, a couple of years before, my mother had started to read me *Oliver Twist*, but had been obliged to put it down because it gave me nightmares. Now, lying full length on the divan in the library, I devoured *The Deemster* by Hall Caine. As I read it I imagined that my parents, by some unlucky stroke, had lost all their money, that we should presently sink into a frightening poverty and be obliged to seek lodgings in one of the more dismal quarters of a large town. I even imagined that my father had got into debt, or into some trouble that was worse than debt, and was on the point of being carried off to prison. So real did this imaginary catastrophe become to me that every day I scanned the red, purple-veined face of the headmaster in the expecta-tion that he would call me to his study and tell me that he had just received—a letter. But he never sent for me, nothing happened, and gradually I recovered my equanimity.

When I cast my mind back over these first two and a half years of school life I am amazed at the quantity of misery that this small boy who went by my name had to suffer. The experience of being harried and tormented all day long for no other reason than that he is considered to be a little different from his fellows is something that grown-up people, with all their superior resources of mind and character, are not generally called on to endure. There was the drab squalor of the football field, the agony of the swimming-baths, where one had only to appear to be ducked, the dreariness of the lessons, the harshness of the masters, the kicks and shoves and spitefulness that met one wherever one went. In particular I remember one torture which the older boys were especially fond of trying on the more timid among the younger ones. They would put them in the racket court and kick a football at them. Round and round the ball would go, bouncing off the walls with a hollow, echoing sound and putting me, when it was my turn for this treatment, almost out of my mind with terror. I had lost all self-respect. I had not even the courage to hate my tormentors.

Once at least I must have been ill. I remember lying, shivering all over, on the long settee in the library. It was covered—I can see it now —with a coarse, dingy material woven in a pattern of dark brown lines and fainter cross-lines. Leather buttons held it together and there was a greasy leather fringe along the seam. From about November on, a faint sickly smell, mingling with the dust on the floor and with the taste of "squashed fly" biscuits, would hang about this place. I connected it with the rats, which every year died poisoned under the boards and rotted in the warmth of the thick, black, hot-water pipes. Workmen came to remove them, taking up the boards as one takes up the roadway over a sewer and revealing an ugly hollow of bricks and beams beneath, but the smell, though it grew gradually fainter, never quite vanished. I realize now that on this occasion I must have had flu. Since the matron never took our temperature unless she could see spots, chills and colds and flus passed unrecognized.

The spot-giving complaints, however, took one at once to the infirmary. Here I went whenever I succumbed to one of the usual children's epidemics. One lay on a bed covered with coarse grey blankets, listening to the rumbling and shrieking of the trains in the cutting outside, and at meal-times ate tepid boiled fish served with equally tepid greens and potatoes; after these came either prunes and custard or that large-grained slimy tapioca which we called cods' eyes. A prematurely stunted skivvy by name Olive, freckle-faced, breastless, with dingy red hair and steel spectacles, aged perhaps twenty, used to read to me every evening from a thick, well-thumbed volume entitled *The*

55

Lamplighter. She belonged to the Salvation Army and I suspect that the book she read to me, though all I can remember of it now is its damp, depressing tone, was a kind of religious tract put into novel form. She greatly feared hell-fire and used to speak of it by some circumlocutory phrase, as people do of cancer. "It—" she would say, "It . . . If you die of a sudden and It gets you, you'll burn for ever and ever. Here, have some more gargle." Her tone made such an impression on me that for a long time after, whenever I heard the word hell-fire, I would have a vision of tapioca, bed-pans and throat gargle, with the white, freckled face of the sky, crossed by wet, leafless trees, pressing against the window.

When I dream, as till I was past forty I used often to do, of this time, I find myself wandering anxiously through cold sunless classrooms, searching for the particular room where I have to be at this hour. Or rather, where I should have been five minutes ago, for the minute hand is already pointing to the first division of the dial and I am that number of minutes late. I have besides not got the book I ought to have—it should be Kennedy's *Elementary Latin Primer*—and what can have happened to my ruler I cannot say. Also my nib is crossed—Phipps minor has seen to that—and my fingers are stained with ink. So that, after hurrying through all those dusty classrooms and running the gauntlet of all those jeering boys, I shall be in triple disgrace: I shall have to listen to the master's bellowing voice as he turns on me: I shall be made to stand up on the form in the sight of everyone and I shall be kept in on the next half-holiday. And then, as likely as not, the dream will change and expand. I am standing in the boot-room passage and a boy who reminds me of a ferret gives me a kick. I am shivering on the edge of the swimming-pool when a cry goes up, "Throw him in the deep end! Duck him!" A creature whose gums and teeth seem to be breaking out of his mouth like the seeds from a cracked pomegranate, says, "I'll pay you out." Hostile faces, hostile gestures, hostile words hem me in like those of the devils in a medieval painting. But they are not devils, only English schoolboys.

Dreams such as this, which once were frequent, provide an evidence that cannot be refuted. The shock of my first years at school was too great. And this brings me to a more general question. There is no misery, I am convinced, to be compared to the misery that is suffered in childhood. Children live very much in the present and have little faculty for hope or faith. Thus, if they are unhappy at their school, they will suffer despairingly, like prisoners who have been given a life sentence, because they cannot imagine it ever ending. This is a thing that parents should take into account before they pack their young son off to a boarding-school.

I now enter with relief upon the middle and more equable period of my prep-school days. The untidy, long-haired, ink-stained, novel-doped little boy whose memories I have inherited is approaching twelve. He was considered clever. He could parse any word in Cicero or Caesar and was well started in Greek, though how this had come about I cannot say. For when I sit here at my table and evoke those far-off school-time hours, I can remember nothing but boredom, drowsiness, hunger and a longing to be anywhere on earth rather than where I was at that moment.

The only subject that interested me at this time was geography, and even in this there was but one branch or department to which I attached much importance—that which concerned itself with oceanic islands. I knew the name and something of the character of every island that was marked on the map of the world that hung on the classroom wall. Some were large, lay close to other lands and were thickly populated. Others, such as Kerguelen or the Cocos Islands or Tristan da Cunha, were small and separated by several thousand miles from the nearest shore. These last were the ones for which I felt the strongest sympathy and attraction—round whose seed-like images on the blue atlas plain my imagination would coil and flow—and any books on the library shelves which I thought might contain an allusion to them were carefully gone through. But a mere visit to one of the islands was not enough to satisfy me. I needed to settle on it. Whenever possible, therefore, some part of prep would be spent in drawing surreptitiously on the back page of my exercise book the favorite of the moment, and since most of the particulars I needed were lacking, I took them freely from my head.

First I drew the island, solitary and uninhabited, and fixed its mountains and its streams. After that I chose a site for my house. A road was built to the port and another road to a more secluded residence. Having accomplished this, the map of the island should have been complete, but a love of planning and general development led me on till I had built harbors, railways, towns and mines and of course settled a thriving population on it. But by this time it had become utterly unfit for me, so that I was forced to migrate to a fresh island, at least two thousand miles distant, and begin the same laborious process over again. For the charm of life on an oceanic island lay precisely in those two thousand miles of water that surrounded it. Two thousand miles from football fields, two thousand miles from Greek conjugations, two thousand miles from old Gabby, our Latin master, and his stink! Till many years after I had grown up I believed that happiness was more easily to be achieved by ridding oneself of the things one did not want than by running after those one lacked.

Oddly enough there was another little boy in my class who had a similar mania to mine. He settled on islands, peninsulas and capes—anywhere, he said, where he could get a footing—in order to bring the blessings of civilization to them. By this he meant—to electrify them. He got his electricity according to circumstances from waterfalls, winds or tides: he set up his plant: he organized the distribution of current and then like myself he moved on somewhere else. Between us we industrialized in the course of a couple of years quite a considerable area of the earth's more scattered surfaces, but possibly because we acted on such very different principles—he out of a conviction of the absolute virtues of electricity, I, in direct contradiction to my most cherished beliefs, under the sheer inescapable pressure of economic law —there was no rivalry between us. Although he would sometimes protest at the unsuitability of my choice when I took one of his newly electrified islands for my hermitage, I never treated his industrial occupations too seriously. And when he moved on from islands and capes to land masses and continents, we turned our backs, as it were, upon one another.

This preoccupation with islands shows that I had some beginnings of a life of my own at this period. I should scarcely have insisted so much upon those two thousand miles unless I had already derived some pleasure from solitude. But in fact the struggle for popularity— which is the one and only passion of all school life, drawing into itself, as the great passions do, almost every other activity and interest—took up (apart from the purely passive addiction to reading) the greater part of my thoughts and energies. To explain the progress I now began to make, I must start with a portrait of one of our masters.

Mr Parker Clark (or Face-ache, as we sometimes called him—not to be confused with Mr Everett Clerke, our history master, commonly known as the Pill) was a young flannel-bagged, Norfolk-jacketed giant who taught us middle-form boys Latin and Greek. He had black curly hair like a Negro, a very loud voice and plenty of good nature. Although he was also the sports master, even those boys who were not good at games liked him. He was famous for his original way of conducting his classes. A boy would stand up to construe a passage which he was supposed to have prepared in prep the night before. At the first serious mistake Mr Clark would put on a frown like thunder and start to shout at him. The boy would then mumble and fall into an even worse howler. "Stand up on your chair," bellowed Mr Clark, getting up himself and striding about the room. "Up on your chair. We all want to look at you. Now try again." Naturally the boy floundered more and more hopelessly. "You're not high enough. Put a box on his chair." A box used to keep papers in was put on his chair and he clambered up on top of it. "Now see if *you* can construe it," he would say, turning to another boy. "You can't either, eh? Up on your chair, then." And before long, unless some cooler head came to the rescue, the whole form would be perched on chairs and boxes upon chairs like so many

Simeon Stylites, with Mr Clark pacing to and fro in front of them and bellowing. As he used to explain to us out of class, he was never angry when he shouted: we need not therefore be too afraid unless we saw him turn deadly pale and speak in a whisper: then, however, we must look out. But he was one of those people who are called boyish (even to us he seemed so) and I never saw him seriously annoyed.

Mr Clark had a number of ideas, considered by himself to be of a daring and even revolutionary nature, which for lack no doubt of a better audience he was fond of letting loose upon us. One of these, I remember, referred to the creation of the world in Genesis. Some learned people, he declared, thought that by the "days" mentioned in this passage were really meant millions of years. And naturally, by the tone in which these words were spoken, we were left to gather that these "some learned people" were right. This method of interpreting Scripture struck me as throwing a flood of light upon the more perplexing of the Bible stories—those, for example, which describe the sun and moon as standing still while an unimportant battle was fought and the mountains as hopping about in their enthusiasm like sheep—so that from this moment the doubts that had begun to assail the natural fundamentalism of my schoolboy mind were arrested.

It was at about this time too that I first began to feel the fascination of those sweeping statements that begin with the word *Really*. The climate of opinion which a boy or young man then ran into—it is the one which prevails through a large part of the world today—suggested that nothing is what it seems to be, but on the contrary is always something else, and that if one wishes to know what this something else really is (and it is of course entirely different to the natural appearance), one must seek the key or explanation that gives it. An absurd example of this relates to railway-carriage wheels. We had read or been told that compressed paper is one of the hardest materials known to science, and then a boy called Mullins, whom we regarded as an authority on such matters, declared that all railway-carriage wheels were made of it. They might *look* as if they were made of steel, but *really*, as every engineer knew, they were made of boiled-down newspapers. I accepted this as being entirely self-evident—did not every scientific statement bear the same paradoxical pattern?—and continued to believe it until many years after I was grown up, when an engineer to whom I happened to mention it laughed at me. Later—that is, after I had passed the age of fifteen—came the impact of atomic theories, social and economic theories, psychological and philosophical theories and the word Really became the inevitable prefix to every serious conversation.

But to return to Mr Clark, another idea of his that made a great impression on me concerned the rise and fall of empires. Pointing to the atlas and to those large, triumphant blots of red that spread over it, he declared that seven empires had risen and fallen since the world began—here he enumerated the Assyrian, the Persian, the Greek, the Roman and so forth—and that some day the British Empire must fall too. This idea shocked me considerably. For one thing I was an ardent patriot, and then there was the serious effect that such changes would have upon geography. Maps would have to be recolored, names changed, national and colonial boundaries redrawn. I wanted to think of those great red blots—and of the blue and yellow and green blots too—going on like the mountains and the rivers for ever.

A considerable part of Mr Clark's conversation ran on his public school. It was a small, obscure place—Pillings, if I remember right, was its name—but we gathered from him that it was *really*, in every respect that counted, the best in England. Certainly neither Eton, Harrow nor Winchester came up to it. I got at all events such an idea of its fame and exclusiveness that, meeting in the holidays with a boy who was bound for Eton and wishing to go one better, I remarked casually, "Well, *I* have my name put down for Pillings." When I found that he had never even heard of it, I decided that there was no need for me to boast any more—he was too ignorant to be worth impressing.

Mr Clark had brought from his school a creed, somewhat unusual in a games master, that little boys are not saved by proficiency in games alone, but also, in specially judicated cases, by the more elusive qualities of dare-devilry and recklessness. In support of this theory he used to instance the great Clive, who had never done well at bat and ball but was as agile as a cat in climbing steeples. Yet he had conquered India! Now it so happened that I was fond of climbing trees. There was one tree in particular overlooking the cricket field where I used to retire with a book when I was supposed to be watching the match. When I had reached the highest ascendable point, which actually was at the very top, I would settle myself into it and look out. Beneath me and all around rolled a sea of sycamore leaves, each leaf horizontally extended, layer above layer, cutting me off completely from the ground. Above, a few white clouds lay about like comfortable sofas in the sleepy sky, while from the direction of the playing field the thud of cricket bats striking on balls made a lazy cushioned sound. Until the school bell rang I was almost as free from interruption as if I had been on my oceanic island.

One afternoon, when I was sitting up there, I dropped my book. As chance would have it, Mr Clark, got up in his white flannels and gaudy Pillings blazer, was just then passing underneath. He called me down in his stentorian voice and sent me back to the match, but I noticed that from this time on he treated me with special kindness. Whether thoughts of Clive and the great empire builders of the past had any-thing to do with this I cannot say, but since he was the most popular master in the school his support helped to remove the more athletic boys' prejudices against me.

At the same time other factors were beginning, though still slowly and uncertainly, to turn the scales in my favor. Even for schoolboys, time passes. The little hunted animal I had been, to whom flight and taking sanctuary had become a second nature, was beginning to change into a more sedate and self-possessed creature. In all schools there is a current which, however often one slips back, carries one inevitably toward the top. The boys above leave, new boys queue up behind and, by the mere passage of time, prestige and popularity are acquired. The last year of my life at Winton House was to be as happy as my first two or three years had been miserable.

DISCUSSION AND INQUIRY

What is unusual about Brenan's experience in prep school is that he was eager to attend and be in the company of other boys. There was no lack of self-confidence in the anticipation of living with and getting along with peers. Perhaps this is why his period of adjustment took several years, for he was ill-prepared for the status quickly given to him as "unpopular." Parents often fail to understand why much of a child's energy is devoted to gaining acceptance of peers. It is easy to see from this selection how miserable one's life can be if he fails in this pursuit. Human beings, especially children, are social animals; and social deprivation can have serious consequences.

The author blames the beginnings of his un-popularity on the kinds of shoes he wore to school. Speculate on some other reasons that might have hindered his acceptance by his schoolmates. Taunting can produce great stress on the child who is the object of ridicule. Have you ever been in such a situation; and can you still remember your feelings? Does peer-group pressure become less important to adults? Can you give examples of peer-group pressure at college, and how it encourages conformity?

Faced with the "stigma of unpopularity," Brenan still had to live from day to day, which to him appeared to be an endless existence. How did he attempt to extract himself from the situation? Which attempts can be classified as overt, and which as defensive?

The selection ends with the line, "The last year of my life at Winton House was to be as happy as my first two or three years had been miserable." Brenan states that with the mere passage of time, popularity, for him, was acquired. Is it merely the passage of time that caused the situation to reverse itself, or is it more likely that the individual accommodated to the situation?

Charles Spencer Chaplin

BIOGRAPHICAL SKETCH

Charles Spencer Chaplin, the son of theatrical parents, was born in London, on April 16, 1889. In 1918, he opened the Chaplin Studios in Hollywood, California, which later merged with the United Artists' Corporation. He has starred in, produced, and directed many films, including City Lights, The Gold Rush, *and* Modern Times; *films that today are considered classics. He has received many awards and honorary degrees during his career.*

SELECTIONS FROM

MY AUTOBIOGRAPHY

ALTHOUGH we were aware of the shame of going to the workhouse, when Mother told us about it both Sydney and I thought it adventurous and a change from living in one stuffy room. But on that doleful day I didn't realize what was happening until we actually entered the workhouse gate. Then the forlorn bewilderment of it struck me; for there we were made to separate, Mother going in one direction to the women's ward and we in another to the children's.

How well I remember the poignant sadness of that first visiting day: the shock of seeing Mother enter the visiting room garbed in workhouse clothes. How forlorn and embarrassed she looked! In one week she had aged and grown thin, but her face lit up when she saw us. Sydney and I began to weep, which made Mother weep, and large tears began to run down her cheeks. Eventually she regained her composure, and we sat together on a rough bench, our hands in her lap while she gently patted them. She smiled at our cropped heads and stroked them consolingly, telling us that we would soon all be together again. From her apron she produced a bag of coconut candy which she had bought at the workhouse store with her earnings from crocheting lace cuffs for one of the nurses. After we parted, Sydney kept dolefully repeating how she had aged.

63

Sydney and I quickly adapted ourselves to workhouse life, but in an overcast sadness. I remember little of incident, but the midday meal at a long table with other children was a warm and expectant affair. It was presided over by an inmate of the workhouse, an old gentleman of about seventy-five, with a dignified countenance, a thin white beard and sad eyes. He elected me to sit next to him because I was the youngest and, until they cropped my head, had the curliest hair. He called me his "tiger" and said that when I grew bigger I would wear a top hat with a cockade and would sit at the back of his carriage with my arms folded. This honor made me very fond of him. But a day or so later a younger boy appeared on the scene with curlier hair than I had and took my place beside the old gentleman, because, as he whimsically explained, a younger and curlier-headed boy always took precedence.

After three weeks we were transferred from Lambeth Workhouse to the Hanwell Schools for Orphans and Destitute Children, about twelve miles out of London. It was an adventurous drive in a horse-drawn bakery van, and rather a happy one under the circumstances, for the country surrounding Hanwell was beautiful in those days, with lanes of horse-chestnut trees, ripening wheat fields and heavy-laden orchards; and ever since, the rich, aromatic smell after rain in the country has always reminded me of Hanwell.

On arriving we were delivered to the approbation ward and put under medical and mental observation before entering the school proper; the reason was that among three to four hundred boys a sub-normal child or a sick one would be unhealthy for the school as well as being in an unhappy situation himself.

The first few days I was lost and miserable, for at the workhouse I always felt that Mother was near, which was comforting, but at Hanwell we seemed miles apart. Sydney and I graduated from the approbation ward to the school proper, where we were separated, Sydney going with the big boys and I with the infants. We slept in different ward blocks, so we seldom saw each other. I was a little over 6 years old and alone, which made me feel quite abject; especially on a summer's evening at bedtime during prayers, when, kneeling with twenty other little boys in the center of the ward in our nightshirts, I would look out of the oblong windows at the deepening sunset and the undulating hills, and feel alien to it all as we sang in throaty off-key voices:

> Abide with me; fast falls the eventide;
> The darkness deepens: Lord, with me abide;
> When other helpers fail, and comforts flee,
> Help of the helpless, O, abide with me.

It was then that I felt utterly dejected. Although I did not understand the hymn, the tune and the twilight increased my sadness.

But, to our happy surprise, within two months Mother had arranged for our discharge, and we were dispatched again to London and the Lambeth Workhouse. Mother was at the gate dressed in her own clothes, waiting for us. She had applied for a discharge only because she wanted to spend the day with her children, intending, after a few hours outside together, to return the same day; Mother being an inmate of the workhouse, this ruse was her only means to be with us.

Before we entered our private clothes had been taken from us and steamed; now they were returned unpressed. Mother, Sydney and I looked a crumpled sight as we ambled out through the workhouse gates. It was early morning and we had nowhere to go, so we walked to Kennington Park, which was about a mile away. Sydney had ninepence tied up in a handkerchief, so we bought half a pound of black cherries and spent the morning in Kennington Park, sitting on a bench eating them. Sydney crumpled a sheet of newspaper and wrapped some string around it and for a while the three of us played catch-ball. At noon we went to a coffee shop and spent the rest of our money on a twopenny teacake, a penny bloater and two halfpenny cups of tea, which we shared between us. Afterward we returned to the park, where Sydney and I played again while Mother sat crocheting.

In the afternoon we made our way back to the workhouse. As Mother said with levity, "We'll be just in time for tea." The authorities were most indignant, because it meant going through the same procedure of having our clothes steamed and Sydney and I spending more time at the workhouse before returning to Hanwell, which of course gave us an opportunity of seeing Mother again.

But this time we stayed at Hanwell for almost a year—a most formative year, in which I started schooling and was taught to write my name—"Chaplin." The word fascinated me and looked like me, I thought.

Hanwell School was divided in two, a department for boys and one for girls. On Saturday afternoon the bathhouse was reserved for infants, who were bathed by the older girls. This, of course, was before I was seven and a squeamish modesty attended these occasions; having to submit to the ignominy of a young girl of fourteen manipulating a facecloth all over my person was my first conscious embarrassment.

At the age of seven I was transferred from the infants' to the older boys' department, where ages ranged from seven to fourteen. Now I was eligible to participate in all the grown-up functions, the drills and exercises and the regular walks we took outside the school twice a week.

Although at Hanwell we were well looked after, it was a forlorn existence. Sadness was in the air; it was in those country lanes through which we walked, a hundred of us two abreast. How I disliked those walks, and the villages through which we passed, the locals staring at us! We were known as inmates of the "booby hatch," a slang term for workhouse.

The boys' playground was approximately an acre, paved with slab-stones. Surrounding it were one-story brick buildings used for offices, storerooms, a doctor's dispensary, a dentist's office and a wardrobe for boys' clothing. In the darkest corner of the yard was an empty room, and recently confined there was a boy of fourteen, a desperate character according to the other boys. He had attempted to escape from the school by climbing out of a second-story window and up onto the roof, defying the officials by throwing missiles and horse-chestnuts at them as they climbed after him. This happened after we infants were asleep; we were given an awed account of it by the older boys the next morning.

For major offenses of this nature, punishment took place every Friday in the large gymnasium, a gloomy hall about sixty feet by forty with a high roof, and, on the side, climbing ropes running up to girders. On Friday morning two or three hundred boys, ranging in age from seven to fourteen years, marched in and lined up in military fashion, forming three sides of a square. The far end was the fourth side, where, behind a long school desk the length of an Army mess table, stood the miscreants waiting for trial and punishment. On the right and in front of the desk was an easel with wrist straps dangling, and from the frame a birch hung ominously.

For minor offenses, a boy was laid across the long desk, face downward, feet strapped and held by a sergeant; then another sergeant pulled the boy's shirt out of his trousers and over his head, then pulled his trousers tight.

Captain Hindrum, a retired Navy man weighing about two hundred pounds, with one hand behind him, the other holding a cane as thick as a man's thumb and about four feet long, stood poised, measuring it across the boy's buttocks. Then slowly and dramatically he would lift it high and with a swish bring it down across the boy's bottom. The spectacle was terrifying, and invariably a boy would fall out of rank in a faint.

The minimum number of strokes was three and the maximum six. If a culprit received more than three, his cries were appalling. Sometimes he was ominously silent, or had fainted. The strokes were paralyzing, so that the victim had to be carried to one side and laid on a gymnasium mattress, where he was left to writhe and wriggle for at least ten minutes before the pain subsided, leaving three pink welts as wide as a washerwoman's finger across his bottom.

The birch was different. After three strokes, the boy was supported by two sergeants and taken to the surgery for treatment.

Boys would advise you not to deny a charge, even if innocent, because, if proved guilty, you would get the maximum. Usually, boys were not articulate enough to declare their innocence.

I was now seven and in the big boys' section. I remember witnessing my first flogging, standing in silence, my heart thumping as the officials entered. Behind the desk was the desperado who had tried to escape from the school. We could hardly see more than his head and shoulders over the desk, he looked so small. He had a thin, angular face and large eyes.

The headmaster solemnly read the charges and demanded: "Guilty or not guilty?"

Our desperado would not answer, but stared defiantly in front of him; he was thereupon led to the easel, and being small, he was made to stand on a soapbox so that his wrists could be strapped. He received three strokes with the birch and was led away to the surgery for treatment.

On Thursdays, a bugle sounded in the playground and we would all stop playing, taking a frozen position like statues, while Captain Hindrum, through a megaphone, announced the names of those who were to report for punishment on Friday.

One Thursday, to my astonishment I heard my name called. I could not imagine what I had done. Yet for some unaccountable reason I was thrilled—perhaps because I was the center of a drama. On the day of the trial, I stepped forward. Said the headmaster: "You are charged with setting fire to the dykes" (the lavatory).

This was not true. Some boys had lit a few bits of paper on the stone floor and while they were burning I came in to use the lavatory, but I had played no part in that fire.

"Are you guilty or not guilty?" he asked.

Nervous and impelled by a force beyond my control, I blurted out, "Guilty." I felt neither resentment nor injustice but a sense of frightening adventure as they led me to the desk and administered three strokes across my bottom. The pain was so excruciating that it took away my breath; but I did not cry out, and, although paralyzed with pain and carried to the mattress to recover, I felt valiantly triumphant.

As Sydney was working in the kitchen, he had not known about it until punishment day, when he was marched into the gymnasium with the others and to his shocked amazement saw my head peering over the desk. He told me afterward that when he saw me receiving three strokes he wept with rage.

A younger brother referred to his older brother as "my young 'un," which made him feel proud and gave him a little security. So occasionally I saw "my young 'un," Sydney, as I was leaving the dining room. As he worked in the kitchen, he would surreptitiously hand me a sliced bread roll with a thick lump of butter pressed between, and I would smuggle it under my jersey and share it with another boy—not that we were hungry, but the generous lump of butter was an exceptional luxury. But these delicacies were not to continue, for Sydney left Hanwell to join the *Exmouth* training ship.

At the age of eleven a workhouse boy had the choice of joining the Army or the Navy. If the Navy, he was sent to the *Exmouth*. Of course, it was not obligatory, but Sydney wanted to make a career of the sea. So that left me alone at Hanwell.

Hair is vitally personal to children. They weep vigorously when it is cut for the first time; no matter how it grows, bushy, straight or curly, they feel are being shorn of a part of their personality.

There had been an epidemic of ringworm at Hanwell and, as it is most contagious, those infected were dispatched to the isolation ward on the first floor overlooking the playground. Often we would look up at the windows and see those wretched boys looking wistfully down at us, their heads shaved all over and stained brown with iodine. They were a hideous sight and we would look up at them with loathing.

Thus when a nurse stopped abruptly behind me in the dining room and parted the top of my hair and announced, "Ringworm!" I was thrown into paroxysms of weeping.

The treatment took weeks and seemed like an eternity. My head was shaved and iodined and I wore a handkerchief tied around it like a cotton picker. But one thing I would not do was to look out of the window at the boys below, for I knew in what contempt they held us.

During my incarceration Mother visited me. She had in some way managed to leave the workhouse and was making an effort to establish a home for us. Her presence was like a bouquet of flowers; she looked so fresh and lovely that I felt ashamed of my unkempt appearance and my shaved iodined head.

"You must excuse his dirty face," said the nurse.

Mother laughed, and how well I remember her endearing words as she hugged and kissed me: "With all thy dirt I love thee still."

Soon afterward, Sydney left the *Exmouth* and I left Hanwell and we joined Mother again. She took a room at the back of Kennington Park and for a while she was able to support us. But it was not long before we were back in the workhouse again. The circumstances that led up to our return were something to do with Mother's difficulty in finding employment and Father's slump in his theatrical engagements. In that brief interlude we kept moving from one back room to another;

it was like a game of draughts—the last move was back to the workhouse.

Living in a different parish, we were sent to a different workhouse, and from there to Norwood Schools, which was more somber than Hanwell; leaves darker and trees taller. Perhaps the countryside had more grandeur, but the atmosphere was joyless.

One day, while Sydney was playing football, two nurses called him out of the game and told him that Mother had gone insane and had been sent to Cane Hill lunatic asylum. When Sydney heard the news he showed no reaction but went back and continued playing football. But after the game he stole away by himself and wept.

When he told me I could not believe it. I did not cry, but a baffling despair overcame me. Why had she done this? Mother, so lighthearted and gay—how could she go insane? Vaguely I felt that she had deliberately escaped from her mind and had deserted us. In my despair I had visions of her looking pathetically at me, drifting away into a void.

We heard the news officially a week later; we also heard that the court decreed that Father must take over the custody of Sydney and me. The prospect of living with Father was exciting. I had seen him only twice in my life, once on the stage, and once when passing a house in the Kennington Road, as he was coming down the front garden path with a lady. I had paused and watched him, knowing instinctively that he was my father. He beckoned me to him and asked my name. Sensing the drama of the situation, I had feigned innocence and said, "Charlie Chaplin." Then he glanced knowingly at the lady, felt in his pocket and gave me half a crown, and without further ado I ran straight home and told Mother that I had met my father.

And now we were going to live with him. Whatever happened, Kennington Road was familiar and not strange and somber like Norwood.

The officials drove us in the bread van to 287 Kennington Road, the house where I had seen my father walking down the garden path. The door was opened by the lady who had been with him at the time. She was dissipated and morose-looking, yet attractive, tall and shapely, with full lips and sad, doelike eyes; her age could have been 30. Her name was Louise. It appeared that Mr. Chaplin was not at home, but after the usual formalities and the signing of papers the official left us in charge of Louise, who led us upstairs to the first landing into the front sitting room. A small boy was playing on the floor as we entered, a most beautiful child of four with large dark eyes and rich brown curly hair: it was Louise's son—my half brother.

The family lived in two rooms and although the front room had large windows, the light filtered in as if from under water. Everything looked as sad as Louise; the wallpaper looked sad, the horsehair furniture looked sad, and the stuffed pike in a glass case that had swallowed another pike as large as itself—the head sticking out of its mouth—looked gruesomely sad.

In the back room she had put an extra bed for Sydney and me to sleep on, but it was too small. Sydney suggested sleeping on the sofa in the sitting room. "You'll sleep where you're told to," said Louise. This caused an embarrassing silence as we walked back into the living room.

Our reception was not an enthusiastic one, and no wonder. Sydney and I had been suddenly thrust upon her, and moreover we were the offspring of Father's estranged wife.

We both sat mutely watching her preparing the table for something to eat. "Here," she said to Sydney, "you can make yourself useful and fill the coal scuttle. And you," she said, turning to me, "go to the cookshop next to the White Hart and get a shilling's worth of corned beef."

I was only too pleased to leave her presence and the whole atmosphere, for a lurking fear was growing within me and I began to wish we were back at Norwood.

Father arrived home later and greeted us kindly. He fascinated me. At meals I watched every move he made, the way he ate and the way he held his knife as though it were a pen when cutting his meat. And for years I copied him.

When Louise told of Sydney's complaining about the small bed, Father suggested that Sydney should sleep on the sitting-room sofa. This victory of Sydney's aroused Louise's antagonism and she never forgave him. She continually complained to Father about him. Although Louise was morose and disagreeable, she never once struck me or even threatened to, but the fact that she disliked Sydney held me in fear and dread of her. She drank a great deal, and this exaggerated my fear. There was something frighteningly irresponsible about her when she was drunk; she would smile with amusement at her little boy with his beautiful angelic face, who would swear at her and use vile language. For some reason, I never had contact with the child. Although he was my half brother, I don't remember ever having exchanged a word with him—of course I was almost four years older than he. Sometimes when drinking Louise would sit and brood and I would be in a state of dread. But Sydney paid little attention to her; he seldom came home until late at night. I was made to come home directly after school and run errands and do odd jobs.

Louise sent us to the Kennington Road School, which was a bleak divertissement, for the presence of other children made me feel less isolated. Saturday was a half-holiday, but I never looked forward to it because it meant going home and scrubbing floors and cleaning knives, and on that day Louise invariably started drinking. While I was cleaning the knives, she would sit with a lady friend, drinking and growing bitterly morose, complaining quite audibly to her friend of having to look after Sydney and me and of the injustice imposed upon her. I remember her saying: "This one's all right" (indicating me), "but the other's a little swine and should be sent to a reformatory—what's more, he's not even Charlie's son." This reviling of Sydney frightened and depressed me and I would go unhappily to bed and lie fretfully awake. I was not yet eight years old, but those days were the longest and saddest of my life.

Sometimes on a Saturday night, feeling deeply despondent, I would hear the lively music of a concertina passing by the back bedroom window, playing a highland march, accompanied by rowdy youths and giggling coster girls. The vigor and vitality of it seemed ruthlessly indifferent to my unhappiness, yet as the music grew fainter in the distance, I would regret its leaving. Sometimes a street crier would pass: one in particular came by every night who seemed to be shouting "Rule Britannia," terminating it with a grunt, but he was actually selling oysters. From the pub, three doors away, I could hear the customers at closing time, singing drunks, bawling out a maudlin, dreary song that was popular in those days:

> For old times' sake don't let our enmity live,
> For old times' sake say you'll forget and forgive.
> Life's too short to quarrel,
> Hearts are too precious to break.
> Shake hands and let us be friends
> For old times' sake.

I never appreciated the sentiment, but it seemed an appropriate accompaniment to my unhappy circumstances, and lulled me to sleep.

When Sydney came in late, which seemed always, he raided the larder before going to bed. This infuriated Louise, and one night when she had been drinking she came into the room and ripped the bedclothes off him and told him to get out. But Sydney was prepared for her. Quickly he reached under his pillow and whipped out a stiletto, a long buttonhook which he had sharpened to a point.

"Come near me," he said, "and I'll stick this in you!"

She reared back, startled. "Why, the bloody young sod—he's going to murder me!"

"Yes," said Sydney, dramatically, "I'll murder you!"

"You wait till Mr. Chaplin comes home!"

But Mr. Chaplin seldom came home. However, I remember one Saturday night when Louise and Father had been drinking, and for some reason we were all sitting with the landlady and her husband in their front-room parlor on the ground floor. Under the incandescent light Father looked ghastly pale, and in an ugly mood was mumbling to himself. Suddenly he reached into his pocket, pulled out a handful of money and threw it violently to the floor, scattering gold and silver coins in all directions. The effect was surrealistic. No one moved. The landlady sat glum, but I caught her roving eye following a golden sovereign rolling to a far corner under a chair; my eye also followed it. Still no one moved, so I thought I had better start picking it up; the landlady and the others followed suit, picking up the rest of the money, careful to make their actions overt before Father's menacing eyes.

One Saturday, after school, I came home to find no one there. Sydney, as usual, was away all day playing football, and the landlady said Louise and her son had been out since early morning. At first I was relieved, for it meant that I did not have to scrub floors and clean knives. I waited until long after lunchtime, then began to get anxious. Perhaps they had deserted me. As the afternoon wore on, I began to miss them. What had happened? The room looked grim and unyielding and its emptiness frightened me. I also began to get hungry, so I looked in the larder, but no food was there. I could stand the gaping emptiness no longer, so in desolation I went out, spending the afternoon visiting nearby marketplaces. I wandered through Lambeth Walk and the Cut, looking hungrily into cookshop windows at the tantalizing, steaming roast joints of beef and pork, and the golden-brown potatoes soaked in gravy. For hours I watched the quacks selling their wares. The distraction soothed me and for a while I forgot my plight and hunger.

When I returned, it was night; I knocked at the door, but no one answered. Everyone was out. Wearily I walked to the corner of Kennington Cross and sat on the curb near the house to keep an eye on it in case someone returned. I was tired and miserable, and wondered where Sydney was. It was approaching midnight and Kennington Cross was deserted but for one or two stragglers. All the lights of the shops began going out except those of the chemist and the public houses, then I felt wretched.

Suddenly there was music. Rapturous! It came from the vestibule of the White Hart corner pub, and resounded brilliantly in the empty square. The tune was "The Honeysuckle and the Bee," played with radiant virtuosity on a harmonium and clarinet. I had never been conscious of melody before, but this one was beautiful and lyrical, so blithe and gay, so warm and reassuring. I forgot my despair and crossed the road to where the musicians were. The harmonium player was blind, with scarred sockets where the eyes had been; and a besotted, embittered face played the clarinet.

It was all over too soon and their exit left the night even sadder.

Weak and tired, I crossed the road toward the house, not caring whether anyone came home or not. All I wanted was to get to bed. Then dimly I saw someone going up the garden path toward the house. It was Louise—and her little son running ahead of her. I was shocked to see that she was limping exaggeratedly and leaning extremely to one side. At first I thought she had been in an accident and had hurt her leg, then I realized she was very drunk. I had never seen a lopsided drunk before. In her condition I thought it best to keep out of her way, so I waited until she had let herself in. A few moments later the land-lady came home and I went in with her. As I crept up the darkened stairs, hoping to get to bed unnoticed, Louise staggered out onto the landing.

"Where the hell do you think you're going?" she said. "This is not your home."

I stood motionless.

"You're not sleeping here tonight. I've had enough of all of you. Get out! You and your brother! Let your father take care of you."

Without hesitation, I turned and went downstairs and out of the house. I was no longer tired; I had got my second wind. I had heard that Father patronized the Queen's Head pub in the Prince's Road, about half a mile away, so I made my way in that direction, hoping to find him there. But soon I saw his shadowy figure coming toward me, outlined against the street lamp.

"She won't let me in," I whimpered, "and I think she's been drink-ing."

As we walked toward the house, he also staggered. "I'm not sober myself," he said.

I tried to reassure him that he was.

"No, I'm drunk," he muttered remorsefully.

He opened the door of the sitting room and stood there silent and menacing, looking at Louise. She was standing by the fireplace, holding on to the mantelpiece, swaying.

"Why didn't you let him in?" he said.

She looked at him bewildered, then mumbled: "You too can go to hell—all of you!"

Suddenly he picked up a heavy clothesbrush from the sideboard and like a flash threw it violently, the back of it hitting her flat on the side of her face. Her eyes closed, then she collapsed unconscious with a thud to the floor as though she welcomed oblivion.

I was shocked at Father's action; such violence made me lose respect for him. As to what happened afterward, my memory is vague. I believe Sydney came in later and Father saw us both to bed, then left the house.

I learned that Father and Louise had quarreled that morning because he had left her to spend the day with his brother, Spencer Chaplin, who owned several public houses round and about Lambeth. Being sensitive to her position, Louise disliked visiting the Spencer Chaplins, so Father went alone, and as a revenge Louise spent the day elsewhere.

She loved Father. Even though very young I could see it in her glance the night she stood by the fireplace, bewildered and hurt by his neglect. And I am sure he loved her. I saw many occasions of it. There were times when he was charming and tender and would kiss her good night before leaving for the theater. And on a Sunday morning, when he had not been drinking, he would breakfast with us and tell Louise about the vaudeville acts that were working with him, and have us all enthralled. I would watch him like a hawk, absorbing every action. In a playful mood, he once wrapped a towel round his head and chased his little son around the table, saying, "I'm King Turkey Rhubarb."

About eight o'clock in the evening, before departing for the theater, he would swallow six raw eggs in port wine, rarely eating solid food. That was all that sustained him day after day. He seldom came home, and, if he did, it was to sleep off his drinking.

One day Louise received a visit from the Society for the Prevention of Cruelty to Children, and she was most indignant about it. They came because the police had reported finding Sydney and me asleep at three o'clock in the morning by a watchman's fire. It was a night that Louise had shut us both out, and the police had made her open the door and let us in.

A few days later, however, while Father was playing in the provinces, Louise received a letter announcing that Mother had left the asylum. A day or two later the landlady came up and announced that there was a lady at the front door to call for Sydney and Charlie. "There's your mother," said Louise. There was a momentary confusion. Then Sydney leaped downstairs into her arms, I following. It was the same sweet, smiling Mother who affectionately embraced us.

Louise and Mother were too embarrassed to meet, so Mother waited at the front door while Sydney and I collected our things. There was no umbrage or ill feeling on either side—in fact, Louise's manner was most agreeable, even to Sydney when she bade him goodbye.

Mother had taken a room in one of the back streets behind Kennington Cross near Hayward's pickle factory, and the acid smell would start up every afternoon. But the room was cheap and we were all together again. Mother's health was excellent, and the thought that she had been ill never entered our heads.

How we lived through this period I have not the remotest idea. Nonetheless, I remember no undue hardships or insoluble problems.

Father's payments of ten shillings a week were almost regular, and, of course, Mother took up her needlework again and renewed her contact with the church.

An incident stands out at that period. At the end of our street was a slaughterhouse, and sheep would pass our house on their way to be butchered. I remember one escaped and ran down the street, to the amusement of onlookers. Some tried to grab it and others tripped over themselves. I had giggled with delight at its lambent capering and panic, it seemed so comic. But when it was caught and carried back into the slaughterhouse, the reality of the tragedy came over me and I ran indoors, screaming and weeping to Mother. "They're going to kill it! They're going to kill it!" That stark, spring afternoon and that comedy chase stayed with me for days; and I wonder if that episode did not establish the premise of my future films—the combination of the tragic and the comic.

School was now the beginning of new horizons: history, poetry and science. But some of the subjects were prosaic and dull, especially arithmetic: its addition and subtraction gave an image of a clerk and a cash register, its use, at best, a protection against being short-changed.

History was a record of wickedness and violence, a continual succession of regicides and kings murdering their wives, brothers and nephews; geography merely maps; poetry nothing more than exercising memory. Education bewildered me with knowledge and facts in which I was only mildly interested.

If only someone had used salesmanship, had read a stimulating preface to each study that could have titillated my mind, infused me with fancy instead of facts, amused and intrigued me with the legerdemain of numbers, romanticized maps, given me a point of view about history and taught me the music of poetry, I might have become a scholar.

Since Mother had returned to us she had begun to stimulate my interest in the theater again. She imbued me with the feeling that I had some sort of talent. But it was not until those weeks before Christmas when the school put on its cantata "Cinderella" that I felt an urge to express all that Mother had taught me. For some reason I was not selected to play in it, and inwardly I was envious and felt that I was better able to play in the cantata than those who had been chosen. I was critical of the dull, unimaginative way the boys played their parts. The Ugly Sisters had no zest or comic spirit. They spoke their lines eruditely with a schoolboy inflection and an embarrassing falsetto emphasis. How I would have loved to play one of the Ugly Sisters, with the tutoring Mother could have given me! I was, however, captivated

75

by the girl who played Cinderella. She was beautiful, refined, aged about fourteen, and I was secretly in love with her. But she was beyond my reach both socially and in years.

When I saw the cantata, I thought it dismal but for the beauty of the girl, which left me a little sad. Little did I realize, however, the glorious triumph I was to enjoy two months later when I was brought before each class and made to recite "Miss Priscilla's Cat." It was a comedy recitation Mother had seen outside a newspaper shop and thought so funny that she copied it from the window and brought it home. During a recess from class, I recited it to one of the boys. Mr. Reid, our schoolteacher, looked up from his work and was so amused that when the class assembled he made me recite it to them and they were thrown into gales of laughter. As a result of this my fame spread, and the following day I was brought before every classroom in the school, both boys and girls, and made to recite it.

Although I had performed and deputized for Mother in front of an audience at the age of five, this was actually my first conscious taste of glamour. School became exciting. From having been an obscure and shy little boy I became the center of interest of both the teachers and the children. It even improved my studies. But my education was to be interrupted when I left to join a troupe of clog dancers, the Eight Lancashire Lads.

~~~~~~

DISCUSSION AND INQUIRY

In recalling the sad little tramp image made famous by Chaplin in the early days of film making, it is hard to imagine that his ability to portray such a sad-comic figure was not aided by his personal experience in an orphanage. What seems to have saved the Chaplin boys was the mother's attempt to keep her family together. Although the Chaplin family setting was unstable at best, it apparently provided some degree of security and acceptance for Charles and his brother. Why are institutions often unable to provide these necessary ingredients for healthy personality development?

Chaplin witnessed a great deal of corporal punishment while in the institution. He was the victim of it after pleading guilty to the charge of setting a fire in the lavatory. He states: "but I

did not cry out . . . I felt valiantly triumphant."
What forces are at work that make a child not
cry out despite the pain? Why the feeling of
triumph? See the selection by George Orwell for
another example of triumph over beating.

Chaplin was deeply affected by the episode
involving the shaving of his head. Getting one's
head shaved appears to be a traumatic experience
for many adults as well as children. More than
one young man in basic training has had to be
physically restrained in the barber chair as his
hair was shaved to the skull bone. How would
you account for such reactions? What would a
Freudian interpretation conclude?

Despite the frequent fighting and drunken
bouts, Chaplin said he perceived that his father
and stepmother were in love. Can children perceive love between parents or step-parents,
despite frequent fighting? How are children able
to perceive true feelings between parents? What
are the clues that reveal these feelings?

James Conant

BIOGRAPHICAL SKETCH

*James Conant, born in Boston in 1893, was a
Harvard man all the way. He was a student there,
a professor, chairman of the chemistry department, and, for twenty years, president of the
college. During his tenure, he was active in educational reform. During the Second World War, as
chairman of the National Defense Research Committee, he was involved as a scientist-administra-
tor in the development of the atom bomb. Later,
under President Eisenhower, he was Ambassador
to the German Federal Republic.*

SELECTIONS FROM

MY SEVERAL LIVES

JOPPA village in the mid-nineteenth century was not, in one respect,
typical of New England. The community had become a stronghold of
one Protestant sect, Swedenborgianism. According to Grandfather
Bryant's account, the teachings of Emanuel Swedenborg came to
Bridgewater in 1818 and to East Bridgewater (Joppa Village) in 1822.
By the time my two grandfathers were raising families, the Swedenborgian or New Jerusalem Church appears to have been the center of
religious life. Grandfather Conant read the lesson on Sunday morning;
Grandfather Bryant gave financial support to the church. My mother
and my father thus shared a rather special religious faith. During the
first fifteen or twenty years of their married life, they journeyed by
trolley car from Dorchester each Sunday morning to attend a Swedenborgian church in Roxbury. I remember the trips and sitting through
the services. I was too young, however, to attend the Sunday school
and was, therefore, never exposed to Swedenborgian doctrine as were
my older sisters.

About the time I entered kindergarten, my father and mother
stopped these weekly journeys. I think their adherence to Swedenborgian doctrine must have been slowly losing strength. There seem to

have been differences of opinion among the faithful. My mother, I remember, used to speak rather forcefully against one group whose interpretation of Swedenborg's writings she did not like at all. I was thus aware at an early age of "schisms" among churchgoers. Far more important was my mother's final and complete condemnation of all trinitarian doctrines. She never attempted to make me a Swedenborgian, perhaps because she had become less convinced as she grew older. She certainly succeeded, however, in making me at an early age more than suspicious of all the standard arguments in favor of Christianity. Of course, I might have reacted against her strong views and joined an Episcopal High Church. As a matter of fact, I have never had the slightest tendency in that direction.

My knowledge of Swedenborgianism comes almost entirely from what my mother told me over a period of years, usually in answer to my questions. The chief characteristic of the faith, she often said, was a firm belief in immortality. Such a belief, however, had nothing to do with rewards and punishments after death. (On the subject of hell-fire religions, no one could be more condemnatory than my otherwise soft-spoken mother.) Passing into the next world, as she always called it, was entering into an existence which alone had real significance. Here was to be found the explanation of the universe. What happened in our material world was of little moment. The reality of the unseen world seemed to be the essence of her belief. The prospect of seeing once again those one had known on earth appeared not to be important. In her old age, my mother often attended a Unitarian church. In many ways, she might have been classified as a Unitarian, as I have usually characterized myself. The Swedenborgian interpretation of death, however, I am inclined to think she never lost. To this extent her religion differed from that of many Unitarians.

My grandmother, of whom I saw so much as a very young child, was an unquestioning Swedenborgian to the end. She calmly assumed the distinction between the spiritual and the material (the "mere physical," my mother would have said). One of the clearest memories of my childhood is the way I learned of my Grandfather Bryant's death when I was five. During one of our daily talks, my grandmother told me that my grandfather had told her he had seen a child coming to him with a bunch of flowers. He is, of course, she said, already in the next world —which news I accepted almost as a matter of fact; she had spoken often of the journey to the next world my grandfather was about to take. I was not shocked. My grandmother was not grieving. She spoke as though my grandfather had just moved into a beautiful sunlit room. Several days later (so I have always maintained in telling the story), when I came home from kindergarten (which was across the street), my mother said quietly, "Your grandfather is in the next world." "Yes,

I know he is," I said with matter-of-factness. "Grandmother has already told me." "But she couldn't have," my mother exclaimed, "it only happened this morning while you were at school."

My mother was gently spoken and theoretically in favor of tolerance of all points of view. But in regard to religion, as I have already indicated, the doctrine of tolerance did not mean to her equal sympathy with all creeds. And in regard to the great issue of her youth, it certainly did not mean any forgiveness of the slaveholders and those who fought under the Stars and Bars. Her strong views led occasionally to strong words of condemnation, usually uttered, to be sure, in the family circle. So, too, as regards current politics, what my mother approved and what she disapproved soon became quite clear in the course of conversation. More often than not, the clear opinion which emerged was not that of the majority of our friends and acquaintances. Mother was basically a dissenter.

The disputes in the Ashmont household between my Republican father and his Democratic father-in-law were before my day. By the time the Spanish War was over, Grandfather Bryant was dead. Public opinion divided sharply in the first year of the new century about the consequences of the American victory. Bryan was running again, this time on a plank of anti-imperialism. I heard little about the candidate but a great deal about the wickedness of the imperialists. The issue was not closed when McKinley was elected. Two of the three aunts whom I saw often were strong anti-imperialists like my mother. Dissent from Republican foreign policy thus became a continuing household attitude. Theodore Roosevelt's accession to the presidency increased the dissent to a point where I am sure it had a reverse effect on me. By the time the new President stood for election in his own right, he had become a hero in my eyes.

What Father's views were, I cannot say. He was massively silent for the most part when my mother and one of her sisters excoriated the Republicans and all their works. Two conclusions I can draw from these memories: I knew from an early age, first, that ladies could be emotionally involved as onlookers of the political scene and, second, that dissent was not only respectable but usually morally correct.

The Spanish War must have increased the normal interest of small boys in soldiers. All my early memories of playing with other boys are related to either playing with lead soldiers in the house or organizing sham battles out of doors. These activities must have pained my mother, who was anything but a militarist. Indeed, a decade later when Theodore Roosevelt was attacking President Woodrow Wilson for his neutrality during the opening years of World War I, I think she would have been glad to have been called a pacifist. In 1900, however, only a fiercely dogmatic pacifist would have intruded ideology into the play world of male children. Two of my friends had older brothers; they liked to be the officers and drill the younger group. Air rifles were the weapons. The battles of the Civil War served vaguely as models. The Memorial Day parades of the local unit of the Grand Army of the Republic kept us aware of the military past.

On this subject, my father was something of a disappointment. He had served as a captain's boy with an East Bridgewater company of a Massachusetts regiment, and later as a master-at-arms on a ship of the Union Navy. In neither capacity did he take part in any fighting. His stories about his war experiences were interesting, particularly the one about his witnessing the naval battle between the *Merrimac* and the *Monitor*. His reminiscenses suffered, however, according to my view, from a lack of any firsthand account of man-to-man combat. Then, too, he was not a member of the Grand Army of the Republic. He had refused to join, my mother said, because he disapproved of the political activities of the organized veterans who were always working for larger pensions. None of my friends' fathers had been old enough to serve at all; so my disappointment was something I kept strictly to myself.

By the time I was nine or ten, playing soldiers in the many vacant lots of Ashmont gave way to playing football and baseball. The older brothers now were acting as coaches. On at least one occasion, they arranged a football game with another group whose "home field" was a vacant lot a mile or two away. There were no goal posts or formal markers. It was strictly a rushing game, for which the players were equipped with a variety of shoulder pads, rubber nosepieces and padded football pants. Our side, of which I was the captain, won by several touchdowns. Such was the only athletic victory in which I had a part.

The next year, the old gang began to break up. The loyalties and interest of some of us were transferred to the schools we had just entered—mine to the Roxbury Latin School.

. . .

One day in the late 1920s, I met the father of one of my boyhood friends. In the course of our exchange, he spoke of my recent appointment as chairman of the chemistry department at Harvard. "I remember," he said, "when you were a small boy playing with vile-smelling chemicals; you started young; you have kept at it ever since; it is an unusually consistent record." I might have replied that among chemists my case was not strikingly unusual. I could have named several of my acquaintances on both sides of the Atlantic who, like myself, had fallen in love with chemistry while still in school.

Sixty years ago, the appeal of chemical experimentation was novel. "Fun with chemistry" sets had not yet been invented; a boy had to be ingenious to accumulate the equivalent with the aid of the local drugstore. The experiments were simple but spectacular. The knowledge acquired about elements and compounds was so foreign to what was discussed in the daily papers or heard about in general conversation that it seemed a passport into a strange and secret land.

I took the first step into the new land of chemistry during my early teens, when I asked to have illuminating gas piped into the shop my father had recently constructed out of a large vestibule in the Dorchester house. There was nothing unusual about my having a shop. Many of my friends had one in the cellar or the attic, but none of them had a workbench with a stopcock to which a Bunsen burner could be attached by means of a piece of rubber tubing. A gas flame on the bench transformed a carpenter's shop into a laboratory. I was now in a position to buy a blast lamp, worked by a foot bellows, which yielded a flame hot enough to melt glass. I started to try my hand at glass blowing, an art in which I never became proficient. Without gas, the experimenter at home had to use the flame of an alcohol lamp, which is at best a feeble instrument for a would-be chemist. With a Bunsen burner, however, one could evaporate solutions to dryness, set up a still for making distilled water and even prepare oxygen gas by heating red oxide of mercury.

Earlier, my scientific interests had centered on electrical phenomena. Electricity, even in its simplest manifestation, was still something of a marvel. Few of the houses I knew had either electric current or a telephone. The electric doorbell was the one standard piece of electrical equipment. I was considered to be very clever by our next-door neighbor because I "repaired" the doorbell by renewing the zinc rod in the battery. A number of my friends could have done the same. It was not uncommon for a boy in those days to monkey with electromagnets, dry and wet batteries, electric buzzers and small motors. In a few years, interest in amateur wireless telegraphy would spread rapidly and widely.

Because I shared in this growing interest in science, my parents had selected the Roxbury Latin School for my college preparation. At that time in Greater Boston, the shift to a college preparatory school for the last six years of secondary education was almost compulsory for anyone who intended to go on to college. Of those who remained in public grammar school for the last two years and then went on to the public high school, few if any attended college. They went to work directly.

The reputation of the Roxbury Latin School was high on many counts and, in spite of the name, high in chemistry and physics. The six-year course was centered on Latin, French, and either Greek or German, with the usual college preparatory course in mathematics. But unlike many of the other preparatory schools in Greater Boston, the building was equipped with laboratories for both physics and chemistry, and all pupils were required to study both subjects in their last two years.

Soon after I entered the six-year course in 1903, a number of circumstances slowly moved the focus of my interest from electricity to chemistry. There were first the occasional visits to my father's "office," a photoengraver's establishment in Boston. Photoengraving had grown out of wood engraving during the last decades of the last century. My father had started his own wood-engraving company in a few rooms in an office building in Boston not long after the close of the Civil War. When the halftone process entered the printing business, a rapidly-growing branch of chemistry entered the commercial world. My father became an applied chemist, though he would have denied any knowledge of the science of chemistry. I am not sure that he could have carried out the complicated set of procedures involved in etching the copperplates, which his son followed so eagerly when he had a chance. He was, however, a competent photographer in the days before dry plates; preparing and developing wet plates was then a complicated chemical operation.

A second incentive was supplied by the teacher of physics and chemistry at the Roxbury Latin School. I doubt if any schoolteacher has ever had a greater influence on the intellectual development of a youth than Newton Henry Black had on mine. His lectures on elementary science to the second-year class were for those days remarkable. They stimulated the interest in science of a good fraction of the class. What appealed to me most were the final lectures on chemistry. My early fascination with the mysteries of photoengraving must have formed a receptive attitude, but at the time I was quite oblivious to any such connection. I simply thought it would be fun to do such simple things as to set up a hydrogen generator at home.

I became one of the small group of boys who brought their sandwiches to the physics laboratory at lunch hour. Almost all the others were concerned with the wireless; they were the forerunners of what became the large group of radio "hams." I had tried my hand at making an induction coil and a radio receiver with no success. So I began discussing my chemical experiments with the other boys, and from time to time with Mr. Black himself. I was not in a frame of mind, however, to desire a real chemical workbench in my home until a clerk in the corner drugstore set me on the path. It was from him that I had purchased the acid necessary for making hydrogen. He took an interest in my chemical interest, and one day suggested that I might take up qualitative analysis. He explained that one could obtain a set of directions as to how to analyze a solution to determine its chemical content. A set of simple reagents, a glass funnel and filter papers and a method of boiling water were all one needed.

During one of the lunch hours at school, I asked Mr. Black about my friend's suggestion. He thought it excellent, named the book I should buy (A. A. Noyes' *System of Qualitative Analysis*) and offered to provide me with solutions to analyze. So began what developed into a tutorial relationship. I received a little bottle every week or so and reported to Mr. Black during one of the noon periods what I had found; for example, silver and tin but no copper or lead. It was an exciting business, and I kept coming back for more unknowns. Before long I began rather systematically to follow the laboratory manual of the high school chemistry text and to study the text itself, which I had previously only looked into as my fancy chose.

DISCUSSION AND INQUIRY

James Conant spent his boyhood in New England at the turn of the century in a religious family of Swedish origin. He writes admiringly of his mother, who was an outspoken dissenter on many political and religious issues of the day, while he expresses some disappointment in his father. His father was neither outspoken on current issues nor able to supply firsthand accounts of combat experiences for the boy, who was interested in war games and lead soldiers. How does a boy rationalize or overcome his disappointment in his father when that father does not live up to his ideal image of masculinity?

James turned his back on all religious teachings early in life. Is this, perhaps, a sample of a child's rebellion against parental beliefs? Under what circumstances are children likely to rebel against family values and beliefs? How might early exposure to acceptance of dissent within the family, particularly among the women, have influenced his political and social beliefs in later life?

James fell in love with chemistry as a young boy in the Roxbury Latin School. His chemistry

*teacher, Mr. Black, became a friend and encour-
aged the boy by supplying him with the necessary books and chemical samples to study qualitative analysis on his own. Conant showed a
great deal of intellectual curiosity and was highly
motivated toward independent study. What other
factors may have contributed to his high achievement motivation? What role might the family
play in creating an environment that will stimu-
ulate self-motivation? Consider your personal
experiences in school. Do you remember a teacher
who played a significant role in your positive
feelings toward education?*

Dwight David Eisenhower

BIOGRAPHICAL SKETCH

Dwight David Eisenhower was born in 1890 in Denison, Texas, and grew up in Abilene, Kansas. In 1915, he graduated from the United States Military Academy at West Point, trained and ready for a long, full military career. He commanded the Allied Expeditionary Force in Western Europe during the Second World War and led the D Day invasion of France on June 6, 1944. Until his nomination for President, he served as Supreme Commander of the Allied Powers in Europe. He served two full terms as President of the United States (1953–1961), and died in Washington, D. C., in 1969.

SELECTIONS FROM

AT EASE:
STORIES I TELL TO FRIENDS

MY EARLIEST memory involves an incident that occurred two or three months before my fifth birthday. I took a long trip to a strange and far-off place—Topeka—for a tough and prolonged war.

My mother's sister, Aunt Minnie, was visiting us. We lived in a little cottage on Second Street in Abilene. It was decided that I would return with her to Topeka where a considerable number of Mother's relatives lived.

It was a day trip and during the course of the morning the heat of the railroad car and the monotony of the noise made me very sleepy. "Does this train have a sleeping car?" I asked her, using a scrap of worldly knowledge I had presumably picked up while listening to a family conversation. "It's not really necessary to go to a sleeping car," my aunt replied. "Just lie down on the seat and I'll make sure you have a good nap." I did and she was right.

After leaving the train, we next had to take a long ride by horse and buggy to my relatives' farm out beyond the northern outskirts of Topeka. I can remember looking down through the floorboards, watching the ground rush past and the horses' feet, which seemed to slide. When we arrived, life became even more confusing. It was peculiar to be surrounded by so many strangers. It seemed to me that there were dozens or hundreds of people—all grownups—in the house. Even though they were, somehow, my family, I felt lonesome and lost among them.

I began to wander around outside. In the rear of the house was an old-fashioned well, very deep, with a wooden bucket and a long rope threaded through a pulley. My uncle Luther found me, fascinated by the well, and he offered a long story about what would happen to me if I fell in. He spoke in such horrible terms that I soon lost any ambition to look over the fearful edge into the abyss below. Looking around for less dreadful diversion, I noticed a pair of barnyard geese. The male resented my intrusion from our first meeting and each time thereafter he would push along toward me aggressively and with hideous hissing noises so threatening my security that five-year-old courage could not stand the strain. I would race for the back door of the house, burst into the kitchen, and tell any available elder about this awful old gander.

Thus the war began. In the early parts of the campaign, I lost a skirmish every half hour and invariably had to flee ignominiously and weeping from the battlefield. Without support, and lacking arms of any kind, it was only by recourse to distressing retreat after retreat to the kitchen door that I kept myself from disaster.

My enemy was that bad-tempered and aggressive gander. I was a little boy, not yet five years old, who was intensely curious about the new environment into which he was thrust and determined to explore its every corner. But the gander constantly balked me. He obviously looked upon me as a helpless and harmless nuisance. He had no intention of permitting anyone to penetrate his domain. Always hopeful that he would finally abandon his threatened attacks on my person, I'd try again and again, always with the same result.

Uncle Luther decided that something had to be done. He took a worn-out broom and cut off all the straw except for a short hard knob which he probably left so that in my zeal, if I developed any, I might not hurt my odd adversary. With the weapon all set, he took me out into the yard. He showed me how I was to swing and then announced that I was on my own.

The gander remained aggressive in his actions, and I was not at all sure that my uncle was very smart. More frightened at the moment of his possible scolding than I was of aggression, I took what was

87

meant to be a firm, but was really a trembling, stand the next time the fowl came close. Then I let out a yell and rushed toward him, swinging the club as fast as I could. He turned and I gave him a satisfying smack right in the fanny. He let out a most satisfactory squawk and ran off. This was my signal to chase him, which I did.

From then on, he would continue his belligerent noises whenever he saw me (and the stick). He kept his distance and I was the proud boss of the back yard. I never make the mistake of being caught without the weapon. This all turned out to be a rather good lesson for me because I quickly learned never to negotiate with an adversary except from a position of strength.

Mother and Father maintained a genuine partnership in raising their six sons. Father was the breadwinner, Supreme Court, and Lord High Executioner. Mother was tutor and manager of our household. Their partnership was ideal. This may sound unbelievable, and only recollected in tranquillity, but I never heard a cross word pass between them. Never did I hear them disagree on a value judgment in family, social, or economic affairs—not that there weren't sufficient causes. I never had any indication that they were annoyed with each other. Before their children, they were not demonstrative in their love for each other, but a quiet, mutual devotion permeated our home. This had its lasting effect on all the boys.

Normally, Father worked six days a week. He usually left the house about 6:30 and came home about 5:00. Family life revolved around him. School, chores, meals, and all other activities—winter and summer —had to be adjusted to meet his requirements. His work was hard and the pay was meager. Because of an early experience—two or three years after he married, a general store in the town of Hope, Kansas, in which he was a partner, went bankrupt—he had an obsession against ever owing anyone a nickel. He would not allow any of us a charge account —not that they were so common then. But either cash was paid or nothing was bought.

That early economic catastrophe left its mark. Father had been given a sizable farm as a wedding present by his father but he so disliked farming that he sold it to form the partnership in the store. For a time, all went well but drought and an invasion of grasshoppers one year—I think it was 1887—ruined the crops of Dickinson County. Father continued to extend credit; he carried the farmers to the end. Then his partner proved too weak to go through the ordeal of facing up to the store's own creditors. Taking what little cash was left, the partner departed one night for parts unknown.

My parents never heard from him again. Although Father's pride was hurt, he set out at once to find any kind of job and patiently started to pay off his former suppliers.

He accomplished this in a relatively few years.

His first job was in Denison, Texas, where I was born. My older and younger brothers were all born in Dickinson County, Kansas; we returned to Kansas when I was less than two years old. There, Father was an engineer in a creamery, later a manager of a gas plant, and finally director of employee savings for a group of public utilities.

My mother, for all her gentleness, was outraged by the injustice of my father's early business venture, specifically at the other partner's disappearance. She began to study law at home. For some years she read legal books, hoping that someday, somewhere, they would meet up with the absconder—fully prepared to take legal action against him. Throughout the years that her sons continued to live under the same roof, this warm, pleasant, mild-mannered woman never ceased to warn them against thieves, embezzlers, chiselers, and all kinds of crooks.

Her household problems were, I realize now, monumental. The least of them was to provide comfortable beds for six boys in three rooms. She skillfully assigned us to beds in such a pattern as to minimize the incidence of nightly fights. She rotated our duties; helping with the cooking, dishwashing, laundry (she never had reason to miss the assistance usually provided by daughters); pruning the orchard, harvesting the fruit and storing it for the winter; hoeing the corn and weeding the vegetable garden; putting up the hay in our immense barn; feeding the chickens and milking the cow. By rotating chores weekly, each son learned all the responsibilities of running the house and none felt discriminated against. The total task of making life happy and meaningful for a family of eight took insight, imagination, and managerial skill.

Mother rarely resorted to corporal punishment and when she did it was a slap on the hand with a ruler or anything handy and lightweight. Instead, she deeply believed in self-discipline and she preached it constantly. According to her, each of us should behave properly not because of the fear of punishment but because it was the right thing to do. Such a philosophy was a trifle idealistic for a platoon of growing boys but in later years we came to understand her ideas better.

Mother took care of minor infractions during the day but anything serious was passed along to Father for settlement. With his family of hearty, active boys, I'm sure that strict discipline was necessary for survival. He certainly was never one for spoiling any child by sparing the rod. If the evidence showed that the culprit had offended deliberately, the application of stick to skin was a routine affair.

Father had quick judicial instincts. Mother had, like a psychologist, insight into the fact that each son was a unique personality and she adapted her methods to each.

Arthur, the first born, gave my parents little trouble. He was studious and ambitious. From my perspective, four years younger, he seemed a man about town. While he had his share of tussles with the rest of us, it is my impression that he was the best behaved. He was not much interested in athletics and still less in fisticuffs with lesser mortals around the house.

Edgar, second in line, was a natural athlete, strong, agile, two years older than I and yet for years we were almost the same size. His superior qualities always made him the victor in our inevitable personal battles. While these never had the ferocity of our fights with other boys —in those cases you stood up and slugged until one gave way—our encounters usually ended up in a highly unscientific wrestling match, with Ed on top.

Being a stubborn sort myself, I found his arm twisting and toe holds not only painful but mortifying. They built up in me a definite intention to get even when I matured enough to battle him on an equal footing. That time was long in coming. Not until I returned from West Point for a vacation in 1913 did I send him an all inclusive challenge—anything he wanted, wrestling, boxing, barefisted or with gloves—or plain rough and tumble. Even then he got the best of me. In his reply from wherever his summer job had taken him, he wrote, "I would be glad to meet you with boxing gloves at forty paces." And he did not come home that season so I was robbed of sweet revenge.[1]

One circumstance that helped our character development: we were needed. I often think today of what an impact could be made if children believed they were *contributing* to a family's essential survival and happiness. In the transformation from a rural to an urban society, children are—though they might not agree—robbed of the opportunity to do genuinely responsible work.

Roy, like Arthur, had no interest in going to college. He wanted to make money. Arthur, following high school, took a course in a local business college, became a competent secretary, and then went on to a career as a well-known and successful banker in Kansas City. Because Ed and I were constantly paired off, and Earl and Milton were much younger that he, Roy was a bit of a lone wolf. (Another brother, Paul,

---

[1] I suppose those qualities of Ed's that I admired most were shown when we were digging a cistern together one day. He was using an adz and I a shovel. We had just struck a clay formation. I was tired of the shovel, and, giving way to my insistence, we traded tools. I raised the adz and swung, bringing it down neatly through the side of his foot. It had to hurt but Ed's shouted exclamation was, "Oh Dwight! Clean through my new twenty-five-cent socks!"

born in 1894, died in infancy of diphtheria. There was an age gap, then, of six years between Roy and Earl.) Roy began working in a drug store even before he entered high school. He was soon the youngest registered pharmacist in Kansas. Eventually he purchased a drug store in Junction City and did a thriving business.

Earl and Milton, who were born only eighteen months apart, became the other set of natural partners. There were few quarrels between them. Earl, because of blindness in his left eye caused in an accident at the age of four, and Milton, who during infancy had undergone an attack of scarlet fever which left him weakened, did not have as robust and disreputable a boyhood as Ed and I enjoyed. Milton turned his energies more to studies and to the arts, particularly the piano. He became good enough to give an occasional recital in school and later organized a dance band which helped provide him with funds for college education. One or two of his teachers tried to induce him to take further training for the concert stage, but another diverted him to newspaper work, which eventually led him to careers in government and higher education.

In appearance, we shared strong family characteristics but there were notable sources for differences. My father was dark and swarthy; my mother a golden blond. The six boys, therefore, were a predictable mixture. Arthur, resembling my father, was dark. Ed's hair was a chestnut color. I was so light that I was often dubbed "The Swede" by opponents in intercity athletics. Roy, like Arthur, was dark, while Earl was a fiery redhead (a contribution from my paternal grandfather). Milton's coloration was more like Ed's. In our late teens, Ed and I were often thought to be twins.

In this position, Ed, Earl, and I were the hot-tempered and quarrelsome element, while Arthur, Roy, and Milton were always credited with more tractable natures.

There was no shortage of causes for friction. Each week, a nickel magazine, *The Saturday Evening Post*, came into the household and each of us asserted our right to have it first. Mother laid down priorities. Anything scarce around the house, especially any favorite food, was much valued and before the argument was finished, overvalued. Ed and I liked to eat between meals. Frequently Mother issued the classic warning, "Now don't be eating so much or you'll spoil your supper." To satisfy our unreasonable appetites but still determined to avoid overindulgence, she would give us an apple, a pear, or now and then a piece of pie or cake. "Now one of you is to divide it" she said, "and the other is to get first choice." This insured fair play but put an almost intolerable burden on the divider.

Both parents were against quarreling and fighting. They deplored bad manners. I did discover one day that my father was far from being a turn-the-other-cheek type. He arrived home early one afternoon as I came in from the school grounds on the run, chased by a belligerent boy of about my own size. Seeing this, my father called: "Why do you let that boy run you around like that?"

Instantly I shouted back, "Because if I fight him, you'll give me a whipping, whether I win or lose!"

"Chase that boy out of here."

This was enough for me. I turned around and it was the suddenness of my counterattack, rather than any fighting prowess, that startled my tormentor, who took off at a rapid pace. I, being faster, was more than overjoyed when I caught him, threw him down to the ground, and voiced threats of violence. He seemed to take these most seriously. In fact, I promised to give him a thrashing every day unless he let me alone. I was rapidly learning that domination of others in this world often comes about or is sought through bluff. But it took me some years to learn that pounding from an opponent is not to be dreaded as much as constantly living in fear of another.

Not that I didn't need allies, even then. On my first day of school, Arthur kept an eye on me as I explored the playground. It was not long before a bigger boy, one who seemed to me almost as big as my father, began to chase me, making noises about biting off my ears. I felt toward him much as I had felt toward the gander, but in this case I had no big stick.

Or thought I did not anyhow. Arthur was as big as my tormentor and after this fellow had chased me around the play yard for what seemed an interminable time, Arthur stepped in and said: "That'll be enough of that. Let him alone."

The boy protested that he was just having fun, and Arthur said sharply, "Have your fun with someone else."

I had found a surprising means of protection—my big brothers. The two of them continued to stand between me and what in those early days was clearly a world of enemies. Most of the enemies, of course, were only teasing. But from the standpoint of a little boy, they were not only tormentors; they represented sheer terror.

In spite of boyish frictions the household and even life outside was exceptionally happy. Though our family was far from affluent, I never heard a word even distantly related to self-pity. If we were poor—and I'm not sure that we were by the standards of the day—we were unaware of it. We were always well fed, adequately clothed and housed. Each boy was permitted to earn his own money and to spend it according to his taste and best judgment. One way to obtain cash was raising and selling vegetables. Another was to get a summer job, or to work in a store after school.

From the beginning of our schooling, Mother and Father encouraged us to go to college. They said constantly, "Anyone who really wants an education can get it." But my father, remembering that he didn't become a farmer as his father had hoped, scrupulously refrained from suggesting courses of study.

His insistence that we go through college recalls one incident that I then looked on as almost tragic. Edgar had decided, early in his high-school days, to follow Arthur's example and earn money for himself rather than go on further in school. For some months he pretended he was going to school while he worked, instead, for the town doctor. One day his continued absence was reported to Father. I never before or after saw him so angry.

At noontime that day, Edgar and I had come home for lunch and Father, in a surprise visit from the creamery, found us in the barn. His face was black as thunder. With no pause for argument, he reached for a piece of harness, a tug it was called, at the same time grabbing Ed by the collar. He started in.

A little over twelve years old at the time, I began to shout to my father to stop. Finally I began to cry as loudly as I could, possibly hoping that Mother would arrive on the scene.

Father stopped his thrashing and then turned on me because I had come up behind him and tried to catch hold of his arms. "Oh, do you want some of the same. What's the matter with you, anyway?"

"I don't think anyone ought to be whipped like that," I said, "not even a dog." Whatever his reason, I suffered no punishment.

Now I know, and I am sure Ed does too, that only through instant and drastic action when he learned about the truancy could my father have persuaded him, a headstrong fellow, to change his attitude toward school. Had it not been for the application of leather, prolonged and unforgettable, my brother might well have become an unhappy handyman in Kansas with no scope for the wide exposition of his economic and political views. Undoubtedly fear that his boy would seriously damage all the years of life ahead provoked my father to a violent display of temper and temporary damage.

Usually, Father was quiet and reserved. Mother was by far the greatest personal influence in our lives. She spent many hours a day with us, while Father's time with us was largely at supper and in the evening. In the end, his desire for his sons' education was fulfilled by four of them. Father secretly hoped Ed would become a doctor. He didn't express this and when Ed decided to go to Michigan to study law, Father approved. All the younger brothers sent Edgar funds on occasion but he worked at the University and essentially financed his own education. My appointment to West Point assured an education for me with no drain on household finances. Ed, remembering the help he received, financed Earl's education at the University of Washington. Milton, by

93

writing for magazines, correcting English papers, and, as I said, playing in a dance band, was able to pay his costs at Kansas State University and later, as the American Vice-Consul at Edinburgh, Scotland, he was able to undertake graduate work there at the University.

This willingness of brothers to aid each other was one consequence of the guidance we received as youngsters. Years later, when Arthur was an authority on grain marketing finance and banking, Edgar a successful lawyer and director of industrial companies, Earl a radio station owner and public relations director of the community newspaper, Milton President of John Hopkins University, and I a first administration Republican President, friends often asked why there had not been a black sheep in the family.

I have often thought about this. The answer lies, I think, in the fact that our family life was free from parental quarreling and filled with genuine, if not demonstrated love. I never knew anyone from a divorced family until I went to West Point. Responsibility was a part of maturing. Concern for others was natural in our small community. And ambition without arrogance was quietly instilled in us by both parents. Part of that ambition was self-dependence. My mother could recite from memory long passages of the Bible (family tradition has it that she once won first prize in her church, as a child in Virginia, by memorizing 1,365 verses in a six-month period). But these were not her only admonitions. Whenever any of us expressed a wish for something that seemed far beyond our reach, my mother often said, "Sink or swim," or "Survive or perish."

I have started to sketch the people who were David and Ida Eisenhower and the Eisenhower boys in Abilene. Like anyone else who searches the corners of his mind, names and faces and places come crowding across my memory. Having set the stage of personalities, so to speak, I would like to tell a few more stories, describe the town of Abilene, and mention others who were a part of it.

. . .

If I can to some extent identify myself with the original family who lived on my farm, I think I may also guess a little about the austerity of life within the primitive cabins that lay in the valley of Marsh Creek. Yet to those of us in a supermarket and jet-powered age, the hazard and harshness of their daily living must remain beyond comprehension.

But I would imagine that the relationship between parents and children, at least, differed little from our lives in Abilene. In their simple faith, in their reliance on a guiding providence, the parents of that distant day could have differed little from my own. Surely, more than one little boy in those rude houses of hewn log remembered all his life and tried to abide by a few familiar words of his father or mother, gently spoken yet as deeply felt as the mountains are rooted in the earth's rocks. With them I am close kin, for just that happened to me.

The year when I was ten, my mother gave permission to Arthur and Edgar, the two older Eisenhower boys, to go out with a group for Halloween "trick or treating." It was upsetting when my father and mother said I was too young to go along. I argued and pleaded until the last minute. Finally, the two boys took off.

I have no exact memory of what happened immediately afterward, but I was completely beside myself. Suddenly my father grabbed my shoulders to shock me back into consciousness. What I had been doing was standing by an old apple tree trunk and pounding it with my bleeding fists, expressing resentment in rage. My father legislated the matter with the traditional hickory switch and sent me off to bed.

Perhaps an hour later, my mother came into the room. I was still sobbing into the pillow, my feelings—among other things—hurt, completely abused and at odds with the entire world. Mother sat in the rocking chair by the bed and said nothing for a long time. Then she began to talk about temper and controlling it. Eventually, as she often did, she drew on the Bible, paraphrasing it, I suppose. This time she said:

"He that conquereth his own soul is greater than he who taketh a city."

Hatred was a futile sort of thing, she said, because hating anyone or anything meant that there was little to be gained. The person who had incurred my displeasure probably didn't care, possibly didn't even know, and the only person injured was myself. This was soothing, although she added that among all her boys, I was the one who had most to learn.

In the meantime, she had set about putting salve on my injured hands and bandaging the worst places, not failing to make the point that I had expressed resentment and only damaged myself.

I have always looked back on that conversation as one of the most valuable moments of my life. To my youthful mind, it seemed to me that she talked for hours but I suppose the affair was ended in fifteen or twenty minutes. At least she got me to acknowledge that I was wrong and I felt enough ease in my mind to fall off to sleep. The incident was never mentioned again. But to this day I make it a practice to avoid hating anyone. If someone's been guilty of despicable actions, especially toward me, I try to forget him. I used to follow a practice— somewhat contrived, I admit—to write the man's name on a piece of scrap paper, drop it into the lowest drawer of my desk, and say to myself: "That finishes the incident, and so far as I'm concerned, that fellow."

The drawer became over the years a sort of private wastebasket for crumbled-up spite and discarded personalities. Besides, it seemed to be effective and helped me avoid harboring useless black feelings. This device applied, of course, to things purely personal. During World War II, there was no question of the deep-seated hatred I felt for Hitler and all that he stood for. But there were ways to deal with him other than the drawer.

Eventually, out of my mother's talk, grew my habit of not mentioning in public anybody's name with whose actions or words I took violent exception. In private, of course, I have not always execised tight control on temper or tongue—my staff, at least, has always held up under these bursts with an attitude of cheerful resignation. A quick explosion, as quickly forgotten, can sometimes be a necessary safety valve. I think my mother might have agreed.

DISCUSSION AND INQUIRY

Dwight presents a picture of a serene, friction-free household with a firm, loving mother and a kind father, who made use of the rod when he or Mother thought it was necessary. Mother apparently dealt with the inconsequential controversies that inevitably arose with six sons in the family; however, she left the corporal punishment for the father. Although there is no mention of negative reactions to this procedure, what might be the outcome of having children wait for their thrashing until Dad comes home? Consider the effect on the relationship between the child and his father as well as the child's image of the role of the male parent. How may this situation at home have contributed to Dwight's feelings about himself as an authority figure?

The author recalls several incidents from his early life—the gander incident, the chase by the belligerent boy, and the Halloween experience—that he claims taught him a number of things: namely, that it is best to negotiate from a position of strength, that a pounding from a foe is superior to living in fear of that opponent, and that hatred is futile. The recollections are of particular interest in light of his record as a military leader and as President of the United States. Is it likely that these events were singularly responsible for shaping his attitudes toward strength, fear and hatred? Can you select specific events from your childhood that you feel taught you an important "lesson" and, therefore, resulted in an enduring point of view?

It is apparent that the Eisenhowers valued education for their children and planned for it from the beginning. The time brother Ed was severely beaten for truancy greatly impressed Dwight, and is viewed by him, in retrospect, as having changed the course of Ed's life. All six boys had a high regard for education and all went on to considerable success. Is it typical for children to value education when it is a value held by their parents? How can one account for those situations where this value exists but is not successfully transmitted to the children?

Dick Gregory

▲▲▲▲▲▲▲▲▲▲▲▲▲▲▲▲▲▲▲▲▲▲▲▲▲▲▲▲▲▲▲▲

BIOGRAPHICAL SKETCH

Dick Gregory was born in St. Louis, Missouri, in 1932. Chicago became the backdrop for his performances as a comedian, and he eventually developed into a well-known nightclub and television personality. Gregory has been politically active for a number of years, concerning himself with the war in Vietnam and the status of minority groups.

▼▼▼▼▼▼▼▼▼▼▼▼▼▼▼▼▼▼▼▼▼▼▼▼▼▼▼▼▼▼▼▼

SELECTIONS FROM

NIGGER

IT'S A SAD and beautiful feeling to walk home slow on Christmas Eve after you've been out hustling all day, shining shoes in the white taverns and going to the store for the neighbors and buying and stealing presents from the ten-cent store, and now it's dark and still along the street and your feet feel warm and sweaty inside your tennis sneakers even if the wind finds the holes in your mittens. The electric Santa Clauses wink at you from windows. You stop off at your best friend's house and look at his tree and give him a ball-point pen with his name on it. You reach into your shopping bag and give something to everybody there, even the ones you don't know. It doesn't matter that they don't have anything for you because it feels so good to be in a warm happy place where grownups are laughing. There are Daddies around. Your best friend's so happy and excited, standing there trying on all his new clothes. As you walk down the stairs you hear his mother say: "Boo, you forgot to say good-by to Richard, say good-by to Richard, Boo, and wish him a. . . ."

Then you're out on the street again and some of the lights have gone out. You take the long way home, and Mister Ben, the grocer, says: "Merry Christmas, Richard," and you give him a present out of the shopping bag, and you smile at a wino and give him a nickel, and you even wave at Grimes, the mean cop. It's a good feeling. You don't want to get home too fast.

98

And then you hit North Taylor, your street, and something catches your eye and you lift your head up and it's there in your window. Can't believe it. You start running and the only thing in the whole world you're mad about is that you can't run fast enough. For the first time in a long while the cracked orange door says: "Come on in, little man, you're home now," and there's a wreath and lights in the window and a tree in the kitchen near the coal closet and you hug your Momma, her face hot from the stove. Oh, Momma, I'm so glad you did it like this because ours is new, just for us, everybody else's tree been up all week long for other people to see, and, Momma, ours is just for us. Momma, oh, Momma, you did it again.

My beautiful Momma smiled at me like Miss America, and my brothers and sisters danced around that little kitchen with the round wooden table and the orange crate chairs.

"Go get the vanilla, Richard," said Momma, "Presley, peel some sweet potatoes. Go get the bread out the oven, Dolores. You get away from that duckling, Garland. Ronald, oh, Ronald, you be good now, stand over there with Pauline. Oh, Richard, my little man, did you see the ham Miz White from the Eat Shop sent by, and the bag of nuts from Mister Myers and the turkey from Miz King, and wouldn't you know, Mister Ben, he. . . ."

"Hey, Momma, I know some rich people don't got this much, a ham, and a turkey, Momma. . . ."

"The Lord, He's always looking out for my boys, Richard, and this ain't all, the white folks'll be by here tomorrow to bring us more things."

Momma was so happy that Christmas, all the food folks brought us and Mister Ben giving us more credit, and Momma even talked the electric man into turning the lights on again.

"Hey, Momma, look here, got a present for Daddy. A cigarette lighter, Momma, there's even a place to scratch a name on it."

"What you scratch on it, Richard, Big Pres or Daddy?"

"Nothing, Momma. Might have to give Daddy's present to old Mister White from the Eat Shop again."

She turned away and when she turned back her eyes were wet. Then she smiled her Miss America smile and grabbed my shoulder. "Richard, my little man, if I show you something, you won't tell nobody, will you?"

"What is it, Momma?"

"I got something for you."

"Oh, Momma, you forgot, everything's under the tree."

"This is something special, just for you, Richard."

"Thanks, Momma, oh, thanks, how'd you know I wanted a wallet, Momma, a real wallet like men have?"

Momma always gave each of us something like that, something personal that wasn't under the tree, something we weren't supposed to tell the other kids about. It always came out, though. Garland and I'd be fighting and one of us would say, "Momma likes me better than you, look what she gave me," and we both found out the other got a secret present, too.

But I loved that wallet. First thing I did was fill out the address card. If I got hit by a car someone would know who I am. Then I put my dollars in it, just like men do. Ran outside that night and got on a streetcar and pulled out my wallet and handed the conductor a dollar.

"Got anything smaller, boy?"

"Sure, Mister," I said and I pulled out my wallet again and took a dime out of the coin purse and snapped it shut and put the dollar back in the long pocket and closed the wallet and slipped it into my back pocket. Did the same thing on the way back home.

Did we eat that night! It seemed like all the days we went without food, no bread for the baloney and no baloney for the bread, all the times in the summer when there was no sugar for the Kool-Aid and no lemon for the lemonade and no ice at all were wiped away. Man, we're all right.

After dinner I went out the back door and looked at the sky and told God how nobody ever ate like we ate that night, macaroni and cheese and ham and turkey and the old duckling's cooking in the oven for to-morrow. There's even whiskey, Momma said, for people who come by. Thanks, God, Momma's so happy and even the rats and roaches didn't come out tonight and the wind isn't blowing through the cracks.

How'd you know I wanted a wallet, God? I wonder if all the rich people who get mink coats and electric trains got that one little thing nobody knew they wanted. You know, God, I'm kinda glad you were born in a manger. I wonder, God, if they had let Mary in the first place she stopped at, would you have remembered tonight? Oh, God, I'm scared. I wish I could die right now with the feeling I have because I know Momma's going to make me mad and I'm going to make her mad, and me and Presley's gonna fight. . . .

"Richard, you get in here and put your coat on. Get in here or I'll whip you."

See what I mean, God, there she goes already and I'm not even cold, I'm all wrapped up in You.

"What's wrong, Richard? Why you look so strange?"

"You wouldn't understand, Momma."

"I would, Richard, you tell me."

"Well, I came out to pray, Momma, way out here so they wouldn't hear me and laugh at me and call me a sissy. God's a good God, ain't He, Momma?"

"Yes, Richard."

"Momma, if I tell you something, would you laugh at me, would you say I'm crazy, would you say I was lying? Momma?"

"What is it, Richard?"

"I heard Him talk to me, Momma."

She put her arm around my shoulders and pulled me against her. "He talks to people, Richard, some people that are real special and good like you. Do me a favor, Richard?"

"Sure, Momma."

"Next time you talk to Him, ask Him to send Daddy home."

"Let me stay up and look out the window with you, Momma."

"Everybody's in bed, Richard."

"All my life, Momma, I wanted to stay up with you on Christmas Eve and look out that window with you, Momma. I won't laugh at you."

"What you mean, Richard?"

"You're waiting on him, ain't you? I know, Momma, every Christmas Eve you take a bath and put on that perfume and those clothes from the rich white folks and get down there on your knees in front of that window looking for Daddy."

"Richard, you better get on to bed."

"I know, Momma, that whiskey ain't for people coming by, that's for Daddy."

"Richard, you go on to bed and when he gets here I'll wake you up."

"No, Momma, I want to sit up with you . . . Momma?"

"Yes, Richard?"

"I shoulda got a present for Mister White, 'cause I know Daddy's coming to get his this year."

There were a lot of things I wanted to tell Momma that night while we sat and waited for Daddy, while we prayed on our knees, and dozed and hugged each other against the cold and jumped up like jacks every time we heard a noise on the street. But I never did. Sometimes I think she knew anyway.

I wanted to say to her, Momma, you remember that day I came home and told you I was at Doctor Jackson's house? And how he liked me, Momma, and told me I'd be a good doctor? How he's going to help me learn to read, and how he told me when it gets too cold to study in my house I could come by his house? Remember that, Momma? It was a lie. I played all that day in a vacant lot.

I guess she knew. She never pressed me for names when I told her about all the people who liked me, all the people I created in my mind,

101

people to help poor folks. I couldn't believe God had made a world and hadn't put none of those people in it.

I made up a schoolteacher that loved me, that taught me to read. A teacher that didn't put me in the idiot's seat or talk about you and your kind. She didn't yell at me when I came to school with my homework all wrinkled and damp. She understood when I told her it was too cold to study in the kitchen so I did my homework under the covers with a flashlight. Then I fell asleep. And one of the other five kids in bed must have peed on it.

I'd go out and sweat and make five dollars. And I'd come home and say, Momma, Mister Green told me to bring this to you. Told me he liked you. Told me he wished he could raise his kids the way you're raising us. That wasn't true, Momma.

Remember all those birthday parties I went to, Momma? Used to steal things from the ten-cent store and give the best presents. I'd come home and tell you how we played pillow kiss and post office and pin the tail on the donkey and how everybody liked me? That was a lie, Momma. One girl cried and ran away when she threw the pillow and it hit me. She opened her eyes and saw she was supposed to kiss me and she cried and ran away.

And on my birthday, Momma, when I came home with that shopping bag full of presents and told you the kids in my class loved me so much they all got me things? That wasn't true. I stole all those little things from the ten-cent store and wrapped them up and put a different kid's name on each one.

"Oh, Richard, if he don't show up this time. . . ."

"He's comin', Momma, it's like you said. He got held up in traffic, the trains were full."

"You know, Richard, your Daddy's a cook, he has to work on Christmas."

"He'll be here, Momma, you go put those clothes back on."

Remember when those people came by and told you how dirty we were, how they didn't want us playing with their kids or coming into their houses? They said we smelled so bad. I was six then, and Presley was almost eight. You cried all night, Momma, and then you told us to stay home until you could get us some new clothes. And you went and hid all the clothes we had. Momma, it was summertime and we couldn't just lay there, crying and watching out the window at the kids play running tag, and rip and run, and get called in for their naps, and get called in for their dinners. And we looked all over for our clothes, down in the basement, in the coal closet, under the stove, and we couldn't find them. And then we went through your things, Momma, and put on the dresses you never wore, the dresses the rich white folks gave you. And then we went outside to play. The people laughed at us when we went outside in your dresses, pointed and slapped their legs. We never played so good as we played that summer, with all those people watching us. When we came off the porch those Negro doctors and lawyers and teachers waiting to get into White's Eat Shop across the street would nudge each other and turn their heads. And when the streetcar stopped on the corner, right in front of our house, the people would lean out the windows and stare. Presley and I would wave at them. We did it all that summer, and after a while nobody bothered us. Everybody got to know that the Gregory boys didn't have clothes so they wore their mother's dresses. We just made sure we were home before you got there, Momma.

"How do I look, Richard?"

"You look okay, Momma."

"These are the best pair of shoes I got, Miz Wallace gave me them, but they're summer shoes."

"What you mean, summer shoes? Those are the black and white ones you never wear. I didn't know they were summer shoes."

"You never see folks wear white shoes in the wintertime."

"People dye them, Momma. I'll dye them for you so you can put them on and Daddy can see you."

"Oh, Richard, there won't be time, they got to dry."

"Don't worry, Momma, you burn the dye and it dries right while you wear it."

I've dyed a lot of shoes, Momma, down on my hands and knees in the taverns, dyeing and shining shoes. I never told you too much about the things I did and the things I saw. Momma, remember the time I came home with my teeth knocked in and my lip all cut? Told you I tripped downstairs. Momma, I got kicked. Right in the face.

It was Saturday afternoon, my big hustling day. I was ten, but I looked like I was seven. There were a lot of people in the tavern, drinking beer, and I was shining this white woman's shoes. They were white and brown shoes, summer shoes. The men sitting at the bar were laughing.

"Hey, Flo, gonna take the little monkey home with you, change your luck?"

She starting laughing. "Maybe I will. Heard these little coons are hung like horses, I'm getting tired of you worms."

"Little monkey's got a tail, Flo, swing from limb to limb."

White and brown shoes. I didn't want to get the brown polish on the white part so I put my other hand on the back of the white woman's leg to steady myself.

"He's got a tail all right. One of you boys can warm me up, but I'm going to get me a black buck to do me right."

One of the white men, a man who wasn't laughing, jumped off his bar stool. "Get your dirty black hands off that white lady, you nigger bastard."

He kicked me right in the mouth.

One of the men who had been laughing came off his stool and grabbed the man who kicked me.

"For Christ's sake, he's just a little kid."

"Mind your goddamn business."

Whop. The fight was on.

The bartender jumped over the bar and grabbed me with one hand and my shoeshine box with the other. "Sorry, boy, it's not your fault, but I can't have you around."

Out on the sidewalk he gave me a five-dollar bill.

When I saw all the blood and pieces of tooth on my shirt, I got scared. Momma would be real angry. So I went over to Boo's house and spent the night. I told Boo if I could get kicked in the mouth a couple more times today, and get five dollars each time, man, I'd be all right.

"What time is it, Momma?"

"Four o'clock, Richard."

"I guess I didn't have to burn them, did I?"

The tavern isn't so bad, Momma. No kid ever runs up and laughs at me because I'm shining shoes. But they sure remind me I'm on relief. And there's another reason I won't quit working the taverns, Momma. In the wintertime it's warmer in there, and in the summertime it's cooler than our house. And even though men spit in my face and kick me in the mouth, Momma, every so often somebody rubs my head and calls me son.

"Why do you believe he's coming, Richard?"

"Oh, Momma, I talked to that man in the backyard, I know he's coming."

"Go on to bed, Richard."

"No, Momma, I'll wait here with you. If I lay over there in the chair, when he comes will you wake me up?"

"Sure I will, Richard. Now get some sleep."

"Okay, Momma."

So many things I wanted to tell you that night, Momma. There was a little girl used to wave to me when I cut through the alley to get onto Taylor, a clean little girl who used to sneak a piece of cake off her table and give it to me. A piece of cake and a glass of Kool-Aid. After a while, I'd finish up my paper route early just to come back and wave at her. After dinner, her Momma and Daddy would go up to the front room and sit around and leave her in the back to do the dishes all alone. I started to help her wash the dishes. I'd creep in up the back porch and she'd let me in and say: "Sh, nobody knows you're here." It was like playing house. I'd just come and stand there at the sink with her every night and help her with the dishes. Then one time her father came back to the kitchen. He grabbed me and shook me and told me how I broke into his house because his daughter wouldn't let no dirty street kid in.

She was crying, scared to death, and she said; "I let him in, Daddy, I let him in, he's my friend."

"No sir, she's lying," I said. "I make her bring me food out, I make her let me in."

He slapped me. He slapped me until I fell down, and when she grabbed onto his arm, crying and screaming to make him stop, he kicked me out of the door to the back porch. He started to choke me.

Then he stopped. "Why you grinning at me like that, you little bastard?"

"Last week when you woke up drunk on this here porch, that was me brought you home. Found you on Sarah Street and brought you home and was so proud leading your black ass down the street 'cause you acted just like my Daddy would. Come out of your drunk every now and then, swinging and fighting. I had to run and duck. People see you and want to jump on you. But I tell them that's my Daddy, he's all right. Leave him alone, that's my Daddy."

He let me go, and he backed away and there was a funny look on his face. He started sweating, and chewing on his lip, and looking around to see if anybody heard what I had said. He opened his mouth, but nothing came out. Then he reached into his pocket and pulled out his wallet. He gave me a dollar. I threw it back at him. I reached into my own hip pocket and pulled out a dollar. My dollar was bigger than his because nobody knew I had mine. And then I walked away.

"God, my little Richard's asleep now and I have to talk to You. I always made a big mistake, God. I sit here every Christmas, times in the summer, too, and pray for his Daddy and never pray for other kids' Daddies. Send them theirs first, and then if You're not too weary, oh, Lawd, send Big Pres home. But when You send him, God, don't send him for me. Send him 'cause the boys need him."

105

"God, my Momma cried herself to sleep so I'm asking You to send Daddy home right away. God, wherever he is let him knock on that door. I'll wait up for him, God, just let him please knock on that door."

Momma, I loved those firemen in St. Louis, so big and tall and strong, rushing out to save people, Negro firemen and white firemen, no difference, they'd rush out and never ask whose house it was, how much money he had, if he was on relief. I'd stand on the corner where they had to pass and I'd wave to them, and sometimes they'd wave back. Sometimes I thought they went out of their way to pass that corner, just so they could wave to me. Then I'd follow them to the fire, and stand there and pray they would put it out fast so none of them would get hurt. I used to count every fireman that went up the ladder and count them as they came back down. Once I saw them use the net to save somebody and they didn't act like they were doing anybody a favor. I'd see them standing around in their uniforms, like they all belonged to the same family, and talk about fires. At the big fires, when the Red Cross came, they'd drink coffee and bite into sandwiches. It's a beautiful thing to watch a man who really deserves the food he eats.

One time I bought an old raincoat with hooks instead of buttons, and a pair of old hip boots. I hid them in the cellar. Nobody knew I had them. Whenever I wanted to feel good I'd put them on and walk around the cellar, pretending I was putting out fires, running up ladders to save people, catching people in my net. Then I'd take them off and walk over to the firehouse and watch them drill and clean the engine and roll up the hose. I'd walk right up to a fireman and say: "Excuse me, mister, but I shore like you all." He'd turn around and say something nice to me. Sometimes, before I knew better, I used to think my Daddy was a fireman somewhere, saving people and saying nice things to kids.

"Momma, Momma, wake up, wake up, Momma. Didya hear it, didya hear it? Somebody's knockin' on the door."

There was a neighbor woman standing at the door when I opened it.
"Let me speak to your mother, Richard."
I left the room like I was supposed to when a grown person came in. But I listened.
"He's here, Lucille, Big Pres been down my house all night scared to come home 'cause he ain't got nothing for the kids but some money. He just got in this evening. Been over my place crying, Lucille, 'cause he went and gambled and won and when he finished winning all the stores was closed."
I ran right in and Momma grabbed me and hugged me. "I told you,

Momma, didn't I tell you he was coming? Go get him, Momma, go and tell him we got everything we want."

I ran back and woke up the kids—"Daddy's home, Daddy's home"—and they tumbled out of bed, all five of them rolling and fighting their way out of the blankets, caught up in the sheet and scrambling around for the socks they lost under the covers and bumping into each other and in such a hurry they got legs and arms all mixed up. But nobody was mad at all. We all ran into the kitchen and jumped up and down while Momma got dressed again, put on the fanciest of the clothes the white folks gave her, clothes she never wore, and fixed her hair and put on lipstick and perfume.

"You don't need that stuff, Momma, just go get Daddy and bring him home."

After Momma left, we quieted down. We sat in the front room by the window and we waited. We hadn't seen him much in five years. We waited a long time because Momma hadn't seen him much in five years either.

"Aw, he's not really here," said Dolores. She was twelve. "Anyway, I don't want to see him."

"I want to see him," said Ronald. He was seven, and he was sitting on the floor, shivering, and holding onto Pauline's hand. Pauline was the baby, she was almost five.

"Oh, man," said Presley, who was fourteen, "I can't wait, he's gonna be so clean, a two-hundred-dollar suit on him."

"Dare anybody, he gonna be wearin' thousand-dollar suits," said Garland, who was nine. "And he'll have a pocketful of money."

"Yeah, a pocketful of money, but no gifts," I said.

"He been busy makin' money," said Garland.

"He's a soldier," said Ronald.

"Momma said he's a cook," said Dolores.

"Big deal."

"What's matter with you, Richard, don't you want to see Daddy?" said Presley.

"Last week I wanted to see him, when the rent man was cussin' Momma."

"He been busy makin' money," said Garland.

Pauline started to cry, and Ronald leaned over and rocked her in his arms. "Ooooh, you be quiet, little rat, you Daddy comin' home, he's a soldier."

"He's a cook," said Dolores, pushing Presley a little to look out the window.

"Shut up, girl," said Presley. "You remember when Daddy carry that old lady cross the street?"

"No."

107

"See, you don't know nothing. Man, was he ever big and clean. He got arms so strong he just picked this old lady right up after she fell off the streetcar and carry her cross the street and up to her house. Everybody saw it."

Presley did a lot of talking that night. I was just thinking. I thought about that time that trampy woman came by and shouted at my Momma. "Goddam husband of yours home?"

"No, he's not," Momma said politely.

"I just want you to know anytime he ain't at your house or my house, he's at some woman's house."

"I appreciate you wouldn't come by here talking like this because the kids can hear you."

"I don't give a damn 'bout your kids. I got some kids for him, too."

Yeah, I thought, Big Pres is coming home. All those nights Momma kept the hallway light on after we went to bed. All those nights she listened to the police news on the radio, listening to hear his name. The times the police came by the house to ask if we'd seen him lately.

Suddenly a taxicab pulled up outside the window and we heard the door slam, and a big, deep voice like nobody's but my Daddy's was saying, "Keep the change, friend." And then all the kids were on their feet and knocking each other down to get to the door, and Ronald dropped Pauline, and everybody was hollering and screaming, and the last thing I heard was my Momma's voice saying, "Don't touch his clothes with your dirty hands, now don't touch his clothes."

I slammed the bedroom door and climbed into bed with my sneakers on and cried. I pulled the blanket over my head, but I could hear all right.

"Man, look at that thousand-dollar suit, see, what'd I tell you, Presley? . . ."

"Lookit, Daddy, lookit, Daddy . . ."

"Hey, Daddy, pick me up after Pauline. . . ."

"Now you get off Big Pres, don't go messing up his clothes with your dirty hands. . . ."

" 'Cille? Where's Richard?"

"Richard, Big Pres is here, come on out." But she was scared to leave him to see if I was okay. When she turned her back he might walk out again.

"Lookit all that money Daddy got. Bet it's a million dollars. . . ."

"Where'd you get all that money, Daddy? . . ."

I could hear him crackling the money in his hand and his big, deep voice saying, "You been a good girl, 'Lores, doin' like your Momma says. . . . You been good, Presley, don't want you growin' up to be like your Daddy now . . . payin' your Momma mind and doin' your school work. . . . How about you, Garland? . . ."

And I lay there and bit the cover and kicked the sheet and cried. Don't want you growing up to be like your Daddy now. Is that what he's worried about? I bit the cover until my gums started bleeding and I didn't stop until my nose was all stuffed up from crying. Don't you worry, Daddy, don't you worry.

After a while, Momma brought him into the bedroom. "Big Pres, Richard waited up all night for you, he knew you were coming. He bought you something for Christmas, Big Pres. You know, he buys you something every Christmas."

She pulled on me. She rolled me over. "What's wrong with you, Richard, you hear me call for you, didn't you hear me say Daddy's home? What are you crying about, Richard, what's wrong with you?"

She didn't tell him what was wrong. No, you got to treat strangers with respect. "Big Pres, he's just jealous, he's just jealous 'cause you didn't pick him up like you picked up the others."

I lay in bed and I looked up at that man and he was ten feet tall. Tallest man I ever saw. He was clean, and he was strong, and he was healthy. He sat down on the bed next to me.

"Don't you sit on that dirty bed, Big Pres," said Momma, and she brushed off his suit and got one of the silk tablecloths the white folks had given her which we never used. She put the tablecloth on top of the sheet, yeah, the one sheet that stayed on the bed for six months. She didn't want Big Pres to get his suit dirty.

"I brought you some money, Richard."

"Don't want it, Daddy."

"Got more for you than I got for the others."

"Still don't want it."

"I'm your Daddy, boy, don't you want to see me?"

"I see you every time I see my Momma on her knees in front of the window cryin' and prayin' you'll come. You oughta thank me 'cause I brought you here, yeah, thank me you never get sick 'cause every night I say my prayers I say bless him wherever he is."

"Richard, I'm going to stay home with you this time, if you want me I'll stay home. You want me to stay, Richard?"

I didn't say anything.

"I'll get a job. Your Momma won't have to work. You want me, Richard?"

I looked at him but I didn't say anything. I guess he meant what he said. The moment he said it, anyway. And I lay there and I was thinking. If you stay, old man, I'll leave. I don't need you, Daddy, not now. I needed you when the boys chased me home, when the man cheated me out of my paper money, needed you every time Boo's Daddy came home at seven o'clock.

" 'Cille, what's wrong with this boy?"

"Don't you worry about him, Big Pres, he's crazy."

That got me mad, Momma forgetting all her love for me to pacify him.

"Yeah, he's crazy. Hey, 'Cille, you got a drink around the house?" She brought out the whiskey. He drank it right out of the bottle.

I got dressed that day and I left the house to play, but I ducked back every half hour to see if he was still there. Once I slipped Boo in to let him peep.

"That's my Daddy, Boo. My Daddy's rich, too, man, pocket full of money."

"Your Daddy ain't got no money. You all on relief."

"Come here, Boo, let me show you something." I walked up to my Daddy and looked at him. It was the first time I walked in and said anything to him. I didn't ask him, I told him.

"Give Boo five dollars, Daddy."

When he reached in and pulled out that pocketful of money, Boo's eyes popped out. He hadn't ever seen that much money in his life. Looked like he had all the money in the world. He looked so fine fumbling through those twenties and tens and fives, and I wondered if it was enough to go over to Mister Ben's and wipe out the back bill and put a little on the front bill.

"You got a good Daddy," said Boo.

I kept slipping back all that day, peeping in to make sure he was still there. Once I thought I almost caught him leaving, all dressed with his brown bag in his hand, but when he saw me he put it down. I'd slip in and I'd hear him telling Momma all the things he was going to do for her. Stay home. Get a job. Get off relief. Give up other women. Take Momma to all the night clubs. She wouldn't have to work for the white folks no more.

"Told you about working so hard for them white folks," he'd say. "Don't want my kids left in this house all by themselves."

She cried. "You mean it, Pres, you really mean it?"

"Yeah, 'Cille."

She got up off her orange-crate chair and put her hands on his face and kissed him.

I walked right in then. "Get your goddamn hands off my Momma."

He beat me, pulled off his belt and beat me across my backside. Momma held me on her lap while he beat me.

"Ha. That's a hell of a man there, that Richard. I beat his ass good, 'Cille, and he don't even cry."

He had little men and he didn't even know it. Every time he hit me I couldn't cry from almost wanting to laugh. I know, old man, couple of days from now you'll be too far away for that belt to reach me.

Momma made me go to bed and she whispered: "Please treat your Daddy nice. For me. Please do it for me."

"I'm the cause of his being here, Momma. I'm the one that asked the Man out back, I prayed for him."

"That's right, Richard."

That night he beat her.

He beat her all through the house, every room, swinging his belt and whopping her with his hand and cussing her and kicking her and knocking her down and telling her all about his women.

"Think you're so goddamn good, bitch," said my Daddy, cracking my Momma across her back with his belt. She whimpered and fell against a little table, knocking over a lamp from the white folks. She bent over to pick up the lamp and Big Pres kicked her in her backside and she fell forward on the linoleum floor. She lay there, her face pressed against the linoleum, sobbing.

"I don't even feel right walking down the street with you," he said, kicking her in the side with his foot. "Walk down the street everybody wants to run up, say hello to you, they look at me like I was dirt."

He grabbed her hair and pulled her up to her knees. Momma looked up at him, tears running down her cheeks. Slap. Right across her face. "I got bitches, women like you never seen, proud to walk down the street with Big Pres." Slap. Momma fell down on her face again.

"Get on your feet, bitch." Momma got up, slowly.

Whop. Momma spun across the front room, back toward the kitchen, like a drunk. Whop. Big Pres had the belt out again, and now he drove her in front of him, around the kitchen table, Momma stumbling over the chairs and the orange crates, Big Pres kicking them out of his way. Whop. Back into the front room, Momma bounced against a soft chair, then against the wall.

"And what the hell you taught Richard, bitch? Hell, whatever you taught him, you ain't gonna turn them all against their Daddy."

She never said a word, just crying, sobbing, trying to stay on her feet, trying not to get hit too hard but never really ducking his hand or his belt. She'd see it coming and close her eyes and put her hands up, but she never tried to get out of the way. The kids were crying and hollering and Ronald and Pauline were hugging each other and Dolores was hiding her face in her hands. Garland and Presley were scared to death. I watched him knock her down, and cuss her, and he was saying the things I wanted to say when she forgot her love for me and told him I was crazy. He left her on the floor, dirty and crying, came over and whopped me across my face so hard that when I knocked into the wall the pictures fell right off their hooks. One was a picture of Jesus, and the other was a piece of wood with the Ten Commandments.

111

And then they were in the kitchen and Big Pres was crying and kissing my Momma and saying he was sorry and how he was going to take care of us and give up his women and get a job.

And Momma kept saying, "No, Big Pres, it's all my fault, it's all my fault, I shouldn't talk like that, they'll be time to get off relief when you're home awhile and get a chance to rest up."

I got up off the floor and I walked into that kitchen. Big Pres was sitting at the table with his face in his hands, and Momma was standing over him, stroking his head. They both were crying. I took down the butcher knife off the wall, the big one with the black handle, and swung at his head. Seen plenty of people swing knives in the taverns and I knew how to cut. Swung right at his head, everything I had, I swung for every kid in the whole world who hated his no-good Daddy.

Momma grabbed my wrist with both her hands and twisted the knife out of my hand.

Big Pres looked up real slow. I guess it's a hell of a thing for a man to look up into his own son's eyes and see murder.

"I'll leave now, 'Cille," he said very softly. "You should have let him hit me, should have let him kill me. I never was any good, never treated you or him right. I need to be dead."

He got up. "Don't beat Richard, 'Cille, don't beat him. I know what I done."

Momma grabbed Big Pres' leg and he kicked her away. He turned and walked out the door. My Momma tried to hold the door open while he closed it behind him.

"No, Big Pres, he didn't mean nothing, Richard's crazy, you know that. . . ."

He turned and kicked her foot out of the door, and slammed it shut. My Momma fell down and slid across the floor, holding the doorknob in her hand.

"Don't leave, Daddy, don't leave, Daddy . . ." the kids were screaming.

I followed him out of the door and down the street. He didn't see me, his head was down, and he walked like the greatest crime in the world had just been committed against him. His head didn't come up again until he walked into a tavern. I walked in behind him and stood near the door where he couldn't see me. He walked right up to a woman sitting at the bar. She was smoking a cigarette and tapping her high heels against the rail.

"Where you been, Big Pres? I been waiting on you for hours."

"I had to beat the bitch's ass for bad mouthing you, Mollie," he said. "But I got a tough little man there, Richard, you should see that little man, beat his ass and he didn't cry."

112

"I been waiting all day, Big Pres. Don't you start telling me about some little bastard you got. Don't even know if it's yours or the . . ."

"Watch your mouth, Mollie. My 'Cille's a good woman, no loose piece of trim like you."

"Sure, who you think buys the bread when you're . . ."

He knocked that bitch right off the stool. He swung that big hand of his and her cigarette went one way and her shoes came off and she went face first on the floor. He stomped that woman like no other man in the world. I got to see my Daddy at his best that night. Two men stood up from tables and started toward Big Pres. He threw back his head and he laughed and he stood over that bitch and his hand came out of his pocket with a razor in it.

"Dare any dirty mother-fucker in this place to come and stop me from stomping this bitch. Hear?"

Nobody moved.

He walked out of there, ten feet tall. My Daddy. I walked over to the woman on the floor and helped her up. She shook me away.

"I'm real sorry, ma'am."

She spat in my face. She didn't know I was Big Pres' boy.

I watched him walk down the street, head up high, hands swinging loose. Big Pres. A real Capone with the whores and the bitches. Heard "I love you" from some broad off the street. But never from his own kids. And that's worth all the sevens falling on all the craps all over the world. He missed it. Missed seeing his kids grow up, missed having his kids crawl into bed with him and lie down and go to sleep because Daddy's sleeping. He missed what I have now. Feeling a little girl put a finger in my mouth, knowing that Daddy will never bite hard. Hearing a little kid say: "Throw me up in the air, Daddy," sure that Daddy will catch her.

Big Pres had to be a lonely man. There must have been times he woke up in a lonely bed, and wanted to give every whore he ever had, every seven, every eleven he ever threw, every wild time he ever had, just to go all the way back and have one of his kids walk up to him and say: "Daddy, I love you."

There must have been times like that. Because I would turn in all the Dick Gregorys in the world and all the night clubs and all the money just to go back to those days and find a Daddy there.

When you have a good mother and no father, God kind of sits in. It's not good enough, but it helps. But I got tired of hearing Momma say, God, fix it so I can pay the rent; God, fix it so the lights will be turned on; God, fix it so the pot is full. I kind of felt it really wasn't His job. And it's a hell of a thing when you're growing up and you're out on the street and you kind of hedge up to a man so he can rub your head and call you son. It's a hell of a thing to hear a man say: I wish my boys were more like the Gregory boys. If Big Pres could only know how people admired the Gregory boys.

Well, Big Pres walked away and left us. Left us to face the cold winters, the hot summers, the Easters with nothing new, the picnics with nothing in the basket. I wonder if it ever dawned on him that he fixed it so we couldn't even go to church one Sunday every year— Father's Day.

I should never have swung at him with that knife. I should have fallen on my knees and cried for him. No kid in the world, no woman in the world should ever raise a hand against a no-good Daddy. That's already been taken care of: A Man Who Destroys His Own Home Shall Inherit the Wind.

When I got back home that night, the knob was back on the door. And the light was on in the hallway. She was sitting up that night, looking out the window. Momma sat like that for the next three or four months, looking out the window, dozing in her chair, listening to the police news. Then she'd go to work without having been to bed.

Sometimes I'd stay up with her, listen to the radio with her, look out the window with her. I tried to make her believe I didn't know she was waiting on him.

. . .

I never learned hate at home, or shame. I had to go to school for that. I was about seven years old when I got my first big lesson. I was in love with a little girl named Helene Tucker, a light-complected little girl with pigtails and nice manners. She was always clean and she was smart in school. I think I went to school then mostly to look at her. I brushed my hair and even got me a little old handkerchief. It was a lady's handkerchief, but I didn't want Helene to see me wipe my nose on my hand. The pipes were frozen again, there was no water in the house, but I washed my socks and shirt every night. I'd get a pot, and go over to Mister Ben's grocery store, and stick my pot down into his soda machine. Scoop out some chopped ice. By evening the ice melted to water for washing. I got sick a lot that winter because the fire would go out at night before the clothes were dry. In the morning I'd put them on, wet or dry, because they were the only clothes I had.

Everybody's got a Helene Tucker, a symbol of everything you want. I loved her for her goodness, her cleanness, her popularity. She'd walk down my street and my brothers and sisters would yell, "Here comes Helene," and I'd rub my tennis sneakers on the back of my pants and wish my hair wasn't so nappy and the white folks' shirt fit me better. I'd run out on the street. If I knew my place and didn't come too close, she'd wink at me and say hello. That was a good feeling. Sometimes I'd follow her all the way home, and shovel the snow off her walk and try to make friends with her Momma and her aunts. I'd drop money on her stoop late at night on my way back from shining shoes in the taverns. And she had a Daddy, and he had a good job. He was a paper hanger.

I guess I would have gotten over Helene by summertime, but something happened in that classroom that made her face hang in front of me for the next twenty-two years. When I played the drums in high school it was for Helene and when I broke track records in college it was for Helene and when I started standing behind microphones and heard applause I wished Helene could hear it, too. It wasn't until I was twenty-nine years old and married and making money that I finally got her out of my system. Helen was sitting in that classroom when I learned to be ashamed of myself.

It was on a Thursday. I was sitting in the back of the room, in a seat with a chalk circle drawn around it. The idiot's seat, the troublemaker's seat.

The teacher thought I was stupid. Couldn't spell, couldn't read, couldn't do arithmetic. Just stupid. Teachers were never interested in finding out that you couldn't concentrate because you were so hungry, because you hadn't had any breakfast. All you could think about was noontime, would it ever come? Maybe you could sneak into the cloakroom and steal a bite of some kid's lunch out of a coat pocket. A bite of something. Paste. You can't really make a meal of paste, or put it on bread for a sandwich, but sometimes I'd scoop a few spoonfuls out of the big paste jar in the back of the room. Pregnant people get strange tastes. I was pregnant with poverty. Pregnant with dirt and pregnant with smells that made people turn away, pregnant with cold and pregnant with shoes that were never bought for me, pregnant with five other people in my bed and no Daddy in the next room, and pregnant with hunger. Paste doesn't taste too bad when you're hungry.

The teacher thought I was a troublemaker. All she saw from the front of the room was a little black boy who squirmed in his idiot's seat and made noises and poked the kids around him. I guess she couldn't see a kid who made noises because he wanted someone to know he was there.

It was on a Thursday, the day before the Negro payday. The eagle always flew on Friday. The teacher was asking each student how much his father would give to the Community Chest. On Friday night, each kid would get the money from his father, and on Monday he would bring it to the school. I decided I was going to buy me a Daddy right then. I had money in my pocket from shining shoes and selling papers, and whatever Helene Tucker pledged for her Daddy I was going to top

115

it. And I'd hand the money right in. I wasn't going to wait until Monday to buy me a Daddy.

I was shaking, scared to death. The teacher opened her book and started calling out names alphabetically.

"Helene Tucker?"

"My Daddy said he'd give two dollars and fifty cents."

"That's very nice, Helene. Very, very nice indeed."

That made me feel pretty good. It wouldn't take too much to top that. I had almost three dollars in dimes and quarters in my pocket. I stuck my hand in my pocket and held onto the money, waiting for her to call my name. But the teacher closed her book after she called everybody else in the class.

I stood up and raised my hand.

"What is it now?"

"You forgot me."

She turned toward the blackboard. "I don't have time to be playing with you, Richard."

"My Daddy said he'd . . ."

"Sit down, Richard, you're disturbing the class."

"My Daddy said he'd give . . . fifteen dollars."

She turned around and looked mad. "We are collecting this money for you and your kind, Richard Gregory. If your Daddy can give fifteen dollars you have no business being on relief."

"I got it right now, I got it right now, my Daddy gave it to me to turn in today, my Daddy said . . ."

"And furthermore," she said, looking right at me, her nostrils getting big and her lips getting thin and her eyes opening wide "We know you don't have a Daddy."

Helene Tucker turned around, her eyes full of tears. She felt sorry for me. Then I couldn't see her too well because I was crying, too.

"Sit down, Richard."

And I always thought the teacher kind of liked me. She always picked me to wash the blackboard on Friday, after school. That was a big thrill, it made me feel important. If I didn't wash it, come Monday the school might not function right.

"Where are you going, Richard?"

I walked out of school that day, and for a long time I didn't go back very often. There was shame there.

Now there was shame everywhere. It seemed like the whole world had been inside that classroom, everyone had heard what the teacher had said, everyone had turned around and felt sorry for me. There was shame in going to the Worthy Boys Annual Christmas Dinner for you and your kind, because everybody knew what a worthy boy was. Why couldn't they just call it the Boys Annual Dinner, why'd they have to give it a name? There was shame in wearing the brown and orange and white plaid mackinaw the welfare gave to 3,000 boys. Why'd it have to be the same for everybody so when you walked down the street the people could see you were on relief? It was a nice warm mackinaw and it had a hood, and my Momma beat me and called me a little rat when she found out I stuffed it in the bottom of a pail full of garbage way over on Cottage Street. There was shame in running over to Mister Ben's at the end of the day and asking for his rotten peaches, there was shame in asking Mrs. Simmons for a spoonful of sugar, there was shame in running out to meet the relief truck. I hated that truck, full of food for you and your kind. I ran into the house and hid when it came. And then I started to sneak through alleys, to take the long way home so the people going into White's Eat Shop wouldn't see me. Yeah, the whole world heard the teacher that day, we all know you don't have a Daddy.

It lasted for a while, this kind of numbness. I spent a lot of time feeling sorry for myself. And then one day I met this wino in a restaurant. I'd been out hustling all day, shining shoes, selling newspapers, and I had googobs of money in my pocket. Bought me a bowl of chili for fifteen cents, and a cheeseburger for fifteen cents, and a Pepsi for five cents, and a piece of chocolate cake for ten cents. That was a good meal. I was eating when this old wino came in. I love winos because they never hurt anyone but themselves.

The old wino sat down at the counter and ordered twenty-six cents worth of food. He ate like he really enjoyed it. When the owner, Mister Williams, asked him to pay the check, the old wino didn't lie or go through his pocket like he suddenly found a hole.

He just said: "Don't have no money."

The owner yelled: "Why the hell you come in here and eat my food if you don't have no money? That food cost me money."

Mister Williams jumped over the counter and knocked the wino off his stool and beat him over the head with a pop bottle. Then he stepped back and watched the wino bleed. Then he kicked him. And he kicked him again.

I looked at the wino with blood all over his face and I went over. "Leave him alone, Mister Williams. I'll pay the twenty-six cents."

The wino got up, slowly, pulling himself up to the stool, then up to the counter, holding on for a minute until his legs stopped shaking so bad. He looked at me with pure hate. "Keep your twenty-six cents. You don't have to pay, not now. I just finished paying for it."

He started to walk out, and as he passed me, he reached down and touched my shoulder. "Thanks, sonny, but it's too late now. Why didn't you pay it before?"

I was pretty sick about that. I waited too long to help another man.

I remember a white lady who came to our door once around Thanksgiving time. She wore a woolly, green bonnet around her head, and she smiled a lot.

"Is your mother home, little boy?"

"No, she ain't."

"May I come in?"

"What do you want, ma'am?"

She didn't stop smiling once, but she sighed a little when she bent down and lifted up a big yellow basket. The kind I saw around church that were called Baskets for the Needy.

"This is for you."

"What's in there?"

"All sorts of good things," she said, smiling. "There's candy and potatoes and cake and cranberry sauce and"—she made a funny little face at me by wrinkling up her nose—"and a great big fat turkey for Thanksgiving dinner."

"Is it cooked?"

"A big fat juicy turkey, all plucked clean for you. . . ."

"Is it cooked?"

"No, it's not. . . ."

"We ain't got nothing in the house to cook it with, lady."

I slammed the door in her face. Wouldn't that be a bitch, to have a turkey like that in the house with no way to cook it? No gas, no electricity, no coal. Just a big fat juicy raw turkey.

I remember Mister Ben, the grocery-store man, a round little white man with funny little tufts of white hair on his head and sad-looking eyes. His face was kind of gray-colored, and the skin was loose and shook when he talked.

"Momma want a loaf of bread, Mister Ben, fresh bread."

"Right away, Richard," he'd say and get the bread he bought three days old from the bakeries downtown. It was the only kind he had for his credit-book customers. He dropped it on the counter. Clunk.

I'd hand him the credit book, that green tablet with the picture of the snuff can on it, to write down how much we owed him. He'd lick the tip of that stubby pencil he kept behind his ear. Six cents.

"How you like school, Richard?"

"I like school fine, Mister Ben."

"Good boy, you study, get smart."

I'd run home to Momma and tell her that the bread wasn't fresh bread, it was stale bread. She'd flash the big smile.

"Oh, that Mister Ben, he knew I was fixin' to make toast."

The peaches were rotten and the bread wasn't fresh and sometimes the butter was green, but when it came to the nittygritty you could always go to Mr. Ben. Before a Jewish holiday he'd take all the food that was going to spoil while the store was shut and bring it over to our house. Before Christmas he'd send over some meat even though he knew it was going on the tablet and he might never see his money. When the push came to the shove and every hungry belly in the house was beginning to eat on itself, Momma could go to Mister Ben and always get enough for some kind of dinner.

But I can remember three days in a row I went into Mister Ben's and asked him to give me a penny Mr. Goodbar from the window.

Three days in a row he said: "Out, out, or I'll tell your Momma you been begging."

One night I threw a brick through his window and took it.

The next day I went into Mister Ben's to get some bread for Momma and his skin was shaking and I heard him tell a lady, "I can't understand why should anybody break my window for a penny piece of candy, a lousy piece of candy, all they got to do is ask, that's all, and I give."

~~~~~~~~~~~~~~~~~~~~~~~~~~~~~~~~~~~~~

DISCUSSION AND INQUIRY

The ordinal position a child has in the family generally influences his personality development. This selection does not tell us whether Richard was the oldest, youngest or in-between sibling, yet he displays certain personality traits that lead the reader to believe he was the oldest boy, if not the oldest of all the children. What characteristics did he display that are most typical of the first-born?

Most of his actions and energy seemed to be directed toward easing his mother's plight. He would lie about his popularity to her and give her money, claiming it was given to him by people who thought she was doing a good job raising her children. He would keep her company during her night-time vigils waiting for his father. Do these actions reveal a lack of egocentrism in Gregory? What does Piaget's theory of intellectual development tell about egocentrism in children? Can you recall times in your childhood when you tried to take over the role of the protector in your family?

Young Richard wanted a father. He gives us

several clues in this passage. Can you find them? Although he desires a father, he rejects Big Pres. Why is this so? The other children seemed eager to accept Big Pres back. Could it simply be that Gregory felt it was not in his mother's best interest to have her husband at home—or is it possible that Gregory enjoyed being the protector and sometime-provider of the family? We cannot be sure of the reasons based on this selection alone, but the reader should be reminded that the motives of children are not always obvious— even to themselves.

Gregory talks of the shame and embarrassment of being poor. He recalls how he would not wear the winter coats given out by a charity because they all looked alike and identified the wearer as a charity case. Is the author telling us that it is shameful to be poor, or that one is made to feel ashamed when one is poor? Why did Dick claim his father was going to make a large donation to the Community Chest? Is this bragging or does it reflect a need to rise above the status of always being the recipient of charity?

John Holloway

BIOGRAPHICAL SKETCH

John Holloway is an eminent scholar of English literature and a well-known poet and essayist. He was born in England in 1920, and is currently a teacher at Queens College in Cambridge, England. Among his many writings are The Victorian Saga, Poems of the Mid-Century, *and* Widening Horizons in English Verse.

SELECTIONS FROM

A LONDON CHILDHOOD

WHEN I was about six and a half, a school doctor with a wrinkled round face and a tooth-brush moustache and a brown suit and very clean hands gave me a medical examination; and having listened to my heart through a stethoscope, he declared it was enlarged, and I had a heart murmur. My mother's knowledge as a nurse and her country dreads and superstitions came together—not for the only time—and she was alarmed. The people at school seemed to care too, and I was not allowed to play rough games in the playground for a year or so—Bertie Crouch the gardener's son chased me vigorously on one occasion, and ended (as such boys could) sliding stylishly up to the fence on his hob-nail boots, only to find Miss Martin standing there waiting to give him a ticking-off for chasing a boy with a weak heart. I was also not allowed to go swimming, later on in my schooldays, and at that time I used to walk to the swimming baths with the others, but then just hang about. It was the same when we marched in a crocodile down to the recreation ground to play football; and this too was why I got partly wheeled when we went back to have a look at the Newby's house. Of course I walked a great deal, but I used to get wheeled as well.

The chief effect of what the doctor said, though, was that after a very long time—quite enough for it to have come too late, I should think, had it really been needed—a camp bed turned up in the school, and I had to take part in lessons, for an hour a day after lunch, lying flat out on it at the front of the class. I suppose I was the star pupil at

121

that little suburban church school (it was in Upper Norwood, a much more stylish part than ours). I hope they would have been at the same trouble for a very dull boy. They might.

Certainly it sounds a bit disagreeable. I viewed the long-awaited coming of that bed with strong dislike, because I thought I should be teased about it by the other children, and somehow treated more severely otherwise by the teachers, to make up. It did not work out like that. My classmates thought it great fun on the first day, but they were full of kindness about it, didn't tease me, and in fact most of them kept off the whole subject. Soon it became a matter of routine, and no one took any notice. Now, I see it as one more sign of how easily children behave in a grown-up way if you give them a chance. It also says a good deal for the teachers in that serene and gentle school, so different from the one I went to when I was eight.

I must have seemed a clever boy to the teachers, because it was decided that I should be entered for the Victoria Scholarship at "The Whitgift"—the well-known public school in Croydon where I could have gone (to the preparatory department at first no doubt) as a day-boy. I learned that there was just one Scholarship open for boys like myself, and I can remember thinking about this with—in a childish sense—much misgiving. It was easy to see that I was the top child in my class, but I was not at all the sort of child who thinks that if a distinction exists, it is for him. I didn't in the least see myself as bound for the Victoria Scholarship. Anyway, Croydon for me meant simply the big High Street and the crowds, and wandering about in the toy department at Kennards. At the same time I was vaguely aware that Mr. Cartwright the headmaster, and the others too, were being quite business-like and serious about it all. I now see that they thought they were going to get that Victoria Scholarship for their little school. Reviewing it all now, I suppose they were quite possibly right. Not that it matters much. Scholastic ability seems to me to go with car-performance or wealth, not beauty or goodness. It is just a possible means to good things, not a good thing in itself. As such it is rather a bore.

Anyhow, Mr. Williams, a young and (as I found him) rather forbidding man, prim and severe, began to coach me in Latin from a slim book with "Elementa Latina" in red down the spine. My mother tried to help me, but really all she could do was hold the book and hear me say "to or for a table" and "with, by or from a table" and "Caesar kills Balbus" and things like that. "O table" made us laugh and mystified us a bit: my mother had done some Latin at school, but "O table" had mystified her then, and the years hadn't changed things. However, in those days the idea that the text book might ask one to learn wrongly, just didn't exist. To learn Latin was to learn *Elementa Latina*. I don't think, even now, that there's any harm in this—for the bookish ones.

When you're young and quick, it doesn't much matter whether your lessons have been rationalized and streamlined by someone clever and up-to-date, or not. The great thing is to be learning and learning.

Yet I don't believe I did very well with my Latin. A restricted family background—however affectionate, however cooperative—hinders a child's academic success because it leaves him doubting its value and unclear as to its upshot. My slim blue book had to be learned alone, and doing homework while all the others were playing, in order to go I didn't really know where or why. In the end, my Latin and all the rest came to nothing, and I got on by another road in another place.

When I was ten and a half—this takes me to a period outside this book, but I shall touch on it for a minute so as to put these years in perspective—I went by myself to watch motorcycle racing on a grass track near Biggin Hill. I thought about where I should get the most exciting views, and I got the answer just right. But ignorance of one important fact caused me trouble. I had been once or twice to the Crystal Palace to watch dirt-track racing with my father: but this had not taught me that amateurs, racing on grass, can leave the track and plough through the spectators. My choice of a point of vantage set me —it would, of course—exactly where this was to happen. I still have a vivid mental picture of the valves of a motorbicycle threshing up and down very close to my face. I picked myself up, realized I was hurt but could run, and set off at a desperate top speed for the tall thick hedge. Here I proposed to hide, and use my handkerchief to deal with the fact that I was bleeding. As I grew aware of the fact that I was really bleeding quite a lot, from the back of my hand, I was intercepted by a St. John's Ambulance man, and in a moment was sitting on the ground, being bandaged up—in several places, not just my hand where a small artery had been severed (I have a slight scar still). I was surrounded of course by a tight-packed circle of gawping strangers. Later I was driven home in a private car, and I think this was the first time I went in one.

Anyhow, all this, though it did me no harm save that it disfigured one finger-nail for a few years, meant that I had to go for the 11+ medical examination swathed in bandages on my leg, arm and face. We were left to think that if I failed to pass, I failed in the whole exam, but I suppose this was simply one more case of how the ignorant and naive are left to suffer; no doubt it was an examination which merely ensured that if a boy needed treatment he got it. I was very much afraid I should fail because of my bandages, though I saw the point when the doctor grinned and said, "that sort of thing makes no difference to me."

Well, the doctor read about my enlarged heart and old murmur in his records, and seemed to take it all seriously. He listened to me, up and down, and more than once, through his instruments. Then he said: "there's nothing wrong with this boy's heart"; and since my mother of course felt that a county school doctor would know more than a primary school one, she was very pleased. But then he went on to declare that there never had been anything wrong with it either. So in all probability the trouble and effort of those years of no games and the camp bed had been wasted. I am grateful for the error, though. I once had the makings of a good wing or wing-three-quarter footballer, a Machiavellian bowler of left-hand breaks, and a lively slosher as batsman. But by the time I had this medical examination, and could "do games" like everyone else, I'd learnt better ways of using my time than running after balls; and never really got drawn in.

The idea that I had a weak heart made my mother do more than ever for me. She used always to meet me for the meal in the middle of the day (at that time there were no meals served at school). Sometimes we used to go to a cook-house in a little row of shops on the way to the Round Pond and the Rookery at Streatham. The cheapest two-course meal was eleven pence, and the dearest was one-and-four. We were served by a burly blue-eyed man, his fair hair greying, his apron very white, his hands very washed. He cooked and served and did everything, with his wife a very small figure in the back of the shop. He made fine apple pies, which had cloves in them. I had never tasted clove in apple before.

But paying this much for dinner (as we called it) was rather a lot for us; so usually my mother used to bring a meal in her shopping basket, and we would take it into Grange Wood Park and eat it there. The Park had once been the grounds of a big house: we wandered about the stables once or twice, but the big Victorian house we didn't go inside. There were long, dark holly-drives, and what was almost a holly wood, with the trees big enough for it to be clear underneath them, and we sheltered there once or twice from the rain. Also there was a big shelter, made of pine-trunks and thatched. We sheltered there too, several times: it seemed to rain quite often on the days we took our lunch in the Park, and we had to watch our shoes for the wet: mine because they were small, and my mother's because they were poor. Besides the hollies, there were many sweet-chestnut trees; and we often tried to find some that we could eat, but never did.

My mother used to bring fine lunches. She must have spent the morning on them. Above all she would bring ginger puddings, which I adored, in our white pudding-basin wrapped in an old towel to keep warm. For me it was like magic, on a cold day, to sit on one of the green slatted benches, and see the towel and then the pudding-cloth come off, and the steam from the pudding fume up. We had plates and spoons, and cornflour sauce and all sometimes: she could see how much this dish made me happy, and she brought it over and over. It was while eating one of these puddings that I first heard the cuckoo: and the note of the cuckoo and the taste of ginger still go together in my mind. Several times we ate our lunch there in the snow, and sharp, sharp cold. When I think of these times I recall the bite of the cold and the hot taste and warm color of the pudding together too. There were jays there as well as the cuckoo; strange and exotic they seemed, and slow-moving—as indeed they are. Once, but only once, we saw the cuckoo that we so often heard. This bird seemed mysterious to me, so often close yet so seldom seen. I thought about the cuckoo a little as one might about the phoenix, as if there were only one.

My mother had what at any rate used once to be the country feeling for all living creatures: whether you like them or not, and quite probably you do not, they are immediately and vividly *there*, as much as any human being. After the time of this book, and when I was nine and we lived further out and in a more rural place, she once woke me up in the middle of the night, and what she wanted me for was to look through her bedroom window at the garden—it was mauve with the moonlight, I see it still—and listen to a nightingale, sitting on a bush not twenty feet away. It meant so much to her, partly because it was the first nightingale she had heard for twenty years: the move we had made was bringing back to her some of the things she had lost when she lost the world of her childhood. I shall never cease to be grateful for how she did such things for me: she was more romantic than was good for her —or others—but the simple fact is that it is better to care than not to care.

She passed caring on to me. I can remember when I was just seven, wanting to go into the road near my school and rescue a toad from the traffic: it must have been a busy time of day, because for once there was a lot of traffic. I was forbidden to do this by an older boy, who was a prefect or something. This was almost the only time he spoke to me, but the thing left its mark so that I can remember his name (it was Nunn) as I remember no one else's at that school except that of my first girl, Beryl Rowe, and Bertie Crouch. I was in deep distress about the toad, which I had to watch lumbering and hopping helplessly. My mother appeared on the scene at just that moment, and Nunn felt his job was finished, and sheered off. I don't think my mother rescued the toad either; in fact, I think it rescued itself.

It's not true that I remember only those names, because I remember another. There was a boy called Mills. He wore grey flannel shorts and a grey jersey, which he had inside his trousers and his belt. Miss Jarvis, who was a fussy old marm we all thought, told him one day that this wasn't the right way to wear his jersey, and that he was to wear it outside. And he blushed as he began to pull it out, and said in shame, "it's all holes, Miss." So she told him to put it back again.

Bertie Crouch's father was a gardener, and they lived in a cottage

125

down the road and the steep hill to Grange Wood Park: I think he was a gardener in the Park somewhere, but we never knew him, and he was certainly not the gardener in a blue serge apron that my mother used to chat with sometimes. Higher up the hill were two other houses. At the top, on the corner by the main road, was a house in Victorian grey brick, almost a Cottage *orné*, that had been the lodge to Grange Wood Manor in its heyday. Mrs. Brown lived here. She was a portly, stately woman well into middle age, and had grey hair, almost golden-white in fact, that she did loosely, in a bun. She and my mother became good friends and we used to go there and have tea after our lunch, or tea after school at four: but then we were usually soon shepherded off, because Mr. Brown was coming in. Sometimes the adults played whist, a game my mother used to like a good deal, and played at home with my father; using a dummy hand, if someone else could be found for a third (they never had four). At the Browns they also taught me to play rummy, and on one occasion must have amused themselves by letting me win, because I won for a long time and got very excited. "I'm determined to win!" I kept saying. My mother was quite cross for the rest of the day, once we left. It must have been silly and troublesome of me; though if you keep it to yourself, the sentiment is all right.

Just down the slope from Mrs. Brown's house was a small white house. It stood inside its own oak fence all round, and house, garden, fence and all stood inside a little wood that ran down the hill. This was where Mrs. Field lived. I think we went into her house only once or twice. It was full of copper ornaments, all spaced out, and white inside the way it was outside. Mrs. Field was a blonde, she had hair of a deep red-gold, which she brushed very smooth. Her husband was a good-looking man, smooth and confident-voiced and breezy. He was nice to us but didn't lose any time. I saw later that the Fields were really much above the Browns in their ways and their aspirations. Those copper pots, that golden hair, and Mrs. Field usually seemed to wear a black costume in her little white house. Perhaps they were (in the 1920s) just a bit "arty." If so, it was a long while before I touched against that world once more.

School stopped at midday and did not begin again until two, and so we had a long lunch-time, and it seemed in a way like the third part of the schoolday, along with the morning and the afternoon, instead of just a gap between them. It was on the way home after school, though, that I used to see my other favorite part of that higher, up-the-hill world of schooldays. Halfway down South Norwood Hill—and immediately beyond the point where Beryl and her mother, walking home with us, would turn off right along White Horse Lane, so it fitted in very well—we could turn off to the left and go down Woodvale Avenue. At the time, this was a private road; "not adopted," they used

126

to call them. It had just a gravel surface, and there were almost no houses in it, at least that I remember. But on either side was a long line of chestnut trees, not the high but the wide, spreading kind, that met overhead in the middle, and made the road twilit and mysterious in my eyes. In autumn the colors were first very rich and warm, then deeper and blacker as the autumn rain soaked into the leaves thick underfoot. They used to be so thick that I found as a child my feet lost touch with the ground; even when I kicked the leaves up, a cloudy puff at every step, I would still be walking on the lower leaves beneath.

It was really no further home this way, but slower because of the walking and because there was more to stop and look at. Sometimes also my mother would run into the gardener from Norhurst; because this road ran along the edge of it. He was a shortish man, but powerfully built, with a masculine, bony face, and wore a grey cap he pulled well down. He spoke in a slow, heavy way; looking back at him now, I think he found my mother attractive, and since he wasn't the flirtatious kind it came out in this wooden doggedness. They talked about the big house and the old days and old people there. He'd not worked at Norhurst when my mother had, but they had many experiences and memories that linked and fitted in to each other, and sometimes they talked a good while. Once or twice the three of us took shelter in the big stables while it rained. They were ordinary Victorian stables with the gently sloping roofs and wide eaves and large flat wall-spaces of their time; but set deep in the chestnuts, with a worn court of granite blocks, and the great doors and gateways that a stable has to have. These stables had a poetry about them. Dimly, they opened up a large country to my imagination; I took in the fact that these great rambling buildings were simply where the horses had lived, were set in some corner, right away from the house itself.

One result of my alleged weak heart was that in my second year at school I used to stay in the classroom during play-time. Miss Bailey, the five-year-olds' teacher, a dear, kind grey-haired woman who is, I think, the only person in my whole childhood whom I can look back on with completely happy feelings, and Miss Martin, the young, be-spectacled teacher for the six-year-olds, who was also a nice woman though a bit sharper, used to make tea together in a small blue-enamelled teapot, and sometimes gave me a cup. Sometimes a handful of other children would stay in too, and each of us would get a biscuit. (How generous those two dear women were! Six or seven biscuits, a good few times a week, must have shown against their wages.) Once, when they were out, and with strong feelings of guilt, I took a second one, of a kind I specially liked: though seeing, really, that my being in a way a special case, down on my camp bed (or supposed to be, anyhow), would soften their disapproval but didn't make it right. Back came

Miss Martin and someone told her what I'd done. She did disapprove:
"You know what *that* is, don't you!" she said to me. I filled with horror.
I knew only one crime worse than stealing, and that was murder. Perhaps I'd end up just where my mother said. "Yes, miss, greedy," said
Bertie Crouch at top speed. He was glad to get one in. Miss Martin
hesitated, and then let it go. I wasn't taken in, though I think I was half
taken in. It was my first experience, so far as I recall, of people with a
vocabulary of grey words only, for a world full of white and black
facts.

All Saints was a church school, and at the age of six we spent a good
deal of time every morning learning the catechism. One phrase in the
catechism gave me much food for thought. This was about "doing my
duty in that station in life in which it hath pleased Providence to call
me." The teachers explained this, in those far-off days, much as I suppose it was explained when it was adopted under Queen Elizabeth:
rich were rich, and poor poor, and you accepted your lot. For my part,
however, I resented the phrase, because it seemed to challenge my right
to try for the Victoria Scholarship. I thought a good deal about this. I
can't remember if I reached for myself, or got by asking a teacher, the
conclusion that it might be exactly to this Victoria Scholarship that in
my case Providence was pleased to issue its call; but certainly I was
aware (in retrospect this surprises me) that if so, a lot more followed,
in that anyone could pull himself up to anywhere, provided only that
his boot-strings were long enough. I didn't, of course, so much as
glimpse the logic behind all this: only, that what had seemed easy to
understand very well was something you couldn't understand at all,
once you really tried.

Natural enough, though: an only child, very close to a most intelligent mother, and talking to her all day long, I was in some degree a
little adult. I really could think: though I hadn't the least idea of either
the rareness of that, or its value. "Why did God save us by turning
himself into just a poor carpenter's son?" Miss Martin asked us once.
Couldn't he, her point was, have done it without quite so deep a
descent . . . ? Nobody could say, till I realized more or less, that if you
did this you showed you thought it was all right to be a poor carpenter,
you weren't stand-offish or snobbish. So I said, more or less, that it was
because God loved us such a lot and wanted to share it. Miss Martin,
impressed, asked if someone had told me that, or I'd guessed it for
myself. But alas! It was to be at least ten years before I got my values
right in this matter. At six, it seemed to me nothing to have guessed,
and much to my credit to have learnt from a sound authority. So I said
my mother had told me, which was altogether a lie. It looks as if my
intelligence was stronger than my moral sense, though not strong
enough. This may still be so.

DISCUSSION AND INQUIRY

John appears to have had an overprotective mother, who oversaw John's life fairly thoroughly. Both the author and his mother would probably claim that the overprotection was thought to be necessary because of the alleged heart condition. What other factor existed in the Holloway family that might have caused John's mother to supervise his life so closely?

John was afraid his special bed in the classroom would cause him to be the object of ridicule. This was not to be the case. Children with particular handicapping conditions are generally accepted by their peers as soon as some initial curiosity is satisfied. Parents with children who wear leg braces, for example, often fear the mocking their child will take from other children. But the self-consciousness is usually the problem of the parent and not the child. Consider then the benefits of placing physically handicapped children in regular classrooms instead of isolating them in a particular room of the school building.

The author claims that the physical restrictions placed on him because of the "heart condition" had the advantage of keeping him from being "drawn in" to sports, and, as a result, he found "better ways" of using his time. What is the importance of athletic activity for the elementary school age child?

Compare this selection with that by Robert Merrill. What are the common characteristics with regard to mother-son relationships?

Chet Huntley

BIOGRAPHICAL SKETCH

Chet Huntley, born in 1911, spent his boyhood in Montana. After attending three different colleges, he received his B.A. from the University of Washington in Seattle. It was in Seattle that he got his first broadcasting job. His career with NBC began in 1955, and reached its peak with the well-known Huntley-Brinkley format. In the course of his career, Chet Huntley won every important award offered for excellence in news coverage.

SELECTIONS FROM

THE GENEROUS YEARS

WHAT is surely my first memory was the absence of Mother for a while and then her return with a small incomprehensible thing, which, I was told, was my sister. My companion, my confidante, my patient, understanding and forgiving Wadine.

I cannot remember when Shep appeared. It seemed to me that he was always there. Out of my own experience, I have subscribed to everything ever said about a boy and his dog, particularly a farm boy.

Shep was an uncertain mixture of shepherd and collie, and I have no sure recollection just how handsome he really was. I recall that his nose was cold, his tongue was warm and friendly on my hands and face, and his fur was made for a small boy to grasp and cling to through romp and roughhouse.

Remembered also are brief instances of fright . . . momentary fear . . . when the lamplight in the little unfinished ranch house revealed dark faces peering through the windowpanes. The whites of eyes were like small luminous orbs in the blackness. Driven by insatiable curiosity about these newcomers to the land where they had hunted, an occasional group of Assiniboin would pay their visit. In the daytime they sat silently on their horses and watched us as we went about the chores. At night they studied us from the darkness, little concerned

130

whether they were detected, and obviously concluding that if the white man insisted on windows in his lodge he must expect the passer-by to look inside. The Indians did us no harm. They only baffled us with their stoicism and imperturbable countenances.

Apparently the Indians had made it clear that communication between themselves and these intruders would be a long and tedious process. The settlers accepted it and made little effort to exchange more than the nod of the head or the universal signal of peaceful intent, which was no more than the raising of one hand. The Indians were in no haste to learn the white man's language, and they were in less haste to use it. The settlers' efforts to converse usually ended in frustration and a kind of embarrassment, for the Indian's response was a detached stare at the horizon or at some vague point just above the rancher's head. It was too soon. Sitting Bull was less than a quarter century dead. On the reservations the old warriors still spun their tales of the last battles, and precious were the legacies of vicarious pride from the exploits of Chief Gall, Crazy Horse, Chief Joseph and the others. A half century later, even in the 1960s, communication between Indian and white man would sometimes falter.

An Indian, searching for stray horses, sat astride his wiry little pony one morning, talking to Dad and Grandpa at the corral gate. A white beaded headband held his long black hair in place, a handsome blanket fell casually from his shoulders. His lean legs were encased in tight-fitting trousers, and his moccasined feet hung easily alongside his horse's belly.

The Indian did Grandpa the customary courtesy of asking for a pipeful of tobacco, for which a "thank you" was never given and never expected. Between puffs on his pipe, the Indian said that the signs told of a mild winter . . . the badgers were dark in color and no white wolves had been seen. Abruptly he turned his horse and trotted off. Conversations with the Indians were refreshingly free of small talk.

Several years later a small Indian band, including two boys my age, rode up to the ranch house as I was engaged in the repair of a halter. They watched me intently as I put the rivets through the leather and rounded them off with a hammer on the anvil. One of the boys returned to his horse and removed the beaded and ornamented hackamore. Half in sign language and half in broken English, he offered to trade his hackamore for my halter plus one dollar. I can recall Grandpa and the other Indians watching and listening with great concentration as the Indian lad and I bargained. Finally I closed the deal with an emphatic gesture of one index finger at the half-joint of the other, and the Indian boy nodded. The Indians smiled in appreciation, and Grandpa, with a great laugh, handed to me a half dollar.

Our horses, however, never responded satisfactorily to the hackamore; they were too accustomed to the bridle and bit. I often watched and admired the Indian boys as they demonstrated their horsemanship. Once or twice I encountered them on the open range land and we raced our mounts. They sat high on their horses' shoulders, almost at the base of the neck, and leaned precariously over the flying mane. They never jeered at my comparatively awkward riding talent, but they were frankly contemptuous of my saddle and bridle. It was clear that it seemed funny to them that this white boy insisted on placing a saddle in the middle of a horse and riding back there where all the bouncing occurred.

. . .

I have been unable to sort out the overlapping attitudes of respect and affection I had for the four adults who made up so much of my childhood. Grandma was the cherished one to whom I went for the ultimate in praise and the one I avoided when I had done something I should not have. She was the final authority on all matters of morality and behavior and manners. Mother was the beautiful repository of love and affection. Dad was the good-natured and tolerant companion rather than guide and counselor. Grandpa, however, was my heroic figure, and I spent much of those early years chasing at his heels.

I learned that Grandma and Mother were unsatisfactory sources of information about animal habits and ranch life. Frequently, I was informed that small boys had no need for answers to such questions. Dad too was something less than candid. But Grandpa told me what I wanted to know . . . bluntly and somewhat vividly. What I failed to learn from him, I picked up easily from the hired hands who worked on the ranch later. Somehow, every association with Grandpa held the promise or the possibility of high adventure.

He never realized, I suppose, what he did for the ego of a small boy when he waived aside the misgivings of Grandma and Mother and took me into town with him. Those were the moments of triumph!

Town was an intense and exciting concentration of sounds and sights and noises and smells—particularly, smells. The dry-goods stores were veritable bazaars of aroma: coffee (in barrels), boxes of dried fish, dried fruit in bulk, kerosene, spices, harnesses and saddles, and smoked meats. The drugstore, with its ice cream parlor in conjunction, was another establishment which sent its array of aromas out across the boardwalk and into the dusty street. There were all the scents of chemicals and medicines, but more powerful was the mouth-watering aroma of the ice cream soda. These odors and scents blended into those of the street, horse manure and harness.

The ice cream parlor and drugstore had its own characteristic sounds and appearances too. The furniture invariably sported elaborately curved metal legs. The seats of the chairs were wooden or sometimes wicker. As the metal legs of the chairs scraped on the floor they created a sound unlike that anywhere else, and the soda faucet hissed and coughed deliciously as it squirted a foaming stream of nectar into the coneshaped container.

On rare occasions in these recent years, I have driven into some small Western town and detected just a trace of that heady combination of aromas—harness, saddle leather, saddle soap and manure; bulk coffee, ice cream soda and kerosene—and I can hear the shouts of the teamsters around the livery stable, the sound of boots and heavy farm shoes on the wooden sidewalks, the jangle of tug chains; and see the dust on Main Street, with the row of storefronts on one side, the Great Northern tracks, the depot and the grain elevators on the other.

Grandpa would place the order at the dry-goods store, then run his errands at the drugstore, the shoe-repair shop, perhaps stop at the bank or the farm-machinery showroom, and collect the mail at the post office. We would have lunch at the counter of a café or grill. That was always a great experience. I never could deduce how Grandpa made our selection so rapidly and conclusively from the myriad offerings on the menu. To the disgust of Grandma and Mother, I thought restaurant food was the finest one could imagine.

The orders placed and the errands completed, Grandpa had a little time for the last and crowning transaction of the day, before getting the team out of the livery stable, picking up the purchases and starting the long drive home. He paid his respects at the saloon!

Another cloud of strange aromas lay behind the swinging doors and the opaque windows: the heady scent of whiskey and stale tobacco smoke. As Grandpa leaned his elbows on the bar, rested one foot on the brass rail, pushed back his hat and exchanged pleasantries with the bartender, I would anticipate the white-aproned proprietor's reach for the ice vat in which, I knew, he kept the most fantastically delicious liquid substance the world had ever known: strawberry soda pop! It occurred to me that Grandpa drank something slightly different. It came out of a larger bottle, which the proprietor merely placed on the bar with a small glass; but I thought Grandpa's drink was sufficiently similar to mine that I had tremendous admiration for his taste and his unbounding wisdom in knowing where these things were available.

Grandpa would satisfy his thirst, buy a couple pints for consumption at the ranch, and we would leave in time to arrive home by dusk and the supper hour.

One trip into town with Grandpa was climactic. He had concluded the various errands and made his customary call at the saloon. It was Saturday afternoon, and there were more customers in the establishment than usual. Grandpa was savoring the aftertaste of his whiskey, and I had taken my bottle of soda to a chair on the other side of the room. An ugly, squat, bull-necked and frightfully powerful man made his way along the bar and stood glowering at Grandpa.

Instinctively, I knew we were in for trouble. I had heard stories about "Rip," and it was obvious that this was he.

Rip was the town bully and terror. He operated a sometime dray or delivery service, and the saloon was his home and office. Rip's chief ambition was to terrorize the town and boast that he had licked or intimidated every man in the area. He was a thoroughly detested beast, and the town was in the process of petitioning the sheriff to chase him out and get rid of him, once and for all.

Rip looked Grandpa up and down, and with a snarl asked, "Are you Bob Tatham?"

I shrank in fright into the back of my chair, trying to look as small and inconspicuous as possible. I also elected a refuge under the pool table in the event things should develop as I had reason to think they might.

Grandpa put down his glass, turned slowly and surveyed his man. "Yes, I'm Bob Tatham," he answered.

"Tatham," sneered Rip, "You've got quite a reputation around here, d'ya know that? They tell me you're quite a fightin' man."

The bartender leaned over the bar and made a feeble effort to intercede. "Now, look here, Rip. Let's not have any trouble. Why don't you just go about your business—"

He was cut short by the persistent challenger. "Mind your business behind the bar, Shorty, you little bastard, I've got me a great big fightin' man."

Grandpa turned and I could see him coiling to avoid any sudden blow. "Rip," he said slowly, "I'm not lookin' for any trouble with you, but if you insist on it, you're gonna' have your hands full."

Rip backed up and the men at the bar stepped aside and retreated toward the rear of the saloon. I slid out of my chair and crouched at the far side of the pool table. Rip lowered his head, clenched his great hairy fists, roared like an enraged lion and charged.

Grandpa's fist wasn't enough to stop the battering-ram assault, but he deflected it. Rip went halfway down, and his head butted Grandpa against the bar. I was now peering out from under the pool table—a thoroughly frightened five-year-old.

Rip shook his head from the blow, backed off and charged again, This time Grandpa caught him as he sprang forward, and the sound of his fist in Rip's face crackled. Rip slid on the floor, knocking over a spitoon. But he got up, blood dripping from his hateful mouth, and charged again.

Twice Rip's great clublike fists caught Grandpa and knocked him across the room; however, they were glancing blows and their damage was minimal. Repeatedly, Grandpa avoided Rip's blind assaults and drove his fists into the distorted and bloody face, but still the enraged bully rushed in. Onlookers called upon Rip to give up, but he did not hear them. Finally Rip was knocked almost on top of the pool table and came up brandishing a cue stick. Grandpa attacked with a series of savage blows, and at last Rip uttered a low moan and sank senseless to the floor.

Someone gave him a cursory examination, propped him into a chair, and drinks were ordered up for Grandpa! Trembling, I came from beneath the pool table. Grandpa looked at me, laughed, and said, "Boy, what the devil are you doing under that table?"

I murmured something about trying to stay out of the way.

"I thought for a while I was gonna' need your help," he said.

Turning to the crowd at the bar, Grandpa said, "Gentlemen, I thank you for the drinks, they'll ease the pain in my hand." He suspected he had broken a small bone, and indeed, he had.

On the way home Grandpa turned and regarded me quizzically for a moment, then smiled and asked, "What are you goin' to say when we get home and they ask you what we did today?"

I hesitated a moment and said, "I'll tell them I had some strawberry pop."

"Stick to that story, boy"—he laughed—"and we'll have some more strawberry pop."

For days Grandpa nursed his tumescent hand and muttered something about getting it caught in the double trees while unhitching the horses. In the barn I saw him vigorously applying horse liniment.

. . .

I was six years old that winter when, following a good harvest, Dad and Mother decided we would spend the severe-weather months in southern Missouri, visiting Grandpa and Grandma. They had gone there a few months earlier to dispose of a farm which Grandma's father had willed to her. Dad and Mother speculated mildly on the possibility of selling the Montana ranch and relocating on the Missouri property.

The ranch was left in the care of a well-recommended fellow, and we journeyed off to Missouri for several months. I can recall very little about this brief interlude beyond Wadine and me tramping to the little rural dry-goods store, the gathering of black walnuts in the woods, and the severe weather which kept us confined to the house. The return to the ranch, however, was vivid.

I was at that age when the bond between boy and dog is enduring. Shep would have explored the Missouri woods and chased the red squirrels, but he would be waiting at the ranch. The caretaker dutifully met us in Saco, and it seemed that Dad and Mother were perpetrating a needless and altogether frivolous delay when they decided to have lunch in town before driving home. Why had the caretaker failed to bring Shep into town? He would always stay with the team of horses whether they were put up in the livery stable or hitched on the street. Seated at the restaurant table, I impatiently restrained the questions concerning Shep until all the talk of livestock and weather and feed had been exhausted. Unable to wait longer, I asked how my dog was.

As casually and heartlessly as if he were announcing the death of a chicken, the caretaker answered, "Oh yeah, the dog . . . he got killed somehow . . . found him up there on the west pasture."

I turned away and rested my head on the back of the chair . . . sick and numb. Homecoming had degenerated into revolting despair. If we had never left, it could not have happened.

And indeed it would not have. We learned later that the caretaker had set out scores of coyote traps and had taken no precaution against Shep's tripping them. He had found Shep in one of the traps, his leg broken, and had shot my dog with his rifle.

Mother's chief concern about the welfare of us children on the ranch was her desperate fear of rattlesnakes. Shep had been a staunch guardian, thrusting Wadine or me aside, barking strenuously for help, frightening the snake away; and several times he had seized the reptile safely behind the head and dispatched it.

Something forever vanished from the ranch when Shep failed to come bounding down the lane to greet us.

One wintry morning, when the windows bore an inch of frosty jungle drawings, Mother cautioned me to bundle up particularly well. A stocking cap was pulled low over my ears and forehead, and a woolen scarf was tied securely over my mouth and nose, forcing me to breathe through it. Mother warned me to go no farther than the barn and then come back in a few minutes, check the themometer on the outside of the house and let her know what it read.

I stepped outside into a strange eeriness. The snow crackled underfoot like shots of a cap pistol. My breath coming through the folds of the scarf created a cloud which hung in the air. I walked a few steps toward the barn and glanced back at the house. From the chimney arose a thin column of smoke that ascended up and up in a straight, clean line. I heard shouts and conversation and realized that I was overhearing the Osiers and the Pinkermans as they worked at their morning chores more than a mile distant. The air was sheer crystal, and tiny fragments of frost danced in it. The livestock were ringed tightly about the strawstack, their heads and shoulders buried deep within its protection.

136

I raced once around the barn, gathered an egg or two from the reluctant hens and ran back toward the house. On the porch I stood on tiptoe to read the thermometer. Seventy-six degrees below zero!

No one remained outside for any length of time that day. As night approached, it grew a little warmer, and by the next day the thermometer was back at a modest 40 below.

Inside, we were comfortable and warm. On the coldest days we dipped into the precious supply of coal, but otherwise most of our heat came from the cow chips.

The evenings were delightful. The family sat about a huge round table over which hung a splendid lamp—an old Coleman gasoline burner, antecedent of the Coleman lantern. Its mesh mantles burned white-hot, and it had to be pumped up. Boasting a great white shade and an attractive handle, by which it could be suspended from the ceiling, it threw off a magnificent white light, hissing contentedly and filling the room with a clean odor.

I have frequently thought of trying to find an old Coleman lamp to hang in my home or office, but I shudder to think what it might do to building inspectors and insurance rates.

About the table Mother and Grandma worked on the pile of mending, or they crocheted and knitted. Grandpa was buried within his newspaper, usually the Kansas City *Star*, which arrived almost a week late. Our mail was now delivered once a week and placed in the mailbox on the ranch gate. Previously we had picked it up in town. Grandpa insisted on the *Star* because it kept him informed of his beloved Kansas City, and its thorough, unyielding Republicanism measured up to his specifications. Dad was usually engrossed in a book. During the war years, I pored over the maps, drawings, cartoons, accounts, and pictures of the action in France, and drew pictures of Germans with spiked helmets.

Under the rays of the friendly lamp, Mother worked with me and taught me to "sound out the letters" and put the words together. I scrawled letters to my uncle who was "somewhere in France."

Mother sent to "Monkey" Ward's for several games. On the big table we played Rook and Old Maid and Authors, while the wind howled outside and blew the icy snow particles against the windows. Frequently Grandma would enter from the kitchen with a heaping bowl of buttered popcorn or a platter of homemade candy. Wadine would sit patiently while Mother or Grandma lavished time and affection on the care of her long blond curls.

On those sub-zero winter nights, the delicate business of going to the toilet on the side of the hill behind the house was something to delay as long as possible. There was certainly no idling in our "bathroom," and no one, in wintertime at least, ever inquired of another if

137

he intended "to stay in there all day." In our family, somehow, the word for body waste came to be "Oh-oh." I have a suspicion it derived from the involuntary expletive when one sat down on that frost-covered seat! In this respect, we males enjoyed a distinct advantage over the opposite sex.

Many winter nights the mysterious gods of the far north put on spectacular displays. The aurora borealis, immense and silent, sent its streamers and shafts of colored light from horizon to zenith. It frequently began with only a great blue-white curtain of light hanging delicately from the northern sky. Then the curtain would rip asunder and explode into fountains, cascades and giant globules of rose, blue-violet, green and amber. One rarely spoke while the northern lights were dancing, for such an incredible show seemed to justify sound. It demanded gigantic peals and waves of overwhelming accompaniment, but it was silent and intimidated into silence anything which might not match its proportions.

. . .

These were years of "learning by doing" . . . the ways and the care of ranch animals. As the steers approached the time for market, I moved them as little as possible, lest they lose their fatty tissue. If they were content to stand in a given area and fatten themselves, it was "money in the bank." If a calf was to be taken away from his mother and reared on skimmed milk so that the cream might be sold, it meant teaching the youngster how to drink from a bucket; and that was a task of unmitigated hell. Before the instruction was complete, patience invariably ran out, calf and instructor were soaked from head to foot in skimmed milk. The sheep always grazed into the wind to prevent flies from despositing eggs in their damp nostrils. Never approach a horse from the rear—always from the front or side—otherwise you might get the daylights kicked out of you. Watch the shoulders of the draft horses carefully, where the collars of their harnesses pulled against them; an ill-fitting collar could ruin a fine animal. Be careful when riding a saddle horse through a gate, lest he brush too closely to the post and bang your knee. When unbridling a horse, always stand to the side of his head, lest he should bolt in a bit of premature surcease from duty and run over you. When releasing horses at the end of the day, try to herd them toward some soft and grassy bit of pasture, lest, as they roll and sport themselves on the ground, they injure a shoulder on a stone and bring on a fistula.

Once in a while a young ewe encountered difficulty dropping her first lamb. When this happened I was the obstetrician because my hands and arms were small. Grandpa lathered my arm with a thick coating of soap suds. The ewes stood patiently while I probed the womb, grasped her lamb by the front feet and pulled steadily and firmly. Grandpa wisely counseled me to avoid bringing up this indelicate subject around Grandma and Mother, for that would have been the end of my obstetrical work. He always chose a place somewhere out of their sight. Even Dad, I think, looked upon the whole operation with something less than enthusiasm.

The growing lambs had to be "docked," and I learned to cut their tails, notch their ears and castrate them, quickly and deftly, and with a minimum of pain.

Occasionally, bad weather struck at lambing time. That meant picking them up the moment they dropped, wrapping them in something warm, and rushing them to the shelter of the barn or even the house.

The herding of the livestock on our own pasturage and on the open range fell, largely, to me for several reasons. I was eager to do it because it gave me the opportunity to ride a horse over the land. Moreover, I was somehow uniquely immune to mosquitoes. They drove everyone else frantic, they could swarm on a lamb and eventually kill it by consuming its blood—but I could ride or walk through dense clouds of them and come off virtually unscathed.

In a deep swale to the west of the ranch house, I noticed that the snow water collected each spring and then flowed down into the basin through a small gap in the hills, and spread out in the general area of the vegetable garden. Painfully aware of the shortage of water during those drought years, I resolved to bestow a magnificent gift upon Grandma and Mother by building a dam at the lower outlet of the swale, to provide water for the garden. I worked like a beaver on my "dam" most of that summer, during every spare moment. I tugged and perspired, digging rocks out of the surrounding hillsides and somehow transporting them to the "dam." I rolled some of them into position. With a tremendous crowbar I employed every form of leverage known to physicists, I hitched Old Bill, one of the farm horses, to the stone boat and hauled rocks on it. I threw considerable quantities of earth in between the rocks and even tamped Russian thistles into the crevices for sealing material.

Somehow, the size of my "dam" was discounted and everyone was too busy to pay any attention to the construction project of a seven-year-old boy.

Winter piled the snow on the back three-twenty, and I began to anticipate the lake which would form behind my "dam" when the spring thaw came. The weather finally turned warmer, and I was amazed at the proportions of my "lake"—it filled the entire swale and trickled over the top of the "dam." In the center, the water was possibly fifteen- or twenty-feet deep!

But my engineering was of brief duration and almost disastrous.

139

During the night the dam gave way, sending a wall of water tumbling down the draw, through the corral, past the barn and into the garden. The next morning, the corral had a deep gorge cut through it, a corner of the barn stood several feet off the ground, and the garden looked like the delta of a river. I was reminded in stern language to leave the physical aspects of the ranch as they were and to consult some of the family elders before undertaking any more ambitious projects.

. . .

In the vicinity of the barnyard grew a fantastic weed which we called "lamb's quarter." Its tender leaves when young made splendid greens, but by late summer it had grown six or seven feet tall, and through this forest of lamb's quarter, Wadine and I played our imaginative games.

It appeared that the ground rules and the objective of our game were somewhat ambiguous, and a considerable portion of the play was given to earnest discussion of how the rules might be refined and codified. There was a "good guy" and a "bad guy," naturally; and again, naturally, I was consistently the "good guy." Wadine not only had a constantly villainous role, but she had a durable name . . . "Joe Harper." Years later she was to tell me that she had frequently become "darned sick and tired of Joe Harper," and that she had longed to play the heroic role just once! The patch of lamb's quarter was the scene of many violent and tense confrontations with the hopelessly antisocial and irascible outcast, but truth, honesty, and virtue always prevailed— until Wadine wearied of Joe Harper and walked into the house.

Rarely has a small boy been blessed with a smaller sister of such character . . . with such a capacity for patience and affection. Wadine was taciturn, a marvelous listener, and she is yet. She would listen gravely, by the hour, to my fanciful boastings and declarations of astounding intent. Wadine solemnly agreed . . . or permitted me to believe she agreed . . . that I would, indeed, ride the stallion right into Saco! I would one day shoot and bring home over my heroic shoulders the carcass of a gray wolf! I would learn to swim and I could run faster than the wind! I could throw and pin Roy Waal with one hand tied behind me and I was not afraid to ride Billy, the Hereford bull! Childish secrets were safe with Wadine. She did not tell our parents when I tried to smoke a stalk of lamb's quarter.

One day, at play, I had been much too rough with Wadine, and Mother seized from the closet the ultimate weapon: the willow switch. With what swelling surge of affection I have recalled over the years how Wadine's eyes gushed with tears as she beseeched Mother to spare me the terrible punishment.

Her "no-nonsense" and steady character were illustrated the day I fell out of the barn loft. Wadine surmises that she may have pushed me, but I doubt it. In any event as we jostled on the brink of the hay trap, I suddenly plummeted through the opening and crashed onto the floor of the barn. As Mother tells the story, Wadine calmly and with magnificent insouciance entered the house and suggested that "Someone should see what is wrong with that boy out there. He can't talk." It must have resulted in a mild concussion, for I had no recollection of the remainder of that day or that evening.

Once in town, when I was engaged in a fight with a schoolmate and I was being badly outpointed, I recall Wadine standing by and sobbing.

. . .

Somewhere, at some vague point in those innocent years, I began going to school. Although I can recall the anticipation of the momentous event, the years have somehow dimmed and all but erased any memory of the first day of a process which would occupy most of the next two decades.

One of the initial undertakings of our new outpost society was the creation of a school system. A school district was created in conformity with the laws and requirements of the state, and the settlers, in duly constituted and recorded assembly, elected a school board and assessed themselves to provide for the construction of a schoolhouse and the hiring of a teacher. It appeared that our land, lying approximately halfway between Stinky Creek and Whitewater, was selected as the ideal site. Consequently, Dad set aside an acre in the extreme northeast corner of our half-section, and the little rectangular one-room schoolhouse, with its row of windowpanes facing southward, and two privies out behind, became known as "the Huntley school."

A generous and deserving woman's club in Saco has long since moved the little building into town, restored it, supplied it with snapshots and photographs of its early clientele, and otherwise preserved it as a reminder of the community's rough-hewn, frontier past.

Our "little white schoolhouse" must be awed and self-consciously out of place in town, among other buildings. It has lost its air of loneliness. It represents no more the hope and confidence of better days to come, but is a monument to human defeat . . . to the immutable and tenacious invincibility of the grassland. The windowpanes, like sad eyes, no longer look out over the West Bench and weep. The simple little schoolhouse, however, has been rescued from the ignominious fate of all the other ranch buildings of the area—which simply vanished and turned the horizon of the benchland back to its unbroken union of land and sky.

The schoolhouse, in addition to its prime function, served as the community center. There were nights when it cast a warm glow into the pasture and down the lane. The old piano thumped merrily, and the fiddle shrilled its sprightly tunes. The rural wives were whirled about the floor, and the men might repair occasionally to the row of teams and rigs hitched outside for cautious nips at a bit of bottled "spirit."

The schoolhouse was occasionally converted to a "house of the Lord," on Sundays when the Methodist "sky pilot" from town was moved to visit our area or when some itinerant missionary or evangelist might appear. And the county agent, too, conducted infrequent meetings in the schoolhouse. I recall one evening meeting at which he applauded my father and grandfather for deemphasizing farming in behalf of cash grain crops to utilize the land for livestock instead. There ensued a general discussion concerning the use of the unclaimed land and cooperative ownership and use of herd bulls.

The auction-supper was the most tried-and-sure method of raising funds for the school or for any other civic project. Each farm wife or eligible daughter prepared a "supper" for two, packed it, wrapped it in the fanciest paper and decoration available, and brought it to the party. After a few hours of dancing, the boxes were sold at auction. The highest bidder for each package received not only the contents but the companionship of the housewife who had prepared it. The auction process was invariably an occasion for good-natured jibing and joking.

The schoolhouse was also the setting for funerals, for christenings, for marriages, and elections. It was, indeed, a community center, in that it housed the collective joys and sorrows of the neighborhood. It administered to the young, it was drafted into service in behalf of the souls and the fortunes of the adults, and it was a temple for the last rites of the aged. Before it was endowed with the distinction of an historical landmark and packed into town, it accrued an aura of stubborn permanency, standing there on its little knoll, by the lane, a quarter mile south of Osier's, for fifty years or more. When ranch buildings of the area sank into the prairie and vanished, the little schoolhouse endured, weathering the succession of seasons, refusing to capitulate to the elements or accidents, withstanding even the vandalism which the combination of automobiles and misguided youth have set loose upon so many rural areas.

Ada Sommers, who had taught school in Wisconsin before venturing to the Montana homestead, and who had volunteered for "a turn or two," was the teacher who introduced me to the excitement of formal learning. Of all the memories of that school, many of them vivid and detailed, I cannot remember learning to read. I do recall that she employed the phonic system of instruction. She flashed the cards on which the letters of the alphabet were printed, and in unison we sounded them. In this respect, I went to school with a liberal "head start" from Mother.

My prejudice in behalf of the phonic system has been strong, but the method has all but disappeared. Here and there it is given a revival—frequently as a kind of curiosity. Our generation of Montana youngsters learned to "sound out" the words, and I cannot recall a youngster in the later grades or in high school who had any difficulty with reading. Spelling, furthermore, seemed to be an effortless and automatic by-product of learning to read.

The Huntley School student body included about a dozen pupils, ranging from the first to the eighth grades, all in one room. In some mysterious way, Mrs. Sommers sorted us out so that each youngster received his share of attention. The one-room school is not the brawling cockpit one might imagine. A small area at the front of the room was reserved for the group or individual whose turn it might be for recitation. Mrs. Sommers pitched her conglomerate classroom in low key, so it was not difficult to concentrate in spite of the hum of the education processes up front. Homework was not spared. I can recall eavesdropping on the recitations of the more advanced pupils, with the result that in later years there was much that came in the nature of review. I had somewhat surreptitiously borrowed instruction from that of Rudy Waal, Steve Osier and Carrie Franklin.

A brand of pipe tobacco marketed at that time was packaged in a gay candy-striped tin container, like a miniature picnic basket. It was the universal lunch box for schoolchildren. Neither Dad nor Grandpa smoked that particular brand, however, so my sister and I usually carried our lunches in gallon Karo syrup pails. In cold weather we ate in the schoolroom; when it was warm we sat outside, with our backs against the building.

The noon hour usually began with a brief period of determined bargaining between Roy Waal and me. Day after day, Roy's, Elena's and Rudy Waal's lunch boxes were stocked with the delicious *flatbrot*, which, frequently, I had watched their mother prepare. It consisted of a thin batter poured directly onto the top of the stove, cooked until small brown spots began to appear, then removed, cut into manageable sections and served with butter. In appearance, texture and taste it was not dissimilar to the thin bread found in Syria and Lebanon, but the Middle East product does not rival the Scandinavian, particularly as it was prepared by Mrs. Waal. In any event, I bartered portions of my lunch each day for generous slices of Roy's Scandinavian bread.

Steve Osier and Danny Pinkerman must have been five or six years older than I, so I was spared any need to struggle to maintain a neutral position in the bitter rivalry which existed between them. A number of school days were marked by vicious fights between Steve and Danny. They never fought on the school grounds or close enough to the building to invite intercession by the teacher. Rather, they had a habit of slipping unobtrusively into a deep ravine about two hundred yards east, and there the bloody struggles would occur. They must have loathed each other with an intense juvenile passion. They would not quarrel or fight with Rudy Waal or Bizgard Kappel, who were the same ages; nor did they bully us younger boys.

A fight between Steve and Danny did not begin with a slanging match or exchanges of insults. At some signal comprehended only by themselves, they would simply disappear into the gully and beat each other unmercifully. On several occasions the fights continued all afternoon. They would fail to return to classes after the lunch period, and the rest of us knew what was going on. At four o'clock, when school was dismissed, we would rush down to the ravine, to find Steve and Danny utterly exhausted, clothing ripped, bloody, but still attacking each other with undiminished fury. Once, these two arch enemies quietly retired from Sunday School to meet in "the gully of honor."

Roy Waal was the only boy of the immediate community who was in my age bracket and in the same grade at school, and we were good companions. Roy profited in all the lore of rifles, hunting, trapping and fast horses absorbed from his older brother, Rudy. I managed to hold my own, however, with second-hand tales of the railroad, borrowed from Dad, and embroidered for the occasion, and the vivid stories I had heard Grandpa tell—stories of his Missouri boyhood, of his experiences as a teamster and a streetcar motorman in Kansas City, or his brief years as a prison guard at the Colorado State Prison at Canyon Ferry.

Roy and I watched meadowlarks and curlews build their ground nests and hatch their young. We killed rattlesnakes and fashioned bracelets by stringing the rattles together. We watched the absorbing processes of animal copulation, birth and death. We caught great bullfrogs out of the Whitewater, explored the hillsides for Indian tools and artifacts, and carved our initials in the carapaces of turtles. We found moss agates and speculated on their beauty should we one day afford the cost of having them cut and polished. We performed great feats of aerial daring and experiment by launching ourselves from the end of the hoist rope in the barn loft: taking off from the highest beam, swooping in a great arc at the end of the rope, then letting go at the precise moment to soar free and land in the big mound of hay at the other end of the loft. We experimented unsatisfactorily with parachutes from the peak of the barn to the straw pile.

Roy and I were devoted and pathological rock throwers. Small boys harbor a primordial attachment to a round, smooth stone, and we were no exception to the rule. The banks of the Whitewater had been denuded down to tremendous gravel beds—billions of rocks worn round and crudely polished by the gigantic churnings of the "Great Glacier"

144

and by the erosion of wind and water. There Roy and I engaged in target practice for hours.

Rock throwing, and my expertise at it, got me into a slight squabble at school. I observed Ivy Osier going into the girls' toilet. Holding in my hand a small, round stone, I found the temptation too great. I was both startled and immensely pleased as the stone flew straight and true to vanish through the small star-shaped air vent in the side of the privy, then clattered and bounced about inside for delightful seconds, followed by agonizing shrieks from the startled Ivy. She emerged, asserting furiously that the stone had hit her. If it did, it was on a belated bounce when its impact would have been spent, but I was in trouble, nevertheless. When I argued unwisely that I had heard the stone bouncing about inside the toilet, it was obvious at once that I was the culprit. It cost me a couple of whacks with a ruler across the back of my throwing hand.

My first three or four years of school were thus spent at the modest little frame building a half mile from home. An intervening half century has not erased the sharp memories of Rudy, Roy and Elena; of Steve, Bertha and Ivy; of Helen and Danny; of Florence and Carrie Franklin; and of Margaret Busche. They were happy, rewarding years despite crop failures, drought, pestilence and numb despair. By any standards we were children of the poor, but we were not aware of it. Our lives and fortunes were full.

~~~~~~~~~~~~~~~~~~~~~~~~~~~~~~~~~~~~~

DISCUSSION AND INQUIRY

Chet Huntley grew up on a Montana farm in a traditional extended-family situation surrounded by loving parents and grandparents. He describes Grandma as the cherished one, Mother the repository of love, Dad as good-natured, and Grandpa as the hero. What more could a little boy ask! His experiences with Grandpa provide the richest memories for Chet. How would you describe their relationship? According to Erik Erikson, a trusting relationship with significant others is a basis for healthy personality development. What evidence do you have that Chet's relationships with his family were trusting relationships?

Chet and his sister, Wadine, enjoyed a very pleasant companionship, free of the jealousies

145

and rivalries often observed between siblings. He recalls his mother's absence and her reappearance with a baby girl, but his recollection of this potentially traumatic event reveals no bitterness or anxiety. Why is this the case in this particular family? How might the extended-family situation mitigate sibling rivalry? What are the possible effects of the closeness and pressures of urban living on the sibling relationship?

Chet recalls many marvelous informal learning experiences during his preschool years as well as vivid memories of his early schooling. The rural environment provided him with rich experiences as he observed the Indians, explored nature, and visited town with Grandpa. (See the selection by Elmer McCollum, who also grew up in a rural setting.) Compare these informal learnings with the more formal school experiences in his one-room school. Compare these experiences with your own schooling. Where and how does learning really occur? Is it possible that all children learn more outside the confines of the classroom? What educational reforms suggest themselves to you after reading about Chet's childhood?

Christine Jorgensen

BIOGRAPHICAL SKETCH

Born George Jorgensen, in 1926, to a happy, stable family in New York, Christine Jorgensen searched for her true identity throughout her early years. George became Christine in Denmark in 1951, through a transsexual operation, which made headlines around the world. In 1953, she was selected Woman of the Year by the Scandinavian Societies of Greater New York for her outstanding contribution to the advancement of medical science and the courageous manner in which she carried herself throughout the ordeal.

SELECTIONS FROM

CHRISTINE JORGENSEN: A PERSONAL AUTOBIOGRAPHY

SOME of the strongest and most enduring of childhood memories are inevitably linked with my paternal grandmother, who exerted a great influence on my early life. There were twenty-six aunts, uncles, and cousins in our Bronx neighborhood, but the matriarch and focal point of the clan was "Grandma Jorgensen." She was a generous, common-sense woman who enriched the lives of our family, friends, and neighbors, enveloping us all in a warm glow of love.

In stature, Grandma was short and pleasantly plump. She chose mostly grey and lavender shades for her clothes, which complemented her white hair. In my mind's eye, even now, I can picture her silvery hair brushed high on her head and topped by a shining knot. Another outstanding thing about her was an aristocratic, "Indian-type" nose, which was a genetic feature of the Petersen family. Dad and Dolly inherited it, while I was endowed with the prominent Petersen ears.

Grandma had small, plump hands that seemed to have a life of

147

their own as they worked incessantly at some form of handiwork: needlepoint, knitting, or crocheting. As the years passed, she met the rudeness of time gracefully, and her hands, particularly, seemed never to age. I remember the scent of lavender that surrounded her. She was always a person of grace and dignity.

As a child, I used to pick violets for her. They were her favorite flower and she had a green thumb for raising the African variety, an ability which I've tried to match, unsuccessfully, for years.

I developed into a frail, tow-headed, introverted child, but I learned early that society laid down firm ground rules concerning my behavior. A little boy wore trousers and had his hair cut short. He had to learn to use his fists aggressively, participate in athletics and, most important of all, little boys didn't cry. Contrary to those accepted patterns, sometimes I did feel like crying, and I must have felt that Grandma understood and didn't disapprove when I ran away from a fist-fight or refused to play rough-and-tumble games. Once, when I ran to her in flight from some childish altercation, she said, "Fighting is the ugliest part of life. To live without fighting is much more important, and much more satisfying."

After Grandpa Jorgensen died in 1927, Grandma lived comfortingly close to our house in the Bronx with her son-in-law and daughter, Helga, Dad's sister. As soon as I was permitted to travel the few blocks to Grandma's house alone, I began to spend many hours with her. I loved listening to the stories about Denmark, told in her soft voice and Danish accent; the customs and traditions of the Old Country and the charming, funny things she did as a child. Always, as we talked, her small hands were busy crocheting doilies or antimacassers and our conversation was accompanied in the background by the ticking of a beautifully carved wall clock which was given to Grandpa in 1868, and is still in my possession today. Occasionally, I was allowed to admire her collection of fine porcelain, at reasonably close range.

I suppose I knew instinctively that I didn't have to tell Grandma when someone had hurt my feelings or when I had been cruelly disappointed. Had I told her of my childish prayer one Christmas when I was five, asking God for a pretty doll with long, golden hair, Grandma might have helped answer that prayer. At least, she would have eased my disappointment when my present turned out to be a bright red railway train.

It must have been about this stage, that I became aware of the differences between my sister, Dolly, and me. Those differences, to me, lay in the order of "masculine" and "feminine" things. Dolly had long blonde hair and wore dresses, both of which I admired but which were not allowed to me, and I was upset and puzzled by this.

148

"Mom," I asked, "why didn't God make us all alike?" My Mother gently explained that the world needed both men and women and there was no way of knowing before a baby was born whether it would be a boy or a girl.

"You see, Brud," she said, "it's one of God's surprises."

"Well," I replied, "I don't like the kind of surprise God made me!"

I believe the spirit of rebellion must have been taking a foothold in me, even though I was a shy and introverted child. Though I don't remember the incident, I've been told that my childish revolt manifested itself one day when I was about four or five, and I went to visit my maternal grandmother, "Nana" Hansen. During the course of a shopping trip, I planted myself solidly in front of a neighborhood store and demanded some candy.

"No," Nana replied, "you're going to eat shortly."

"Then I'll go home," I answered, and started on my way. Nana followed, block after block, but at a distance. Reaching another candy store, I stopped, turned to see Nana regarding me, and said, "Candy now?"

"No," came the prompt and firm reply. True to my word, I plodded my determined way home. Evidently, I was a willful one even at that age.

In 1928, the nation was riding at a prosperous high tide and reflecting that spirit was one of the popular song hits of the time, "Happy Days Are Here Again." Newly elected President Herbert Hoover was proclaiming " a chicken in every pot and a car in every garage." Wall Street's ticker tape machines clattered away at a great rate and stocks rose to new heights. The Jorgensen Realty and Construction Company expanded its credit and continued to build more houses. Even the death, in 1927, of Grandpa Jorgensen, one of the company's founders, didn't stop its meteoric rise.

But "The Roaring 20's" were about to quiet down to a whimper. October 29, 1929, was the beginning of one of the darkest periods in American financial history, for it ushered in the Great Depression. With the sudden, swift market crash on "Black Thursday," everything lost value, the economic stability of the country was destroyed, and the Jorgensen Construction Company was swept along with the wreckage of countless others. Fifteen houses, built by the company on bank credit and mortgages, stood in lonely vacancy in the New York area. A few of them sold for a tenth of their original cost; others the family couldn't give away. Even our home on Dudley Avenue was in jeopardy for awhile. Dad and his brother Bill had all their resources in those buildings, even including Grandma Jorgensen's money. The stock certificates were worthless and, as Dad said, "Good for nothing but papering a wall." As I was only three years old at the time, I

149

don't recall that financial catastrophe, but many years later, I took Dad's pronouncement literally and papered a wall behind the bar in my home with those colorful, worthless certificates.

In the wake of the Depression, Mom and Dad managed to survive and keep a car, a house, and a family intact. Dad had cashed in his government insurance and funds were low, but he worked at various jobs in the building trade in order to keep going.

After the crash, when her children contributed to her support, Grandma had an efficient, if unusual system of bookkeeping. She had a sheaf of envelopes, each marked and set aside for a specific purpose: "Birthdays," "Christmas," "Funeral" (her own), "Crocheting cotton," etc. When one of the envelopes was empty, Grandma was "broke" in that department and she would never think of taking from one to satisfy the needs of another. After noting Grandma's unique accounting system, I tried to set up one of my own. Of course, my weekly allowance never seemed to find its way into the envelopes, but the feeble attempt was probably the first to make me aware of the principles of thrift.

A couple of years after the demise of Dad's company, and totally unaware of the drastic changes in the lives and fortunes of the Jorgensen's, I began to prepare for the great adventure of going to school. I remember that I anticipated school with a great deal of excitement, for my one great ambition at that period was to learn to read. Dolly could already decipher meaning from the printed pages and I imagine I didn't want to be outdone. The daily arrival of newspapers and the large library of books at home were a constant frustration, and attempts to get others to read to me were futile more often than not. Dad, who was an avid reader, always seemed to me to know so much. He'd point to the newspaper and heatedly discuss an item and, later, when I tried to get some meaning from the printed symbols, I met with no success. School was the place where I could learn to read and I looked forward to it eagerly. When I was five-and-a-half, the day finally arrived, and I went to Public School 71, within walking distance of our home.

During my first week in kindergarten, I met a little boy named Carl, the first new friend with whom I wasn't shy. Carl came from Swedish parents and as we were both Scandinavians, we had common family backgrounds. Diabetic children were relatively unknown at that time and I can remember watching with fascination one day, when his Mother gave him an insulin shot. We became fast friends and all through our school life together, Carl was my one uncritical ally.

We often appeared in school plays and that was one of the activities I loved best of all. "Play-acting" was fun and I could hide my shyness behind the façade of someone else, in a shining world of fantasy. I remember my first role was as an organ-grinder's monkey, and by the time I was in the third grade, I'd graduated to the most cherished of all character parts, Mickey Mouse. The long rubber tail and suffocating mask were a mark of distinction and I wore them proudly.

At some time during that period, I acquired a set of marionettes. I never seemed to tire of manipulating the tiny figures in their fanciful world.

Outwardly, I was a very submissive child, but the sense of rebellion must have been growing rapidly within me and established itself more openly the following summer, when Mom and Dad sent me to a boys' summer camp, located at Dover Furnace, New Jersey.

Camp Sharparoon was a typical vacation camp, operated in what seemed to me then a far too-militant manner. The day's schedule was posted each morning on a bulletin board, and, although I was too young to read the notice in detail, I was sure in advance that I wasn't going to like the "orders of the day." The first day's regimen confirmed my fears when we flew from one activity to another, commanded by the shrill, piercing sound of a whistle.

High on the mountainside above the camp was a large rock with a gigantic letter "S" painted on it, and the penalty for an infraction of the rules was the job of painting the "S". A fearful, whispered rumor told of the many boys who had fallen to instant death from that dizzying height, while painting the camp symbol. The story held me in terror for several days, until I finally realized that it was, of course, false.

I fell a victim to other tricks played on the newcomers, when I was told that a "Sky Hook" and a "Jericho Pass" were absolutely essential to every camp member. I don't remember why the Sky Hook was necessary, but a Jericho Pass had no little importance, as I was informed that it was the only thing that would permit use of the latrines. Finally, in dire circumstances, I rushed around the camp looking for someone to give me the vital Jericho Pass until a sympathetic senior counselor put a stop to my frantic search. My relief—in several aspects—was so great that it is, even now, memorable.

I can still remember that a desire for seclusion grew more positive with each passing day, and my plans never included others. There was more freedom in carrying out those plans alone and, therefore, less chance of being made to feel ridiculous, strange, or different.

"Hey, George, c'mere!" I was often ordered to join the other boys in a game. It seemed to me then it was always like that, just when I was having fun on my own. I resented these intrusions so much that I began devising ways of disappearing for a whole day, but when I returned, I knew I'd have to face the discipline of the counselors.

After a few miserable days of inadequately trying to fight against the regimentation, I made a tearful but determined request to be taken home. "I want to come home," was all I wrote on the penny postcard that I sent to Mom and Dad.

No one could understand why I was so unhappy or why I delighted in visiting Dolly when Mom and Dad took me on a trip to the girls' camp, some distance away. Somehow, I felt more at ease, more comfortable there. The girls didn't call me "sissy" or ask me if I was really a girl dressed in boys' clothes, like the boys at Camp Sharparoon did.

Fortunately, neither of my parents saw any reason for forcing me to continue something I disliked so violently, so each summer after that I was shipped off, with a blanket roll and a few dollars in pocket money, to relatives who owned a farm in northern New York State.

Many of the leisure hours on the farm were spent at an old familiar "swimmin' hole" in the area. Like the children at the summer camp, the neighboring farm boys couldn't understand me either. To them I was "that strange little kid from the city."

"C'mon, George," they challenged. "Why don't you swim in your birthday suit like we do?"

I remember that I wanted so much to have them admire me and be included as a member of the gang, but I shrank back in confusion and fear. "I get too cold in the water," I lied. Though I liked to swim and was a good swimmer, I couldn't break the habit of wearing a complete swimsuit with both top and bottom. I have no doubt that my embarrassment stemmed from shyness and a natural modesty which I had learned at home.

There were other ways in which I didn't measure up to the acceptable standards of a budding young male, as one of my school teachers was to point out so graphically and cruelly.

Most youngsters are acquisitive and prone to annoy adults with the oddities they collect and hoard. To a childish mind, anything from tattered comic books to a chipped marble are considered rare and valuable treasures to be admired, cherished, and sometimes even traded. In that respect, at least, I wasn't any different from other children.

I can't recall how, but when I was eight, I had in some way acquired one of those rich treasures: a small piece of needlepoint which I kept hidden in my school desk. Occasionally, I would reach in my desk and touch it, or if no one was watching, I'd take it out and admire it secretly. I didn't display it openly, probably sensing the derision that might result.

After recess one day, I was astonished to find that the lovely piece of handiwork had disappeared from my desk. Even now, I remember that I was heartbroken, for one of the small pleasures of my life had been lost or misplaced. Or had it been stolen?

Our teacher called the class to order and stood beside her desk, apparently waiting for the last echoes of childish freedom to die. She must have sensed her triumph as she paused significantly for complete attention. "George Jorgensen, come here," she commanded. "I'd like you to come up, too, Mrs. Jorgensen, so you can hear what this boy has to say."

I turned to see Mom, quietly making her way from the back of the classroom. In distress over my loss, I hadn't noticed her sitting there before. In growing panic, I wondered what Mom was doing in class. She hadn't told me that she was coming to school. The teacher must have asked her, but why? Mothers were asked to school only when the kids did something wrong, and I wondered what I had done.

In the silence that followed, the teacher took an object from her desk. "Is this yours?" she asked, with a prim little smile, holding the precious needlepoint just beyond my reach.

"Yes," I answered. I felt the quick sting of tears, the blood rushing to my face and heard a hot little breath sucked in behind me in excitement. I reached out to take the needlepoint from her hand, but she withdrew it sharply and faced my mother.

"Mrs. Jorgensen, do you think that this is anything for a red-blooded boy to have in his desk as a keepsake? The next thing we know, George will be bringing his knitting to school!"

There were titters from the class which she didn't try to silence. I glanced at Mom. Her lips were quivering and her face was flushed. "I'll take care of it," she said quietly, and guided me ahead of her out of the classroom. We walked home in silence. From time to time she brushed tears from her eyes and even now I recall my feeling of humiliation and confusion. In some way I had hurt her. I wasn't sure just how, but I think I knew that the teacher had hurt her even more. For the first time in my life, I felt the most destructive of all emotions, hate. That woman had cheapened something I loved and, in some way, had injured my Mother. I was no doubt too young to realize that a love for beauty was not the sole property of either a male or female, but the teacher's attempt to form that link seemed wrong to me, even then.

Mom never mentioned the incident after that, but to me it has remained a vivid memory. From then on, except for ansuers to direct questions, I never spoke to the teacher again and I know now how much I must have resented her. I didn't realize that her own tragedy lay in ignorance and a lack of understanding. In her callousness, she couldn't comprehend the fact tnat in order to follow the normal pattern of development, I needed help, not ridicule.

As I often did when I was troubled, I went to visit my beloved Grandma Jorgensen and told her what had happened. She went to one of her great wooden chests and lovingly unwrapped many samples of her own superb needlework. She handed me a small, exquisitely crocheted doily and explained to me something of the joy and satisfaction she had known in making an object that was both useful and beautiful.

"You mustn't mind if other people can't see or feel a sense of beauty, too, George," she told me gently.

Grandma's explanation seemed more real to me than the teacher's ridicule. I thought that I knew what beauty was in my own way and that it was a mistake to categorize it as either masculine or feminine.

But Grandma was always my champion when others laughed at my "sissified" ways. I've been told that once, at the age of four, I had insisted on carrying a miniature cane and wearing a beret wherever I went. "Never mind," she said, "it's his way of expressing the yearning for dignity in his life."

I remember I was about eleven or twelve years old when my sister Dolly began to notice my outstanding feminine mannerisms. One day when we were walking home from school, Dolly said, "Why do you carry your books that way? It looks silly for a boy!" I was carrying my books up in my arms, just as she carried hers. It was something I'd never been aware of before.

I thought a great deal about those books during the following few days. "Does the way in which one carried books have to be 'boyish' or 'girlish'?" I wondered. I tried carrying them at my side, but it was awkward and I kept dropping them, so I simply went back to the old, more comfortable method.

A few years later, when Dolly was in college, she devoted a thesis to the effects of environment on the development of a child. I never read the thesis, but was told I was the subject of it and that she had won considerable acclaim for her work in analyzing my feminine ways and attributing them partially to the fact that I played with girls so much as a child.

At the time, I was angry, though I never mentioned it. I felt that a very personal thing had been explored and exposed and I didn't like being used as the subject for such a disclosure. Undoubtedly, my distress stemmed from fear and the total self-absorption of my thirteen years and, therefore, blinded me to her motives. Today, I know that she was deeply concerned and was trying to help me by searching for more understanding within herself. In a way, she was shouldering the problem and facing it squarely; a giant step for the average college girl in 1939, when such subjects as the "feminine" boy were not openly discussed.

How many of my emotions could be attributed to this early environment I couldn't determine then, of course, but deep within myself, even at that early age, I felt that all these basic feelings were an integral part of me and not highly influenced by outside conditions.

154

~~~~~~

DISCUSSION AND INQUIRY

George wanted a doll for Christmas at age five, but found a train under the tree. His treasured possession at age eight was a piece of needlepoint instead of a chipped marble, and he preferred visiting his sister's summer camp to attending his boys' camp. He claims that his interest in feminine things and his feelings about himself as a male were part of his being and not influenced by outside conditions. Do you agree? How influential was Grandma, who obviously supported his interest in "feminine things?" Looking back at these "feminine" interests in light of his decision to become "Christine," it is easy to say that there was evidence of atypical behavior before age five. However, consider what is masculine or feminine to a young child. How atypical is it for a young boy to enjoy playing with dolls? At what point does a boy usually make a masculine role identification and what are the outside pressures that precipitate adoption of masculine mannerisms and interests? Were there pressures in George's life that counteracted such an identification?

When George went to school, he was particularly fond of "play acting," which, he says, provided a façade and helped him hide his shyness. Again, looking at this in light of the adult Jorgensen, it is easy to say that he always wanted to be someone else. Remember, however, that school-age children often participate comfortably in school plays or backyard "shows." In these roles, they clown around, fight, and show affection in ways which would be totally unacceptable to them if they were being themselves. What purpose do these "play acting" opportunities serve for the child? Compare this "play acting" to preschoolers' role playing. What are some socially acceptable adult behaviors that parallel role play and "play acting" in children?

~~~~~~

Helen Keller

BIOGRAPHICAL SKETCH

Helen Keller was born in Alabama in 1880. She was a normal, healthy baby during infancy. At eighteen months, she was afflicted with a near-fatal disease, which resulted in total loss of sight and hearing. With the help of her dedicated teacher and friend, Anne Sullivan, Helen learned to speak. A cum laude *graduate of Radcliffe College, she became a writer and lecturer. Much of her life was devoted to working for the American Foundation for the Blind. She died at the age of 88.*

SELECTIONS FROM

THE STORY OF MY LIFE

THE beginning of my life was simple and much like every other little life. I came, I saw, I conquered, as the first baby in the family always does. There was the usual amount of discussion as to a name for me. The first baby in the family was not to be lightly named, every one was emphatic about that. My father suggested the name of Mildred Campbell, an ancestor whom he highly esteemed, and he declined to take any further part in the discussion. My mother solved the problem by giving it as her wish that I should be called after her mother, whose maiden name was Helen Everett. But in the excitement of carrying me to church my father lost the name on the way, very naturally, since it was one in which he had declined to have a part. When the minister asked him for it, he just remembered that it had been decided to call me after my grandmother, and he gave her name as Helen Adams.

I am told that while I was still in long dresses I showed many signs of an eager, self-asserting disposition. Everything that I saw other people do I insisted upon imitating. At six months I could pipe out "How d'ye," and one day I attracted every one's attention by saying "Tea, tea, tea" quite plainly. Even after my illness I remembered one of the words I had learned in these early months. It was the word "water,"

156

and I continued to make some sound for that word after all other speech was lost. I ceased making the sound "wah-wah" only when I learned to spell the word.

They tell me I walked the day I was a year old. My mother had just taken me out of the bath-tub and was holding me in her lap, when I was suddenly attracted by the flickering shadows of leaves that danced in the sunlight on the smooth floor. I slipped from my mother's lap and almost ran toward them. The impulse gone, I fell down and cried for her to take me up in her arms.

These happy days did not last long. One brief spring, musical with the song of robin and mockingbird, one summer rich in fruit and roses, one autumn of gold and crimson sped by and left their gifts at the feet of an eager, delighted child. Then, in the dreary month of February, came the illness which closed my eyes and ears and plunged me into the unconsciousness of a new-born baby. They called it acute congestion of the stomach and brain. The doctor thought I could not live. Early one morning, however, the fever left me as suddenly and mysteriously as it had come. There was great rejoicing in the family that morning, but no one, not even the doctor, knew that I should never see or hear again.

I fancy I still have confused recollections of that illness. I especially remember the tenderness with which my mother tried to soothe me in my waking hours of fret and pain, and the agony and bewilderment with which I awoke after a tossing half sleep, and turned my eyes, so dry and hot, to the wall, away from the once-loved light, which came to me dim and yet more dim each day. But, except for these fleeting memories, if, indeed, they be memories, it all seems very unreal, like a nightmare. Gradually I got used to the silence and darkness that surrounded me and forgot that it had ever been different, until she came— my teacher—who was to set my spirit free. But during the first nineteen months of my life I had caught glimpses of broad, green fields, a luminous sky, trees and flowers which the darkness that followed could not wholly blot out. If we have once seen, "the day is ours, and what the day has shown."

. . .

I cannot recall what happened during the first months after my illness. I only know that I sat in my mother's lap or clung to her dress as she went about her household duties. My hands felt every object and observed every motion, and in this way I learned to know many things. Soon I felt the need of some communication with others and began to make crude signs. A shake of the head meant "No" and a nod, "Yes," a pull meant "Come" and a push, "Go." Was it bread that I wanted? Then I would imitate the acts of cutting the slices and buttering them.

157

If I wanted my mother to make ice-cream for dinner I made the sign for working the freezer and shivered, indicating cold. My mother, moreover, succeeded in making me understand a good deal. I always knew when she wished me to bring her something, and I would run upstairs or anywhere else she indicated. Indeed, I owe to her loving wisdom all that was bright and good in my long night.

I understood a good deal of what was going on about me. At five I learned to fold and put away the clean clothes when they were brought in from the laundry, and I distinguished my own from the rest. I knew by the way my mother and aunt dressed when they were going out, and I invariably begged to go with them. I was always sent for when there was company, and when the guests took their leave, I waved my hand to them, I think with a vague remembrance of the meaning of the gesture. One day some gentlemen called on my mother, and I felt the shutting of the front door and other sounds that indicated their arrival. On a sudden thought I ran upstairs before any one could stop me, to put on my idea of a company dress. Standing before the mirror, as I had seen others do, I anointed mine head with oil and covered my face thickly with powder. Then I pinned a veil over my head so that it covered my face and fell in folds down to my shoulders, and tied an enormous bustle round my small waist, so that it dangled behind, almost meeting the hem of my skirt. Thus attired I went down to help entertain the company.

I do not remember when I first realized that I was different from other people; but I knew it before my teacher came to me. I had noticed that my mother and my friends did not use signs as I did when they wanted anything done, but talked with their mouths. Sometimes I stood between two persons who were conversing and touched their lips. I could not understand, and was vexed. I moved my lips and gesticulated frantically without result. This made me so angry at times that I kicked and screamed until I was exhausted.

I think I knew when I was naughty, for I knew that it hurt Ella, my nurse, to kick her, and when my fit of temper was over I had a feeling akin to regret. But I cannot remember any instance in which this feeling prevented me from repeating the naughtiness when I failed to get what I wanted.

In those days a little colored girl, Martha Washington, the child of our cook, and Belle, an old setter and a great hunter in her day, were my constant companions. Martha Washington understood my signs, and I seldom had any difficulty in making her do just as I wished. It pleased me to domineer over her, and she generally submitted to my tyranny rather than risk a hand-to-hand encounter. I was strong, active, indifferent to consequences. I knew my own mind well enough and always had my own way, even if I had to fight tooth and nail for it. We spent a great deal of time in the kitchen, kneading dough balls, helping make ice-cream, grinding coffee, quarreling over the cake-bowl, and feeding the hens and turkeys that swarmed about the kitchen steps. Many of them were so tame that they would eat from my hand and let me feel them. One big gobbler snatched a tomato from me one day and ran away with it. Inspired, perhaps, by Master Gobbler's success, we carried off to the woodpile a cake which the cook had just frosted, and ate every bit of it. I was quite ill afterward, and I wonder if retribution also overtook the turkey.

The guinea-fowl likes to hide her nest in out-of-the-way places, and it was one of my greatest delights to hunt for the eggs in the long grass. I could not tell Martha Washington when I wanted to go egg-hunting, but I would double my hands and put them on the ground, which meant something round in the grass, and Martha always understood. When we were fortunate enough to find a nest I never allowed her to carry the eggs home, making her understand by emphatic signs that she might fall and break them.

The sheds where the corn was stored, the stable where the horses were kept, and the yard where the cows were milked morning and evening were unfailing sources of interest to Martha and me. The milkers would let me keep my hands on the cows while they milked, and I often got well switched by the cow for my curiosity.

The making ready for Christmas was always a delight to me. Of course I did not know what it was all about, but I enjoyed the pleasant odors that filled the house and the tidbits that were given to Martha Washington and me to keep us quiet. We were sadly in the way, but that did not interfere with our pleasure in the least. They allowed us to grind the spices, pick over the raisins and lick the stirring spoons. I hung my stocking because the others did; I cannot remember, however, that the ceremony interested me especially, nor did my curiosity cause me to wake before daylight to look for my gifts.

Martha Washington had as great a love of mischief as I. Two little children were seated on the veranda steps one hot July afternoon. One was black as ebony, with little bunches of fuzzy hair tied with shoe-strings sticking out all over her head like corkscrews. The other was white, with long golden curls. One child was six years old, the other two or three years older. The younger child was blind—that was I—and the other was Martha Washington. We were busy cutting out paper dolls; but we soon wearied of this amusement, and after cutting up our shoestrings and clipping all the leaves off the honeysuckle that were within reach, I turned my attention to Martha's corkscrews. She objected at first, but finally submitted. Thinking that turn and turn about is fair play, she seized the scissors and cut off one of my curls, and would have cut them all off but for my mother's timely interference.

Belle, our dog, my other companion, was old and lazy and liked to sleep by the open fire rather than to romp with me. I tried hard to teach her my sign language, but she was dull and inattentive. She sometimes started and quivered with excitement, then she became perfectly rigid, as dogs do when they point a bird. I did not then know why Belle acted in this way; but I knew she was not doing as I wished. This vexed me and the lesson always ended in a one-sided boxing match. Belle would get up, stretch herself lazily, give one or two contemptuous sniffs, go to the opposite side of the hearth and lie down again, and I, wearied and disappointed, went off in search of Martha.

Many incidents of those early years are fixed in my memory, isolated, but clear and distinct, making the sense of that silent, aimless, dayless life all the more intense.

One day I happened to spill water on my apron, and I spread it out to dry before the fire which was flickering on the sitting-room hearth. The apron did not dry quickly enough to suit me, so I drew nearer and threw it right over the hot ashes. The fire leaped into life; the flames encircled me so that in a moment my clothes were blazing. I made a terrified noise that brought Viny, my old nurse, to the rescue. Throwing a blanket over me, she almost suffocated me, but she put out the fire. Except for my hands and hair I was not badly burned.

About this time I found out the use of a key. One morning I locked my mother up in the pantry, where she was obliged to remain three hours, as the servants were in a detached part of the house. She kept pounding on the door, while I sat outside on the porch steps and laughed with glee as I felt the jar of the pounding. This most naughty prank of mine convinced my parents that I must be taught as soon as possible. After my teacher, Miss Sullivan, came to me, I sought an early opportunity to lock her in her room. I went upstairs with something which my mother made me understand I was to give to Miss Sullivan; but no sooner had I given it to her than I slammed the door to, locked it, and hid the key under the wardrobe in the hall. I could not be induced to tell where the key was. My father was obliged to get a ladder and take Miss Sullivan out through the window—much to my delight. Months after I produced the key.

When I was about five years old we moved from the little vine-covered house to a large new one. The family consisted of my father and mother, two older half-brothers, and, afterward, a little sister, Mildred. My earliest distinct recollection of my father is making my way through great drifts of newspapers to his side and finding him alone, holding a sheet of paper before his face. I was greatly puzzled

160

to know what he was doing. I imitated this action, even wearing his spectacles, thinking they might help solve the mystery. But I did not find out the secret for several years. Then I learned what those papers were, and that my father edited one of them.

My father was most loving and indulgent, devoted to his home, seldom leaving us, except in the hunting season. He was a great hunter, I have been told, and a celebrated shot. Next to his family he loved his dogs and gun. His hospitality was great, almost to a fault, and he seldom came home without bringing a guest. His special pride was the big garden where, it was said, he raised the finest watermelons and strawberries in the county; and to me he brought the first ripe grapes and the choicest berries. I remember his caressing touch as he led me from tree to tree, from vine to vine, and his eager delight in whatever pleased me.

He was a famous story-teller; after I had acquired language he used to spell clumsily into my hand his cleverest anecdotes, and nothing pleased him more than to have me repeat them at an opportune moment.

I was in the North, enjoying the last beautiful days of the summer of 1896, when I heard the news of my father's death. He had had a short illness, there had been a brief time of acute suffering, then all was over. This was my first great sorrow—my first personal experience with death.

How shall I write of my mother? She is so near to me that it almost seems indelicate to speak of her.

For a long time I regarded my little sister as an intruder. I knew that I had ceased to be my mother's only darling, and the thought filled me with jealousy. She sat in my mother's lap constantly, where I used to sit, and seemed to take up all her care and time. One day something happened which seemed to me to be adding insult to injury.

At that time I had a much-petted, much-abused doll, which I afterward named Nancy. She was, alas, the helpless victim of my outbursts of temper and of affection, so that she became much the worse for wear. I had dolls which talked, and cried, and opened and shut their eyes; yet I never loved one of them as I loved poor Nancy. She had a cradle, and I often spent an hour or more rocking her. I guarded both doll and cradle with the most jealous care; but once I discovered my little sister sleeping peacefully in the cradle. At this presumption on the part of one to whom as yet no tie of love bound me I grew angry. I rushed upon the cradle and overturned it, and the baby might have been killed had my mother not caught her as she fell. Thus it is that when we walk in the valley of twofold solitude we know little of the tender affections that grow out of endearing words and actions and companionship. But afterward, when I was restored to my human heritage, Mildred and I grew into each other's hearts, so that we were content to go hand-in-hand wherever caprice led us, although she could not understand my finger language, nor I her childish prattle.

. . .

Meanwhile the desire to express myself grew. The few signs I used became less and less adequate, and my failures to make myself understood were invariably followed by outbursts of passion. I felt as if invisible hands were holding me, and I made frantic efforts to free myself. I struggled—not that struggling helped matters, but the spirit of resistance was strong within me; I generally broke down in tears and physical exhaustion. If my mother happened to be near I crept into her arms, too miserable even to remember the cause of the tempest. After awhile the need of some means of communication became so urgent that these outbursts occurred daily, sometimes hourly.

My parents were deeply grieved and perplexed. We lived a long way from any school for the blind or the deaf, and it seemed unlikely that any one would come to such an out-of-the-way place as Tuscumbia to teach a child who was both deaf and blind. Indeed, my friends and relatives sometimes doubted whether I could be taught. My mother's only ray of hope came from Dickens's "American Notes." She had read his account of Laura Bridgman, and remembered vaguely that she was deaf and blind, yet had been educated. But she also remembered with a hopeless pang that Dr. Howe, who had discovered the way to teach the deaf and blind, had been dead many years. His methods had probably died with him; and if they had not, how was a little girl in a far-off town in Alabama to receive the benefit of them?

When I was about six years old, my father heard of an eminent oculist in Baltimore, who had been successful in many cases that had seemed hopeless. My parents at once determined to take me to Baltimore to see if anything could be done for my eyes.

The journey, which I remember well, was very pleasant. I made friends with many people on the train. One lady gave me a box of shells. My father made holes in these so that I could string them, and for a long time they kept me happy and contented. The conductor, too, was kind. Often when he went his rounds I clung to his coat tails while he collected and punched the tickets. His punch, with which he let me play, was a delightful toy. Curled up in a corner of the seat I amused myself for hours making funny little holes in bits of cardboard.

My aunt made me a big doll out of towels. It was the most comical, shapeless thing, this improvised doll, with no nose, mouth, ears or eyes —nothing that even the imagination of a child could convert into a face. Curiously enough, the absence of eyes struck me more than all the other defects put together. I pointed this out to everybody with provoking persistency, but no one seemed equal to the task of providing the doll with eyes. A bright idea, however, shot into my mind, and the problem was solved. I tumbled off the seat and searched under it until I found my aunt's cape, which was trimmed with large beads. I pulled two beads off and indicated to her that I wanted her to sew them on my doll. She raised my hand to her eyes in a questioning way, and I nodded energetically. The beads were sewed in the right place and I could not contain myself for joy; but immediately I lost all interest in the doll. During the whole trip I did not have one fit of temper, there were so many things to keep my mind and fingers busy.

When we arrived in Baltimore, Dr. Chisholm received us kindly: but he could do nothing. He said, however, that I could be educated, and advised my father to consult Dr. Alexander Graham Bell, of Washington, who would be able to give him information about schools and teachers of deaf or blind children. Acting on the doctor's advice, we went immediately to Washington to see Dr. Bell, my father with a sad heart and many misgivings, I wholly unconscious of his anguish, finding pleasure in the excitement of moving from place to place. Child as I was, I at once felt the tenderness and sympathy which endeared Dr. Bell to so many hearts, as his wonderful achievements enlist their admiration. He held me on his knee while I examined his watch, and he made it strike for me. He understood my signs, and I knew it and loved him at once. But I did not dream that that interview would be the door through which I should pass from darkness into light, from isolation to friendship, companionship, knowledge, love.

Dr. Bell advised my father to write to Mr. Anagnos, director of the Perkins Institution in Boston, the scene of Dr. Howe's great labors for the blind, and ask him if he had a teacher competent to begin my education. This my father did at once, and in a few weeks there came a kind letter from Mr. Anagnos with the comforting assurance that a teacher had been found. This was in the summer of 1886. But Miss Sullivan did not arrive until the following March.

Thus I came up out of Egypt and stood before Sinai, and a power divine touched my spirit and gave it sight, so that I beheld many wonders. And from the sacred mountain I heard a voice which said, "Knowledge is love and light and vision."

. . .

The most important day I remember in all my life is the one on which my teacher, Anne Mansfield Sullivan, came to me. I am filled with wonder when I consider the immeasurable contrasts between the two lives which it connects. It was the third of March, 1887, three months before I was seven years old.

On the afternoon of that eventful day, I stood on the porch, dumb, expectant. I guessed vaguely from my mother's signs and from the hurrying to and fro in the house that something unusual was about to happen, so I went to the door and waited on the steps. The afternoon sun penetrated the mass of honeysuckle that covered the porch, and fell on my upturned face. My fingers lingered almost unconsciously on the familiar leaves and blossoms which had just come forth to greet the sweet southern spring. I did not know what the future held of marvel or surprise for me. Anger and bitterness had preyed upon me continually for weeks and a deep languor had succeeded this passionate struggle.

Have you ever been at sea in a dense fog, when it seemed as if a tangible white darkness shut you in, and the great ship, tense and anxious, groped her way toward the shore with plummet and sounding-line, and you waited with beating heart for something to happen? I was like that ship before my education began, only I was without compass or sounding-line, and had no way of knowing how near the harbor was. "Light! give me light!" was the wordless cry of my soul, and the light of love shone on me in that very hour.

I felt approaching footsteps. I stretched out my hand as I supposed to my mother. Some one took it, and I was caught up and held close in the arms of her who had come to reveal all things to me, and, more than all things else, to love me.

The morning after my teacher came she led me into her room and gave me a doll. The little blind children at the Perkins Institution had sent it and Laura Bridgman had dressed it; but I did not know this until afterward. When I had played with it a little while, Miss Sullivan slowly spelled into my hand the word "d-o-l-l." I was at once interested in this finger play and tried to imitate it. When I finally succeeded in making the letters correctly I was flushed with childish pleasure and pride. Running downstairs to my mother I held up my hand and made the letters for doll. I did not know that I was spelling a word or even that words existed; I was simply making my fingers go in monkey-like imitation. In the days that followed I learned to spell in this uncomprehending way a great many words, among them *pin, hat, cup* and a few verbs like *sit, stand* and *walk*. But my teacher had been with me several weeks before I understood that everything has a name.

One day, while I was playing with my new doll, Miss Sullivan put my big rag doll into my lap also, spelled "d-o-l-l" and tried to make me understand that "d-o-l-l" applied to both. Earlier in the day we had had a tussle over the words "m-u-g" and "w-a-t-e-r." Miss Sullivan had tried to impress it upon me that "m-u-g" is *mug* and that "w-a-t-e-r" is *water*, but I persisted in confounding the two. In despair she had dropped the subject for the time, only to renew it at the first opportunity. I became impatient at her repeated attempts and, seizing the new doll, I dashed it upon the floor. I was keenly delighted when I felt the fragments of the broken doll at my feet. Neither sorrow nor regret followed my passionate outburst. I had not loved the doll. In the still, dark world in which I lived there was no strong sentiment or tenderness. I felt my teacher sweep the fragments to one side of the hearth, and I had a sense of satisfaction that the cause of my discomfort was removed. She brought me my hat, and I knew I was going out into the warm sunshine. This thought, if a wordless sensation may be called a thought, made me hop and skip with pleasure.

We walked down the path to the well-house, attracted by the fragrance of the honeysuckle with which it was covered. Some one was drawing water and my teacher placed my hand under the spout. As the cool stream gushed over one hand she spelled into the other the word *water*, first slowly, then rapidly. I stood still, my whole attention fixed upon the motions of her fingers. Suddenly I felt a misty consciousness as of something forgotten—a thrill of returning thought; and somehow the mystery of language was revealed to me. I knew then that "w-a-t-e-r" meant the wonderful cool something that was flowing over my hand. That living word awakened my soul, gave it light, hope, joy, set it free! There were barriers still, it is true, but barriers that could in time be swept away.

I left the well-house eager to learn. Everything had a name, and each name gave birth to a new thought. As we returned to the house every object which I touched seemed to quiver with life. That was because I saw everything with the strange, new sight that had come to me. On entering the door I remembered the doll I had broken. I felt my way to the hearth and picked up the pieces. I tried vainly to put them together. Then my eyes filled with tears; for I realized what I had done, and for the first time I felt repentance and sorrow.

I learned a great many new words that day. I do not remember what they all were; but I do know that *mother, father, sister, teacher* were among them—words that were to make the world blossom for me, "like Aaron's rod, with flowers." It would have been difficult to find a happier child than I was as I lay in my crib at the close of that eventful day and lived over the joys it had brought me, and for the first time longed for a new day to come.

· · ·

I had now the key to all language, and I was eager to learn to use it. Children who hear acquire language without any particular effort; the words that fall from others' lips they catch on the wing, as it were, delightedly, while the little deaf child must trap them by a slow and often painful process. But whatever the process, the result is wonderful. Gradually from naming an object we advance step by step until we have traversed the vast distance between our first stammered syllable and the sweep of thought in a line of Shakespeare.

At first, when my teacher told me about a new thing I asked very few questions. My ideas were vague, and my vocabulary was inadequate; but as my knowledge of things grew, and I learned more and more words, my field of inquiry broadened, and I would return again and again to the same subject, eager for further information. Sometimes a new word revived an image that some earlier experience had engraved on my brain.

I remember the morning that I first asked the meaning of the word, "love." This was before I knew many words. I had found a few early violets in the garden and brought them to my teacher. She tried to kiss me; but at that time I did not like to have any one kiss me except my mother. Miss Sullivan put her arm gently round me and spelled into my hand, "I love Helen."

"What is love?" I asked.

She drew me closer to her and said, "It is here," pointing to my heart, whose beats I was conscious of for the first time. Her words puzzled me very much because I did not then understand anything unless I touched it.

I smelt the violets in her hand and asked, half in words, half in signs, a question which meant, "Is love the sweetness of flowers?"

"No," said my teacher.

Again I thought. The warm sun was shining on us.

"Is this not love?" I asked, pointing in the direction from which the heat came, "Is this not love?"

It seemed to me that there could be nothing more beautiful than the sun, whose warmth makes all things grow. But Miss Sullivan shook her head, and I was greatly puzzled and disappointed. I thought it strange that my teacher could not show me love.

A day or two afterward I was stringing beads of different sizes in symmetrical groups—two large beads, three small ones, and so on. I had made many mistakes, and Miss Sullivan had pointed them out again and again with gentle patience. Finally I noticed a very obvious error in the sequence and for an instant I concentrated my attention on the lesson and tried to think how I should have arranged the beads. Miss Sullivan touched my forehead and spelled with decided emphasis, "Think."

In a flash I knew that the word was the name of the process that was going on in my head. This was my first conscious perception of an abstract idea.

For a long time I was still—I was not thinking of the beads in my lap, but trying to find a meaning for "love" in the light of this new idea. The sun had been under a cloud all day, and there had been brief showers; but suddenly the sun broke forth in all its southern splendor.

Again I asked my teacher, "Is this not love?"

"Love is something like the clouds that were in the sky before the sun came out," she replied. Then in simpler words than these, which at that time I could not have understood, she explained: "You cannot touch the clouds, you know; but you feel the rain and know how glad the flowers and the thirsty earth are to have it after a hot day. You cannot touch love either; but you feel the sweetness that it pours into everything. Without love you would not be happy or want to play."

The beautiful truth burst upon my mind—I felt that there were invisible lines stretched between my spirit and the spirits of others.

From the beginning of my education Miss Sullivan made it a practice to speak to me as she would speak to any hearing child; the only difference was that she spelled the sentences into my hand instead of speaking them. If I did not know the words and idioms necessary to express my thoughts she supplied them, even suggesting conversation when I was unable to keep up my end of the dialogue.

This process was continued for several years; for the deaf child does not learn in a month, or even in two or three years, the numberless idioms and expressions used in the simplest daily intercourse. The little hearing child learns these from constant repetition and imitation. The conversation he hears in his home stimulates his mind and suggests topics and calls forth the spontaneous expression of his own thoughts. This natural exchange of ideas is denied to the deaf child. My teacher, realizing this, determined to supply the kinds of stimulus I lacked. This she did by repeating to me as far as possible, verbatim, what she heard, and by showing me how I could take part in the conversation. But it was a long time before I ventured to take the initiative, and still longer before I could find something appropriate to say at the right time.

The deaf and the blind find it very difficult to acquire the amenities of conversation. How much more this difficulty must be augmented in the case of those who are both deaf and blind! They cannot distinguish the tone of the voice or, without assistance, go up and down the gamut of tones that give significance to words; nor can they watch the expression of the speaker's face, and a look is often the very soul of what one says.

. . .

It was my teacher's genius, her quick sympathy, her loving tact which made the first years of my education so beautiful. It was because she seized the right moment to impart knowledge that made it so pleasant and acceptable to me. She realized that a child's mind is like a shallow brook which ripples and dances merrily over the stony course of its education and reflects here a flower, there a bush, yonder a fleecy cloud; and she attempted to guide my mind on its way, knowing that like a brook it should be fed by mountain streams and hidden springs, until it broadened out into a deep river, capable of reflecting in its placid surface, billowy hills, the luminous shadows of trees and the blue heavens, as well as the sweet face of a little flower.

Any teacher can take a child to the classroom, but not every teacher can make him learn. He will not work joyously unless he feels that liberty is his, whether he is busy or at rest; he must feel the flush of victory and the heart-sinking of disappointment before he takes with a will the tasks distasteful to him and resolves to dance his way bravely through a dull routine of textbooks.

My teacher is so near to me that I scarcely think of myself apart from her. How much of my delight in all beautiful things is innate, and how much is due to her influence, I can never tell. I feel that her being is inseparable from my own, and that the footsteps of my life are in hers. All the best of me belongs to her—there is not a talent, or an aspiration or a joy in me that has not been awakened by her loving touch.

DISCUSSION AND INQUIRY

The word determination *seems to describe the central theme of this selection. Helen, deaf and blind, was determined to conquer her own frustrations by learning all she could. The Kellers were equally determined to find a teacher for Helen. Anne Sullivan displayed as much determination in teaching her pupil. It was fortunate for Helen that her parents were of some means to be able to search for and hire a tutor. The advantages of wealth cannot be overlooked.*

Helen soon realized that her ability to communicate with others was extremely limited, and she became an angry, hostile, and aggressive child. Might the anger and tantrums of a normal toddler be caused in part by the frustration of limited communication? What is meant by the term developmental lag? *Does it apply in the case of Helen Keller?*

One of problems of the parents and teachers of handicapped children is determining what behaviors are normal and what behaviors are speci-

fically related to the handicap. Helen viewed her newborn sister as an intruder and was very jealous. She also kicked the shins of one of her nursemaids with some regularity. Do these behaviors fall in the range of normalcy?

After that wonderful event in which Helen made the connection between words and their meanings, her teacher could not keep up with her thirst for knowledge. The most difficult meanings to grasp were those of abstract terms such as love and think. Do all children have difficulty in grasping the meaning of abstractions? In Piaget's theory of intellectual growth, at what stage would the comprehension of abstractions take place? Choose several abstractions and attempt to explain their meanings to a child of 6, a child of 9, and a child of 13. Describe the results.

Arthur Koestler

BIOGRAPHICAL SKETCH

*Arthur Koestler, who was born in Budapest in
1905, was resoundingly established as a political
writer with an international reputation upon the
publication of his second novel,* Darkness at
Noon. *Esteemed as a scientist and philosopher,
his essays, novels, and autobiographical books
display a broad range of knowledge and insight
into the plight of men and countries.* Arrow in
the Blue *is the first volume of a four-part autobiographical series.*

SELECTIONS FROM

ARROW IN THE BLUE

I WAS born in the eighth year of my parents' marriage, their first and
only child, when my mother was thirty-five. Everything seems to have
gone wrong with my birth: I weighed over ten pounds; my mother's
labor lasted two days and almost killed her. The whole unsavory
Freudian Olympus, from Oedipus Rex to Orestes, stood watch at my
cradle.

As might well be expected in the case of an only child born to a
woman on the threshold of middle age and frustrated by a self-
imposed exile, my mother's love was excessive, possessive, and capricious. Plagued by her recurrent migraines, she was subject to abrupt
changes of mood, from effusive tenderness to violent outbursts of
temper, so that in my earliest years I was constantly tossed about from
the emotional climate of the tropics to the arctic and back again.

From my third year onward I was given into the charge of a long
succession of foreign governesses—*Fräuleins, Mademoiselles,* and
Misses, who succeeded each other at intervals of various lengths until I
was twelve. None of them stayed longer than a year. One pretty
Fräulein vanished under mysterious circumstances because, as I learned
later, a distant cousin of mine, one of the villain's sons, got her in
the family way. An English Miss was sent packing after a fortnight

when my mother found out from a photograph in her room that she had been a horseback rider in a circus. Another must have been a sadist, for my memories of her consist only of the series of elaborate punishments she inflicted on me. All these foreign governesses of the pre-1914 era had apparently come to far-away Hungary because of some freak event or catastrophe in their lives: they were the type who, had they been born men, would have joined the Foreign Legion. I still own a photograph, dated 1910, which shows a group of these weird and forbidding females assembled with their unhappy charges in the Budapest Zoo. They looked like a group of convicts in a women's prison, uniformed in bustles, cheap fur-trimmed coats, muffs, feather boas, and feathered hats.

Second in importance, both in our household and as a neurosis-forming factor, was Bertha, the parlormaid. Her full name was Miss Bertha Búbala. She had a son called Béla Búbala who was approximately my age, born out of wedlock, and boarded out in the country. Bertha was a bony, horse-faced woman with a grudge against life which had bitten into her character and turned it acid; she was devoted to and tyrannized by my mother, and tyrannized me in turn.

I was in her care during the intervals between governesses. These periods sometimes lasted several weeks or months and, as my mother was frequently bedridden, Bertha was the one stable factor in the flux of events, and held unrestricted sway over me. The guiding rule of her reign was that the accused is guilty unless proved innocent. The memory of my early years seems to consist of a continuous series of crimes which brought in their wake an equally monotonous succession of punishments and disgraces. Though it was impossible to know beforehand whether an action constituted a crime or not, there never was any doubt in my mind about my guilt. One acquired guilt automatically, in the same way one's hands grew dirty as the day wore on: and to be in disgrace was the natural outcome of this process.

Thus the first major fact that took root in my mind was the consciousness of guilt. These roots grew quickly, silently, and greedily, like a eucalyptus tree, under the driftsand of early experience.

My mother not only tolerated but encouraged Bertha's despotism, for she saw in it the Spartan touch which would prevent me from being "spoilt." That children should not be spoilt, and that they must be ruled with an "iron rod," was a basic tenet of Victorian education in general, and of the Hitzigs in particular. This conviction led to another reversal of the legal code. In the normal walks of life everything is permitted that is not forbidden by law. In my childhood everything was forbidden that was not expressly permitted.

The home which is the stage of my early memories was a typical middle middle-class flat of the turn of the century, stuffed with plush curtains, antimacassars, tassels, fringes, lace covers, bronze nymphs, cuspidors, and Meissen stags at bay; and the inevitable polar-bear skin between the piano and the potted palm. All these objects were NOT TO BE TOUCHED; outside the nursery the flat was a forest of forbidden trees and poison-ivy.

The list of major offences included: to be noisy; to answer back; to offend Bertha; to speak in the presence of strangers without being spoken to; to omit saying "please" and "thank you very much"; to ask for a second helping without waiting for it to be offered. But these were all explicit, identifiable offences; the dark menace of life consisted in acquiring guilt without noticing it.

I was rarely chastised by my parents; punishment mostly took the form of Being In Disgrace. Disgrace started by being made to stand "in the corner," face to the wall; this was followed by "not being spoken to" for several hours and sometimes for a day or two,until the ceremony of formal forgiveness took place. It consisted in the recital of a formula of contrition and the solemn promise never to be bad again followed by the formal statement of forgiveness. There was also an intermediary state between complete disgrace and absolution. In this state one was spoken to and permitted to speak, but only about matters of strict necessity; it was, in diplomatic parlance, a condition of being recognised *de facto* but not *de jure*.

I only remember a single occasion on which I was acquitted of a charge by Bertha. This event was so exceptional that its recall, after some thirty years, is still accompanied by emotion. Noticing one day that I was in disgrace again, I asked Bertha what I had done. For there were two kinds of disgrace: one which began with an official declaration, based on a specific charge; and another, undeclared one, of which one only became aware by noticing that one was "not being spoken to." In the latter case inquiry into the nature of the crime was expected and in order. When I made my inquiry, Bertha compressed her lips and observed a few seconds of bitter silence as she usually did when spoken to by me. Then she issued the formal statement, which was both accusation and verdict: I had moved a china figurine several inches from its appointed and consecrated place on the mantelpiece. At that moment my mother chanced to enter the room and, having overheard part of Bertha's indictment, remarked offhandedly that it was she who had moved the object to its new location. The unparalleled event of her having taken my side against Bertha, and of Bertha letting me off with a grudging "watch out in the future," caused such a surge of relief and gratitude within me that I recognized its echo many years later on those blessed and rare occasions when a drill sergeant or a prison guard suddenly revealed himself in a humane light. The fact that this unexpected reprieve made so deep an impression seems to reveal an early acceptance of guilt, and of the deservedness of any punishment that might be meted out.

In all this, my father hardly enters the picture. He was too absorbed in his chimerical world of envelope-cutting machines and radio-active soap to interfere with my education. Besides, he was painfully aware of his own ignorance in matters of learning, and it must have been agony for him to cope with a precocious bookworm of a child whose questions he was unable to answer. He loved me tenderly and shyly from a distance, and later on took a naïve pride in seeing my name in print.

Our shyness was mutual; from my earliest schooldays to the end of his life we never established any intellectual contact, and never had a single conversation of an intimate nature. Nor did we ever quarrel; we liked and respected each other with the guarded reserve of strangers thrown together on a train journey. Though he was half mad in one way and I in another, we instinctively turned toward each other our saner aspects. On the whole it was a more courteous and civilized relationship than I have ever had with anybody over so long a period of time.

All my earliest memories seem to group themselves about three dominant themes: guilt, fear, and loneliness.

Of the three, fear stands out most vividly and persistently. My formative experiences seem to consist of a series of shocks.

The first that I remember occurred when I was between four and five years old. My mother dressed me with special care, and we went for an outing with my father. This in itself was unusual; but even more peculiar was the strange and apologetic manner of my parents as they led me down Andrássy Street, holding on firmly to both my hands. We were to visit Dr. Neubauer, they said; he was going to take a look at my throat and give me a cough medicine. Afterward, as a reward, I was to have some ice-cream.

I had already been taken to Dr. Neubauer the week before. He had examined me, and had then whispered with my parents in a manner which had aroused my apprehensions. This time we were not kept waiting; the doctor and his woman assistant were expecting us. Their manner was oily in a sinister way. I was made to sit in a kind of dentist's chair; then, without warning or explanation, my arms and legs were tied with leather straps to the frame of the chair. This was done with quick, deft movements by the doctor and his assistant, whose breathing was audible in the silence. Half senseless with fear, I craned my neck to look into my parents' faces, and when I saw that they, too, were frightened the bottom fell out of the world. The doctor hustled them both out of the room, fastened a metal tray beneath my chin, prised my chattering teeth apart, and forced a rubber gag between my jaws.

There followed several indelible minutes of steel instruments being thrust into the back of my mouth, of choking and vomiting blood into the tray beneath my chin; then two more attacks with the steel instruments, and more choking and blood and vomit. That is how tonsillectomies were performed, without anæsthesia, A.D. 1910, in Budapest. I don't know how other children reacted to that kind of thing. In all probability I must have been sensitivized by some earlier, forgotten traumatic experience for I reacted with a shock that was to have a lasting effect.

Those moments of utter loneliness, abandoned by my parents, in the clutches of a hostile and malign power, filled me with a kind of cosmic terror. It was as if I had fallen through a manhole, into a dark underground world of archaic brutality. Thenceforth I never lost my awareness of the existence of that second universe into which one might be transported, without warning, from one moment to the other. The world had become ambiguous, invested with a double meaning; events moved on two different planes at the same time—a visible and an invisible one—like a ship which carries its passengers on its sunny decks, while its keel ploughs through the dark phantom world beneath.

It is not unlikely that my subsequent preoccupation with physical violence, terror, and torture derives partly from this experience, and that Dr. Neubauer paved the way for my becoming a chronicler of the more repulsive aspects of our time. This was my first meeting with "Ahor"—the irrational, Archaic Horror—which subsequently played such an important part in the world around me that I designed this handy abbreviation for it. When, years later, I fell into the hands of the régime which I dreaded and detested most, and was led in handcuffs through a hostile crowd, I had the feeling that this was but a repetition of a situation I had already lived through—that of being tied, gagged, and delivered to a malign power. And when my friends perished in the clutches of Europe's various dictators, I could, in writing about them, without much effort put myself in their place.

It may seem that I am exaggerating the effects of an experience which consisted, after all, in one of the most trivial surgical interventions carried out in a somewhat clumsy and brutal manner. More precisely, it may be thought that the study of psychiatry has equipped the author with a kind of dramatic hindsight. No one can guarantee the correctness of his memory; but the fact is that for more than a year after that experience I lived in a strange fantasy world of my own,

174

playing hide-and-seek with an evil power which persecuted me. This power was personified by our gentle family physician, Dr. Szilagyi.

Shortly after the tonsil operation, I was in bed with an upset stomach. Dr. Szilagyi examined me, and after the usual consultation with my mother behind closed doors, he remarked with a jovial pat on my cheek: 'Well, well! The best thing to do seems to be to cut your tummy open with a knife.' With that he contentedly departed in his morning coat and striped trousers, carrying his black leather bag—and in it, no doubt, lay the knife.

I was old enough to understand that Dr. S.'s remark was meant to be a joke. But with the precocious child's uncanny ear for nuances, I caught an undertone which was not jocular. In fact, Dr. Szilagyi had discussed with my mother the advisability of getting rid of my appendix.

For a long time thereafter, my days became divided into dangerous and secure halves. The dangerous half was the morning, when the doctor made the rounds of his patients. The safe half was the afternoon when he received them in his consulting room. The situation was complicated by my father's habit of taking me on some mornings for rides in a hired horse-cab; while he was visiting his business acquaintances, I was left waiting in the cab. Before Dr. Szilagyi's threat had got hold of me, I used to enjoy those morning rides. Now I dreaded them because, while alone in the cab, I felt particularly vulnerable and exposed; if Dr. S. happened to pass by, he might remember his threat, snatch me out of the cab and take me with him. So on every outing I pestered my father to take a closed carriage instead of an open one. The closed carriages had little curtains which you could pull across the windows. As soon as my father got out of the cab, I pulled the curtains tight.

My obsession took even more extravagant forms. Once a fortnight I had to accompany my father to the barber's shop to have my hair cut. The shop had an ill-lit back room which was reflected in the mirror in front of the barber's chair. When the door was opened I could catch a glimpse of the back room and vaguely distinguished several strange instruments which hung from hooks. The instruments became somehow associated with the knife that was to cut my tummy open, and the barber's shop became another place of terror.

It never occurred to me to confess my fears to my parents nor to ask for their protection; and I had no playmates to confide in. Since they had sided with Dr. Neubauer and trapped and betrayed me, they could no longer be trusted; the very mention of the matter might remind them of the temporarily shelved and forgotten project and hasten its execution. I must have had at that period a greater capacity for dissimulation than in later years, for my parents never guessed what went

175

on in my private underworld. But then, most children are like that: while unable to keep a secret referring to the world of facts, they are perfect conspirators in defence of the world of their fantasies.

I cannot recall how long this attack of mild paranoia lasted; but it must have persisted for some months because in the meantime the seasons changed, and the weather became too warm for closed and curtained cabs. I was sent to school just after my sixth birthday, and by that time this particular obsession had dissolved.

A second series of upheavals, which would have affected even a normal child, occurred between my ninth and tenth year. I set fire to our home, underwent two operations, and witnessed a disastrous conflict between my parents. The last mentioned of these shocks was the worst, but for evident reasons cannot be discussed; it involved a succession of lurid and harrowing scenes which, apart from their frightening nature *per se*, taught me the anguish of split loyalties. All my experiences of that critical year were silhouetted against this background—which, for the time being, must remain a blank.

The year was 1914–15. The outbreak of the First World War had ruined my father's business in Budapest; we had given up our flat and moved to Vienna. From then on we never again had a permanent home.

The first station in our nomadic wanderings was a boarding-house called Pension Exquisite; it was, and probably still is, on the fifth floor of an old building in the heart of Vienna, facing St. Stephen's Cathedral. One afternoon, at a time when the conflict between my parents was at its height, I was left alone in our rooms in the Pension. I was depressed, and thought that the glow of some colored candles which my mother had bought would create a pleasant change of atmosphere. I lit them, put them on the window sill and, becoming absorbed in my reading, forgot all about them—until one of the candles fell into a wastepaper basket and set it alight. I tried to extinguish the flames by waving the basket in the air; and when the flames grew too hot, hurled it against the gauze curtains. The room, like every self-respecting boarding-house room of the period, was richly draped with velvet and plush, and the fire spread rapidly. I was too frightened of being punished to call for help, and tore in a frenzy at the burning curtains in the thickening smoke. The next thing I remember is waking up on the bed of Fräulein Schlesinger, a teacher of French who lived in the boarding-house and with whom I was very much in love. My parents' return coincided with the arrival of the fire brigade; some three or four rooms facing the Cathedral were gutted before the fire was brought under control. I was not punished, not even in disgrace; the heroic dimensions of my misdeed had evidently transcended the limits of any possible retribution.

Not long after this event, I was again reading in my room one lonely afternoon when suddenly there was a loud report, and a hard object hit me on the back of the head, knocking me momentarily unconscious. A big can of tinned beans which had been standing on the radiator cover had exploded, presumably under the effect of fermentation. The elaborately far-fetched nature of this further catastrophe made the inmates of the Pension Exquisite regard me as a boy endowed with somewhat awe-inspiring potentialities, and I was much sought after for table-lifting seances, a popular pastime in those days.

Next, Dr. Szilagyi's long-standing threat materialized: an abscess on the appendix got me on the danger list. Feigning sleep, I overheard a conversation from which I gathered that I was to be operated on the next day. I was taken to the hospital in an ambulance. It was a bright, clear, winter morning; as we crossed the lovely courtyard of Vienna's Imperial Palace, small flakes of snow began to whirl down from the sunny sky. Through the window next to my pillow in the ambulance, I watched hungrily the dance of the white crystals in the air, and while I did so a curious change of mood came over me. I believe that in those moments I became for the first time aware of the gentle but overwhelming impact of beauty, and of the feeling of one's own self peacefully dissolving in nature as a grain of salt dissolves in the ocean. At the beginning of the journey I had watched the faces of passers-by in the street with impotent envy; they laughed and talked, their morrow would be like yesterday; only I was set apart. Under the snowflakes in the courtyard of the palace, I no longer minded; I felt reconciled and at peace.

That journey in the ambulance was a turning-point. A few moments of terror were still to come: being wheeled into the operating theatre; and the panic of suffocation under the ether. But the phantoms of the nether-world had been made to retreat by some other power of even more mysterious origin. As it turned out, they were not routed, but merely forced to fall back to prepared positions.

I was told that the appendectomy, which had failed the first time, had to be repeated. I was now treated as a brave boy who is never afraid of the big bad wolf; but in fact I was in mortal fear of the ether mask, of a repetition of the choking agony before going under. The old enemy, Ahor, had appeared in a new guise. Then, one day, while reading the *Tales of Munchausen,* I had an inspiration. The chapter I was reading was the delightful story of the boastful Baron falling into a bog and sinking deeper and deeper. When he has sunk down to his chin, and his remaining minutes seem to be counted, he saves himself by the simple expedient of grabbing his own hair and pulling himself out.

I was so delighted with the Baron's escape that I laughed aloud—

and in that same instant found the solution to the problem which had been haunting me. I was going to pull myself out of the bog of my fears by holding the ether mask myself over my face until I passed out. In this way I would feel that I was in control of the situation, and that the terrible moment of helplessness would not recur.

I mentioned the idea to my mother who understood instinctively, and induced the surgeon to satisfy my whim. Although the operation was too long delayed and I again had to be rushed to hospital in the same ambulance, along the same road, I felt no fear when I put the mask on my face under the encouraging grin of the anæsthetist.

Since that episode I have learned to outwit my obsessions and anxieties—or at least to come to a kind of *modus vivendi* with them. To arrive at an amicable arrangement with one's neuroses sounds like a contradiction in terms—yet I believe that it can be achieved, provided one accepts one's complexes and treats them with respectful courtesy, as it were, instead of fighting them and denying their existence. It is my profound belief that man has the power to pull himself by his own hair out of the mire. The Baron in the Bog, abbreviated "Babo," conqueror of "Ahor," has become for me both a symbol and a profession of faith.

The closing episode of this education by shock occurred when I was thirteen. I had become an addict of the science-fantasies of Jules Verne. While reading a scene from *A Tour of the Moon*, a long forgotten memory of my earliest days suddenly emerged with extraordinary vividness in my mind; and this was followed by an equally extraordinary sense of quietude and relief.

The content of the chapter I was reading is as follows: As the cannon-ball carrying the explorers toward the moon travels through space, one of the animals aboard, a little fox-terrier, dies. After some hesitation the explorers decide to throw the corpse out through the airtight hatch. This is done; and then the passengers, looking through the thick glass window, realise to their horror that the body of the dog is flying on a course parallel to their own through space. They thought it would drop away, but the carcass shares the momentum of the cannon-ball, just as an object thrown from the window of a moving railway carriage shares the momentum of the train; and outside the earth's atmosphere there is no friction to act as a brake. Gradually the carcass increases its distance from the window, impelled by the persistence of the gentle thrust which had sent it through the hatch; but though slowly receding, it maintains its parallel speed and keeps abreast of the window. The dead fox-terrier has become a planet or a meteor which will continue to travel in its dark elliptic orbit round the earth through eternity.

Reading this scene, it occurred to me that perhaps one day criminals, instead of being hanged or electrocuted, might be pushed out into space from rocket-ships. The cosmic temperature of absolute zero would for ever preserve their bodies from decay. To have these astral corpses floating around the earth as permanent satellites might be inconvenient and give rise to various superstitions, but for this there was an easy remedy: at the moment of the expulsion, one had only to steer the rocket in the open orbit of a parabola instead of the closed orbit of an ellipse. The corpse would then follow the course not of planets but of comets: perform one semicircular sweep round the sun and then recede deeper and deeper into interstellar space, past the fixed stars and the spiral nebulae, into infinity.

I considered this method quite practicable not only for executions but for disposing of the dead in general. After all, it had become a practice to cremate them and strew their ashes to the winds. To release the dead from their bondage to the earth and send them off on their eternal journey through space, transformed into silent comets with hands folded on their breasts, was a thought full of peace and consolation, and my nearest approach to the idea of immortality; it made of death an enviable adventure. The comfort was not so much in the idea of conserving the body, afloat in the cosmic refrigerator, but in the fact that, however many eons of light-years they travelled along their parabola, they could never *fall out* of this world.

It was during this reverie that the long-buried memory slipped into my consciousness as unobtrusively as if it had always been there. It was the memory of a scene that had taken place—though this may seem hard to believe—when I was a little over two years old. I had been locked up in the unlighted bathroom in punishment for some offence. I was in the throes of a wild panicky fear that I would have to stay for ever in the dark and would never see my mother again, nor the light of day, nor anything else. Then there was a blank in my memory, or rather a black patch, like the sudden darkness on the screen when the film breaks in the projecting room. Next I remembered crashing head-foremost against the iron support under the washbasin; this was followed by a sudden flood of light as my mother flung open the door and rushed to the rescue, while I howled in an ecstasy of relief, self-pity, and love. I also remembered having registered with satisfaction her worried and self-reproachful antics; and the dim, nascent cloud of a thought, which in coherent language would amount to: "That will teach her!"

That was the scene which came back to me so unexpectedly when, while dreaming of space-ships and comets, I discovered that, alive or dead, one cannot fall out of this world. The memory had lost its poisoned sting, the primeval horror of the dark prison. It seems to me that since then I have been more or less free of the fear of death—

though not of the fear of the act of dying, with its painful and degrading paraphernalia. As I grow older, this latter fear increases, like the apprehension of a painful operation to which one submits only reluctantly—though one knows that it is for one's good.

~~~~~~

DISCUSSION AND INQUIRY

Born of older parents, Arthur was an only child who felt that the conditions surrounding his birth inevitably led to his mother's love being excessive, possessive, and capricious. Is this always true for children born of older parents? William Allen White felt it inevitable that he would be spoiled because he, too, was an only child of older parents. (See the selection by William Allen White.) In Arthur's case, mother and despotic Bertha both ascribed to "rule by the iron rod" to ensure that he would not be "spoiled." As he describes himself in this selection, would you say they were successful in avoiding the "spoiled child syndrome?" In their effort to avoid spoiling Arthur, they created an environment for him that induced fear and guilt. Is this the only alternative to spoiling? Compare the outcomes of William Allen White's upbringing to that of Koestler's. What are the conditions conducive to spoiling? What is your definition of a spoiled child? Poll some of your friends to see what this bandied-about term means to them. Is there general agreement on the definition of "spoiled child?"

The evil power created by Koestler, which he named Ahor, became a strong force in his life. Fearful fantasies emerged through the use of this demon; and young Koestler was unwilling to discuss this with any adult. Would it have helped if the author had playmates or several siblings to whom he could have confided his fears? Are children embarrassed to reveal fantasies to adults for fear of rejection? Certainly Koestler's fear of the tonsillectomy was legitimate. How could this experience have been made to be less frighten-

ing? Part of the basis of fear itself in both children and adults is the feeling of a lack of control over the situation. Young Koestler evidently perceived this notion as evidenced by his request to handle the ether mask during the second appendectomy. What other kinds of control might be put in the hands of children to reduce the common fears they face? What were some of your childhood fears, and how did you cope with them? Koestler invented Babo to conquer Ahor. Did you create an imaginary character to help cope with some of your fears?

Elmer Verner McCollum

BIOGRAPHICAL SKETCH

Elmer Verner McCollum, an eminent scientist who is widely known for his discoveries and writings on nutrition, was born on a Kansas farm in 1879. After completing undergraduate study at the University of Kansas and graduate study at Yale University, Dr. McCollum accepted a teaching position at Yale. His pioneering research on the chemistry of foods attracted wide attention and resulted in his appointment to the faculty of Johns Hopkins University. His widespread influence in the field of nutrition is illustrated by the way his writings have shaped courses in nutrition and meal planning. Among those writings, along with scores of contributions to periodicals, are The Newer Knowledge of Nutrition *and* A History of Nutrition.

SELECTIONS FROM

FROM KANSAS FARM BOY TO SCIENTIST

EARLY in the morning of March 3, 1879, Mother was delivered of her first son and fourth child, by Aunt Sarah Ramsey, who accommodated neighbors needing the service of a midwife and whom I remember seeing on several occasions in my childhood. She was a solemn-looking woman with a quiet voice and dignified manner. On Sundays she always wore a black dress. She enjoyed the distinction of being called "Aunt Sarah" by all who knew her. When her duties were performed, Father took her home in the farm wagon.

March was a busy month for farmers, and as soon as she was up and around Mother put me in the care of my eldest sister, Effie, then ten years old, who was required to assist in every way possible about the house and farmyard. I was a new and demanding obligation and a great

182

nuisance to her. Years later she told me that in my infancy she hated me.

Mother busied herself with her garden, chickens, and dairy cows, and did a minimum of housekeeping beyond preparing meals for the family. Indeed there was little incentive for housekeeping in the crowded home in which she lived.

I was reported to have started well as to growth and comfort, but before many months I had an experience which might well have cost me my life. When I was seven months old Mother found herself pregnant and was faced with a perplexing problem. She believed that she should wean me early and conserve her strength for the next baby, Burton, my only brother and her last child. The cause of her concern was how to feed me. It was the firm belief among women in that period that a baby fed cow's milk would surely die. This belief was based on sound observation, but there was no known explanation for it. Bottle-fed babies generally developed severe gastrointestinal infection, which was in many instances fatal. Had anyone at that period understood the simplest principles of hygiene the cause would have been apparent to any intelligent observer. Although in summer, when they were in pasture, cows were clean, they were attended by swarms of flies. The flies explored milk pails inside and out. To remove visible contaminants, we poured freshly drawn milk through a cloth strainer, which was rinsed after use but was never sterilized by boiling water. It was hung to dry and was immediately covered with flies in summer. They fed on the milk residues until the cloth became dry, and the odor of food attracted flies all through the day. They deposited numerous specks, or droppings, which adhered to the cloth. At the next milking the newly drawn milk was poured through this unclean cloth and became heavily seeded with microorganisms. Since flies on the farm had access to both human and animal excreta, and to utensils and the cloth strainer, scarcely any milk was fit to be fed to an infant, especially in the warm months.

Mother's solution of the problem of feeding me after weaning did credit to her intelligence. She decided to give me milk to which mashed potato was added, the mixture then being boiled to make a soup. For variety and added palatability she also gave me chicken broth daily. On this diet I should probably have grown satisfactorily except for the fact that everything I ate had been thoroughly heated. Twenty-eight years after I was born two Norwegian investigators, Holst and Froelich, discovered that any thoroughly dry or any heated diet would induce scurvy in guinea pigs. Mother anticipated them, using a human subject. She knew nothing of this disease, not even its name, even in her old age.

Between 1905 and 1938 I visited Mother each summer in Lawrence,

Kansas. I repeatedly asked her to tell of her experiences with me as an infant and she never varied in her account of my illness. She said that when I was about ten months old, brown spots appeared in many places on my skin and that my joints became swollen and so sensitive that I screamed when handled. I had swollen and bleeding gums. Mother and her friends had no idea what ailed me. She took me to a Dr. Elder, whose son was my uncle by marriage to a sister of Mother's. He must have had about the minimum of medical education for even a country doctor of that period. He advised her that my trouble arose from inability to erupt my teeth, and thereupon assisted nature by cutting into the gum ridges with a small pocket knife which he removed from his pocket and did not attempt to clean. He cut all around both the upper and lower arches and left me in a dreadful condition. Mother related that she doubted this treatment benefited me, because my condition continued to grow steadily worse.

That I was suffering from scurvy is shown by the event which brought about my rapid recovery. We had an apple orchard and every year kept apples through the winter by making a conical pile of them on coarse grass, covering them with dry grass and shoveling earth on the grass-covered cone to prevent the fruit from freezing. When I was about one year old Mother peeled apples which had been kept over winter in this manner, and by chance she held me on her lap while I puled in misery. She had despaired of my survival. By chance she sought to pacify me by giving me the apple scrapings, and she observed that I seemed to like them. Mother often, throughout her life, said she believed that what the appetite called for the system needed, and from this clue she fed me apple scrapings freely every day from then on. She said that I was noticeably improved within two or three days, and continued to get better steadily. Spring was at hand, and soon she gave me other uncooked vegetable foods. Wild strawberries were abundant on the open prairie, and I was given the juice of these by early May. My recovery was uneventful.

I do not know whether the cutting of my gums was deep enough to injure the tooth buds, or whether they were damaged by hemorrhage in their vicinity owing to capillary fragility. Both my temporary and permanent teeth were of poor quality and began early to decay. Almost from the time I can first remember I had toothache. I discovered that the pain was lessened by keeping cold water in my mouth. Many hours I spent in applying cold water to an aching tooth by filling and emptying my mouth as the water became warm. I used water fresh from the well. Someone told Mother that application of a clove to the cavity of an aching tooth was a good remedy for toothache, and so she kept a supply for my use. Oil of cloves contains eugenol, an anesthetic. Its application as a crushed clove freed me from pain.

When I was about ten years old, Dr. Logan Cox began to extract my aching teeth. No money was spent on dental work for me until I was thirteen years old, when Mother had a dentist in Fort Scott fill with gold the cavities on the margins of my upper central incisors, for the sake of my appearance. Nothing further was done to save my teeth until I was in high school and earned the money myself to have a dentist place amalgam fillings in several decayed teeth.

From my earliest recollections I suffered from frequent colds and respiratory infections which Mother called croup, and from time to time had severe throat infections. I had from early childhood adenoids and large inflamed tonsils, which I could see in the mirror.

Mother's favorite remedy for chest trouble was rubbing on goose grease. She always kept a jar of this and with age it became highly rancid. She believed that high odor was one of its virtues and did not impair its remedial value. Many times in winter I was sent to school smelling so high that it was a subject for remark among the children with whom I was associated. Her remedy for sore throat was application to my neck of a slice of fat pork dusted with black pepper. It was kept in place by wrapping my neck in an old woolen stocking. Naturally I was reluctant to go to school with such social disabilities, for they were laughed at by the children; and I was the object of many an unfeeling witticism which humiliated me. But Mother had no fear of breaking the morale of a child by giving it an inferiority complex. There was never any doubt about the soundness of her judgment. She would listen to no protests from me, but commanded me to go along to school and bear up under her therapeutic measures. My embarrassment was somewhat softened by the circumstance that some children in school wore "stink-bags" suspended about their necks to ward off disease. These were filled with medicines, prominent among which was asafetida. The belief that these would keep the Devil away was attractive but is now not accepted by many. Some of our itinerant farmhands wore these bags, and I had assurances from them that they were of value in warding off disease.

That my general health was fairly good is attested by daguerreotypes of me at ages four and eight years. My brother and I were generally racing about the farm, from time to time wrestling and pummeling each other to settle our differences; so it is evident that I had considerable vitality.

Among my earliest recollections was the fear that Burt and I suffered when left alone in the house of evenings in bad weather while other members of the family were out doing the milking and caring for the horses, hogs, and poultry. There was nothing else to do with us. As it grew dark we became alarmed from a sense of loneliness and abandonment, and were sometimes in tears when the first member of the family

185

finished work and came to the house and lit the kerosene lamp. In warm dry weather, from infancy, we tagged along with the grownups to the barnyard at chore time and watched their activities. We often became sleepy and were aroused and piloted, half awake, and put to bed. Since we went barefoot we had to submit to the ordeal of having our feet washed in cold water just drawn up from the well.

When I was about six years old my brother and I had an experience that made us fear darkness and imps lurking there. It came about through my sisters reading ghost stories published in the Toledo *Blade*, a weekly newspaper to which Father subscribed. The stories told of spooks and spoopendykes. Sister Harriet, or Hattie, as she was called in the family, was five years older than I. She either read the stories or heard them related by my older sisters and found that she could magnify herself in our eyes by narrating as her own the experiences described. She told how she had seen, after nightfall, strange creatures of darkness appear from various places about the farmyard and even in the house. She had not been afraid of the ghosts, spooks, and spoopendykes, she said, and had stood up to them and they had disappeared.

The bedroom on the second floor of our house had a small door in the wall, large enough for a man to creep through into the low attic over the kitchen in case of fire. Hattie told of seeing goblins emerge from that door at night. These stories she related to us as we accompanied her on errands, like bringing in the cows from pasture, and never before other members of the family. She told us not to say anything to Mother about these adventures with unearthly creatures, since it would worry her. The information was given us in confidence and we were to keep it secret. We did as we were told, but we became afraid of the dark, expecting to be momentarily pounced upon by spooks. For some months we insisted that a lighted lantern be left in our bedroom as a protection. Had Mother known what sister Hattie had told us, she would have been made sorry for her misdeeds. Eventually we forgot about spooks. It seems strange that we did not tell Mother the whole story.

Our farm was a wonderful place for small boys to learn by observation. Among my earliest recollections was toddling behind Mother as she looked after brooding hens. Each hen was kept in a coop while she incubated her clutch of eggs, to secure her against molestation. Every morning Mother took the hen off her nest to eat and drink. While the hen scolded, ate, and sipped water, Mother placed the eggs for a short time in a pail of water to restore moisture lost by evaporation. I am not certain that this was of advantage, but she believed eggs tended to dry out, and that they hatched better if wet daily. When the incubation period terminated she showed us eggs with the chick's beak protruding through the shell. Occasionally we saw a chick which, after breaking the shell with its beak, had rested for a time and then by a supreme effort broke the shell into approximately equal halves and freed itself. We became familiar with the manner in which the mother hen cared for her brood after they were off the nest. We were never permitted to handle young chicks.

My brother and I watched the operations of preparing the soil, planting seeds, the emergence of the young plants and the later stages of growth. We witnessed the methods of tillage. While still small, we were required to pull and shell peas and beans and to help prepare other garden vegetables for cooking.

Father had built a stone ice-house at a time before my memories begin. Each winter it was filled with ice from a pond or the small river near our farm. The ice cakes were packed in sawdust. We had only enough ice for cooling drinking water, and for making ice cream on occasions when we had company. For cooling milk we let the deep tin cans down a cistern to half immersion in the water, which was in summer cool only by comparison with the high temperature of the atmosphere.

At evening Mother would turn the windlass to wind the ropes to which the cans were attached, and bring them up. These deep cans had a layer of cream about five inches thick which she skimmed for making butter. Burt and I toddled after her from infancy to watch this operation. It was her custom to give each of us a spoon and let us eat clabber after the cream was taken off. All my life I have regarded sour milk as one of the most appetizing of foods.

We observed the churning operation in which small particles of butter first became visible, and then coalesced into a mass of butter; saw it washed and molded into one-pound cakes with a decorative sculptured sheaf of wheat on top. We were interested in Mother's account of why she kneaded yeast into bread dough; saw the rising process and the emergence from the oven of baked loaves or biscuits. We asked many questions about "why" in all the familiar operations of the kitchen.

Out of doors we watched the currying and harnessing of horses and the mending of farm implements, the shelling of corn, grinding of sickles of mowers and reapers, axes, scythes, and corn knives. Father was handy at any kind of cobbling and make-do repair work. He did this to save time, since the blacksmith shop was in the village of Redfield, three miles away, and the trip on horseback or by wagon was too time-consuming to be made often. I believe that observation of so many kinds of operations, including the care of animals and plants, and being required at an early age to participate in the work of the farmyard, was much more valuable to me than playing with mechanical toys as is the rule today in cities. The urban child scarcely ever sees an adult at work requiring skill, and rarely has opportunity to make things for himself.

As very small boys Burt and I were curious about what kind of animals lived in the different-sized holes which we saw here and there on the farm or on the open prairie. Our first experiment to find an answer was made by placing a box over the hole and then pouring water in it until its occupant was forced to come out and enter our trap. It was a pocket gopher. After inspecting him for a time, we set him free.

In summer we frequently found creatures which interested us. Among these were bugs, worms, and flying insects. On several occasions we determined to follow a tumblebug as it rolled its inch-thick ball of cow-dung, using its hind feet for pushing and proceeding backward. From time to time it would leave the sphere and run about to get its bearings, then start again pushing its burden with its head pointing away from the ball. We never found where its journey ended, for its progress was slow, and the distance of its journey too long for us to keep watch over it. We examined with curiosity creatures turned up by the plow, but nobody could answer any of our questions about them or tell us their names.

There were two cow-ponds in our pastures, and these afforded us never-failing interest because of the abundance and variety of plant and animal life. Our chief interest was in frogs of several kinds, and at least two kinds of insects which could walk on water. Turtles' noses were visible here and there at the surface, and after breathing for a time they submerged. Wasps came to secure mud for nest-building; birds came to drink, and there was usually a water snake somewhere about the pond. We were alert and enthusiastic observers of pond life and would have welcomed instruction from someone versed in natural history, but we knew no one who had any scientific knowledge of the wild creatures we saw.

When we were little boys we had no picture-books, and nobody taught us anything about wildlife. We were never told stories, except sister Hattie's experiences with ghosts. No effort was made to teach us to read until we were sent to school at five years of age. Until I was six years old, brother Burt was almost my only companion. We saw for short periods children of neighbors when they came to visit us, or when Mother visited her friends. When we were out of doors in good weather we never had a dull moment. In spring and summer we explored the orchard, the hedgerows, and pastures, looking for birds' nests. When we found one we visited it frequently and kept watch over the progress of its owners in egg-laying and incubating, and later the feeding of the young.

When I was five and a half years old my three sisters took me with them to Pleasant Hill School, two miles distant. Not infrequently the roads were all but impassable after rains, and dragging me along the roadside on the grassy margins was a difficult task. Mud stuck to our shoes, and picked up long grass stems which acted as a binder, so that the accumulation of mud in matted grass grew rapidly in weight and dimensions. Frequently it was necessary to pause at a fence post to mechanically disengage the mass and get a fresh start. Often, in wet weather, I was worn out when we reached the schoolhouse.

The only incident that lives in my memory of my first year in district school made a deep and lasting impression on me. A girl of my age and I were the only pupils of what was called the chart class. The chart had leaves a yard square, which were turned over backward as each leaf's lesson was completed. On each leaf were large letters of the alphabet, and pictures to assist the little learner. *A* was shown with an axe, *B* with a box, *C* with a cat, etc. Our teacher, a girl of perhaps eighteen years, told the little girl to say "ox," but she sulked and remained silent. She refused obstinately to respond to teacher's commands, whereupon teacher resorted first to threats, then to thrashing her with a little switch of Osage orange. The child was in hysterics and would not say the required word. The teacher kept flailing her, but did not succeed in humbling her. In my memory is the record that this terrifying scene continued through the greater part of the afternoon session, but I was so frightened and resentful that memory may be distorted. None of the older children said a word in protest to the disgraceful exhibition. I never heard that the parents objected to the cruel treatment of their child.

The following summer a new schoolhouse was built one mile north of our house. It was a one-room house, with desk seats for perhaps thirty children. I believe there were never more than twenty children attending. It was heated by a big coal-burning Round Oak stove. My sister Effie, then about seventeen years old, was the first teacher. At about fifteen she had taken a training course at what was called the Normal School, in Fort Scott. She had been granted a teacher's certificate when not quite sixteen and had already taught one winter at Turkey Creek School, seven miles west of our home.

Although Mother had attended school only two winters she had given much care to the early education of her eldest daughter. Effie taught but one year in our new school, where I was a pupil until the age of seventeen. During the last five years it was necessary for me to enter school late and leave early to help with the farm work in autumn and spring because of Father's illness.

Mother was so busily occupied with household duties and the care of poultry, butter-making, and the garden, that she had no spare time and never attempted to teach her sons at home, as she had done with

189

her first child. Mother never petted us, but never failed to pause in her work to praise us for bringing her flowers, strawberries we picked on the prairie, a nice apple, or other gifts which we thought she would like. We had deep affection for her and appreciated her compliments. When she addressed us it was generally as a command, always in a firm tone, to keep away from horses' heels, out of the way of the bull, and away from sows with young pigs. Many of her commands were for keeping us out of danger, but as soon as we could perform useful services, we were commanded to carry corncobs to the kitchen to feed the stove, gather wild strawberries in spring, and search the farmyard for eggs. Hens had ideas of their own about desirable nesting places, so that one might find an egg in a manger, the hayloft, or about a haystack, and such places had to be searched.

Not infrequently we did things which were forbidden. Mother's method of punishment was to call us to her and reprimand us with severe looks and accusation of disobedience. She then told us to stand in a corner, face the wall, and reflect on how naughty we had been. After perhaps ten minutes she would call us to her and ask if we were sorry for what we had done. We always were sorry. She then asked whether, if she let us off this time, we would never do such a thing again. We always promised, and were released. We walked slowly and humbly a few steps from the door and then skipped away entirely free from unpleasant emotion and entered again upon the pursuit of happiness.

If our offense was great she would send us to a clump of shrub not far from the house to fetch switches for her use in whipping us. The shrub had red bark. I have never seen it growing elsewhere. It seemed designed by nature for chastising small boys. When each delivered a switch to Mother, she stood us in the corner for a few minutes, then called us to her, had us put our toes even with a crack in the floor and lectured us severely for our misdeed, while holding the switch threateningly. After we had promised to behave better she released us, and our spirits rose like a thermometer taken out of ice water in summer. Off we went, bent upon our own designs for entertainment.

Mother never struck us with the switch, nor spanked us with the open hand. For small offenses she would sometimes, especially when we were very little boys, hold her hands over her face and pretend to weep. We could never witness this scene without melting into tears. We promised to be good, her face brightened into smiles with astonishing promptness, and the incident was soon forgotten.

Mother had great fear of tornadoes, and when weather conditions favored this type of storm she looked worried and spoke of the danger that seemed imminent. We felt deep concern for her at such times, and our spirit for play was dampened until she appeared more cheerful.

I was extremely fortunate in having such a superior brother as my constant companion throughout the first twelve years of my life. At about age seven or eight we began to associate somewhat with near-neighbor children, but we were generally alone together, exploring our surroundings. I cannot imagine what my thoughts and interests would have been had I not had him for a companion to play with and to develop small-boy plans for doing things to make life more interesting. I believe we were better off alone than we would have been with more group associations with boys near our ages, and I believe that the farm afforded an almost ideal environment for us to awaken our mental faculties and to enjoy life. The few boys we associated with at intervals were all less imaginative and less observant than we. When we had played hide-and-seek, or a "one-eyed cat" ball game or mumblety-peg or marbles with neighbor boys, or boys we saw less frequently as the result of neighborly visiting, we were, as I remember, always a little happier when the visitors left and we were again on the run like a pair of twins.

. . .

The only playthings Mother ever bought us were a little red wagon, an occasional pocketknife, and harmonicas. All other things which we became interested in for utility or amusement we fabricated ourselves. At a neighbor's we saw a "figure-four" box-trap for catching rabbits, and forthwith made several of them and tried them out. The trap consisted of three sticks, accurately notched so that when fitted together, one standing upright, one horizontally, and the third at a forty-five degree angle to both the others, they formed a stable support for one edge of a box. On the end of the horizontal stick we impaled part of an ear of corn for bait. When a rabbit found the bait and nibbled it the sticks were dislodged from their notches and the box fell over the rabbit, confining it until we visited the trap and captured it. The idea was sound, but the abundance of food in the fields made this type of trap of little value, since rabbits found plenty to eat without searching a trap.

We designed a treadle trap, which was operated by the rabbit following a trail of corn grains leading over a nearly balanced board. When it stepped beyond the fulcrum the treadle tipped, opening the way into the boxlike trap and bringing to view more corn. Another step and the treadle tipped so as to close the opening and deliver the rabbit into the box. But we learned that baited traps were of value only when deep snow or sleet covered the fields and prevented animals from finding food readily.

We had much better success by nailing together four boards so as to form a hollow-log structure, closing one end except for a small hole to admit light. We laid this beside an Osage orange hedge where rabbits were sheltered from sight, and then drove them out of their hiding

191

places. They would run along the hedge and dart in again and again, but from time to time one would see the dark entrance to our trap and dart into it for shelter. We then pulled him out and marched straight to the house to show our prize to Mother and enjoy her praise of our success.

By removing the pith from foot-long stems of elder and fitting them with ramrods we made popguns, which operated with wads of wet paper and made entertaining pops. We designed a fly-gun with a short strong wooden bow which, when released, propelled a short blunt-headed arrow at high velocity. With this we could shoot flies sitting on a wall at a distance of about one foot. We made tops, bows and arrows, crossbows, kites, and slingshots of the type with which David smote Goliath. With these we could hurl a pebble at least twice as far as we could with the arm. We made sleds, wooden mallets for hulling walnuts, a net-weaving set consisting of a round stick on which we tied twine to form meshes, and a shuttle to carry the twine through the loop in tying the knot. With this outfit we made small seines and with them scooped minnows from shallow water in cow-ponds. We once constructed a fiddle, but the tone was so disappointing that we gave up further efforts in that direction.

As small boys Burt and I were almost exclusively interested in birds and mammals, especially in hunting and trapping game creatures. We devoted very little time to considering the lilies of the field. We examined rather minutely the structures which made up flowers of many kinds which were abundant on the prairie. We knew the names of a few weeds, given them by farmers.

With each year of advance in age we were assigned new work and responsibility. At six or seven we were often annoyed at being called from our play or construction enterprises to turn the grindstone for sharpening mower sickles, axes, corn knives, or scythes; or to churn cream, pick beans or peas or other garden products, and prepare them for cooking. Sometimes Mother would call us loudly from the kitchen door and when we arrived would direct us to catch two roosters which were fighting and pen them up to stop their mutilating each other. In a day or two they forgot their feud and were released.

Churning cream was a laborious task for small boys. Cream does not soon turn to butter and buttermilk unless it is of proper acidity and temperature. Since Mother had no better way to test acidity and temperature than by taste and touch, sometimes churning required an hour or more of turning the crank. I recall one occasion when we were worn and tired before the butter would "come," and Burt remarked that churning was "tedisum."

As we grew stronger we were assigned such tasks as cutting weeds,

192

hoeing the garden, carrying jugs of water to men working in the fields, and feeding skim milk to calves. While we were small boys we always worked together, keeping up conversation about making things we wanted and about plans for hunting and fishing. We often stood and talked when we were supposed to be at work. On many occasions Mother stepped out of the house to call to us to stop talking and get on with the job. We always obeyed without resentment, but soon slackened our efforts and started talking again.

Somehow we came into possession of a catalog of a sporting goods house in Kansas City. The pictures of guns, ammunition, fishing tackle, games, especially baseball equipment, and magic lanterns fired our imaginations and made us long to possess these attractive articles. But we had no money with which to buy them and often discussed ways of obtaining some. Opportunity came when our parents offered to pay us a bounty for killing rats. We were promised five cents for each rat killed.

Our farmyard was at that time badly infested with them. They killed young chickens, gnawed holes in corncribs and bins in the barn, and ate and soiled much grain. Our first efforts at rat-catching were directed to digging them out of their burrows, or with the aid of Fanny, a small terrier given us by a neighbor, scaring them out of their shelters under outbuildings and trying to dispatch them with sticks. The results were disheartening, because much effort yielded few rats. We set to thinking of ways to increase our efficiency and came up with a plan which promised opulence for little work.

It was in summer, and the cows, which were brought morning and evening to the barnyard for milking, spent days and nights in pasture. Absence of animals, except the work horses in the barn, meant a dearth of scattered food about the barn, and the rat population ran short of food, at other seasons plentiful. In the barn were two large bins in which Father stored bran and shorts that he brought home in the wagon on his trips to Fort Scott. The rats were eating this dry feed, which when chewed became sticky and gummed up their mouths. Their only other source of food was eggs and young chickens.

Burt and I reasoned that we might entice the rats into a hollow-log type of trap similar to that we had used to catch rabbits, by wetting the mill-feed to make it more acceptable and putting it into the trap. We constructed such a trap, closed at one end by crossed wires, but left it open at the other end so that light could shine through. We equipped the open end with a sliding board that fitted between strips of wood like the endgate of a wagon box. To this board we attached a string, which we carried to the ceiling, where it passed through a ring and thence to the barn door. By pulling the string we could raise the gate of the trap. The string outside the barn door was wound around a nail and tied so as to keep the gate suspended.

We wet bran and laid it in a thin line on the barn floor leading to the openings of the trap, into which we put a generous quantity of the wet food. At twilight many rats emerged from their hiding places and quickly learned that a fine evening meal awaited them. After training them through three evenings we were ready to make the first catch. Each evening we had listened outside the barn door and could hear rats inside the long box squealing and quarreling over the feast. Now when sounds indicated that rats were crowding each other inside, we unwound the cord and let down the endgate. We hurried in and placed the end of the trap in a large grain bag, drew out the board closing the trap, and by lifting the opposite end poured the rats into the bag and dispatched them, by the stone-age-man method.

Our first catch was forty-two rats. We at once reset the trap and within half an hour sprang it again. A third catch was made that evening, the total number of rats captured and killed being sixty-three. It was all the work of little more than an hour. We proudly carried our sorry-looking harvest to the house to exhibit it to our parents and sisters, and in high spirits went to bed. The next morning we were much disappointed when Mother told us that we were to receive only one cent for each rat we had caught. I still marvel that my parents did not hesitate to go back on the agreement they had made with us. However, we soon forgave and forgot this breach of promise. On succeeding nights we practically rid the premises of rats and turned to other enterprises.

We next laid plans for earning money by selling garden vegetables at a stone quarry a mile and a half from our house. We continued this through three summers. The quarry was worked by a small colony of German immigrants; some of them lived in shanties and others were housed in a long barrack-like house owned by the foreman, George Bowman, who with his wife and two of her sisters kept a boarding house. Burt and I made many trips there on foot carrying a bushel basket of lettuce, string beans, radishes, green peas, and other vegetables, which we sold to the Bowmans. Knowing that we had no other customers, they cheated us badly. Unaware of values, we were satisfied with as little as thirty to fifty cents for our entire load. This money we were permitted to spend as we wished. It went for fishing tackle, bamboo rods, knives, and a few other things. In an entire summer we could earn no more than five or six dollars in this way.

We met with other disappointments in expectation of making money by caring for runty pigs. Each spring our sows produced about a hundred young. After weaning, these shoats were kept on green pasture during the day. Morning and evening they were fed corn in the barnyard lot, together with what we called slop. This consisted of water, bran, shorts, skim milk, and buttermilk. This mixture we poured into the end of a long trough while pigs crowded each other on both sides competing lustily for the drink as it flowed along. Those nearest the source of supply had the advantage over those further along, and since the stream rapidly thinned as mouths drank it in, the pigs near the lower end of the trough got little or no slop. A few weak ones were entirely crowded away. Since the milk was an important supplement for the corn, these pigs did not grow and soon exhibited runtiness.

Several summers Burt and I were told that if we would take out the runts from the pen and feed them separately we might have them for our own. This we did, and with plenty of food and no competition they grew rapidly and became salable porkers by the time the other hogs were ready to go to market. But when we asked for the money which they brought Mother said she would buy us new clothes instead of giving us the cash. We felt cheated but took our disappointment without remonstrating. It was a great mistake, but we did not harbor any grudge against our parents for misrepresenting situations to us. On no other occasions than these of the rat bounty and the runty pigs did they fail to keep their promises to us.

When I was ten years old I learned that a neighbor boy had sold an exceptionally fine skunk skin for a dollar. This seemed to me big money, and I resolved to exploit the skunk resources of our neighborhood. Brother Burt did not share my enthusiasm for this enterprise. Through the autumn and winter I explored the area for two miles in every direction and killed about a dozen skunks, skinned them, and sold the pelts in Fort Scott. The average price I received was not over fifty cents.

While hunting and trapping skunks I could not avoid being sprayed with their scent. I reeked of their nauseous odor, and there was loud protest from members of the family when I came into the house. While the strong odor was disagreeable to me, I considered tolerating it an exhibition of heroism. I was not in the least humiliated by being a great nuisance to the family, but persisted in renewing contacts with the fetid animals in a spirit of daring without attempting to defend myself against scolding and reprimands from every member of the household. After one year of this I gave it up.

We began as very small boys to ask to be permitted to have guns for shooting rabbits and wildfowl, which were numerous. Father never used a gun and never did any hunting. He had an old musket which he had long ago traded for in exchange for three chickens. Grandfather Kidwell had an old rusty breechloading shotgun, which he gave to me at my request. Burt and I were permitted to load these old guns and go

195

out together to shoot game when I was about eleven and Burt under ten years old. My recollection of our conduct on these occasions is that we were quite aware of all the necessary precautions to take, and that we were careful never to point a gun at each other.

Owing to the serious illness of Father I began plowing, harrowing, and planting in the spring of my eleventh birthday. My brother, being younger, had less strenuous duties. As a result we were obliged to work separately most of the time. Our life together, which had been so close and so mentally beneficial and mutually satisfactory, was over.

DISCUSSION AND INQUIRY

Elmer McCollum found the family farm in Kansas a wonderful place for a small boy to learn by observation. He had few commercial toys and he saw no books until he went to school at age five; however, his life was full of rich learning experiences. He and his brother, Burt, engaged in creative play ventures using only raw materials found in their natural environment. How can you account for this farm boy's inventiveness? Did Chet Huntley show the same innovative skills in making use of materials from the natural environment? (See the selection by Chet Huntley.) Does the rural child have more opportunities for creative play and use of materials? Does life in the ghetto provide the same opportunities?

Elmer's mother used many old-fashioned remedies, several of which included odorous rubs and poultices, as she treated his frequent attacks of colds and croup. She was not concerned about his humiliation as he became the victim of unfeeling attacks from classmates because he smelled bad. The author doesn't say much about his exclusion from his peer group, but it is of interest to speculate about his feelings and the concomitant behavior resulting from his relegated social position in the classroom. Did he feel inferior? Perhaps he did, because he mentions the fact that his mother didn't mind breaking one's morale by giving him an inferiority complex. Did he excel academically to compensate for his in-

feriority feelings? What ways do children use to show adults that they feel inferior or have a poor self-image? Eleanor Roosevelt suffered from inferiority feelings. How did her behavior reveal her feelings about herself? (See the selection by Eleanor Roosevelt.)

Punishment for Elmer was usually a reprimand from his mother and a period of isolation, after which he was to apologize and promise not to disobey again. She rarely, if ever, used corporal punishment, even though she threatened occasionally to use the switch. She held no grudges —both the McCollum boys found they could skip away happily after one of these encounters with her. Evaluate her method of punishment. What are the positive (negative) aspects of her approach to controlling unacceptable behavior? How did her punishments affect the relationships between herself and her sons? What is the difference between discipline and punishment?

John D. McKee

BIOGRAPHICAL SKETCH

John D. McKee was born in 1919 with cerebral palsy. The doctors informed his parents that he would never walk, but he did—at the age of six. He spends much of his spare time writing articles concerning the kinds of obstacles the handicapped person must face in order to have a productive, happy life. Among the many periodicals he has written for are The Atlantic Monthly *and* Today's Health.

SELECTIONS FROM

TWO LEGS TO STAND ON

THE weather was near blizzard conditions that day in December. It was the kind of hard, biting cold that a Midwestern winter produces. Early in the evening there was a knock on the door of a small cottage in Emporia, Kansas. A young housewife, heavy with child, found a little boy standing on the doorstep with homemade pine wreaths clutched in blue, gloveless hands.

His face was pinched with cold, and the wind whipped through his worn, thin coat. Would the lady buy a wreath? She would, and she would invite the little waif to warm himself before the fire. This was a sad way, she thought, for a little boy to be spending his time, and so near Christmas, too.

The little boy did not tarry long, but his face remained in the woman's memory for long years afterwards. Especially would she remember his blue-cold hands and the clumsily contrived wreaths they held.

My mother always associated the little boy and the Christmas wreaths with my birth, for at 8:30 that evening I made an all-too-sudden appearance into the world. I arrived about two months ahead of schedule, much to the consternation of my mother, and of my father, who at the moment was on the other end of his run as a Middle Division brakeman on the Santa Fe Railroad.

I weighed in at a scant two and a half pounds. Officially, I was christened John DeWitt—John for my mother's older brother, and DeWitt for my father—but anyone could see at a glance that all that name was too much of a load for me to drag around, and almost immediately the name was shortended to Jack.

I was born at home and there was no incubator available; so I was bundled into a clothesbasket and surrounded by hot water bottles and hot bricks wrapped in flannel. Apparently I thrived on this hot-house treatment. When I was only a few days old, Dad could cradle me in his hand, only my feet and legs hanging down his arm. A short time later, the man who delivered the groceries expressed himself thus: "My, ain't he growed! Why, put him on a piller and you couldn't of found him!"

My impatience to get into the world, and what are perhaps the results of that impatience, must be my excuse for setting down this premature attempt at autobiography. Autobiographies, I realize, are usually reserved for persons who—full of years, memories, and an extensive vocabulary—have an uncontrollable urge to Tell All. The urge may be traced to any one of several circumstances. The writer might have made a fortune, climbed the Matterhorn, built bridges in the Andes, or organized a society for the prevention of something-or-other. In another category, there are those who have Known Everybody and who have Done Everything. Lately, it seems the Teller of All must have suffered the vicissitudes of a chicken ranch, must have roughed it in the woods, or must have grown up—amid alternate tears and laughter—in the wilds of San Francisco or Greenwich Village or some other such exotic place to have lived a life worth telling about.

I have neither done nor have I been any of these things. I just got here a little early and happened to be born cerebral-palsied. It seems to me, however, that in telling my own story, I might be telling at least a part of the story of thousands of other cerebral-palsied persons and of those other thousands of human beings handicapped in one way or another—persons whose story needs to be told and who are, it may be, neither as articulate as I am nor as fortunate as I have been.

There didn't seem to be anything the matter with me at the beginning. At the age of four months, I weighed fourteen pounds. By the time I was fourteen months old, I was putting words together into sentences.

On the other hand, as the months went on, it became apparent that something was terribly amiss with my body. It was not only that I made no attempt to crawl, I was a year old before I could even sit up by myself.

It was about this time that Mother took me to a clinic. The doctor gave me a thorough examination and checked each item on the examination card "O. K." until he came to the feet and legs. There he put a big X, and under "Remarks," he wrote, "Spastic. Suggest stretching exercises."

"All I knew from that," Mother says, "was that there was something wrong. I had no idea what spastic meant, and the doctor didn't explain."

Long afterward Mother told me that while she was carrying me she had slipped and fallen on the icy sidewalk. That may have been what caused my premature birth, and it may also have been what injured the motor nerve centers of my brain and sent me into the world a spastic. The injury which causes cerebral palsy may occur before, during, or following birth. It may be that, the birth process beginning early, I suffered cerebral anoxia, a lack of oxygen in the brain which is caused by premature cessation of the oxygen supply from the mother to the foetus, a cessation which causes damage to brain tissues.

Whatever the cause, the results are somewhat similar to crossed wires in a telephone exchange. It's as if you rang Smith's number and got Jones. If a cerebral-palsied person sends a mental signal to his foot for action, his arm may tighten in sympathetic, or even independent, action. The wires are crossed somewhere.

I am not only peculiar in respect to normal humanity; I am a somewhat strange specimen among cerebral-palsied persons. I gather, from conversation and from reading, and also from the surprised comments of a cerebral palsy specialist who recently examined me, that though monoplegia and periplegia—the loss of the use of one or two limbs— is not uncommon, triplegia certainly is. In my case, the spasticity settled only in my right leg and arm and slightly in my left leg. My left hand and arm were left entirely free of the paralysis, so that, for instance, while I use only the index finger on my right hand for typing, all the fingers of my left hand are called into action.

Add to this peculiarity the blessing of speech. Approximately 97 per cent of the victims of cerebral palsy have defective speech, if they can talk at all. When the paralysis hits the muscles of the throat and tongue, the muscles which control swallowing and speech, even breathing and digestion sometimes become problems.

Correction or alleviation of the cerebral-palsied person's speech difficulty is the first step in his rehabilitation. For communication is even more important than the ability to walk or use the hands, and if the cerebral-palsied person is to be made a useful member of society, he must first be taught to talk.

Until not long ago (and, in fact, there are probably still some instances of it) the cerebral-palsied were looked upon as mentally defective. It is true that some 30 per cent of cerebral-palsied children are not educable, but that fact is not inherent in cerebral palsy itself.

Still, parents have hidden cerebral-palsied children away in their homes, because they were bewildered and ashamed at what they had brought into the world. Cerebral-palsied persons have been committed to homes for the feeble-minded, simply because they have been unable to express themselves and demonstrate their intelligence.

Circumstantial evidence is against us in many cases. The average victim of cerebral palsy is often not attractive to look at. His facial muscles may contract uncontrollably, so that he grimaces and grins for no apparent reason. Unable to swallow correctly, he may drool continually. He spills his food and struggles painfully with each word he utters.

I have been spared the facial contortions and the drooling, the garbled speech and the inverted breathing, but I still have to watch myself carefully when I eat in company. Eating out could have been one of the hardest things for me to learn. But in this, as in all things, my parents refused to let me think of myself as different from my brothers or from other normal people.

At home with my family, I was perfectly relaxed. If I spilled something at the table, it was only as if one of my brothers spilled his milk or dropped his bread butter-side-down on the floor. Once in a while, if I was having a particularly tough time and was spreading my food around the dining room with a lavish hand, Mother would say, "Why don't you sit on the floor, Jack? Anything that falls up, we'll hand down to you." In the laugh that followed, the tension was broken, and I could usually finish my meal with a minimum of spilling.

From my own experience it seems to be that my parents' attitude is the only one to adopt with the problem of cerebral palsy, and my cerebral-palsied friends who have solved their problem take a remarkably similar view.

I met Hubert when he was going to McPherson College and I was attending Kansas Wesleyan University. Hubert's walking problem was as difficult as mine. His speech was so troublesome as to make recitation a chore. Penmanship, in his violently shaking hands, was a scrawl. Yet he was in his junior year in college, and when I met him, he was returning from Iowa, where he had hitchhiked to attend a national students' meeting.

We met in the college dining hall, and since our conversation was not nearly finished by the end of the meal, I invited him to my room. Hubert had had trouble getting the food from the plate to his mouth, and the area around his plate showed it. But the only reference he made to his troubles came when we were ready to leave. "I'll be ready to go," he said, grinning and reaching for a drink with both shaking hands, "just as soon as I spill some more water."

The preceding, then, is by way of introduction to some of the problems I brought with me when I appeared on the scene two months early, on December 22, 1919. These are but a few of the problems which my parents faced then and which I now face. Many of the problems have been conquered; some of them remain unsolved today. But the mystery of why I am as I am and the continuing challenge the mystery presents have always intrigued me.

This will be the story of one person's struggle with what the world chooses to call a handicap. It will also be the story of what has been done, by myself, and by a great many others, to overcome the handicap, and it will contain, too, something of a fairly simple—and, I hope, unpretentious—philosophy I have evolved from being from the beginning different from my fellows.

There will necessarily be much about my body in this story, because my body has required more time, more attention, more study, and more intimate knowledge than does that of most persons. My body is not only the carriage of my mind and spirit and personality: its very difference has helped to shape them. If there is anything at all that makes this record worth-while, it is that difference.

The wearing out of a shoe sole at the center instead of at the toe, the longer and yet longer times between falls, even the first time I willed my toes to move and they moved—not the leg from the hip or knee, not even my foot, moving from the ankle, but the toes, moving independently—these are real little miracles, perhaps worth recording for their own sake.

There must have been some dark days indeed between the time Mother took me to the clinic and the time I was two years old. Most of the progress which has been made in the treatment of cerebral palsy has taken place in my own lifetime, and in those early days, at least among the doctors who saw me, diagnosis was usually the end of the line. Treatment was by trial and error if there was any treatment at all. The long struggle to get me on my feet was carried on at first almost entirely by my father and mother.

With a pillow behind me and a pillow propping me up on either side, I could sit up by the time I was a year old. Sometime between my first and second birthdays, I began to sit up alone, and by the time I was two—way behind schedule—I had finally begun to crawl. Although it was a red-letter day when I finally began to get over the floor under my own power, part of the difficulty I was to have later became apparent then. When I crawled, I thrust my arms ahead of me. Then I drew up my legs, both at the same time, with the action originating from the hip. There was no reciprocal action between the arms and legs, or between the legs themselves. It was to be years before any sort of reciprocation, necessary almost above all else for walking, was obtained.

But I was crawling. At last I was moving, regardless of how awkwardly. Now at last there must be some hope for my walking.

The day I first hunched myself across the floor marked a beginning and an end. It was the end of a period of black bewilderment and despair for my parents, when but for hope and faith there was no evidence at all that I would ever move from my bed; and the beginning of an almost equally frustrating period, when for years I did not progress beyond crawling, and it did not look as if I ever would. But it was a beginning in more than that. For I could move about. I could crawl about the house, and later, out in the yard, and my world began to expand. Of course, I still had to wake Mother or Dad in the night. It would be several years before I could turn over in bed by myself.

I sometimes think that the greatest difference between me and the rest of mankind is simply that I started more slowly than people normally do. I can hope, at least, that I am a tortoise of sorts. Though I was left at the post when the race began, and though there is very little likelihood that I shall ever pass any of the field, at least I shall finish. For, though I move slowly, I have done most of the things that human beings do. Gradually I am accumulating the experience of a full life, and if I live long enough, I have no doubt that my life, in the end, will have been as full, as interesting, and as useful as will the lives of those who have come into the world more fully equipped than I.

. . .

The last bell rang and I got up to leave. Another parents' day at the second grade was over, and I was in a hurry to join my mother in the back of the room. I hurried down the aisle, holding to the desks on either side to make sure I didn't fall.

Another mother came up the aisle like a ship in full rigging. She crashed into me, said something apologetically and went sailing on up the aisle.

Mother swooped down on me, helped me to my feet, and said, "Can't you look where you're going, Jack? You might have been hurt!"

When we got home, she stood me up in front of her and said, "I'm sorry I spoke to you that way, Jack, but when that woman knocked you down, I just had to say something or burst, and it was too late to say anything to her."

That was one of the few times I ever saw either of my parents show their feelings when I fell or got bumped; and they had more than enough opportunities.

Fortunately for me, my parents made me feel that I was missing none of the adventure of living. I went to Sunday school and church with them. I remember the fiddle squeaking and the guitar and drums beating out the rhythms of the square dance at the open-air pavilion at

Shoft's Chicken Dinner Farm. I remember sitting in the dugout on Sunday afternoons and cheering Dad, who played second base for the Hardy town team. I went to a carnival one time and rode with Mother on the Ferris wheel. It stopped when we were at the top of the wheel, and I looked out and saw all the twinkling lights of the carnival and, fanned out away from me, all the lights of the town below. I remember how Mother laughed when I asked her, "Momma, do we have to get off now?"

I sometimes went on my mother's hip, and sometimes my father carried me. I graduated to a cart, and later, when my brothers were born, I shared the buggy—but where my family went, I went.

By the time I was five years old, I must have crawled a couple of thousand miles on my hands and knees. My shoes had to be repaired every week, and, even at that, they had to be replaced every month. I used to crawl around the front yard of our home in Nebraska and once almost made friends with a rattlesnake before Mother discovered us and killed the rattler with a hoe.

But the thing I remember most and best before the operations is the firelit fall evening that I tried my first step. This was in the Brace Period. There had already been the White Pill Period, the Osteopathic Period, the Chiropractic Period, and the Electric Shock Period. There was yet to come the He'll-Grow-Out-Of-It Period, and finally, the Operations Period.

My parents were determined to see that I got every possible opportunity. If there was a chance that something would help me walk, let me play with the other kids in the neighborhood, they were going to take that chance. They never gave up, even for a little while, and Mother said she prayed a lot.

The Brace Period came with our move to Concordia, Kansas, and the consequent addition of yet another doctor who thought he might know how to help me. The braces were steel and leather affairs that could be locked at the knees. With them on I could stand up and walk around, as long as I had something to hang onto. The big problem was lack of balance. Like most spastics, I had almost no sense of balance, and like most spastics, I was deathly afraid of falling. As long as I was holding to something, I was all right, but put me alone in the middle of a room and I went rigid with fright.

"He seems to have no control of his muscles," the doctor said. "If there were only some way we could teach him to control the muscles of his legs and feet, perhaps he could learn to walk."

Dad thought about that. He thought about it all that week, and the next Saturday afternoon, he said, "Mary, get me a pair of Jack's old shoes." Then he went down in the basement, and when he came back, he had a can of gray paint, a paint brush, and a heavy carpenter's pencil.

Mystified, Mother and I followed him out the back door, I with my braces locked, stumping along stiff-legged, holding Mother's hand. Dad spent that afternoon outlining my footprints on the back sidewalk with black pencil and painting in the outlines with gray paint. Then he planted some lengths of steel pipe on either side of the walk and strung heavy, insulated wire between the evenly spaced pipe lengths at just the right height for my hands.

"Now, Jack," he said, "as soon as the paint dries, you begin walking. You will practice putting your feet down in those footprints, and maybe someday we can take those braces off. What do you say?"

What did I say? I could hardly wait till the paint dried!

At first it was fun. I clung tightly to the guidelines, and hour after hour practiced putting my feet in those gray prints. But the game soon wore off, and often I hung swinging to the guidelines, petrified because I had stumbled and started to fall.

"How did the walking go today?" Dad would ask when he got home from work, and Mother would say, "He walked a long way today, De-Witt. He did fine. He started to fall once, but he caught himself and went right on walking."

Or she would say, "Jack's getting lazy. I had to take the vegetables out to the porch to peel them today, so I could watch him and make sure he walked."

After I learned to walk between the lines, however, and was at least a little less afraid of falling, they left me alone a good deal of the time, patrolling my beat. There are some things you can't learn with your parents hovering over you, and out on that back sidewalk, with nobody holding me up as I wobbled the length of the walk and back, I got my first small taste of independence.

That was how the score stood, on that gray fall afternoon in Kansas, over a quarter of a century ago. I was, at long last, on my feet. I was walking, after a fashion, but I could never have any sort of independent existence as long as I had to lean on something or hold to something to maintain my equilibrium. There were not always going to be walls or doors or banisters to cling to.

I had been out walking between the lines, missing the painted footprints as often as I hit them with my erratic feet, but still plodding uncertainly up and down the walk. Any time I got tired or downhearted, I could quit, for I was alone this day, but something of what I had learned, something that had been instilled in me since birth, would not let me quit. If I had not been told there was something better, if I had not been gently pushed and helped and goaded on, who knows but what I might right now be flat on my back in a bed from which I would never rise?

At any rate, I had walked until twilight came and the weather turned chilly. Then Mother came out and helped me into the house.

We had a winding, open stairway, leading from the living room, the first step of which protruded from the newel post and made a convenient seat for a five-year-old boy. As a matter of fact, it was one of my favorite places in the house. It wasn't exactly a chair, but it was a good place to sit.

It was something out of the ordinary, and it gave me a feeling of private ownership. Perhaps that was because no one else ever sat there or could, my little behind being the only one that would fit the seat.

Mother brought me into the living room, unlocked my braces, and set me on the stairway ledge. The sudden change from the nippy air of the out of doors to the enveloping warmth of the big, potbellied German heater was almost too much for me. I grew drowsy and daydreamed. I saw myself grown up, walking down the street straight and tall between Mother and Dad, swinging my arms naturally at the sides, keeping my knees straight without benefit of braces. I saw myself pitching a baseball game, quarterbacking a football team, running races, jumping, climbing trees.

The room was cheery with the red glow from the stove and the light of the old-fashioned three-bulb brass chandelier, and the smell of supper cooking on the stove came deliciously from the kitchen. It was the in-between time of day, when play was done and there was still a little time for dreaming before supper and bed.

I sat there with all the warmth and dreams around me, and I looked at the big library table only two steps away. Could I walk to it? After all it was only two steps. Just two steps without guidelines, without a chair or a wall or a person to cling to.

Two steps into nothing, or two steps that might mean the beginning of walking wherever I wanted to go. I might fall and hit my head on the table. I might get one step away from the safety of the stairway and freeze with fright. I might fall. I might fall. I might fall. The thought kept pounding through my head, and I was shaking with fear. Because I had fallen—become overbalanced in a chair, or pulled myself up to a table or a chair and had walked, hanging on, and had tripped and fallen—and because I did not know yet how to fall, I had hit hard and it had hurt.

But another thought was hammering to get in. I could hear Dad say, "Pick 'em up and lay 'em down, Jack. You won't fall. You can walk." I remembered Mother watching me from the back porch, and how proud she was when I tottered the length of the walk and back, missing the footprints only twice. I was going to walk. My mother and father said I could.

Suddenly I quit thinking. I pulled myself up slowly, clinging like grim death to the newel post. I stood there for a moment, gathering my courage and listening for Mother. I wanted to be sure she didn't know what I was doing. If I fell, I wanted to be able to crawl back to the stairway and sit down before she discovered it; and if I made it to the table, I wanted to surprise her.

Pans were rattling reassuringly in the kitchen. I took one step and wavered. I stood for a split second on one foot, unable in my sudden panic to bring the other foot forward.

Then the trailing foot came around, and I fell forward, reaching for the table. My fingers clutched at the edge of the table and I pulled myself erect. I made it!

My parents have given me many things, but the greatest gift they ever gave me was courage—the courage to take two steps.

DISCUSSION AND INQUIRY

"Why don't you sit on the floor, Jack? Anything that falls up we'll hand down to you." This kind of humor, combined with parental love and support enabled Jack to enjoy his childhood despite his physical limitations. His determination to succeed cannot be solely attributed to his parents' urging, but also to the emotional climate of the household. It allowed Jack to decide for himself that he would walk because he wanted to, thus encouraging autonomy. Some parents of handicapped children push their child too hard. Other parents, never overcoming the disappointment, become detached and indifferent. What would be the result of these extreme attitudes on the handicapped child? What would be the results of these parental attitudes on the normal child?

Young McKee was not hidden by his parents. He was taken to ball games, fairs, and Sunday school. In his own words, "Fortunately for me, my parents made me feel that I was missing none of the adventure of living . . . where my family went, I went." Can you relate their family closeness with the development of self-concept?

Would you consider McKee's mother to be overprotective? Compare her with the mothers of John Holloway and Robert Merrill. (See the selections by John Holloway and Robert Merrill.)

Robert Merrill

BIOGRAPHICAL SKETCH

Moishe Miller, a little boy born in Brooklyn in 1919, grew up to be Robert Merrill, one of the great baritone opera stars of the century. He was launched on his great career after winning the Metropolitan Auditions in 1945. Since that day, he has appeared in many, many operatic performances. In 1970, he had his Broadway debut as Tevye, in Fiddler on the Roof.

SELECTIONS FROM

ONCE MORE FROM THE BEGINNING

BUT God gave Lotza Miller a third try. [Two previous children born to Lotza Miller had died in infancy.] I was born on top of the kitchen table in Williamsburg on South Second Street. Lotza—now Lillian—clasped me to her breast as no Jewish mother had ever clasped any Jewish boy before. It seems I looked just like the talented infant girl who had died. I was a treasure so dear that I might just as well have been named Ruby or Diamond instead of Moishe. No boy was ever loved with such a vengeance, smothered with so much devotion, and weakened by such strength. By the time I was conscious of what was going on in my world, Momma and Poppa were engaged in a war of attrition, and home was an armed camp. My arrival and subsequent survival in this world demanded that the Millers do better. My mother's dissatisfactions became greater by the day, her ambitions wilder. Her contempt of my gentle father was to know no end.

Sadly enough, my father was never to do any better. He was then a sewing-machine operator in a factory and was earning more money than he had ever earned before. His salary was about twenty-five dollars a week. For a man with no ambition, this was a fortune. He had never dreamed he could bring home so much money. Actually, Poppa had never dreamed at all. If Momma had only gotten off his back, he would have been the happiest of men—with his little son and all the cloth he could ever sew in a never-ending assembly line.

Pop would have been satisfied to live in one room forever without steam heat, without air, without a view, without hot water. To my father, life was a gift that needed no extra wrappings. You worked and you ate and you washed it down with some cold seltzer. And you listened to some good music on your Victrola—like Cantor Rosenblatt, maybe, or that great opera singer Caruso, who had a Yiddish throb in his voice and sang those minor Italian melodies that so attracted Jewish immigrant listeners. And Pop did love to hear his Lotza sing at local affairs, although her ambitions were a source of irritation to him.

Pop was a peasant philosopher. Life was supposed to be a struggle. You worked and brought up a family and tried to be a good person. And you had a trade. Singing was not a trade unless you were a cantor, and even then it wasn't exactly a trade. He felt you could be a good person without all the rigmarole of religion, and only out of respect to the memory of his own parents did he attend synagogue on the High Holidays. Mom *bensched* the candles on Friday night simply out of superstition, and every Sabbath of her life the white cloth and the candles were placed on the table. She wasn't going to be the one to break the ritual and possibly bring the wrath of God down on her household. It was easier to continue, and the neighbors would have been shocked otherwise. Didn't she sing at weddings and *bar mitzvahs*? And, after all, she *was* Jewish.

Now that I had arrived on the scene—better late than never—followed shortly by my brother Gidalia, Momma began applying the pressure that was to create a permanent strain on the family. There was always something just beyond our reach—and she was going to get it. But her good and unimaginative husband could extend himself just so far, and then the nagging and the arguments would begin and the Polish profanities would fly from my sweet father's lips. He would be driven, at the end of a hard day's work, from gentle fatigue to a screaming rage. "I should never have married so young!" was the announcement Poppa made every few days. I knew that my mother, who never let go of the reins, drove him to these tantrums, and I resented her; but without her energy and drive, we all would have lived and died on South Second Street.

Poverty may be romantic to those who have never known it first-hand. *La Bohème* is glamorous only if Rudolfo and Mimi are attractive and in particularly good voice. If it's snowing outside that immense skylight that looks out over the roofs of gay Paree, so much the better.

But South Second Street was not a Paris slum designed by Guy Pène du Bois. It was a filthy, roach- and baby-infested, chalk-marked block that got the sun for a few minutes at high noon and for the rest of the day lay in shadows as if under a cloud. It was ugly, gray, and foul, and across its face in colored chalk was a scrawled message to its inhabitants: "Drop dead!"

In winter it was damp, freezing, and cheerless, except for that moment after a blizzard when the freshly shoveled piles of snow made great white hills that lined the street and became fortresses to play on. But they were soon stained yellow and brown by little boys and dogs. If the weather held, they became filthy, disease-ridden battlefields that sent many a boy to the hospital. Kids would be found half-dead and blue where they had fallen through the snow and been left for hours. Our flat had no heat, and I would be so frozen in the morning that I couldn't relieve myself.

The spring thaw would make the gutter a flooded sewer, our own little road-company Venice. When summer arrived, the street would steam with smells and heat that drove everybody to the roofs or fire escapes. I can see the hairy bellies of the men and the sagging breasts of the new mothers hanging over the rusted iron balconies. There wasn't much privacy on South Second Street. The whole libretto was played out without shame. Birth and death—with everything in between—were played out in a great big circus; my family was part of it, balancing on a clothesline—without a net, a daredevil act, believe me. The death-defying immigrants! Watch them! Don't take your eyes off them! Any moment may be their last!

I can still hear the screaming sirens and mothers and kids. The ambulance was a frequent visitor on our street, for it seemed that every few days a small child would fall from a window or fire escape, suffocate in a dumbwaiter, or be run over while the Momma was cooking, washing, or tending another of her brood. The jam of humanity was such that the loss was barely noticed by anybody but the mother herself—who was too busy to mourn but aged ten years overnight. No one on South Second Street looked young, not even the kids.

During a heat wave, everyone hung from the tenement windows like limp, wrinkled wash or sat on the stoops like garbage until four in the morning or climbed to the dirty roof for that last breath of air.

Through all this, my mother tried to keep me at her side. If it had been possible, I would have been breast-fed straight through high school. Momma trusted no storekeeper, no restaurant, nobody. My brother Gidalia was something else. Gilbert, as he was soon to be called, was always outgoing. I was a different story. From the beginning I was saved from experiencing any fun that was available on the block. My mother, without a doctor's diploma, was the greatest diagnostician in the business and decided I was a cardiac case. I was forbidden to play dangerous games in the dangerous street with the dangerous boys. I wasn't allowed to play in the dangerous school, and later, through some

collusion, she produced a doctor's note to exempt me from the dangerous gymnasium. Her head would shake tragically as she spoke of my
"leaking valve" and my blood pressure.

Living on the sixth floor of a walk-up, *schlepping* groceries and a
baby carriage, my mother kept in training. If you didn't die of a heart
attack before you were twenty-one in that house, you could live forever. Up and down, up and down, and God forbid she forget the string
beans or beets for pickling. But *I* never had to make these trips—not
me. Moishe was a cardiac case. "He's got a murmur, the kid! *Oi!* High-
strung like a violin." For me, Momma would lower bread-and-jelly,
fruit, or a dime for the store on a string from the window. Lifting a fork
to my mouth was the only exercise she allowed me, and when I wanted
to play in the street she would shanghai me to the docks.

After negotiating with the captain of a tugboat under the Williamsburg Bridge, she would take me for a ride in the "fresh salt air," dragging Gidalia on a short lead so that he would not fall overboard.

"Look at the color in the sailor's cheeks, singer mine. That's from
living such a healthy life. Breath in, *meine kind.* In! Out! In! Out!
Gidalia, if you fall in the water and drown, I'll break every bone in the
body! Moishe, darling, take a deep breath . . . deeper. That's it. Let it
out, Moishe. *Let it out, already!*"

My kid brother, unlike me, always got his own way. He had per-
fected the convulsion to a high art. When he wanted something, he
could hold his breath longer than an Olympic swimmer. He would lie
on the floor kicking his feet and turning navy blue. For a second-act
curtain, he would become stiff and his eyes would roll up to the top of
his head. He didn't fool me for a moment, but it worked. Even if
Momma did suspect a fraud, it was awfully hard to prove—each fit
could have been the real one. Gil was smart. He was the fox who kept
crying wolf. He had found his way of fighting Momma. I had not.

Momma discovered I could sing the moment I let out my first cry.
To my mother, my delivery was a debut. All through my first years, I
almost died of embarrassment every time she asked me to entertain the
aunts and uncles. Invariably, I refused, and when she made it clear that
she was going to have her way—and she always did—I sang, but only
after I had turned all the lights out or gone into the bathroom and
closed the door. When everyone laughed, Momma would say, "It's all
right. First things first. He'll start on radio. That's bad? Nobody'll see
him, but he'll sing. Music is in his blood from me and my own Poppa."
Then she forced piano lessons on me through a teacher who was a
friend of hers. I practiced on a thirdhand upright she got somewhere.
I was so afraid that the kids outside would find out that—hot as it was
—I would close every window so no one could hear me practicing. I

literally sweated through my scales. I got up to Clementi for two hands and that was the end of the piano.

Momma was convinced that music was in my blood, but she wasn't convinced that my blood was very good. So I had to drink beef blood.

With all our money problems, I cannot say we ever starved. Through the miracle of Momma's organization, there was always a broth on the stove or bread in the oven, always marrowbones and the luxury of beef blood. In good time and bad, there was always enough to eat. In fact, with my lack of exercise and her constant feeding, I was puffing up like a spongecake. It wasn't bad enough that I spoke only Yiddish. Now I was quite accurately called "Fatso" by the kids on the block.

My first relief from my Yiddishe Momma was Public School 19. It was a dirty, dingy, overcrowded school, but I was on my own from nine to three. To my classmates, I was a complete freak—a human knish. I was ridiculed unmercifully, and it might have been in this setting, as I first learned to speak English, that I began to stutter. Of course, it could also have been on the Fourth of July, when after stealing two dollars from my mother's drawer in the kitchen, Gidalia and I were caught by my father. Poppa gave me the beating of my life and then locked me out of the house, naked for everyone to jeer at. Luckily for him, my brother was considered too young for such character building. I cried and scratched at the door, pleading to be let back in.

Momma was petrified. "Abe! He'll catch pneumonia!"

But this one time, Poppa was boss. "Better yet, maybe he'll catch honesty."

Poppa's idea of discipline didn't stop me from loving him, nor did the punishment stop me from joining the other kids in ransacking the food boxes that sat outside the windows and on fire escapes in the days before refrigerators. Ice for the icebox cost money, and winter itself was employed to keep the food fresh. But we kids were fresher; when I could escape my mother's watchful eye or when she was out singing at a wedding, I'd tag along with the gang to steal fruit and milk and potatoes, which we put on long sticks and cooked over a fire in an empty lot. The tenement basement and the empty lot—those were the shifting scenes of my childhood.

I never saw that famous tree that grows in Brooklyn. I saw no green except cabbage, until the day we visited my mother's cousin Guzik in Massachusetts. Guzik was a shoemaker who had settled his little family in a small house on the outskirts of Worcester. My brother and I went wild at the sight of the trees and grass and frightened our country cousins.

A tree was such a novelty to us that we were first stunned by its bigness and then overjoyed by its beauty. We chased around it, banged ourselves against it, climbed it, made love to it. That day in Worcester was an important one in my life. It was the first time I had ever seen beauty, the first time I'd ever seen a living thing reach up to the sky, green against the blue, tall and straight and dignified. Imagine. Just a tree—but my first.

We actually saw cherries growing on trees that day and picked them in such a state of excitement that we threw them at each other instead of eating them. Who ever knew where cherries came from? From Finkel's store!

In my day there were no parks or playgrounds in our neighborhood —no place to play even if your mother would let you. In the hot months, P. S. 19, with its handball courts and playing area, was closed; we kids would have to climb over the high chicken-wire fence that senselessly separated us from a place to play.

We had to do something, of course. We were considered social outcasts if we didn't steal pennies off the newstands and flatten them into the size of nickels on the trolley tracks. Then when we sneaked into the Congress movie theater, we would use them to get Suchard chocolates from the boxes on the backs of the seats. Any corset drying on a clothesline lost its stays—we used them for swabbing out the peanut machines in the subway. There we sneaked in under the turnstile, or if the entrance was an unattended revolving door, three or four of us would squeeze in for one nickel. We also swiped bamboo shoe trees and smoked ourselves green in the gills in some basement.

Whenever I could escape my jailer, I did. And most of the time it was to play baseball. At first we played in the streets, with hydrants and fat old ladies peeling vegetables as our bases, and then in vacant lots surrounded by torn election posters of smiling candidates long since defeated. Barely readable were their promises of parks and playgrounds —but no matter their party, there was no ice cream and cake for the kids, and no place to play but the sandlots. And how I loved baseball!

But it's hard to be sentimental about the old neighborhood, because I remember too many ugly things—like the Black Hand, the scourge of P. S. 19. For three years I didn't go to the school toilet because of the awful story that a boy was found dead there with a disembodied hand at his throat. The legend was so powerful that no child was allowed to go to the bathroom without a teacher. I wouldn't go at all. Even the police, mystified by the sworn testimony of children and faculty, suggested extreme caution, although their eyes glazed with skepticism whenever the Hand was mentioned.

They never took the Hand into custody, but the superstitious immigrant parents—volatile Italians, dramatic Jews, and mystic Irish, peasants all—were only too ready to believe any old wives' tale. My own mother used to pull my earlobes every time someone looked at me cross-eyed. This was supposed to dispel the curse cast by the evil eye. It's a wonder that I have my ears left. She would pull on them like a milkmaid and then, uncertain that the Devil was gone, would spit in the air around me. If Satan didn't get you, Momma's head cold would.

Williamsburg was tough on Easter Sunday, but there is no way of conveying what Halloween was like.

I will never forget one Halloween. I couldn't have been more than ten. After school, I played in the shadow of the Williamsburg Bridge. The cobblestoned street at its entrance was the spot where the Republic Theatre stood, and it was also the scene of absolute horror. I found myself walking across the bridge with a few of the kids I palled around with when I could escape Momma's eye. We had decided to stand over the water and drop stones and yell at the boats and barges that passed beneath us. We also wanted to see the Woolworth Building, which was the tallest in the whole world, and the rest of Manhattan's skyscrapers, so we walked to the middle of the bridge.

It was beautiful there, and I can still feel the bite of that autumn wind on my cheeks as I caught sight of what looked like a carpet unfolding toward us from the Manhattan side. It was all so fast and terrible. A gang from the Lower East Side had spotted us. We stood paralyzed with fear as the mob rolled toward us brandishing long stockings filled with stones and flour, pieces of rubber hose, the pockets of their jackets filled with rocks.

They were bigger than we were, and I remember their hats—old fedoras with the brims cut off and scalloped or turreted like a medieval crown and covered with campaign buttons of all kinds and colors— made them look like kings of the gutter. The attack was silent at first because they all wore high-laced sneakers with big solid circles on the ankles.

Somebody yelled, "Cheese it! They'll kill us! Run!" and our frozen tableau splintered into fragments, melting, receding, flowing to the Brooklyn side of the bridge, with this mob of cutthroats now screaming after us.

My heart grew big in my chest as I tried to keep up with the hysterical retreat, but my mother had fed me too well. I was fat and slow and further overweighted with bulky sweaters under my jacket and overcoat. The woolen scarf my mother had knit was strangling me. My buddies were screaming blue streaks ahead of me, disappearing, being squeezed by the parallel lines of the bridge, while the profane threats of the enemy were directly behind me. It could have been a loose shoelace or just the end of my strength, but the mob was on top of me.

The police found me beaten to a pulp, left in the wake of the juggernaut, torn, bleeding, and unconscious. I came to in the station house, vaguely aware that they were trying to find my family. My stricken

215

mother soon rushed in and took me to a nearby clinic, vowing that she would never let me out of her sight again.

When I recovered, my physical exercise was limited to digging for pickles and herring in the barrels of brine that stood in front of the butcher and grocery stores. Momma, always out for the best, would make me reach to the bottom of the barrel, so my arm always smelled. After school I was not out of her sight for a second; I had to spend my time shopping with her. Baseball was out until both Momma and I recovered from the massacre. I recovered much sooner than she.

~~~~~~

DISCUSSION AND INQUIRY

An overprotective "Yiddishe Momma," a passive father, and a flat on the sixth floor of a walk-up in Brooklyn set the first stage for Robert Merrill. Overprotection and smothering occur in families in response to various needs: sometimes the needs of the mother, and sometimes the needs of the child. What were some of the factors that could have contributed to the smothering that young Merrill experienced? Compare and contrast this situation with that of John Holloway, who was also overprotected. (See the selection by John Holloway.) What are the possible outcomes of overprotection?*

School was an escape for Robert—it provided six hours of relief from Momma. It was, however, ugly and unpleasant for the boy, who was a fat, unathletic stutterer and, in at least one instance, fair game for the gang who beat and taunted him unmercifully. He only mentions his stuttering briefly, but it is of interest in light of his final career choice. His stuttering began when he learned English. What other factors were operating at this time in his life that may have contributed to his speech problem? There are a number of hypotheses about the etiology of stuttering.

* Schaefer's Circumplex may be useful in projecting about behavioral outcomes when children are reared in different emotional climates. See E. S. Schaefer, "Converging Conceptual Models for Maternal Behavior and for Child Behavior," ed. by J. C. Glidwell, *Parental Attitudes and Child Behavior* (Springfield, Ill.: Charles C Thomas, 1961).

> *Investigate the various explanations for stuttering and the suggested methods for handling the problem.*

Anne Moody

BIOGRAPHICAL SKETCH

Anne Moody's racial consciousness was aroused in Mississippi, where her parents worked on a plantation. Born there in 1940, she lived with them in the segregated shacks set aside for the Negro workers. In 1959, she entered Natchez College (Louisiana) on a basketball scholarship. Two years later, she transferred to Tougaloo College. There she joined the NAACP, with which she has been working since then for the betterment of her people.

SELECTIONS FROM

COMING OF AGE IN MISSISSIPPI

I'M STILL haunted by dreams of the time we lived on Mr. Carter's plantation. Lots of Negroes lived on his place. Like Mama and Daddy they were all farmers. We all lived in rotten wood two-room shacks. But ours stood out from the others because it was up on the hill with Mr. Carter's big white house, overlooking the farms and the other shacks below. It looked just like the Carter's barn with a chimney and a porch, but Mama and Daddy did what they could to make it livable. Since we had only one big room and a kitchen, we all slept in the same room. It was like three rooms in one. Mama them slept in one corner and I had my little bed in another corner next to one of the big wooden windows. Around the fireplace a rocking chair and a couple of straight chairs formed a sitting area. This big room had a plain, dull-colored wallpaper tacked loosely to the walls with large thumbtacks. Under each tack was a piece of cardboard which had been taken from shoeboxes and cut into little squares to hold the paper and keep the tacks from tearing through. Because there were not enough tacks, the paper bulged in places. The kitchen didn't have any wallpaper and the only furniture in it was a wood stove, an old table, and a safe.

Mama and Daddy had two girls. I was almost four and Adline was a crying baby about six or seven months. We rarely saw Mama and Daddy because they were in the field every day except Sunday. They would get up early in the morning and leave the house just before daylight. It was six o'clock in the evening when they returned, just before dark.

George Lee, Mama's eight-year-old brother, kept us during the day. He loved to roam the woods and taking care of us prevented him from enjoying his favorite pastime. He had to be at the house before Mama and Daddy left for the field, so he was still groggy when he got there. As soon as Mama them left the house, he would sit up in the rocking chair and fall asleep. Because of the solid wooden door and windows, it was dark in the house even though it was nearing daybreak. After sleeping for a couple of hours, George Lee would jump up suddenly, as if he was awakened from a nightmare, run to the front door, and sling it open. If the sun was shining and it was a beautiful day, he would get all excited and start slinging open all the big wooden windows, making them rock on their hinges. Whenever he started banging the windows and looking out at the woods longingly, I got scared.

Once he took us to the woods and left us sitting in the grass while he chased birds. That night Mama discovered we were full of ticks so he was forbidden to take us there any more. Now every time he got the itch to be in the woods, he'd beat me.

One day he said, "I'm goin' huntin'." I could tell he meant to go by himself. I was scared he was going to leave us alone but I didn't say anything. I never said anything to him when he was in that mood.

"You heard me!" he said, shaking me.

I still didn't say anything.

Wap! He hit me hard against the head; I started to boohoo as usual and Adline began to cry too.

"Shut up," he said, running over to the bed and slapping a bottle of sweetening water into her mouth.

"You stay here, right here," he said, forcing me into a chair at the foot of the bed. "And watch her," pointing to Adline in the bed. "And you better not move." Then he left the house.

A few minutes later he came running back into the house like he forgot something. He ran over to Adline in the bed and snatched the bottle of sweetening water from her mouth. He knew I was so afraid of him I might have sat in the chair and watched Adline choke to death on the bottle. Again he beat me up. Then he carried us on the porch. I was still crying so he slapped me, knocking me clean off the porch. As I fell I hit my head on the side of the steps and blood came gushing out. He got some scared and cleaned away all traces of the blood. He even tried to push down the big knot that had popped up on my forehead.

219

That evening we sat on the porch waiting, as we did every evening, for Mama them to come up the hill. The electric lights were coming on in Mr. Carter's big white house as all the Negro shacks down in the bottom began to fade with the darkness. Once it was completely dark, the lights in Mr. Carter's house looked even brighter, like a big lighted castle. It seemed like the only house on the whole plantation.

Most evenings, after the Negroes had come from the fields, washed and eaten, they would sit on their porches, look up toward Mr. Carter's house and talk. Sometimes as we sat on our porch Mama told me stories about what was going on in that big white house. She would point out all the brightly lit rooms, saying that Old Lady Carter was baking tea cakes in the kitchen, Mrs. Carter was reading in the living room, the children were studying upstairs, and Mr. Carter was sitting up counting all the money he made off Negroes.

I was sitting there thinking about Old Lady Carter's tea cakes when I heard Mama's voice: "Essie Mae! Essie Mae!"

Suddenly I remembered the knot on my head and I jumped off the porch and ran toward her. She was now running up the hill with her hoe in one hand and straw hat in the other. Unlike the other farmhands, who came up the hill dragging their hoes behind them, puffing and blowing, Mama usually ran all the way up the hill laughing and singing. When I got within a few feet of her I started crying and pointing to the big swollen wound on my forehead. She reached out for me. I could see she was feeling too good to beat George Lee so I ran right past her and headed for Daddy, who was puffing up the hill with the rest of the field hands. I was still crying when he reached down and swept me up against his broad sweaty chest. He didn't say anything about the wound but I could tell he was angry, so I cried even harder. He waved goodnight to the others as they cut across the hill toward their shacks.

As we approached the porch, Daddy spotted George Lee headed down the hill for home.

"Come here boy!" Daddy shouted, but George Lee kept walking.

"Hey boy, didn't you hear me call you? If you don't get up that hill I'll beat the daylights outta you!" Trembling, George Lee slowly made his way back up the hill.

"What happen to Essie Mae here? What happen?" Daddy demanded.

"Uh . . . uh . . . she fell offa d' porch 'n hit her head on d' step . . ." George Lee mumbled.

"Where were you when she fell?"

"Uhm . . . ah was puttin' a diaper on Adline."

"If anything else happen to one o' these chaps, I'm goin' to try my best to *kill* you. Get yo'self on home fo' I . . ."

220

The next morning George Lee didn't show up. Mama and Daddy waited for him a long time.

"I wonder where in the hell could that damn boy be," Daddy said once or twice, pacing the floor. It was well past daylight when they decided to go on to the field and leave Adline and me at home alone.

"I'm gonna leave y'all here by yo'self, Essie Mae," said Mama. "If Adline wake up crying, give her the bottle. I'll come back and see about y'all and see if George Lee's here."

She left some beans on the table and told me to eat them when I was hungry. As soon as she and Daddy slammed the back door I was hungry. I went in the kitchen and got the beans. Then I climbed in to the rocking chair and began to eat them. I was some scared. Mama had never left us at home alone before. I hoped George Lee would come even though I knew he would beat me.

All of a sudden George Lee walked in the front door. He stood there for a while grinning and looking at me, without saying a word. I could tell what he had on his mind and the beans began to shake in my hands.

"Put them beans in that kitchen," he said, slapping me hard on the face.

"I'm hungry," I cried with a mouth full of beans.

He slapped me against the head again and took the beans and carried them into the kitchen. When he came back he had the kitchen matches in his hand.

"I'm goin' to burn you two cryin' fools up. Then I won't have to come here and keep yo' asses every day."

As I looked at that stupid George Lee standing in the kitchen door with that funny grin on his face, I thought that he might really burn us up. He walked over to the wall near the fireplace and began setting fire to the bulging wallpaper. I started crying. I was so scared I was peeing all down my legs. George Lee laughed at me for peeing and put the fire out with his bare hands before it burned very much. Then he carried me and Adline on to the porch and left us there. He went out in the yard to crack nuts and play.

We were on the porch only a short time when I heard a lot of hollering coming from toward the field. The hollering and crying got louder and louder. I could hear Mama's voice over all the rest. It seemed like all the people in the field were running to our house. I ran to the edge of the porch to watch them top the hill. Daddy was leading the running crowd and Mama was right behind him.

"Lord have mercy, my children is in that house!" Mama was screaming. "Hurry, Diddly!" she cried to Daddy. I turned around and saw big clouds of smoke booming out of the front door and shooting out of cracks everywhere. "There, Essie Mae is on the porch," Mama said.

"Hurry, Diddly! Get Adline outta that house!" I looked back at Adline. I couldn't hardly see her for the smoke.

George Lee was standing in the yard like he didn't know what to do. As Mama them got closer, he ran into the house. My first thought was that he would be burned up. I'd often hoped he would get killed, but I guess I didn't really want him to die after all. I ran inside after him but he came running out again, knocking me down as he passed and leaving me lying face down in the burning room. I jumped up quickly and scrambled out after him. He had the water bucket in his hands. I thought he was going to try to put out the fire. Instead he placed the bucket on the edge of the porch and picked up Adline in his arms.

Moments later Daddy was on the porch. He ran straight into the burning house with three other men right behind him. They opened the large wooden windows to let some of the smoke out and began ripping the paper from the walls before the wood caught on fire. Mama and two other women raked it into the fireplace with sticks, broom handles, and anything else available. Everyone was coughing because of all the smoke.

Soon it was all over. Nothing had been lost but the paper on the wall, although some of the wood had burned slightly in places. Now that Daddy and Mama had put out the fire, they came onto the porch. George Lee still had Adline in his arms and I was standing with them on the steps.

"Take Essie Mae them out in that yard, George Lee," Daddy snapped.

George Lee hurried out in the yard with Adline on his hip, dragging me by the arm. Daddy and the farmers who came to help sat on the edge of the porch taking in the fresh air and coughing. After they had talked for a while, the men and women wanted to help clean up the house but Mama and Daddy refused any more help from them and they soon left.

We were playing, rather pretending to play, because I knew what was next and so did George Lee. Before I could finish thinking it, Daddy called George Lee to the porch.

"Come here, boy," he said. "What happened?" he asked angrily. George Lee stood before him trembling.

"Ah-ah-ah-went tuh th' well—tuh get a bucketa water, 'n when ah come back ah seen the house on fire. Essie Mae musta did it."

As he stood there lying, he pointed to the bucket he had placed on the edge of the porch. That seemed proof enough for Daddy. He glanced at me for a few seconds that seemed like hours. I stood there crying, "I didn't, I didn't, I didn't," but Daddy didn't believe me. He snatched me from the porch into the house.

222

Inside he looked for something to whip me with, but all the clothes had been taken off the nails of the walls and were piled up on the bed. It would have taken hours for him to find a belt. So he didn't even try. He felt his waist to discover he was wearing overalls. Nothing was in his reach. He was getting angrier by the second. He looked over at the wood stacked near the fireplace. "Oh my God," I thought, "he's goin' to kill me." He searched through the wood for a small piece. There was not one to be found. Moving backward, he stumbled over a chair. As it hit the floor a board fell out. He picked it up and I began to cry. He threw me across his lap, pulled down my drawers, and beat me on my naked behind. The licks came hard one after the other.

Screaming, kicking, and yelling, all I could think of was George Lee. I would kill him myself after this, I thought. Daddy must have beaten me a good ten minutes before Mama realized he had lost his senses and came to rescue me. I was burning like it was on fire back there when he finally let go of me. I tried to sit down once. It was impossible. It was hurting so bad even standing was painful. An hour or so later, it was so knotty and swollen I looked as if I had been stung by a hive of bees.

This was the first time Daddy beat me. But I didn't speak to him or let him come near me, as long as my behind was sore and hurting. Mama told me that he didn't mean to beat me that hard and that he wasn't angry at me for setting the fire. When I kept crying and telling her that George Lee started the fire, she told Daddy that she thought George Lee did it. He didn't say anything. But the next morning when George Lee came he sent him back home. Mama stayed with us the rest of the week. Then the following week Mama's twelve-year-old brother Ed came to keep us.

A week or so after the fire, every little thing began to get on Daddy's nerves. Now he was always yelling at me and snapping at Mama. The crop wasn't coming along as he had expected. Every evening when he came from the field he was terribly depressed. He was running around the house grumbling all the time.

"Shit, it was justa waste o' time. Didn't getta nuff rain for nuthin'. We ain't gonna even get two bales o' cotton this year. That corn ain't no good and them sweet potatoes jus' burning up in that hard-ass ground. Goddamn, ah'd a did better on a job than this. Ain't gonna have nuthin' left when Mr. Carter take out his share." We had to hear this sermon almost every night and he was always snapping at Mama like it was all her fault.

During the harvest, Daddy's best friend, Bush, was killed. Bush was driving his wagon when his horses went wild, turning the wagon over

223

in the big ditch alongside the road. It landed on his neck and broke it. His death made Daddy even sadder.

The only times I saw him happy any more were when he was on the floor rolling dice. He used to practice shooting them at home before every big game and I would sit and watch him. He would even play with me then, and every time he won that money he would bring me lots of candy or some kind of present. He was good with a pair of dice and used to win the money all the time. He and most of the other men gambled every Saturday night through Sunday morning. One weekend he came home without a cent. He told Mama that he had lost every penny. He came home broke a few more times. Then one Sunday morning before he got home one of the women on the farm came by the house to tell Mama that he was spending his weekends with Florence, Bush's beautiful widow. I remember he and Mama had a real knockdown dragout session when he finally did come home. Mama fist-fought him like a man, but this didn't stop him from going by Florence's place. He even got bolder about it and soon went as often as he liked.

Florence was a mulatto, high yellow with straight black hair. She was the envy of all the women on the plantation. After Bush's death they got very particular about where their men were going. And they watched Florence like a bunch of hawks. She couldn't even go out-doors without some woman peeping at her and reporting that she was now coming out of the house.

Mama had never considered Florence or any of the other women a threat because she was so beautiful herself. She was slim, tall, and tawny-skinned, with high cheekbones and long dark hair. She was by and far the liveliest woman on the plantation and Daddy used to delight in her. When she played with me she was just like a child herself. Daddy used to call her an overgrown wildchild and tease her that she had too much Indian blood in her.

Meantime, Mama had begun to get very fat. Her belly kept getting bigger and bigger. Soon she acted as if she was fat and ugly. Every weekend, when she thought Daddy was with Florence she didn't do a thing but cry. Then one of those red-hot summer days, she sent me and Adline to one of the neighbors nearest to us. We were there all day. I didn't like the people so I was glad when we finally went home. When we returned I discovered why Mama had gotten so fat. She called me to the bed and said, "Look what Santa sent you." I was upset. Santa never brought live dolls before. It was a little bald-headed boy. He was some small and looked as soft as one of our little pigs when it was born.

"His name is Junior," Mama said. "He was named for your daddy."

My daddy's name was Fred so I didn't understand why she said the baby's name was Junior. Adline was a year old and walking good. She cried like crazy at the sight of the little baby.

While I stood by the bed looking at Mama, I realized her belly had gone down. I was glad of that. I had often wondered if Daddy was always gone because her belly had gotten so big. But that wasn't it, because after it went down, he was gone just as much as before, even more.

Next thing I knew, we were being thrown into a wagon with all our things. I really didn't know what was going on. But I knew something was wrong because Mama and Daddy barely spoke to each other and whenever they did exchange words, they snapped and cursed. Later in the night when we arrived at my Great-Aunt Cindy's place, all of our things were taken from the wagon and Daddy left.

"Where is Daddy goin'?" I cried to Mama.

"By his business," she answered.

Aunt Cindy and all the children stood around the porch looking at him drive the wagon away.

"That dog! That no-good dog!" I heard Mama mumble. I knew then that he was gone for good.

"Ain't he gonna stay with us?" I asked.

"No he ain't gonna stay with us! Shut up!" she yelled at me with her eyes full of water. She cried all that night.

We were allowed to stay with Aunt Cindy until Mama found a job. Aunt Cindy had six children of her own, all in a four-room house. The house was so crowded, the four of us had to share a bed together. Adline and I slept at the foot of the bed and Mama and the baby at the head. Aunt Cindy had a mean husband and our presence made him even meaner. He was always grumbling about us being there. "I ain't got enough food for my own chillun," he was always saying. Mama would cry at night after he had said such things.

Mama soon got a job working up the road from Aunt Cindy at the Cooks' house. Mrs. Cook didn't pay Mama much money at all, but she would give her the dinner leftovers to bring home for us at night. This was all we had to eat. Mama worked for the Cooks for only two weeks. Then she got a better job at a Negro café in town. She was making twelve dollars a week, more than she had ever earned.

About a week after she got the new job she got a place for us from the Cooks. Mrs. Cook let Mama have the house for four dollars a month on the condition that Mama would continue to help her around the house on her off day from the café.

The Cooks lived right on a long rock road that ran parallel to Highway 24, the major highway for Negroes and whites living between Woodville and Centreville, the nearest towns.

225

To get to our house from the road you entered a big wooden gate. A little dirt road ran from the gate through the Cooks' cattle pasture and continued past our house to a big cornfield. The Cooks planted the corn for their cattle. But often when Mama didn't have enough money for food she would sneak out at night and take enough to last us a week. Once Mrs. Cook came out there and put up a scarecrow. She said that the crows were eating all the corn. When Mama came home from the café that evening and saw the scarecrow, she laughed like crazy. Then she started taking even more corn. She had a special way of stealing the corn that made it look just like the crows had taken it. She would knock down a few ears and leave them hanging on the stalks. Then she'd drop a few between the rows and pick on a few others. I don't remember everything she did, but before that season was over, Mrs. Cook had three more scarecrows standing.

Right below the cornfield, at the base of the hill, was a swampy area with lots of trees. The trees were so thick that even during the day the swamp was dark and mysterious looking. It looked like an entirely different world to us, but Mama never let us go near it because she said it was full of big snakes, and people hunted down there and we might get killed.

Our little house had two rooms and a porch. The front room next to the porch was larger than the little boxed-in kitchen you could barely turn around in. Its furniture consisted of two small beds. Adline and I slept in one and Mama and Junior in the other. There was also a bench to sit on and a small tin heater. Our few clothes hung on a nail on the wall. In the kitchen there was a wood stove with lots of wood stacked behind it, and a table. The only chair we had was a large rocking chair that was kept on the porch because there was no room in the house for it. We didn't have a toilet. Mama would carry us out in back of the house each night before we went to bed to empty us.

Shortly after we moved in I turned five years old and Mama started me at Mount Pleasant School. Now I had to walk four miles each day up and down that long rock road. Mount Pleasant was a big white stone church, the biggest Baptist church in the area.

The school was a little one-room rotten wood building located right next to it. There were about fifteen of us who went there. We sat on big wooden benches just like the ones in the church, pulled up close to the heater. But we were cold all day. That little rotten building had big cracks in it, and the heater was just too small.

Reverend Cason, the minister of the church, taught us in school. He was a tall yellow man with horn-rimmed glasses that sat on the edge of his big nose. He had the largest feet I had ever seen. He was so big, he towered over us in the little classroom like a giant. In church he

226

preached loud and in school he talked loud. We would sit in class with his sounds ringing in our ears. I thought of putting cotton in my ears but a boy had tried that and the Reverend caught him and beat him three times that day with the big switch he kept behind his desk. I remember once he caught a boy lifting up a girl's dress with his foot. He called him up to his desk and whipped him in his hands with that big switch until the boy cried and peed all over himself. He never did whip me. I was so scared of him I never did anything. I hardly ever opened my mouth. I don't even remember a word he said in class. I was too scared to listen to him. Instead, I sat there all day and looked out the window at the graveyard and counted the tombstones.

One day he caught me.

"Moody, gal! If you don't stop lookin' out that window, I'll make you go out in that graveyard and sit on the biggest tombstone out there all day." Nobody laughed because they were all as scared of him as I was.

We used the toilets in back of the church. The boys' toilet was on one side and girls' on the other. The day after Reverend Cason yelled at me, I asked to be excused. While in the toilet I thought to myself, "I can stay out here all day and he won't even know I'm out here." I began to spend three and four hours a day in the toilet and he didn't even miss me, until a lot of other kids caught on and started doing the same thing. About three weeks or so later about five of us girls were in the toilet at the same time. We had been out there almost an hour. We were standing behind the partition in front of the toilet giggling and making fun of Reverend Cason when all of a sudden we heard him right outside.

"If y'all don't come outta that toilet right this second, I'll come in there and drown you!"

We peeped from behind the partition and saw Reverend Cason standing there with that big switch in his hand.

"Didn't I say come outta there! If I have to come in there and getcha, I'm goin' to beat yo' brains out!"

"Reverend Cason, I ain't finished yet," I said in a trembling voice.

"You ain't finished? You been in there over three hours! If y'all don't get outta there—" Then he was silent. I peeped out again. He was coming toward the door.

I ran out and headed for the classroom, followed by the rest of the girls. When we got around in front of the church we met up with a bunch of boys running from the boys' toilet. We all scrambled in the door. There were only two students sitting in class. I sat in my seat and didn't even breathe until I heard Reverend Cason's big feet hit the bottom step. He came through the door puffing and shouting, but he was so tired from yelling and chasing us that he didn't even beat us. After that he wouldn't excuse us until recess. And then he would have to round us up and bring us back to class.

Every morning before Mama left for the café, she would take us across the road to Grandfather Moody. I would leave for school from there and he would keep Adline and Junior until I came home. My grandfather lived with one of my aunts. He was a very old man and he was sick all the time. I don't ever remember seeing him out of his bed. My aunt them would leave for the field at daybreak, so whenever we were there, my grandfather was alone.

He really cared a lot for us and he liked Mama very much too, because Mama was real good to him. Sometimes my aunt them would go off and wouldn't even fix food for him. Mama would always look to see if there was any food left for him in the kitchen. If there wasn't, she would fix some batty cakes or something for him and he would eat them with syrup.

Often when Mama didn't have money for food, he gave her some. I think he felt guilty for what his son, my daddy, had done to us. He kept his money in a little sack tied around his waist. I think that was his life savings because he never took it off.

Some mornings when Mama would bring us over she would be looking real depressed.

"Toosweet, what's wrong with you?" Grandfather would ask in a weak voice. "You need a little money or something? Do Diddly ever send you any money to help you with these children? It's a shame the way that boy run around gambling and spending all his money on women."

"Uncle Moody, I ain't heard nothin' from him and I don't want to. The Lord'll help me take care o' my children."

"I sure wish he'd do right by these chaps," Grandfather would mumble to himself.

Soon after school was over for the year, Grandfather got a lot sicker than he was before. Mama stopped carrying us by his place. She left us at home alone, and she would bake a pone of bread to last us the whole day.

One evening she came in from work looking real sad.

"Essie Mae, put yo' shoes on. I want you to come go say good-bye to Uncle Moody. He's real sick. Adline, I'm gonna leave you and Junior by Miss Cook. I'm gonna come right back and y'all better mind Miss Cook, you hear?"

"Mama, why I gotta say good-bye to Uncle Moody? Where he's goin'?" I asked her.

228

"He's goin' somewhere he's gonna be treated much better than he's treated now. And he won't ever be sick again," she answered sadly.

I didn't understand why Mama was so sad if Uncle Moody wasn't going to be sick any more. I wanted to ask her but I didn't. All the way to see Uncle Moody, I kept wondering where he was going.

It was almost dark as we walked up in my aunt's yard. A whole bunch of people were standing around on the porch and in the yard. Some of them looked even sadder than Mama. I had never seen that many people there before and everything seemed so strange to me. I looked around at the faces to see if I knew anyone. Suddenly I recognized Daddy, squatting in the yard in front of the house. He had a knife in his hand. As Mama and I walked toward him, he began to pick in the dirt. He glanced up at Mama and he had that funny funny look in his eyes. I had seen it before. He looked like he wanted us back so bad, but Mama was mean. She had vowed that she would never see him again. As they stood there staring at each other, I was reminded of the first time I saw him after he left us, when we lived with my Great-Aunt Cindy. It was Easter Sunday morning. Mama, Aunt Cindy, and all the children were sitting on the porch. We were all having a beautiful time. It was just after the Easter egg hunt and we were eating the eggs we had found in the grass. Mama was playing with us. She had found more eggs than all of us and she was teasing and throwing eggshells at us.

As I was dodging eggshells and giggling at Mama, I saw Daddy coming down the road. I jumped off the porch and ran to meet him, followed by the rest of the children. He gave me lots of candy in a big bag and told me to share it with the others. As we walked back to the porch, I could see Mama's changing expression. Daddy was grinning broadly. He had something for Mama in a big bag he carried with care in his arms.

I don't remember what they said to each other after that. But I remember what was in the big bag for Mama. It was a hat, a big beautiful hat made out of flowers of all colors. When she saw the hat, Mama got real mad. She took the hat and picked every flower from it, petal by petal. She threw them out in the yard and watched the wind blow them away. Daddy looked at her as if he hated her, but there was more than hate in it all. This was just how he looked out in the yard now as he sat picking in the dirt.

I was very frightened. I thought at first he would kill Mama with the knife. Mama stared at him for a while, then went straight past him into the house, leaving me in the yard with him.

"Come here, Essie Mae," he said sadly. I walked to him, shaking. "They say you is in school now. Do you need anything?" he asked. I

229

was so afraid I couldn't answer him. He felt in his pocket. Out of it came a roll of money. He gave it to me, smiling. I took it and was about to smile back when I saw Mama. She came out of the house and snatched the money from me and threw it at him. Then Daddy got up. This time I was sure he would hit Mama. But he didn't. He only walked away with that hurt look in his eyes. Mama grabbed me by the arm and headed out of the yard, pulling me behind her.

"Ain't ah'm gonna say good-bye to Uncle Moody?" I whined.

"He told me to tell you good-bye," she snapped. "He's sleeping now."

That night we had beans for supper, as usual. And all night I wondered why Mama threw back the money Daddy gave me. I was mad with her because we ate beans all the time. Had she taken the money, I thought, we could have meat too.

. . .

Now that school was out and there was no one for us to stay with, we would sit on the porch and rock in the rocking chair most of the day. We were scared to go out and play because of the snakes. Often as we sat on the porch we saw them coming up the hill from the swamp. Sometimes they would just go to the other side of the swamp. But other times they went under the house and we didn't see them come out. When this happened, we wouldn't eat all day because we were scared to go inside. The snakes often came into the house. Once as I was putting wood in the stove for Mama, I almost put my hands on one curled up under the wood. I never touched the woodpile again.

One day we heard Mrs. Cook's dog barking down beside the swamp at the base of the cornfield. We ran out to see what had happened. When we got there, the dog was standing still with his tail straight up in the air barking hysterically. There, lying beside a log, was a big old snake with fishy scales all over his body. Adline, Junior, and I stood there in a trance looking at it, too scared to move. We had never seen one like this. It was so big it didn't even look like a snake. It looked like it was big enough to swallow us whole. Finally the snake slowly made its way back into the swamp, leaving a trail of mashed-down grass behind it.

When Mama came home that evening from the café, we told her all about the snake. At first, she didn't believe us, but we were shaking so that she had us go out back and show her where we had seen it. After she saw the place next to the log where it had been lying and the trail it left going to the swamp, she went and got Mr. Cook. For days Mr. Cook and some other men looked in the swamp for that snake, but they never did find it. After that Mama was scared for us

230

to stay at home alone, and she began looking for a house in town closer to where she worked. "Shit, snakes that damn big might come up here and eat y'all up while I'm at work," she said.

In the meantime, she got our Uncle Ed, whom we liked so much, to come over and look after us every day. Sometimes he would take us hunting. Then we wouldn't have to sit on the porch and watch those snakes in that boiling hot summer sun. Ed made us a "niggershooter" each. This was a little slingshot made out of a piece of leather connected to a forked stick by a thin slab of rubber. We would take rocks and shoot them at birds and anything else we saw. Ed was the only one who ever killed anything. He always carried salt and matches in his pockets and whenever he'd kill a bird he'd pick and roast it right there in the woods. Sometimes Ed took us fishing too. He knew every creek in the whole area and we'd roam for miles. Whenever we caught fish we'd scrape and cook them right on the bank of the creek. On those days we didn't have to eat that hard cold pone of bread Mama left for us.

Sometimes Ed would keep us in the woods all day, and we wouldn't hunt birds or fish or anything. We just walked, listening to the birds and watching the squirrels leap from tree to tree and the rabbits jumping behind the little stumps. Ed had a way of making you feel so much a part of everything about the woods. He used to point out all the trees to us, telling us which was an oak, and which was a pine and which bore fruit. He'd even give us quizzes to see if we could remember one tree from another. I thought he was the smartest person in the whole world.

One day Ed was late coming and we had resigned ourselves to spending the whole day on the porch. We rocked for hours in the sun and finally fell asleep. Eventually Ed came. He locked the house up immediately and rushed us off the porch. He told us he was going to surprise us. I thought we were going to a new creek or something so I begged him to tell me. He saw that I was upset so finally he told me that he was taking us home with him.

As we were walking down the rock road, it occurred to me that I had never been home with Ed and I was dying to see where he lived. I could only remember seeing Grandma Winnie once, when she came to our house just after Junior was born. Mama never visited Grandma because they didn't get along that well. Grandma had talked Mama into marrying my daddy when Mama wanted to marry someone else. Now that Mama and Daddy had separated, she didn't want anything to do with Grandma, especially when she learned that her old boyfriend was married and living in Chicago.

231

Ed told us that he didn't live very far from us, but walking bare-footed on the rock road in the boiling hot sun, I began to wonder how far was "not very far."

"Ed, how much more longer we gotta go? These rocks is burning my foots," I said.

"Ain't much further. Just right around that bend," Ed yelled back at me. "Why didn't you put them shoes on? I told you them rocks was hot." He waited on me now. "Oughter make you go all the way back to that house and put them shoes on. You gonna be laggin' behind comin' back and we ain't never gonna make it 'fore Toosweet get off o' work!"

"Mama told us we ain't supposed to wear our shoes out round the house. You know we ain't got but one pair and them my school shoes."

"Here it is, right here," Ed said at last. "Essie Mae, run up front and open that gate." By this time he was carrying Junior on his back and Adline half asleep on his hip.

I ran to the gate and opened it and rode on it as it swung open. We entered a green pasture with lots of cows.

"Is that where you stay?" I asked Ed as I pointed to an old wooden house on the side of a hill.

"Is any more houses down there?" Ed said, laughing at me. "See that pond over there, Essie Mae!" he called as I ran down the hill. "I'm gonna bring y'all fishing over here one day. Boy, they got some big fishes in there! You shoulda seen what Sam and Walter caught yesterday."

I glanced at the pond but ran right past it. I didn't have my mind on fishing at all. I was dying to see Grandma Winnie's house and Sam and Walter, Ed's younger brothers, and his sister Alberta whom I had never met. Ed had told me that George Lee was now living with his daddy and stepmother. I was glad because I didn't want to run into him there.

Alberta was standing in the yard at the side of the house feeding the big fire around the washpot with kindling. Two white boys about my size stood at her side. I looked around for Sam and Walter. But I didn't see them.

"Ed, what took you so long? I oughta made you tote that water fo' you left here," Alberta shouted at Ed as she turned and saw us.

"I had to tote Adline and Junior all the way here. You must think um superman or something," Ed answered angrily.

"I ain't asked you what you is! You just git that bucket and fill that rinse tub up fulla water!" Alberta shouted. "Sam, yo'n Essie Mae help Ed with that water. And, Walter, take Adline and Junior on that porch outta the way."

I stood dead in my tracks with my mouth wide open as the two white boys jumped when Alberta yelled Sam's and Walter's names. One boy ran to the wash bench against the house and got a bucket and the other picked up Junior, took Adline by the hand, and carried them on the porch.

"Essie Mae! Didn't I tell you to help Sam and Ed with that water?" Alberta yelled at me.

"Where is Sam and Walter?" I asked with my eyes focused on the white boy on the porch with Adline and Junior.

"Is you blind or somethin'? Get that bucket and help tote that water," Alberta yelled.

I turned my head to look for Ed. He was headed for the pond in front of the house with a bucket in his hand. "Ed!" I shouted, still in a state of shock. He turned and looked at me. I stood there looking from Ed to the white boys and back to Ed again, without saying anything. Ed opened his mouth to speak but no words came. A deep expression of hurt crossed his face. For a second he dropped his head to avoid my eyes. Then he walked toward me. He picked up another bucket and handed it to me. Then he took me by the hand and led me to the pond.

As we walked toward the pond, one of the white boys ran ahead of us. He climbed through the barbed-wire fence right below the levee of the pond. Then he turned and pushed the bottom strand of the wire down to the ground with his foot and held the middle strand up with his hands, so Ed and I could walk through. I began to pull back from Ed but he clutched my hand even harder and led me toward the fence. As we ducked under, I brushed against the white boy. Jerking back, I caught my hair in the barbed-wire overhead.

"Essie Mae, watch yo' head 'fore you git cut! Wait, wait, you got your hair caught," the white boy said as he quickly and gently untangled my hair from the wire. Then he picked up the bucket I had dropped and handed it to me. Ed didn't say one word as he stood beside the fence watching us.

The white boy caught me by the hand and attempted to pull me up the levee of the pond. I pulled back. Still holding my hand, he stopped and stared at me puzzled. "Come on, Essie Mae!" yelled Ed, giving me an "it's O.K., stupid" look as he ran up the levee past us. Then the white boy and I followed Ed up the hill holding hands.

As we toted water from the pond, I kept watching the white boys and listening to Alberta and Ed call them Sam and Walter. I noticed that they treated them just like they treated me, and the white boy called Sam was nice to me just like Ed. He kept telling me about the fish he and Walter had caught and that I should come and fish with them sometimes.

After we finished toting the water, we went on the porch where

Adline, Junior, and Walter sat. Adline had a funny look on her face. I could tell that she was thinking about Sam and Walter too. Before the evening was over, I finally realized that the two boys actually were Ed's brothers. But how Ed got two white brothers worried me.

On our way back home, Ed carried us through the woods. As we walked, he talked and talked about the birds, the trees, and everything else he could think of, without letting me say a word. I knew he didn't want to talk about Sam and Walter, so I didn't say anything. I just walked and listened.

I thought about Sam and Walter so much that night, it gave me a headache. Then I finally asked Mama:

"Mama, them two boys over at Winnie's. Ed say they is his brothers. Is they your brothers?"

"What boys?" Mama asked.

"Over at Winnie's. They got two boys living with her about my size and they is the same color as Miss Cook. . . ."

"What did y'all do over at Winnie's today? Was Winnie home?" Mama asked as if she hadn't heard me.

"No, she was at work. Wasn't nobody there but Alberta and those two boys. . . ."

"What was Alberta doing?" Mama asked.

"She was washing and we toted water from the pond for her. Them boys is some nice and they say they is kin to us. Ain't they your brothers, Mama?"

"Look, don't you be so stupid! If they's Winnie's children and I'm Winnie's too, don't that make us sisters and brothers?" Mama shouted at me.

"But how come they look like Miss Cook and Winnie ain't that color and Alberta ain't that color and you . . ."

" 'Cause us daddy ain't that color! Now you shut up! Why you gotta know so much all the time? I told Ed not to take y'all to Winnie's," she shouted.

Mama was so mad that I was scared if I asked her anything else she might hit me, so I shut up. But she hadn't nearly satisfied my curiosity at all.

While Mama was working at the café in town, she began to get fat. She often told us how much she could eat while she was working. So I didn't think anything of her slowly growing "little pot." But one day after taking a good look, I noticed it wasn't a little pot any more. And I knew she was going to have a baby. She cried just about every night, then she would get up sick every morning. She didn't stop working until a week before the baby was born, and she was out of work only three weeks. She went right back to the café.

Mama called the baby James. His daddy was a soldier. One day the soldier and his mother came to get him. They were real yellow people. The only Negro near their color I had ever seen was Florence, the lady my daddy was now living with. The soldier's mother was a stout lady with long thin straight black hair and very thin lips. She looked like a slightly tanned white woman. Mama called her "Miss Pearl." All the time they were in our house, Mama acted as though she was scared of them. She smiled a couple of times when they made general comments about the baby. But I could tell she didn't mean it.

Just before the soldier and Miss Pearl left, Miss Pearl turned to Mama and said, "You can't work and feed them other children and keep this baby too." I guess Mama did want to keep the little boy. She looked so sad I thought she was going to cry, but she didn't say anything. Miss Pearl must have seen how Mama looked too. "You can stop in to see the baby when you are in town sometimes," she said. Then she and the soldier took him and drove away in their car. Mama cried all night. And she kept saying bad things about some Raymond. I figured that was the name of the soldier who gave her the baby.

At the end of that summer Mama found it necessary for us to move into town, in Centreville, where she worked. This time we moved into a two-room house that was twice the size of the other one. It was next to where a very poor white family lived in a large green frame house. It was also located on one of the main roads branching off Highway 24 running into Centreville. We were now a little less than a mile from the school that I was to attend, which was on the same road as our house. Here we had a sidewalk for the first time. It extended from town all the way to school where it ended. I was glad we lived on the sidewalk side of the road. Between the sidewalk and our house the top soil was sand about two feet deep. We were the only ones with clean white sand in our yard and it seemed beautiful and special. There was even more sand for us to play in in a large vacant lot on the other side of our house. The white people living next to us only had green grass in their yard just like everybody else.

A few weeks after we moved there, I was in school again. I was now six years old and in the second grade. At first, it was like being in heaven to have less than a mile to walk to school. And having a sidewalk from our house all the way there made things even better.

I was going to Willis High, the only Negro school in Centreville. It was named for Mr. C. H. Willis, its principal and founder, and had only been expanded into a high school the year before I started there. Before Mr. Willis came to town, the eighth grade had been the limit of schooling for Negro children in Centreville.

For the first month that I was in school a Negro family across the street kept Adline and Junior. But after that Mama had them stay at home alone and, every hour or so until I came home, the lady across the street would come down and look in on them. One day when I came home from school, Adline and Junior were naked playing in the sand in front of our house. All the children who lived in town used that sidewalk that passed our house. When they saw Adline and Junior sitting in the sand naked they started laughing and making fun of them. I was ashamed to go in the house or recognize Adline and Junior as my little sister and brother. I had never felt that way before. I got mad at Mama because she had to work and couldn't take care of Adline and Junior herself. Every day after that I hated the sand in front of the house.

Before school was out we moved again and I was glad. It seemed as though we were always moving. Every time it was to a house on some white man's place and every time it was a room and a kitchen. The new place was much smaller than the last one, but it was nicer. Here we had a large pasture to play in that was dry, flat, and always closely cropped because of the cattle. Mama still worked at the café. But now she had someone to keep Adline and Junior until I came home from school.

One day shortly after Christmas, Junior set the house on fire. He was playing in the front room. We had a small round tin heater in there and Junior raked red-hot coals out of it onto the floor and pushed them against the wall. I was washing dishes in the kitchen when I looked up and saw flames leaping toward the ceiling. I ran to get Junior. The house had loose newspaper tacked to the walls and was built out of old dry lumber. It was burning fast.

After I had carried Junior outside, I took him and Adline up on a hill a little distance away. The whole house was blazing now. I stood there with Junior on my hip and holding Adline by the hand and suddenly I thought about the new clothes Mama had bought us for Christmas. These were the first she had ever bought us. All our other clothes had been given to us. I had to get them. I left Adline and Junior on the hill and ran back to the house. I opened the kitchen door and was about to crawl into the flames and smoke when a neighbor grabbed me and jerked me out. Just as she pulled me away, the roof fell in. I stood there beside her with tears running down my face and watched the house burn to the ground. All our new Christmas clothes were gone, burned to ashes.

We had only lived there for a few months and now we moved again to another two-room house off a long rock road. This time Mama quit the job at the café to do domestic work for a white family. We lived in their maid's quarters. Since Mama made only five dollars a week, the white woman she worked for let us live in the house free. Mama's job was now close to home and she could watch Adline and Junior herself.

Sometimes Mama would bring us the white family's leftovers. It was the best food I had ever eaten. That was when I discovered that white folks ate different from us. They had all kinds of different food with meat and all. We always had just beans and bread. One Saturday the white lady let Mama bring us to her house. We sat on the back porch until the white family finished eating. Then Mama brought us in the house and sat us at the table and we finished up the food. It was the first time I had seen the inside of a white family's kitchen. That kitchen was pretty, all white and shiny. Mama had cooked that food we were eating too. "If Mama only had a kitchen like this of her own," I thought, "she would cook better food for us."

~~~~~~~~~~~~~~~~~~~~~~~~~~~~~~~~~~

DISCUSSION AND INQUIRY

Because of economic necessity, Anne and her younger sister, Adline, were often cared for during the day by a changing assortment of friends and relatives. Anne's experiences with her 8-year-old Uncle George were not very pleasant. Perhaps, however, we should give consideration to George's point of view. Should any 8-year-old be given the responsibility of caring for two young children without adult supervision? How hard it must have been to restrict his 8-year-old interests. He wasn't even allowed to take the children into the woods after the tick incident. Restricted to the small house and yard, one wonders if George deliberately mistreated the girls in an effort to be relieved of the awesome responsibility. (See the selection by Gertrude Berg, in which the issue of children having authority over other children is considered.)

Anne recalls vividly the unjust beating given to her by her father, who believed George's version of how the house caught fire. As an adult, can you recall a punishment you once received that you considered unjust? Why do such memories stay with us so clearly?

Anne experienced many moves, desertion by her father, and her mother's out-of-wedlock pregnancy. Can such experiences affect a child's perception of the family structure? It becomes clear that the concept of family will have different meanings and considerations to individuals based on their childhood experiences. Does "family" have varying connotations among ethnic groups, or is it economic status that is the influential factor?

Anne received little preparation and realistic explanation about those things that had a direct effect on her existence, such as pregnancy, death, and the separation of her parents. Is there an age at which children should be told exactly what is happening and what is real? Each family decides for itself what realities are to be introduced to its children and at what age—the stork versus the womb, the tooth fairy versus daddy placing the money under the pillow, death versus "a long journey." How would you handle these situations?

At one point, Anne meets, for the first time, two cousins who are white. She is confused by their existence and their relationship to her. The incident is another example of the lack of preparation given to her to face such a reality. Does her mother's explanation satisfy her curiosity? What additional questions might Anne have asked had she not been warned that her mother might beat her?

While in elementary school, Anne and her peers found that sitting in the lavatory was much more pleasant than sitting in the classroom. This practice of getting out of the classroom either to go to the bathroom or roam the halls is still very much with us. Does this say anything about our public schools and their ability to hold the interest of many children?

Kwame Nkrumah

BIOGRAPHICAL SKETCH

Kwame Nkrumah, the former president of Ghana, was born in 1909 in the western province of the Gold Coast. He received a degree from the Prince of Wales College and later attended Lincoln University in Pennsylvania. He became General Secretary of the United Gold Coast Convention in 1947, but broke away to start the revolutionary Convention People's Party. After spending one year as a political prisoner, he was released and was elected the first prime minister of the Gold Coast. In 1957 he declared independence for his country, Ghana, and became president of the Republic in 1960. He died in 1972.

SELECTIONS FROM

GHANA: THE AUTOBIOGRAPHY OF KWAME NKRUMAH

THE only certain facts about my birth appear to be that I was born in the village of Nkroful in Nzima around mid-day on a Saturday in mid-September.

Nzima lies in the extreme south-west of the Gold Coast and covers an area of about a thousand square miles stretching from the river Ankobra on the east to the river Tano and its lagoons on the west. It has a population of about 100,000 people, and was known to Europeans for many years as Apollonia because it was on the feast day of St. Apollo that the white man first set foot in Nzima Land.

In the outlying areas of the Gold Coast nobody bothered to record the dates of births, marriages and deaths, as is the custom of the western world. Such happenings were remarkable only because they provided a cause for celebration. By tribal custom it was enough for a mother to assess the age of her child by calculating the number of national festivals that had been celebrated since its birth. In most cases,

239

however, even this was unknown as nobody was concerned very much with age: time did not count in those peaceful communities.

The national festival of Nzima is called Kuntum. According to my mother's calculations, forty-five Kuntums have taken place since I was born, which makes the year of my birth 1912.

On the other hand, the priest who later baptized me into the Roman Catholic Church recorded my birth date as 21st September, 1909. Although this was a mere guess on his part, I have always used this date on official documents, not so much because I believed in its accuracy, but insofar as officialdom was concerned, it was the line of least resistance. It was not until recently that I came to realize how near the mark this guess must have been.

For recently, I spent a short holiday in Nzima and had the opportunity to revisit some of my childhood haunts and to recapture the past. As I sat with some friends on the sea shore at Half Assini our eyes were drawn to the rusty bulk of the *Bakana*, a cargo boat owned by the British and African Steam Navigation Company, which had been wrecked in 1913 and had come to rest on the sea shore.

The *Bakana* had been a landmark to me for so long that I had never realized how significant a part it could play in throwing light on my age. One of my friends asked what had happened and whether I could remember it. Although I was certainly no older than three or four years at the time, I can well remember being told the story of this disaster.

On the night of 27th August, 1913, the *Bakana*, on her way back from Nigeria to the United Kingdom with a cargo of oil, got into difficulties in a particularly heavy surf between Dixcove and Half Assini. In spite of the efforts of the captain to turn the ship seaward, the *Bakana* was dragged by a strong current nearer and nearer the shallow water until she got her propeller embedded in about five feet of sand. Two ships, the *Ebani* and the *Warri* arrived the following day and endeavored to pull her out to sea, but the *Bakana* refused to be moved. The master, Captain Richard Williams, then gave orders to abandon ship and the crew and a few passengers were safely lowered into surf boats and taken ashore. The surf boat which was carrying the captain to one of the other ships capsized and he was drowned. His body was recovered from the sea and he was buried in the center of Half Assini where, although the gravestone has suffered by erosion, it is still possible to read most of the inscription: "Captain Richard Williams, who perished in the surf, August 28th 1913, aged 40 years. . . . Day dawns and the shadows flee away."

I remember more vividly, however, the stories that circulated about the cause of the shipwreck, how the god of the river Ama Azule, wishing to visit his goddess of the neighboring river Awianialuanu, had

240

planned this disaster in order that he should have a boat at his command. The superstition surrounding this was strengthened by the fact that the *Bakana* was actually dragged nearer and nearer to the mouth of the river until eventually she reached its mouth, where she lies today, firmly embedded in the sand, a huge rusty shell, deserted by all but the surf that destroyed her, but majestic still in spite of her torn and broken masts and her gaping hull.

In fact the people of Half Assini still say that they see the lights of a ship—believed to be the *Bakana*—as she sets out to sea at night and ploughs her way to Awianialuanu.

My mother confirms the fact that I was a small boy at the time and that the event occurred some little time after she had brought me from Nkroful to live with my father in Half Assini. Assuming, therefore, that the year of my birth was 1909, the Saturday nearest to the middle of September in that year was the 18th. It seems likely, therefore, that I was born on Saturday, 18th September, 1909.

On the day I was born there was much celebration and beating of drums in the village of Nkroful, not, I may say, in honor of my birth, but in connection with the funeral rites of my father's mother who had died a short while before. As far as the Akan tribe (of which the Nzimas form a part) is concerned, funerals receive far greater honors than do births and marriages. The ceremonial rites performed for the dead presuppose the existence of a supernatural world and, in order that they should not be deprived of comfort there, they are buried with gold, clothes and other necessities of life. Continuous wailing is carried out by relatives and friends of the deceased person, and this goes on throughout the first few days. During the third week following the death a ceremony of remembrance of all the deceased members of the clan is held, commencing with the offering of libations to the spirits and ending in the small hours of the morning with games, dancing and feasting.

And so, on that particular day in Nkroful, my birth was of very little interest to the villagers. I am told, however, that there was a good deal of commotion going on where I was, for I apparently took so long to show any signs of life that my mother had given up all interest in me as she believed me to be dead. This is not as heartless as it may sound for it is a strong belief among the Akans that if a mother mourns the death of her child she will become sterile, and this, to an African woman, is the worst thing that can befall her.

But my female relatives, having dragged themselves away from the funeral celebrations, would not give in so easily. They were determined to put life into me and proceeded to make as much noise as they could with cymbals and other instruments, at the same time jolting me about

241

—and even stuffing a banana into my mouth in an effort to make me cough and so draw breath. They finally succeeded in arousing my interest and, their job completed, handed me back to my anxious mother, a yelling and kicking Saturday's child.

Great importance is attached by the Akans to the day of the week on which a child is born for this determines his platonic soul. They believe that a man is possessed of three souls; the blood soul (or *moyga*) transmitted by the female and considered synonymous with the clan, the *ntoro* which is transmitted by the male and the *okra*, or platonic soul. In order that there should be no mistake about the *okra*, a specific name is given to the child according to the day of the week on which he was born. A male child born on Sunday is called Kwesi; if born on Monday he receives the name Kodjo. And so on. For a boy born on Saturday the name is Kwame. There are other superstitions surrounding a child's birth. For instance, the first child is supposed to be less bright, the third child to be precocious and incorrigible, the ninth child to bring good luck and the tenth child to bring misfortune. Sometimes the fear of bad luck at the birth of a tenth child is so strong that the infant may be smothered at birth or during early infancy.

Whilst I can claim to fall into the pattern of things by being born on a Saturday and bearing the name of Kwame, it is surely disheartening that I was the first and only child of my mother and am therefore, according to tradition, less bright than average!

Nkroful is a typical West African village composed of mud and wattle houses and bamboo compounds. The ground is high and stony leading down via a steep escarpment to a stream on one side and to a swampy lake on the other. I lived there with my mother until I was nearly three years old when we left to join my father who was a goldsmith in Half Assini.

Half Assini is about fifty miles from Nkroful and is on the borders of the French Ivory Coast and the Gold Coast. It is unfortunate for Nzimas that the Tano river and the Ayi Lagoon into which it drains were taken to form the boundary between the two countries, for the people had set up fishing villages all round the lake and are now divided. This has caused much discontent because of customs authorities, language and other barriers which they encounter when crossing from one side to the other.

Many of them still travel on foot the longer way round by the sea shore. Every day, even today, it is a common sight to see women with the heaviest of loads on their heads set off at a trotting pace on their seven-hour journey. And when they arrive at their destination they are still trotting! In these days it is also quite a common thing to see lorries travelling by this route, but this can only be done when the tide is low.

There were no lorries in the days of my childhood, indeed there were

242

not even proper roads, and when I left Nkroful with my mother it was necessary to make the journey to Half Assini on foot travelling through Esiama and along the sea shore. This took nearly three days and we had to spend two nights in the villages en route. At other times when we used to journey into the bush together and we could not complete our journey in one day, we would sleep out in the open forest. I remember helping my mother to collect pieces of wood and dead leaves in order to make a fire to keep wild animals away. I had no fears of such things myself; like all small children I had complete confidence in my mother.

And she was a most worthy and vigilant protector. Although she allowed me a lot of freedom and I never felt myself tied to her apron strings, she was always at hand when I needed her and she had a knack of knowing my wants without either of us speaking a word. She never seemed to use her voice to command; there was something about her presence, her quiet, decisive movements, that placed her above most people and gave her a natural leadership.

My father was a man of strong character, extremely kind and very proud of his children. Although I was probably one of the most wilful and naughtiest of children, I can never remember his lifting a finger against me. As a matter of fact I can only remember my mother beating me really hard on one occasion. That was when, because I couldn't get my own way about something, I spat into a pan of stew that was being prepared for the family meal.

We were a large family, for, although I was the only child of my mother and father, my father had quite a number of children by other wives whom he married by native custom. Polygamy was quite legal and even today it is quite in order for a man to have as many wives as he can afford. In fact the more wives a man can keep the greater is his social position. However unconventional and unsatisfactory this way of life may appear to those who are confirmed monogamists, and without in any way trying to defend my own sex, it is a frequently accepted fact that man is naturally polygamous. All the African has done is to recognize this fact and to legalize, or to make socially acceptable, a thing which has been done and will doubtless continue to be done by man as long as he exists. It is interesting to note that divorce in this polygamous community is negligible compared with countries practicing monogamy, especially when divorce can be obtained so much more easily than in a monogamous society. For a marriage can be brought to an end for any of the following reasons: adultery, barrenness or impotency, drunkenness, sexual incompatibility, the quarrelsome nature of the woman, inharmonious relationship with a mother-in-law, and discovery of marriage within one's own clan.

All members of a clan are considered to be blood relations, and if a

243

marriage takes place between two of the members, it is believed that the whole clan will be visited by the wrath of the gods. In my parents' case, for instance, both were of the same tribe, but my father was of the Asona clan and my mother was from the Anonas. As heredity is governed by the matrilineal line, I belong not to my father's clan, as would be the case in western marriages, but to my mother's. My father's line descends through the eldest son of his sister, a member of the Asona clan.

Apart from our immediate family, which consisted of about fourteen people in all, there always seemed to be relatives staying with us and our little compound was usually full of people. It is a custom among Africans that any relative, however distant the relationship may be, can at any time arrive at your home and remain under your roof for as long as he wants. Nobody questions his arrival, how long he intends staying or his eventual departure. This hospitality is sometimes very much abused, for if one member of the family does well for himself he usually finds his compound filled to capacity with men and women, all claiming some distant kinship, and all prepared to live at his expense until the money runs out.

My family lived together very peaceably and I can remember very few quarrels. The women of the house used to take turns each week to cook the meals and look after my father and at the same time they either worked in the fields or did some petty trading in order to supplement the family income. It was a wonderful life for us children with nothing to do but play around all day. Our playground was vast and varied, for we had the sea, the lagoon and the thrill of unexplored bush all within easy reach.

But we had no toys. I remember one of our playmates, whose father had made some money, one day produced a child's bicycle and was to be found daily pedalling it up and down the beach. We were extremely envious of him and longed to be allowed to ride it, but he was very possessive and rarely let the thing out of his sight. Today, however, it is he who may be envious of other people, for his father died and left the family not only penniless, but also unequipped to make their own living.

It was probably this bicycle that inspired my half-brothers to build one of a sort out of two iron hoops that they found. What I remember most about that incident is the way they treated me almost as a mascot and something rather sacred. Although they all wanted to sit on the contraption and be the first to try it out, I was placed on the seat and held firmly in case I should come to harm.

Looking back on the kindness and consideration with which they always treated me, I sometimes wonder whether they did not in their heart of hearts regard me as a spoilt little brat. Probably they were so afraid that I would run home screaming to my mother, whom they held in high regard, that they were careful to give me no cause for complaint. Certainly my mother rarely denied me anything and doubtless I took advantage of this, but I believe that she tried not to make her affection too obvious because whenever she was serving our meals, she always gave me mine last. I insisted on sleeping in her bed until, of my own free will, I decided to join my half-brothers, and I remember how I used to be angry when my father came to sleep in our bed and I insisted on sleeping between them. Several times he tried to explain to me that he was married to my mother, but I told him that I also was married to her and that it was my job to protect her.

Unlike most growing children, I was very rarely ready for my food. In fact my mother used to get worried because of the trouble she had in forcing me to eat. She discovered that I would sometimes wake up hungry in the night and so she formed the habit of putting some baked plantain under my pillow so that if I woke at any time through hunger, I could eat this and go back to sleep. I very rarely ate a meal during the day and only returned from my games in the evening to eat the food that had been prepared. My parents never complained about this and once they realized that I was flourishing in spite of my small and irregular meals, they ceased to worry.

Although there were plenty of children with whom I could play, my happiest hours were spent alone. I used to wander off on my own and spend hours on end quietly observing the birds and the lesser animals of the forest and listening to their numerous and varied calls. Sometimes, however, I was not content merely to sit and watch them; I wanted to touch and caress them. It was not long, therefore, before I devised a means of trapping them—not to kill but to bring home as pets. Many times I returned with a squirrel, a bird, a rat or a land crab. On one occasion I remember refusing to go with my mother on a journey unless she allowed me to take a pet bird along with me. Clutching the small cage against my body I suppose I either smothered the poor thing or else killed it with fright. Anyhow, we had not gone more than five miles when I suddenly discovered that my precious bird was dead. This caused me so much distress that my mother was unable to console me and there was no alternative but to return home.

I had heard many stories about ghosts, for such things are a very real part of tribal society. Instead of being afraid of these tales, however, I remember sitting for long enough on my own wishing that I could die simply because I should then rank among those privileged souls who could pass through walls and closed doors, sit among groups of people unobserved and make a general nuisance of themselves!

I do not know whether this longing for things supernatural indicated psychic power, but my mother has many times related the following incident which occurred one day, when, strapped to her back in the normal manner of a young African child, I was travelling with her on one of our frequent journeys together. It happened that she had to wade through a stream on the way and, as we neared the center, I suddenly cried out in excitement that I was standing on a fish. Although startled by my sudden and noisy outburst, my mother was even more surprised when she discovered to her utter amazement that she had actually trapped a fish with one of her feet. It ended happily, for she managed to catch it and we had it for dinner that evening.

To strangers I must have appeared a strange and difficult child. Few would have believed that the small boy who kept himself in the background with his finger in his mouth or who would make himself scarce for hours on end, could, when roused, spit fire like a machine gun and use every limb and finger nail in defending his idea of justice. Two men in particular ran away from me in horror.

The first was a policeman who, in the course of his duty, reprimanded one of my half-brothers for doing some kind of mischief on the beach. As he grabbed hold of my brother's arm I was indignant and began to pound him with sand at such a rate and with such force that he let his victim go and ran away. He reported the matter to my father and I received a severe telling off, but I was sure I could detect a twinkle of amusement in my father's eyes.

The second man was in love with one of my half-sisters and came to our compound to ask her hand in marriage. At first I did not understand who he was or what he had come for until in the general excitement someone explained to me that he had come to take my sister away in marriage. I yelled and screamed like one possessed and kicked at the poor love-sick man until he was forced to run from the compound!

I soon learned, however, that life for a growing boy was not all play; at least, not for boys with parents like mine. Although my mother had never had the benefit of formal education herself, she was determined that I should be sent to school at the earliest opportunity. My father, probably due to my mother's persuasive power, was strongly in favor of this also. Even though I could often get around my father, I knew that once my mother's mind had been made up there was nothing I could do about it.

I found my first day at school so disappointing that I ran away determined never to return. But my mother turned a deaf ear to my raging protests and quietly but determinedly dragged me by the arm each morning and deposited me in the schoolroom. Eventually I realized that I had lost the battle and decided that as I was going to be forced to stay there, I might as well get to like it and do what I could to learn something. To my surprise I soon found that I enjoyed my lessons and looked forward to going to school, even though we lived in fear and trembling of the teacher because of his firm and active belief in the adage—"Spare the rod and spoil the child." I disliked being forced to do things against my will, for I had not been accustomed to it, and I used to think what a paradise school would be if we were left in peace to do our studies without the presence of the schoolmaster.

All the various grades were housed in one room and the master used to teach a class at a time. It must have been a hard job for him, and we did not do anything to ease his lot. Luckily I was keen on learning, so keen in fact, that soon my only dread was that my father might one day be unable to afford the school fees, which at that time amounted to threepence a month. Because of this I started rearing a few chickens which I sold for sixpence each. By this means I could not only help to meet the school fees, but I had money to buy books as well. In addition, any fears about my father's poverty were quite unfounded because I can never remember him denying any of us anything we asked and he was particularly generous where I was concerned.

One thing in particular stands out in my mind during my early schooldays, probably because it was my first lesson in discipline. We were not fond of the teacher because of his frequent use of the stick, often we thought without just cause. One day we learned that an inspector was coming to the school and immediately saw our chance of getting our revenge on the master. We got together and decided to play truant for the whole day during the inspector's visit. My one regret was that I was not able to see the expression on the inspector's face when he found an empty classroom or, better still, the look of horror and amazement on the face of the teacher. It must certainly have caused him much embarrassment, but the following morning he got the last laugh, for, as soon as we showed our faces, he was waiting for us with his stick. We were each stripped naked and given twenty-four lashes on our bare bottoms. This hurt so much that for the next three days I was quite unable to sit down at my school desk. But whatever injury this caused to my body and my pride, I knew well enough that I had deserved it. And from that day I have always learnt to accept punishment that I feel I have justly earned, however humiliating this may be.

At about this time I came under the influence of a Roman Catholic priest, a German called George Fischer. This large and well-disciplined man seemed to take a liking to me and he did much to help me in my studies. In fact he became almost my guardian during my early school days and so relieved my parents of most of the responsibility with regard to my primary education. My father was not at all religious but my mother was converted to the Catholic faith and it was through her and Father Fischer that I was also baptized into the Roman Catholic Church.

In those days I took my religion seriously and was very often to be found serving at Mass. As I grew older, however, the strict discipline of

Roman Catholicism stifled me. It was not that I became any less religious but rather that I sought freedom in the worship of and communion with my God, for my God is a very personal God and can only be reached direct. I do not find the need of, in fact I resent the intervention of a third party in such a personal matter. Today I am a nondenominational Christian and a Marxist socialist and I have not found any contradiction between the two.

Probably it was the same fear that my aspirations might be held in check by the Roman Catholic Church that made me afraid of getting myself tied up with women. In those days my fear of women was beyond all understanding. I remember there used to be a young girl who lived a short way from my home and she used to wait for hours in a little lane dividing our compound from the next one. If I happened to come out into the lane she used to approach me and try to start a conversation with me. When she saw that I simply stared at her like a frightened animal, she probably thought I was shy and so she bravely whispered to me that she loved me. I was horrified and abused her as if she had hurt me. I rushed in and told my mother of the wickedness of the girl. My mother laughed and said, "You should be flattered, my boy. What is wrong with somebody being fond of you?"

The girl was persistent in her advances and she started bringing tempting dishes of food which she gave to my mother for me to eat. As soon as I knew that this girl had provided the food, I refused to eat any of it; it was days before my mother could persuade me to eat anything.

I have never outgrown that feeling toward women. It is not fear today, but something deeper. Perhaps it is a dread of being trapped, of having my freedom taken away or being in some way overpowered. And I have the same feelings about money and organized and obligatory religion. All three of them represent to my mind something that should play a very minor part in a man's life, for once one of them gets the upper hand, man becomes a slave and his personality is crushed.

Perhaps if I had heeded the passionate words of the girl in the lane I would have been content to spend the rest of my days with her in Half Assini teaching at the local school or following in my father's trade. But things didn't work out that way.

~~~~~~~~~~~~~~~~~~~~~~~~~~~~~~~~~~~~

DISCUSSION AND INQUIRY

Based on tradition and superstition, Kwame, who was his mother's first and only child, was expected to be less bright than average. Is there any evidence to support the notion that first or only children are less bright? How might such a superstition have started? When such an expectation exists, is it likely that a first-born will be treated differently from the other children in the family? Is there any evidence that Kwame's experiences in his extended-family setting were altered based on the expectation that he was less bright than other children in the family?

Kwame describes his family life as peaceful and relatively free of quarreling. It was an extended family in the African tradition: one father had a number of wives and many children. Although his own mother was primarily responsible for him, Kwame had a number of caretakers and many playmates. He has fond memories of those days when he and his half-brothers roamed their vast playground and made their own toys from scraps and natural materials in the bush or on the beach. Consider some of the advantages of spending one's childhood in such a setting. Compare Kwame's early experiences with those of Chet Huntley, who was also a member of an extended family. (See the selection by Chet Huntley.)

George Orwell

BIOGRAPHICAL SKETCH

George Orwell (the pseudonym for Eric Arthur Blair) was born in India in 1903. He joined the Indian police force after he was graduated from high school, but not finding his calling there, he returned to England, where he received his formal education, and became a journalist. He moved to Spain during the civil war there, and reported on that conflict. His critical essays appeared in the London Observer and Times, *and he earned the first annual award from the* Partisan Review. *Some of his better known works are* Animal Farm *and* 1984. *He died in 1950.*

SELECTIONS FROM

SUCH, SUCH WERE THE JOYS

SOON after I arrived at Crossgates (not immediately, but after a week or two, just when I seemed to be settling into the routine of school life) I began wetting my bed. I was now aged eight, so that this was a reversion to a habit which I must have grown out of at least four years earlier.

Nowadays, I believe, bed-wetting in such circumstances is taken for granted. It is a normal reaction in children who have been removed from their homes to a strange place. In those days, however, it was looked on as a disgusting crime which the child committed on purpose and for which the proper cure was a beating. For my part I did not need to be told it was a crime. Night after night I prayed, with a fervor never previously attained in my prayers, "Please God, do not let me wet my bed! Oh, please God, do not let me wet my bed!" but it made remarkably little difference. Some nights the thing happened, others not. There was no volition about it, no consciousness. You did not properly speaking *do* the deed: you merely woke up in the morning and found that the sheets were wringing wet.

After the second or third offence I was warned that I should be beaten next time, but I received the warning in a curiously roundabout

250

way. One afternoon, as we were filing out from tea, Mrs. Simpson, the headmaster's wife, was sitting at the head of one of the tables, chatting with a lady of whom I know nothing, except that she was on an afternoon's visit to the school. She was an intimidating, masculine-looking person wearing a riding habit, or something that I took to be a riding habit. I was just leaving the room when Mrs. Simpson called me back, as though to introduce me to the visitor.

Mrs. Simpson was nicknamed Bingo, and I shall call her by that name for I seldom think of her by any other. (Officially, however, she was addressed as Mum, probably a corruption of the "Ma'am" used by public school boys to their housemasters' wives.) She was a stocky square-built woman with hard red cheeks, a flat top to her head, prominent brows and deepset, suspicious eyes. Although a great deal of the time she was full of false heartiness, jollying one along with mannish slang ("*Buck* up, old chap!" and so forth), and even using one's Christian name, her eyes never lost their anxious, accusing look. It was very difficult to look her in the face without feeling guilty, even at moments when one was not guilty of anything in particular.

"Here is a little boy," said Bingo, indicating me to the strange lady, "who wets his bed every night. Do you know what I am going to do if you wet your bed again?" she added, turning to me. "I am going to get the Sixth Form to beat you."

The strange lady put on an air of being inexpressibly shocked, and exclaimed "I-should-think-so!" And here occurred one of those wild, almost lunatic misunderstandings which are part of the daily experience of childhood. The Sixth Form was a group of older boys who were selected as having "character" and were empowered to beat smaller boys. I had not yet learned of their existence, and I mis-heard the phrase "the Sixth Form" as "Mrs. Form." I took it as referring to the strange lady—I thought, that is, that her name was Mrs. Form. It was an improbable name, but a child has no judgement in such matters. I imagined, therefore, that it was *she* who was to be deputed to beat me. It did not strike me as strange that this job should be turned over to a casual visitor in no way connected with the school. I merely assumed that "Mrs. Form" was a stern disciplinarian who enjoyed beating people (somehow her appearance seemed to bear this out) and I had an immediate terrifying vision of her arriving for the occasion in full riding kit and armed with a hunting whip. To this day I can feel myself almost swooning with shame as I stood, a very small, round-faced boy in short corduroy knickers, before the two women. I could not speak. I felt that I should die if "Mrs. Form" were to beat me. But my dominant feeling was not fear or even resentment: it was simply shame because one more person, and that a woman, had been told of my disgusting offence.

A little later, I forget how, I learned that it was not after all "Mrs.

Form" who would do the beating. I cannot remember whether it was that very night that I wetted my bed again, but at any rate I did wet it again quite soon. Oh, the despair, the feeling of cruel injustice, after all my prayers and resolutions, at once again waking between the clammy sheets! There was no chance of hiding what I had done. The grim statuesque matron, Daphne by name, arrived in the dormitory specially to inspect my bed. She pulled back the clothes, then drew herself up, and the dreaded words seemed to come rolling out of her like a peal of thunder:

"REPORT YOURSELF to the headmaster after breakfast!"

I do not know how many times I heard that phrase during my early years at Crossgates. It was only very rarely that it did not mean a beating. The words always had a portentous sound in my ears, like muffled drums or the words of the death sentence.

When I arrived to report myself, Bingo was doing something or other at the long shiny table in the ante-room to the study. Her uneasy eyes searched me as I went past. In the study Mr. Simpson, nicknamed Sim, was waiting. Sim was a round-shouldered curiously oafish-looking man, not large but shambling in gait, with a chubby face which was like that of an overgrown baby, and which was capable of good humor. He knew, of course, why I had been sent to him, and had already taken a bone-handled riding crop out of the cupboard, but it was part of the punishment of reporting yourself that you had to proclaim your offence with your own lips. When I had said my say, he read me a short but pompous lecture, then seized me by the scruff of the neck, twisted me over and began beating me with the riding crop. He had a habit of continuing his lecture while he flogged you, and I remember the words "you dir-ty lit-tle boy" keeping time with the blows. The beating did not hurt (perhaps as it was the first time, he was not hitting me very hard), and I walked out feeling very much better. The fact that the beating had not hurt was a sort of victory and partially wiped out the shame of the bed-wetting. I was even incautious enough to wear a grin on my face. Some small boys were hanging about in the passage outside the door of the ante-room.

"D'you get the cane?"

"It didn't hurt," I said proudly.

Bingo had heard everything. Instantly her voice came screaming after me:

"Come here! Come here this instant! What was that you said?"

"I said it didn't hurt," I faltered out.

"How dare you say a thing like that? Do you think that is a proper thing to say? Go in and REPORT YOURSELF AGAIN!"

This time Sim laid on in real earnest. He continued for a length of time that frightened and astonished me—about five minutes, it seemed

252

—ending up by breaking the riding crop. The bone handle went flying across the room.

"Look what you've made me do!" he said furiously, holding up the broken crop.

I had fallen into a chair, weakly snivelling. I remember that this was the only time throughout my boyhood when a beating actually reduced me to tears, and curiously enough I was not even now crying because of the pain. The second beating had not hurt very much either. Fright and shame seemed to have anesthetized me. I was crying partly because I felt that this was expected of me, partly from genuine repentance, but partly also because of a deeper grief which is peculiar to childhood and not easy to convey: a sense of desolate loneliness and helplessness, of being locked up not only in a hostile world but in a world of good and evil where the rules were such that it was actually not possible for me to keep them.

I knew that bed-wetting was (a) wicked and (b) outside my control. The second fact I was personally aware of, and the first I did not question. It was possible, therefore, to commit a sin without knowing that you committed it, without wanting to commit it, and without being able to avoid it. Sin was not necessarily something that you did: it might be something that happened to you. I do not want to claim that this idea flashed into my mind as a complete novelty at this very moment, under the blows of Sim's cane: I must have had glimpses of it even before I left home, for my early childhood had not been altogether happy. But at any rate this was the great, abiding lesson of my boyhood: that I was in a world where it was *not possible* for me to be good. And the double beating was a turning point, for it brought home to me for the first time the harshness of the environment into which I had been flung. Life was more terrible, and I was more wicked, than I had imagined. At any rate, as I sat on the edge of a chair in Sim's study, with not even the self-possession to stand up while he stormed at me, I had a conviction of sin and folly and weakness, such as I do not remember to have felt before.

In general, one's memories of any period must necessarily weaken as one moves away from it. One is constantly learning new facts, and old ones have to drop out to make way for them. At twenty I could have written the history of my schooldays with an accuracy which would be quite impossible now. But it can also happen that one's memories grow sharper after a long lapse of time, because one is looking at the past with fresh eyes and can isolate and, as it were, notice facts which previously existed undifferentiated among a mass of others. Here are two things which in a sense I remembered, but which did not strike me as strange or interesting until quite recently. One is that the second beating seemed to me a just and reasonable punishment. To get one beating, and then to get another and far fiercer one on top of it, for being so unwise as to show that the first had not hurt—that was quite natural. The gods are jealous, and when you have good fortune you should conceal it. The other is that I accepted the broken riding crop as my own crime. I can still recall my feeling as I saw the handle lying on the carpet—the feeling of having done an ill-bred clumsy thing, and ruined an expensive object. *I* had broken it: so Sim told me, and so I believed. This acceptance of guilt lay unnoticed in my memory for twenty or thirty years.

So much for the episode of the bed-wetting. But there is one more thing to be remarked. This is that I did not wet my bed again—at least, I did wet it once again, and received another beating, after which the trouble stopped. So perhaps this barbarous remedy does work, though at a heavy price, I have no doubt.

. . .

I had learned early in my career that one can do wrong against one's will, and before long I also learned that one can do wrong without ever discovering what one has done or why it was wrong. There were sins that were too subtle to be explained, and there were others that were too terrible to be clearly mentioned. For example, there was sex, which was always smouldering just under the surface and which suddenly blew up into a tremendous row when I was about twelve.

At some preparatory schools homosexuality is not a problem, but I think that Crossgates may have acquired a "bad tone" thanks to the presence of the South American boys, who would perhaps mature a year or two earlier than an English boy. At that age I was not interested, so I do not actually know what went on, but I imagine it was group masturbation. At any rate, one day the storm suddenly burst over our heads. There were summonses, interrogations, confessions, floggings, repentances, solemn lectures of which one understood nothing except that some irredeemable sin known as "swinishness" or "beastliness" had been committed. One of the ringleaders, a boy named Horne, was flogged, according to eyewitnesses, for a quarter of an hour continuously before being expelled. His yells rang through the house. But we were all implicated, more or less, or felt ourselves to be implicated. Guilt seemed to hang in the air like a pall of smoke. A solemn, black-haired imbecile of an assistant master, who was later to be a Member of Parliament, took the older boys to a secluded room and delivered a talk on the Temple of the Body.

"Don't you realize what a wonderful thing your body is?" he said gravely. "You talk of your motor-car engines, your Rolls-Royces and Daimlers and so on. Don't you understand that no engine ever made is fit to be compared with your body? And then you go and wreck it, ruin it—for life!"

He turned his cavernous black eyes on me and added sadly:

"And you, whom I'd always believed to be quite a decent person after your fashion—you, I hear, are one of the very worst."

A feeling of doom descended upon me. So I was guilty too. I too had done the dreadful thing, whatever it was, that wrecked you for life, body and soul, and ended in suicide or the lunatic asylum. Till then I had hoped that I was innocent, and the conviction of sin which now took possession of me was perhaps all the stronger because I did not know what I had done. I was not among those who were interrogated and flogged, and it was not until the row was well over that I even learned about the trivial accident that had connected my name with it. Even then I understood nothing. It was not till about two years later that I fully grasped what that lecture on the Temple of the Body had referred to.

At this time I was in an almost sexless state, which is normal, or at any rate common, in boys of that age; I was therefore in the position of simultaneously knowing and not knowing what used to be called the Facts of Life. At five or six, like many children, I had passed through a phase of sexuality. My friends were the plumber's children up the road, and we used sometimes to play games of a vaguely erotic kind. One was called "playing at doctors," and I remember getting a faint but definitely pleasant thrill from holding a toy trumpet, which was supposed to be a stethoscope, against a little girl's belly. About the same time I fell deeply in love, a far more worshipping kind of love than I have ever felt for anyone since, with a girl named Elsie at the convent school which I attended. She seemed to me grown up, so I suppose she must have been fifteen. After that, as so often happens, all sexual feelings seemed to go out of me for many years. At twelve I knew more than I had known as a young child, but I understood less, because I no longer knew the essential fact that there is something pleasant in sexual activity. Between roughly seven and fourteen, the whole subject seemed to me uninteresting and, when for some reason I was forced to think of it, disgusting. My knowledge of the so-called Facts of Life was derived from animals, and was therefore distorted, and in any case was only intermittent. I knew that animals copulated and that human beings had bodies resembling those of animals: but that human beings also copulated I only knew, as it were reluctantly, when something, a phrase in the Bible perhaps, compelled me to remember it. Not having desire, I had no curiosity, and was willing to leave many questions unanswered. Thus, I knew in principle how the baby gets into the woman, but I did not know how it gets out again, because I had never followed the subject up. I knew all the dirty words, and in my bad moments I would repeat them to myself, but I did not know what the worst of them meant, nor want to know. They were abstractly wicked, a sort of verbal charm. While I remained in this state, it was easy for me to remain ignorant of any sexual misdeeds that went on about me, and to be hardly wiser even when the row broke. At most, through the veiled and terrible warnings of Bingo, Sim and all the rest of them, I grasped that the crime of which we were all guilty was somehow connected with the sexual organs. I had noticed, without feeling much interest, that one's penis sometimes stands up of its own accord (this starts happening to a boy long before he has any conscious sexual desires), and I was inclined to believe, or half-believe, that *that* must be the crime. At any rate, it was something to do with the penis—so much I understood. Many other boys, I have no doubt, were equally in the dark.

After the talk on the Temple of the Body (days later, it seems in retrospect: the row seemed to continue for days), a dozen of us were seated at the long shiny table which Sim used for the scholarship, under Bingo's lowering eye. A long, desolate wail rang out from a room somewhere above. A very small boy named Ronald, aged no more than about ten, who was implicated in some way, was being flogged, or was recovering from a flogging. At the sound, Bingo's eyes searched our faces, and settled on me.

"*You see,*" she said.

I will not swear that she said, "You see what you have done," but that was the sense of it. We were all bowed down with shame. It was *our* fault. Somehow or other we had led poor Ronald astray: *we* were responsible for his agony and his ruin. Then Bingo turned upon another boy named Heath. It is thirty years ago, and I cannot remember for certain whether she merely quoted a verse from the Bible, or whether she actually brought out a Bible and made Heath read it; but at any rate the text indicated was:

"Who shall offend one of these little ones that believe in me, it were better for him that a millstone were hanged about his neck, and that he were drowned in the depth of the sea."

That, too, was terrible. Ronald was one of these little ones; we had offended him; it were better that a millstone were hanged about our necks and that we were drowned in the depth of the sea.

"Have you thought about that, Heath—have you thought what it means?" Bingo said. And Heath broke down into tears.

Another boy, Beacham, whom I have mentioned already, was similarly overwhelmed with shame by the accusation that he "had black rings round his eyes."

"Have you looked in the glass lately, Beacham?" said Bingo. "Aren't you ashamed to go about with a face like that? Do you think everyone doesn't know what it means when a boy has black rings round his eyes?"

Once again the load of guilt and fear seemed to settle down upon me.

Had *I* got black rings round my eyes? A couple of years later I realized that these were supposed to be a symptom by which masturbators could be detected. But already, without knowing this, I accepted the black rings as a sure sign of depravity, *some* kind of depravity. And many times, even before I grasped the supposed meaning, I have gazed anxiously into the glass, looking for the first hint of that dreaded stigma, the confession which the secret sinner writes upon his own face.

These terrors wore off, or became merely intermittent, without affecting what one might call my official beliefs. It was still true about the madhouse and the suicide's grave, but it was no longer acutely frightening. Some months later it happened that I once again saw Horne, the ringleader who had been flogged and expelled. Horne was one of the outcasts, the son of poor middle-class parents, which was no doubt part of the reason why Sim had handled him so roughly. The term after his expulsion he went on to South Coast College, the small local public school, which was hideously despised at Crossgates and looked upon as "not really" a public school at all. Only a very few boys from Crossgates went there, and Sim always spoke of them with a sort of contemptuous pity. You had no chance if you went to a school like that: at the best your destiny would be a clerkship. I thought of Horne as a person who at thirteen had already forfeited all hope of any decent future. Physically, morally and socially he was finished. Moreover I assumed that his parents had only sent him to South Coast College because after his disgrace no "good" school would have him.

During the following term, when we were out for a walk, we passed Horne in the street. He looked completely normal. He was a strongly built, rather good-looking boy with black hair. I immediately noticed that he looked better than when I had last seen him—his complexion, previously rather pale, was pinker—and that he did not seem embarrassed at meeting us. Apparently he was not ashamed either of having been expelled, or of being at South Coast College. If one could gather anything from the way he looked at us as we filed past, it was that he was glad to have escaped from Crossgates. But the encounter made very little impression on me. I drew no inference from the fact that Horne, ruined in body and soul, appeared to be happy and in good health. I still believed in the sexual mythology that had been taught me by Bingo and Sim. The mysterious, terrible dangers were still there. Any morning the black rings might appear round your eyes and you would know that you too were among the lost ones. Only it no longer seemed to matter very much. These contradictions can exist easily in the mind of a child, because of its own vitality. It accepts—how can it do otherwise?—the nonsense that its elders tell it, but its youthful body, and the sweetness of the physical world, tell it another story. It was the same with Hell, which up to the age of about fourteen I officially believed in. Almost certainly Hell existed, and there were occasions when a vivid sermon could scare you into fits. But somehow it never lasted. The fire that waited for you was real fire, it would hurt in the same way as when you burnt your finger, and *for ever*, but most of the time you could contemplate it without bothering.

DISCUSSION AND INQUIRY

Bedwetting by older children still draws strong emotional reactions from parents in many homes. At Crossgates, it was apparently something that would not be tolerated. The attitude taken by the Headmaster and his wife further reinforced the guilt feelings that young Orwell had about the episodes. The danger of confirming guilt is that it can result in the seemingly logical conclusions such as those made by Orwell with regard to himself and his world. Can you recall your own bedwetting incidents? Did you feel guilty? How did you handle the matter?

Reinforcement of guilt is further exemplified in the Temple of the Body lecture given by one of the teachers to the boys suspected of masturbating. Orwell had hoped he was not guilty, but concluded he was when he was told he was one of the worst offenders. It was two years later before he understood exactly what masturbation was, but until then, he assumed his guilt lay in the fact that his penis was sometimes erect. The need for sex education for children is clear. How does one educate the adults, especially those who deal with children?

Compare Orwell's selection with that of Arthur Koestler. (See the selection by Arthur Koestler.) What similarities exist in their descriptions of their boyhood days?

Relying on the descriptions of Sim and Bingo as well as the general atmosphere of Crossgates, can you find evidence of sources of material for Orwell's novel 1984, a book about a society where Big Brother is always watching, inhibiting freedom?

Satchel Paige

BIOGRAPHICAL SKETCH

By the time Satchel Paige was twenty, he was playing pro baseball with the Birmingham Black Barons in a stadium not far from his birthplace, Mobile, Alabama. In the 1930s he played winter baseball with other black players in Latin America. His pitching helped the Kansas City Monarchs win the Negro World Series of 1942 and the pennant in 1946. In 1948, Paige, recognized as a great pitcher, joined the major leagues. In 1952, he pitched for the American League All-Star team. He was made coach of the Atlanta Braves in 1969.

SELECTIONS FROM

MAYBE I'LL PITCH FOREVER

IT DON'T matter what some of those talkers say, I wasn't born six feet, three and a half inches tall, weighing a hundred and eighty pounds and wearing size fourteen shoes.

And there wasn't a baseball in my hand, either.

I was just a baby like any other baby born south of Government Street, down by the bay in Mobile. That was where all the Negroes lived and if it hadn't been for my right arm, I probably would have ended up there.

After I hit the top, every couple of months just about I got my name in the papers when those writers played guessing games about when I was born. I never put a stop to it and my family and my buddies didn't help because they kept giving different dates. You see, nobody paid much attention when us kids by the bay was born. There were so many of us I guess it just didn't matter much.

But the government paid attention and there's a birth certificate in Mobile saying I was born July 7, 1906. Now I know it's made out for a LeRoy Page, but my folks started out by spelling their name "Page" and later stuck in the "i" to make themselves sound more high-tone.

But my Mom didn't put much stock in that certificate. She told a

259

reporter in 1959 that I was fifty-five instead of fifty-three; said she had it down in her Bible. Seems like Mom's Bible would know, but she ain't ever shown me the Bible. Anyway, she was in her nineties when she told the reporter that and sometimes she tended to forget things.

There are all kinds of other dates floating around, too, but I'll go by that birth certificate. It doesn't really make any difference how old I tell people I am. They've been carrying on so long about my age, nobody will believe what I say. Like that old gent I ran into in 1947. He was eighty-three and quit playing in 1910, but he swore he played against me.

I just let them talk.

Our place on South Franklin Street was called a "shotgun" house because the four rooms were one behind the other, just a straight shot from the front door to the back.

I was the seventh of eleven children in that little shack. My Dad, John, was a gardener, but he liked to be called a landscaper. My Mom, Lula, was a washerwoman. She was the real boss of our house, not Dad.

John, Jr., and Wilson were my older brothers and Julia, Ellen, Ruth, and Emma Lee were my older sisters. After I was born, Clarence, Inez, Palestine, and little Lula came along. Ruth, Emma Lee, and Clarence all died before I ever quit pitching. Clarence drowned in a boat accident on the Great Lakes.

My Dad died in that house of ours, when I was about eighteen, I guess, although I don't remember for sure.

I only remember pieces and snatches about him. He wasn't hardly a part of my life. We didn't talk too much, but after I started playing baseball as a kid he used to ask me ever so often, "You want to be a baseball player 'stead of a landscaper?"

"Yes," I'd answer and he'd just nod his head like he was satisfied.

Those first few years I was no different from any other kid, only in Mobile I was a nigger kid. I went around with the back of my shirt torn, a pair of dirty diapers or raggedy pieces of trousers covering me. Shoes? They was somewhere else.

Us kids played in the dirt, getting it on our faces so the gnats want to come around. We played in the dirt because we didn't have toys. We threw rocks. There wasn't anything else to throw. And we ran and we chased around. Then we raced for the bay and washed the dirt off. Only we didn't just go anywhere on the bay. Just to certain parts.

The white man got all the rest.

Outside of playing like that, there wasn't much else Negro kids could do in Mobile. Mighty few of them had money for anything like a show.

260

But I didn't play all the time. Everybody got to work when there are thirteen mouths to stuff. By the time I was about six, all my older brothers and sisters had steady jobs, even Wilson, who was only about nine or ten. We all gave our money to Mom so she could get food. She took real pains with what she bought. That was why I can't remember us ever missing a meal.

We didn't always have a belly-busting dishful, but we had something. Mom made sure everybody got their share. She'd stand at the table and ladle out the food, looking real close at each spoonful.

When there wasn't money for store food, we went fishing. There was always plenty of fish around Mobile.

But even with the fish, it was poverty-stricken living before I knew what that meant.

Mom had me in W. H. Council School by the time I was about six or seven years old, but I didn't go too often. The first few times I missed, Mom came looking for me. Finally, she got kind of used to it. Fact was, she didn't put real big store by book learning. It ended up so she didn't get nearly as mad when I missed school as she got when I didn't come home with any money for food from selling empty bottles I'd found in the alleys and trash bins.

When I was still about seven, Mom decided my bottle selling wasn't enough and that I had to get me a job somewhere to help out more. You'd have thought I was fifty or sixty years old the way they worried about my work.

Finally, Mom remembered some of the kids around the neighborhood worked down at the depot, toting bags and satchels.

"You're goin' down there tomorrow," Mom said.

I told her playing would be more fun, but she didn't listen to me.

The next day I was down there, dragging a bag. I got a dime for it. We weren't going to be eating much better if I made only a dime at a time so I got me a pole and some ropes. That let me sling two, three, or four satchels together and carry them at one time. You always got to be thinking to make money.

My invention wasn't a smart-looking thing, but it upped my income.

The other kids all laughed.

"You look like a walking satchel tree," one of them yelled.

They all started yelling it. Soon everybody was calling me that, you know how it is with kids and nicknames. That's when LeRoy Paige became no more and Satchel Paige took over. Nobody called me LeRoy, nobody except my Mom and the government.

A lot of the kids shortened Satchel to Satch. Later, some even called me Satchmo, but not because I blew a mean trumpet like Louie Armstrong. I just blow that fast ball—blow it right by the hitters.

When spring came, I got me some work picking up empty bottles and sweeping up at Eureka Gardens. That was a semi-pro baseball park and the Mobile Tigers played there a lot.

Watching those semi-pro ballplayers got me kind of interested in throwing. Only I couldn't afford a baseball. So I took up rock throwing.

That's when I first found out I had control. It was a natural gift, one that let me put a baseball just about where I wanted it about anytime I wanted to.

I could hit about anything with one of those rocks. Like the day Mom sent me out in the back yard to get us a bird from our chicken coop.

Three chickens came prancing along the path toward me. The one in the middle looked the plumpest. I picked up a rock. The chickens were about thirty feet from me. I took aim and threw. There was a squawking and feathers flew and two chickens went tearing off. The third one, the one in the middle, was knocked dead on the ground.

After that I used to kill me flying birds with rocks, too. Most people need shotguns to do what I did with those rocks.

It didn't take me long to find out that rocks were good for something besides knocking over birds. They made a real impression on a kid's head or backside. I had plenty of chances to use rocks that way, too. Chester Arnold and Julius Andrews and some of my other buddies all were guys who played hookey a lot, just like me, and they liked trouble even better than me. When we weren't fishing, we were out looking for trouble. And we found it. Then I'd start throwing rocks.

Our biggest fights came on the way home from school. We went right by a white school and a big gang from there was always out waiting for us. When we got close, the rocks started flying. I crippled up a lot of them, and I mean it. It got so bad they had to put a policeman there.

Maybe I got into all those fights because I wasn't real smart and didn't take too good to books. But maybe it was because I found out what it was like to be a Negro in Mobile. Even if you're only seven, eight, or nine, it eats at you when you know you got nothing and can't get a dollar. The blood gets angry. You want to go somewhere, but you're just walking. You don't want to, but you got to walk.

Those fights helped me forget what I didn't have. They made me a big man in the neighborhood instead of just some more trash.

Mom didn't take to my fighting. I once tried to fool her, but I found out you don't fool a church-going woman much.

"You been fighting again?" she yelled after seeing how I was sweaty and messed up.

"No. Just playing."

"I know different," she said.

Smack. She caught me one on the ear. She hit harder than I ever got hit in a fight. I used to think she'd hit me because she didn't know how I felt. She didn't know how it was when they told me I couldn't swim where the white folks did.

Then I realized maybe she did.

She must have been chased away from the white man's swimming places. She must have gotten run off from the white man's stores and stands for just looking hungry at a fish.

She must have heard those men yelling, "Get out of here, you no-good nigger."

She must have heard it. I guess she learned to live with it.

. . .

Since I threw those rocks so straight, I guess it was just natural that I started firing a baseball.

By the time I was ten years old, I was throwing it harder than anybody in the neighborhood. I also was belting it farther. When Wilbur Hines, the coach of the team at W. H. Council School, held baseball tryouts that year, I figured I was ready even if I were just ten.

I made the team. It was easy for me. When I was ten and when I was fifty, there was one thing I could do—play baseball. And you better believe it.

Hines put me in the outfield; sometimes he let me play first base, but I didn't do any pitching. I never gave it much thought.

I kept pounding that ball and playing the outfield until a game about halfway through the season. They'd knocked two of our pitchers out of the box in the first inning so Hines decided to try me.

I was all arms and legs. I must have looked like an ostrich. When I let go of the ball, I almost fell off that mound. But that ball whipped past three straight batters for strike-outs. I kept pumping for eight more innings. When I was done I had struck out sixteen and hadn't given up a hit. We were behind, six to nothing, when I started. When I was done we were ahead, eleven to six.

"That was some throwing, boy," Hines told me after the game.

"You know it. I showed them who was number one around here."

"You sure did," he said. "From now on you're number one with me, too—number one pitcher."

Even though I was a kid, I soon became pretty well known all over the South Side as just about the best school pitcher they ever saw around there.

There weren't too many even up in the high schools who could throw as hard and sure as I did. And when those kids my age came up

263

to the plate and I threw my trouble ball, they just wet their pants or cried. That's how scared they were of my speed.

With all those kids I played with on the baseball team, I guess I should have had a lot of friends. But even when I was a kid, I was pretty much of a loner.

That's how it was then and how it always is.

Maybe I didn't have time for other kids because every day was a busy one for me—I worked at the ball park, I toted bags, I played baseball. That kept me pretty busy, but I always had time for trouble. That is, I had time for trouble until 1918.

I was walking home from a game. My clothes were dirty and stained. It was getting dark.

I walked by this store and stopped. Unless you've gone around with nothing, you don't know how powerful a lure some new, shiny stuff is. I turned and looked in the window. There must have been thirty or forty toys there.

I went in the store. I don't know why. I didn't have any money.

Then I saw all those toy rings, those gold bands, and those blue and red and green and black stones.

I looked around. No one was watching.

I grabbed a handful, stuffed them in my pocket.

"Hey, what're you doing?" someone yelled at me.

I looked around. This big white man was coming down on me. I ran. He caught me by the front door.

They dragged me down to police headquarters. Then they got my Mom and even talked to the truant officer. They knew all about my playing hookey and being in trouble with those gang fights and rock throwing.

But they let me go home with my Mom. They told us to see the truant officer the next morning.

Mom cried when they got her down to the station. She cried all the way home. I thought she'd never stop. I don't guess she did until after we'd all been in bed half the night.

She hadn't spanked me. After the police quit yelling, no one had yelled at me. I just didn't understand that. No one had hit me. I guessed things couldn't be as bad as they seemed at first.

But in the morning Mom still looked worried. Her eyes were red and she moved real slow.

"We goin' to see that truant officer?" I asked.

"Yes. Get dressed."

We walked to the truant officer's place. The truant officer was the same woman who'd been chasing me for a couple of years. I don't know her name. I just called her Mrs. Meanie.

She talked . . . about the rings . . . about fights . . . about school . . .

about playing hookey. I never thought anybody could talk that much. It wasn't a court hearing or anything like that. Just this truant officer, my Mom, and me.

Then she quit talking, but only for a minute. When she started in again it didn't make much sense to me, but it was all written down in a book in the county courthouse in Mobile:

"On this day, the twenty-fourth of July, 1918, LeRoy Paige is ordered committed to the Industrial School for Negro Children at Mount Meigs, Alabama."

"No!" screamed by Mom. "Not for just that little bit of junk!"

Then I was scared. Real scared. I cried.

I couldn't stop shaking.

~~~~~~~~~~~~~~~~~~~~~~~~~~~~~~~~~~~~~

DISCUSSION AND INQUIRY

Truancy, gang fights with whites, and stealing were the things that put Satchel Paige on the road to delinquency. He found himself in the Industrial School for Negro Children at Mount Meigs, Alabama, before he reached his teens. He lived in poverty before he knew what it meant. His truancy record was appalling, but note that he was reinforced by his mother, who put little value on formal learning. How does a child acquire values? What experiences did the Paige family, or, for that matter, many Negro families have that might create a negative attitude toward schooling? Helen Sekaquaptewa also found her family cooperative in her truancy from school. (See the selection by Helen Sekaquaptewa.) How and why do attitudes toward learning vary among sub-cultures in the United States?

Participation in interracial gang fights, which provided opportunities for Satchel to develop his pitching arm, was also used against him in establishing evidence for sending him to the Industrial School. Peer-group contact becomes very important to the school-age child, and neighborhood gangs or secret organizations are popular at that time. Were the gangs or gang fights in Satchel's neighborhood unusual? What purpose did they serve for him and for his friends?

Finally, stealing trinkets was the offense that

brought about a confrontation with the law. What do you feel were the reasons for his stealing? Is it unusual for children to "steal"? When and how does a child usually learn about property rights? When can a child really be said to be stealing? Can you remember "borrowing" things from the store (or from a friend) when you were a child? How did you do it? How did you feel about it? How did your family handle it? Police records reflect a disproportionate amount of delinquency among black children. Investigators have found, however, that delinquent-type behaviors are just as common among white, middle-class children. How would you account for this apparent discrepancy?

Eleanor Roosevelt

BIOGRAPHICAL SKETCH

Eleanor Roosevelt was born in 1884 in New York City. At age twenty-one she married her cousin, Franklin Delano Roosevelt, who later became President of the United States. During his terms in office, she was actively involved in political and philanthropic causes. These interests continued after the death of her husband, and she became well-known in her own right. She died in 1962.

SELECTIONS FROM

THE AUTOBIOGRAPHY OF ELEANOR ROOSEVELT

I WAS a shy, solemn child even at the age of two, and I am sure that even when I danced I never smiled. My earliest recollections are of being dressed up and allowed to come down to dance for a group of gentlemen who applauded and laughed as I pirouetted before them. Finally, my father would pick me up and hold me high in the air. He dominated my life as long as he lived, and was the love of my life for many years after he died.

With my father I was perfectly happy. There is still a woodeny painting of a solemn child, a straight bang across her forehead, with an uplifted finger and an admonishing attitude, which he always enjoyed and referred to as "Little Nell scolding Elliott." We had a country house at Hempstead, Long Island, so that he could hunt and play polo. He loved horses and dogs, and we always had both. During this time he was in business, and, added to the work and the sports, the gay and popular young couple lived a busy social life. He was the center of my world and all around him loved him.

Whether it was some weakness from his early years which the strain of the life he was living accentuated, whether it was the pain he endured from a broken leg which had to be set, rebroken and reset, I do not know. My father began to drink, and for my mother and his brother Theodore and his sisters began the period of harrowing anxiety which was to last until his death in 1894.

My father and mother, my little brother and I went to Italy for the winter of 1890 as the first step in the fight for his health and power of self-control. I remember my father acting as gondolier, taking me out on the Venice canals, singing with the other boatmen, to my intense joy. I loved his voice and, above all, I loved the way he treated me. He called me "Little Nell," after the Little Nell in Dickens' *Old Curiosity Shop*, and I never doubted that I stood first in his heart.

He could, however, be annoyed with me, particularly when I disappointed him in such things as physical courage, and this, unfortunately, I did quite often. We went to Sorrento and I was given a donkey so I could ride over the beautiful roads. One day the others overtook me and offered to let me go with them, but at the first steep descent which they slid down I turned pale, and preferred to stay on the high road. I can remember still the tone of disapproval in my father's voice, though his words of reproof have long since faded away.

I remember my trip to Vesuvius with my father and the throwing of pennies, which were returned to us encased in lava, and then the endless trip down. I suppose there was some block in the traffic, but I can remember only my utter weariness and my effort to bear it without tears so that my father would not be displeased.

My mother took a house in Neuilly, outside of Paris, and settled down for several months, as another baby was expected the end of June. My father entered a sanitarium while his older sister, Anna, our Auntie Bye, came to stay with my mother. It was decided to send me to a convent to learn French and to have me out of the way when the baby arrived.

The convent experience was an unhappy one. I was not yet six years old, and I must have been very sensitive, with an inordinate desire for affection and praise, perhaps brought on by the fact that I was conscious of my plain looks and lack of manners. My mother was troubled by my lack of beauty, and I knew it as a child senses these things. She tried hard to bring me up well so that my manners would compensate for my looks, but her efforts only made me more keenly conscious of my shortcomings.

The little girls of my age in the convent could hardly be expected to take much interest in a child who did not speak their language and did not belong to their religion. They had a little shrine of their own and often worked hard beautifying it. I longed to be allowed to join them, but was always kept on the outside and wandered by myself in the walled-in garden.

Finally, I fell a prey to temptation. One of the girls swallowed a penny. Every attention was given her, she was the center of everybody's interest. I longed to be in her place. One day I went to one of the sisters and told her that I had swallowed a penny. It must have been evident that my story was not true, so they sent for my mother. She took me away in disgrace. Understanding as I do now my mother's character, I realize how terrible it must have seemed to her to have a child who would lie.

I remember the drive home as one of utter misery, for I could bear swift punishment far better than long scoldings. I could cheerfully lie any time to escape a scolding, whereas if I had known that I would simply be put to bed or be spanked I probably would have told the truth.

This habit of lying stayed with me for years. My mother did not understand that a child may lie from fear; I myself never understood it until I reached the age when I realized that there was nothing to fear.

My father had come home for the baby's arrival, and I am sorry to say he was causing a great deal of anxiety, but he was the only person who did not treat me as a criminal!

The baby, my brother Hall, was several weeks old when we sailed for home, leaving my father in a sanitarium in France, where his brother, Theodore, had to go and get him later on.

We lived that winter without my father. I slept in my mother's room, and remember the thrill of watching her dress to go out in the evenings. She looked so beautiful I was grateful to be allowed to touch her dress or her jewels or anything that was part of the vision which I admired inordinately.

Those summers, while my father was away trying to rehabilitate himself, we spent largely with my grandmother at her Tivoli house, which later was to become home to both my brother Hall and me.

My father sent us one of his horses, an old hunter which my mother used to drive, and I remember driving with her. Even more vividly do I remember the times when I was sent down to visit my great-aunt, Mrs. Ludlow, whose house was next to ours but nearer the river and quite out of sight, for no house along that part of the river was really close to any other.

Mrs. Ludlow was handsome, sure of herself, and an excellent housekeeper. On one memorable occasion she set to work to find out what I knew. Alas and alack, I could not even read! The next day and every day that summer she sent her companion, Madeleine, to give me lessons in reading. Then she found out that I could not sew or cook and knew nothing of the things a girl should know. I think I was six.

I surmise that my mother was roundly taken to task, for after that

Madeleine became a great factor in my life and began to teach me to sew.

I still slept in my mother's room, and every morning I had to repeat to her some verses which I had learned in the Old or the New Testament. I wish I could remember today all the verses I learned by heart that summer.

Sometimes I woke up when my mother and her sisters were talking at bedtime, and many a conversation not meant for my ears was listened to with great avidity. I acquired a strange and garbled idea of the troubles around me. Something was wrong with my father and from my point of view nothing could be wrong with him.

If people only realized what a war goes on in a child's mind and heart in a situation of this kind, I think they would try to explain more than they do, but nobody told me anything.

We moved back to New York, the autumn that I was seven, to a house which my mother had bought and put in order on East 61st Street, two blocks from Auntie Bye, who lived at Madison Avenue and East 62nd Street. She had Uncle Ted's little girl, Alice, with her a great deal, and that winter our first real acquaintance began. Already she seemed much older and cleverer, and while I admired her I was always a little afraid of her, and this was so even when we were grown and she was the "Princess Alice" in the White House.

That winter we began a friendship with young Robert Munro-Ferguson, a young man sent over from England by an elder brother to make his way in the world. My father and mother had known the elder brother, Ronald (later Lord Novar), and so had Auntie Bye. The boy was taken into her house, given a start in Douglas Robinson's office, and became a dear and close friend to the entire family.

My mother always had the three children with her for a time in the late afternoon. My little brother Ellie adored her, and was so good he never had to be reproved. The baby Hall was always called Josh and was too small to do anything but sit upon her lap contentedly. I felt a curious barrier between myself and these three. My mother made a great effort; she would read to me and have me read to her, she would have me recite my poems, she would keep me after the boys had gone to bed, and still I can remember standing in the door, often with my finger in my mouth, and I can see the look in her eyes and hear the tone of her voice as she said, "Come in, Granny." If a visitor was there she might turn and say, "She is such a funny child, so old-fashioned that we always call her 'Granny.'" I wanted to sink through the floor in shame.

Suddenly everything was changed! We children were sent out of the house. I went to stay with my godmother, Mrs. Henry Parish, and the boys went to my mother's aunt, Mrs. Ludlow. My grandmother left her own house and family to nurse my mother, for she had diphtheria and there was then no antitoxin. My father was sent for, but came too late from his exile in Virginia. Diphtheria went fast in those days.

I can remember standing by a window when Cousin Susie (Mrs. Parish) told me that my mother was dead. This was on December 7, 1892. Death meant nothing to me, and one fact wiped out everything else. My father was back and I would see him soon.

Later I knew what a tragedy of utter defeat this meant for him. No hope now of ever wiping out the sorrowful years he had brought upon my mother—and she had left her mother as guardian for her children. He had no wife, no children, no hope.

Finally it was arranged that we children were to live with my grandmother Hall. I realize now what that must have meant in dislocation of her household, and I marvel at the sweetness of my two uncles and the two aunts who were still at home, for never by word or deed did any of them make us feel that we were not in our own house.

After we were installed, my father came to see me, and I remember going down into the high-ceilinged, dim library on the first floor of the house in West 37th Street. He sat in a big chair. He was dressed all in black, looking very sad. He held out his arms and gathered me to him. In a little while he began to talk, to explain to me that my mother was gone, that she had been all the world to him, and now he had only my brothers and myself, that my brothers were very young and that he and I must keep close together. Someday I would make a home for him again, we would travel together and do many things which he painted as interesting and pleasant, to be looked forward to in the future.

Somehow it was always he and I. I did not understand whether my brothers were to be our children or whether he felt that they would be going to a school and later be independent.

There started that day a feeling which never left me, that he and I were very close and someday would have a life of our own together. He told me to write to him often, to be a good girl, not to give any trouble, to study hard, to grow up into a woman he could be proud of, and he would come to see me whenever it was possible.

When he left I was all alone to keep our secret of mutual understanding and to adjust myself to my new existence.

The two little boys had a room with Madeleine and I had a little hall bedroom next to them. I was old enough to look after myself, except that my hair had to be brushed at night. Of course, someone had to be engaged to take me out, to and from classes, and to whatever I did in the afternoons. I had governesses, French maids, German maids. I walked them all off their feet. They always tried to talk to me, and I wished to be left alone to live in a dreamworld in which I was the heroine and my father the hero. Into this world I withdrew as soon as I went to bed and as soon as I woke in the morning, and all the time I was walking or when anyone bored me.

I was a healthy child, but now and then in winter I would have a sore throat and tonsillitis, so cold baths were decreed as a daily morning routine—and how I cheated on those baths! Madeleine could not always follow me up, and more hot water went into them than would have been considered beneficial had anyone supervised me.

My grandmother laid great stress on certain things in education. I must learn French. My father wished me to be musical. I worked at music until I was eighteen, but no one ever trained my ear! Through listening to my aunt Pussie play I did gain an emotional appreciation of music. She was a fascinating and lovely creature and her playing was one of the unforgettable joys of my childhood.

I would have given anything to be a singer. I felt that one could give a great deal of pleasure and, yes, receive attention and admiration! Attention and admiration were the things through all my childhood which I wanted, because I was made to feel so conscious of the fact that nothing about me would attract attention or would bring me admiration.

. . .

Looking back I see that I was always afraid of something: of the dark, of displeasing people, of failure. Anything I accomplished had to be done across a barrier of fear. I remember an incident when I was about thirteen. Pussie was ill with a bad sore throat and she liked me to do things for her, which made me very proud. One night she called me. Everything was dark, and I groped my way to her room. She asked if I would go to the basement and get some ice from the icebox. That meant three flights of stairs; the last one would mean closing the door at the foot of the stairs and being alone in the basement, making my way in pitch-black darkness to that icebox in the back yard!

My knees were trembling, but as between the fear of going and the fear of not being allowed to minister to Pussie when she was ill, and thereby losing an opportunity to be important, I had no choice. I went and returned with the ice, demonstrating again the fact that children value above everything else the opportunity to be really useful to those around them.

Very early I became conscious of the fact that there were people around me who suffered in one way or another. I was five or six when my father took me to help serve Thanksgiving dinner in one of the newsboys' clubhouses which my grandfather, Theodore Roosevelt, had started. He was also a trustee of the Children's Aid Society for many years. My father explained that many of these ragged little boys had no homes and lived in little wooden shanties in empty lots, or slept in vestibules of houses or public buildings or any place where they could be moderately warm, yet they were independent and earned their own livings.

Every Christmas I was taken by my grandmother to help dress the Christmas tree for the babies' ward in the Post-Graduate Hospital. She was particularly interested in this charity.

Auntie Gracie took us to the Orthopedic Hospital which my grandfather Roosevelt had been instrumental in helping Dr. Newton Schaefer to start and in which the family was deeply interested. There I saw innumerable little children in casts and splints. Some of them lay patiently for months in strange and curious positions. I was particularly interested in them because I had a curvature myself and wore for some time a steel brace which was vastly uncomfortable and prevented my bending over.

Even my uncle Vallie, who at this time was in business in New York, a champion tennis player and a popular young man in society, took me to help dress a Christmas tree for a group of children in a part of New York City which was called "Hell's Kitchen." For many years this was one of New York's poorest and worst sections. I also went with Maude and Pussie to sing at the Bowery Mission, so I was not in ignorance that there were sharp contrasts, even though our lives were blessed with plenty.

Though he was so little with us, my father dominated all this period of my life. Subconsciously I must always have been waiting for his visits. They were irregular, and he rarely sent word before he arrived, but never was I in the house, even in my room two long flights of stairs above the entrance door, that I did not hear his voice the minute he entered the front door. Walking downstairs was far too slow. I slid down the banisters and usually catapulted into his arms before his hat was hung up.

My father never missed an opportunity for giving us presents, so Christmas was a great day and I still remember one memorable Christmas when I had two stockings, for my grandmother had filled one and my father, who was in New York, brought one on Christmas morning.

One more sorrow came to my father the winter that my mother died. My little brother Ellie never seemed to thrive after my mother's death. Both he and the baby, Josh, got scarlet fever, and I was returned to my cousin Susie and, of course, quarantined.

The baby got well without any complications, but Ellie developed diphtheria and died. My father came to take me out occasionally, but the anxiety over the little boys was too great for him to give me a good deal of his time.

On August 14, 1894, just before I was ten years old, word came that my father had died. My aunts told me, but I simply refused to believe it, and while I wept long and went to bed still weeping I finally went to sleep and began the next day living in my dreamworld as usual.

My grandmother decided that we children should not go to the funeral, and so I had no tangible thing to make death real to me. From that time on I knew in my mind that my father was dead, and yet I lived with him more closely, probably, than I had when he was alive.

. . .

We children stayed at Tivoli in summer now with a nurse and governess, even if the others were away, and there were hot, breathless days when my fingers stuck to the keys as I practiced on the piano but I never left off any garments and, even in summer, we children wore a good many. I would roll my stockings down and then be told that ladies did not show their legs and promptly have to fasten them up again!

The house at Tivoli was big, with high ceilings and a good many rooms, most of them large. My grandfather had furnished it down-stairs in a rather formal way. There were some lovely marble mantel-pieces and chandeliers for candles. We had neither gas nor electricity. We had lamps, but often went to bed by candlelight. There were some vitrines with lovely little carved ivory pieces, one tiny set of tables and chairs I loved to look at, and also silver ornaments and little china and enameled pieces collected from various parts of the world.

The library was filled with standard sets of books, besides my grandfather's religious books. A good deal of fiction came into the house by way of my young aunts and uncles. It is astonishing how much Dickens, Scott and Thackeray were read and reread, particularly by Eddie.

On the second and third floors there were nine master bedrooms and four double servants' rooms and one single one. These servants' rooms were much better than those in the town house, but no one thought it odd that there was no servants' bathroom.

There were just two bathrooms in this large house, but it never occurred to us that it was an inconvenience or that it really made much work to have to use basins and pitchers in our own rooms.

We children had to take two hot baths a week, though I think my grandmother could still remember the era of the Saturday night baths. I was expected to have a cold sponge every morning.

My grandmother let me follow her about in the early mornings when she was housekeeping, and I carried to the cook the supplies of flour, sugar and coffee that she so carefully weighed out in the storeroom.

Today few servants would be content to cook in the semidarkness which reigned in that big, old-fashioned kitchen, with a large stone areaway all around it, over which was the piazza, which left only a small space for the light to filter in. The room where the servants ate had one door leading into the areaway. The laundry was a little better, because there were two doors leading out onto the terrace, and here I spent many hours.

Our wash—and what a wash it was—was done by one woman, Mrs. Overhalse, without the aid of any electric washing machine or irons. She had a washboard and three tubs and a wringer and a little stove on which were all weights of irons. The stove was fed with wood or coal.

Mrs. Overhalse was a cheerful, healthy soul, apparently able to direct her own household, come and wash all day for us, and then go back at night and finish up on her farm. She had a number of children. She taught me to wash and iron, and though I was not allowed to do the finer things, the handkerchiefs, napkins and towels often fell to my lot, and I loved the hours spent with this cheerful woman.

Pussie had an artistic temperament, and there would be days when I would go to Maude for comfort, for Pussie would not speak to anyone. Gradually I came to accept it as part of her character and to be grateful for all the lovely things she did, and wait patiently for the storms to pass.

She took me one summer with my governess to Nantucket Island for a few days—an exciting trip for a child who never went anywhere except up and down the Hudson River. After a few days I think she was bored with us; in any case, she left. The governess did not have enough money to get us home. Pussie was to return, but she forgot all about us. Finally my grandmother was appealed to and sent enough money to pay our bill and get us home.

When my young aunts and uncles were away, I was much alone. This solitude encouraged my habit of taking a book out into the fields or the woods and sitting in a tree or lying under it, completely forgetting the passage of time. No one tried to censor my reading, though occasionally when I happened on a book that I could not understand and asked a difficult question before people, the book would disappear. I remember this happened to Dickens' *Bleak House*. I spent days hunting for it.

Certain things my grandmother insisted on. On Sundays I might not read the books that I read on weekdays. I had to teach Sunday school to the coachman's little daughter, giving her verses to learn, hearing her recite them, and then seeing that she learned some hymns and collects and the catechism. In turn, I must do all these things myself and recite to my grandmother.

Every Sunday the big victoria came to the door and we went to church, and my seat usually was the little one facing my grandmother.

Unfortunately, the four miles were long, and I was nearly always nauseated before we reached the church, and equally so before we reached home.

I could not play games on Sunday, and we still had a cold supper in the evenings, though we did not live up to the cold meal in the middle of the day that had been my grandfather's rule.

Madeleine did succeed in teaching me to sew. I hemmed endless dish towels and darned endless stockings. Madeleine caused me many tears, for I was desperately afraid of her. I used to enjoy sliding down the moss-grown roof of our icehouse, and got my white drawers completely covered with green. I went to my grandmother before I went to Madeleine, knowing that my grandmother would scold less severely.

I was not supposed to read in bed before breakfast, but as I woke at five practically every morning in summer and was, I am afraid, a self-willed child I used to hide a book under the mattress. Woe to me when Madeleine caught me reading!

I have no recollection now of why she frightened me. As I look back it seems perfectly ludicrous, but I did not even tell my grandmother how much afraid I was until I was nearly fourteen years old, and then I confessed, between sobs, as we were walking in the woods. How silly it all seems today.

A few things I wanted desperately to do in those days. I remember that when I was about twelve Mr. Henry Sloane asked me to go west with his daughter, Jessie. I do not think I ever wanted to do anything so much in all my life, for I was fond of her and longed to travel. My grandmother was adamant and would not allow me to go. She gave me no reasons. It was sufficient that she did not think it wise. She so often said "no" that I built up a defense of saying I did not want to do things in order to forestall her refusals and keep down my disappointments.

She felt I should learn to dance, and I joined a dancing class at Mr. Dodsworth's. These classes were an institution for many years, and many little boys and girls learned the polka and the waltz standing carefully on the diamond squares of the polished hardwood floor.

My grandmother decided that because of my being tall and probably awkward I should have ballet lessons besides, so I went once a week to a regular ballet teacher on Broadway and learned toe dancing with four or five other girls who were going on the stage and looked forward to the chance of being in the chorus and talked of little else, making me very envious.

I loved it and practiced assiduously, and can still appreciate how much work lies behind some of the dances which look so easy as they are done on the stage.

DISCUSSION AND INQUIRY

Eleanor Roosevelt's envy of her mother and the great love she felt for her father were themes that dominated her early life. Both parents died before she reached puberty, leaving this plain, anxious, nail-biting little rich girl only memories of a beautiful mother and an alcoholic father. Eleanor knew, even as a child, that she was homely, and she was very much aware of her mother's beauty. Adults underestimate the importance of plainness and general physical appearance to a child. Whether shortcomings are real or perceived as real makes little difference in their impact on the child. Furthermore, feelings about appearance and looks can spread to general feelings of inadequacy. For example, "I not only look bad, but I am bad, I am stupid and I am inadequate." In Eleanor's case, she was indeed plain—a fact that was constantly brought to her attention by stated and unstated "messages" from her mother. The very presence of her beautiful mother made her unattractiveness more conspicuous to her and everyone around her. Children find ways to compensate for their negative feelings about themselves. How did Eleanor compensate for her feelings? It may be interesting to speculate about the relationship between feelings about oneself and one's concern for others. Like Eleanor Roosevelt, Joan Baez regarded herself as plain and unattractive—in adult life these individuals displayed great social awareness and an expanded social consciousness. (See the selection by Joan Baez.)

The love Eleanor felt for her father endured long after his death. After her mother's death, she fantasized about the life she would someday enjoy with her father. Is this an unusual fantasy for girls her age? According to Freud, all children form strong attachments to the parent of the opposite sex during the Oedipal period, which occurs between the ages of 4 to 6. Was Eleanor's attachment more exaggerated than most? How did her relationship with her mother affect the attachment to her father? (See the selection by Jean-Paul Sartre, in which he presents his personal views about the Oedipus complex.) What explanation other than a Freudian explanation might be given for her strong feelings for her father?

Lillian Roth

BIOGRAPHICAL SKETCH

Born in 1910, Lillian Roth was a star by the age of 5, and remained on the stage throughout most of her life. She was married five times. She lived a glamorous life during the roaring twenties, and succeeded in making and losing a million dollars before she was 30. Her instant stardom did not bring her happiness, however; her painful battle with alcoholism became widely known through her book I'll Cry Tomorrow, *published in 1954.*

SELECTIONS FROM

I'LL CRY TOMORROW

I HAVE thought of many ways to start my story. I could begin it at a moment of triumph, when as a Hollywood star my escorts to a world premiere were Gary Cooper and Maurice Chevalier, when three of my pictures were running simultaneously on Broadway, and I earned $3,500 for an afternoon's work. That would be a glamorous beginning.

I could begin it at an awful moment, when I stood before an open window, behind me years of alcoholic horror and degradation, about to leap to the pavement eleven stories below. That would be a melodramatic beginning.

Or I could begin it at the age of thirty-four, when as an ex-inmate of a mental institution, I was released to start my life over again. But that might be a puzzling beginning, and difficult for some to understand.

Perhaps, as my husband Burt suggests, the way to tell it is the way it happened, allowing it to unfold in the order dictated by whatever mysterious forces mold us into the persons we become. "That's the only way it will make sense," he cautioned me. "Tell it as it happened."

This is how it happened, then.

My life was never my own. It was charted before I was born.

My parents were hopelessly stagestruck, and as a result, I literally waited for my very first entrance cue in a theater. My mother, who

279

had firm ideas about pre-natal influence, spent as much time in theaters as she could. She laughed and cried with Eva Tanguay and Nora Bayes and Sarah Bernhardt, delighted to think that in some occult fashion her enjoyment was shared by the child she carried. She wanted me to be a singer; and because her greatest idol, almost to the point of worship, was Lillian Russell, I was named for her when I finally arrived on December 13, 1910.

My father saw another future for me. He dreamed of me as a great dramatic actress. Born Arthur Rutstein in Russia, he had been brought to Boston, my mother's birthplace, when he was four. Handsome, happy-go-lucky, and gifted with contagious charm, he played a bit part in "Peck's Bad Boy" at sixteen. To hear him describe it, he was the star. For years my mother laughingly chided him for never getting over it—and teased him about his voice. Dad's voice was an off-key tenor, and temperamental in the high ranges, but it didn't stop him from teaming up with a friend who played the accordion, and singing on the Boston ferry for coins tossed by the passengers. When Dad took Mother along for the ride, during his courtship, he called it "serenading" her. She would sigh with the memory. "Juliet had her Romeo and I had my Arthur. Sometimes I think I suffered more than she did." Actually, Mother didn't mind, because it meant more money to go to more shows.

Arthur was 24, working in his father's produce market by day and ushering in theaters by night, when he first met my mother, Katie Silverman. They were married soon after. My baby sister Ann made her appearance two and a half years after me.

I have often tried to trace my parents' passionate love for the theater. Perhaps it answered some deep need in them. Perhaps it was the result of unfulfilled dreams about which I never knew. My mother, a strong-willed but emotional woman, felt that show people—those with real talent, and she was a stern critic—were the chosen of the gods. "We took you to see the greats and near-greats," she told me when I was old enough to understand. "They all had something to offer, or they wouldn't be up there making people laugh and cry." She had a small, sweet singing voice herself. "That's all I had, Lilly baby, but there was a lot of harmony in my soul, and I gave you that."

Dad, however, was always acting, forever putting on a show for us. He gave a song everything: his left hand over his heart, his right outstretched to a cruel unfeeling world, big tears rolled down his cheeks as he sang, "Just a Cousin of Mine," or "Please, Mr. Conductor, Don't Put Me Off the Train, My Poor Old Mother is Waiting, Waiting for Me in Pain." I remember, in a room off the parlor, bouncing on my little bed to the rhythm of his songs. It was Dad who taught

280

me recitations and despite my shyness brought me out to recite before Sunday company.

Whatever the case, the stage was my life and that of my sister Ann as far back as I can remember.

Ann and I were not alike. No matter how miserable I felt when called upon to perform for guests, I never rebelled. Dad would say, "Lillian is so good. She always minds me. Stand up, darling, and do something for us." Ann, however, refused. Dad might plead, beg, threaten—she would not budge. I was also a silent child, keeping much to myself. My father sometimes worried aloud. "She's so quiet, Katie," he would say. "You ought to find out what she thinks about, what goes on in that little head of hers." Mother would pick me up and hug me. "Oh, Arthur, what can she be thinking of? She's only a baby!"

I thought—and felt—many things. Looking back now, I know that what I felt most during my childhood was fear—and loneliness. I feared my mother's displeasure. Though she loved me, she was a perfectionist. Quick to kiss, she was quick to slap. Her dedication to my career was single-minded: to her the theater was the magic door to everything she dreamed for her Lilly, and she would allow nothing to get in the way. My sense of loneliness is more difficult to explain. I was lonely for—I knew not what. I always felt inadequate. No matter what I was told, I thought every other child was prettier, more charming, more likable—in short, nicer than I. I never liked the person I was, and later, I found alcohol helped me run away from myself.

In 1916 we moved to New York, to a cold-water walk-up on 43rd Street, between Ninth and Tenth Avenues. Arthur, who was always going to make a million, thought he'd find more opportunities in the big city. Even more important was the fact that New York was the center of show business.

Hearing that jobs were available for talented little girls, Katie used to dress Ann and me each morning near the coal stove in the kitchen, and then make the rounds with us of the producers and theatrical agents. Their offices were invariably crowded. Each was like the other —a desk, a bored girl behind it, and the same answer, day after day: "Nothing doing." Mother refused to be discouraged. One blustery winter's day in 1916 she dropped in with us at Educational Pictures. Yes, there was a job, then and there—for me!

It was to be my first assignment in show business, to pose as Educational Pictures' screen trademark, a living statue holding a lamp of knowledge.

Katie's excitement as she signed me in possessed me too. It was always to be like that. Her wish became mine. In later years I always looked into the wings, where she stood during my act, to see what her face said. A smile meant I had done well. The merest shadow of a frown, that my performance wasn't perfect, no matter what the critics wrote the following morning.

Now, in preparation for my first job, she undressed me and a fatherly looking old gentleman with a cigar clenched in his teeth started to paint me with white body makeup. When lunch time came, Katie left me in his charge while she and Ann went out to buy sandwiches for all of us, including the old gentleman. Left alone with me, he went to the door, looked outside, and locked it. "Cold in here," he said. I had been standing on a box. "Better lie down, where it's warm," he said, taking me in his arms and carrying me to a couch near the stove. He painted my thighs, then worked his brush upwards and began painting me where it made me uneasy.

He daubed me with the brush, again and again, on the same part of my anatomy. The cigar moved from one corner of his mouth to the other, and then back again. "Only five years old," he said. "My, you're a nice little girl."

I covered my eyes with my hands. I knew there was something wrong in what he was doing, but I couldn't stop him or cry for help. If Katie found out, something terrible would happen. She would scream, her face would contort, and I could not bear to hear her scream or to see her face like that.

When he heard her footsteps in the hall, he hurriedly unlocked the door and stood me up on the box again; he was just finishing my feet when Katie came in and spread out our lunch.

An unknown fear held my tongue. I never told her. But for years afterward I dreamed constantly about a man with a cigar in his mouth, who locked me up in a room and did dreadful things to me. A popular Admiration Cigar advertisement at the time pictured a smiling, moon-faced man with a cigar in his mouth, and he was repeated, cigar and face, on and on into infinity, growing smaller and smaller in the background. Whenever I caught sight of him in subway or trolley ads, I shut my eyes tightly and hid my face in Katie's skirts until all his heads faded away.

Katie learned that Sam Goldwyn was producing motion pictures in Fort Lee, New Jersey, across the Hudson River. If Educational Films could use me, why not Goldwyn? Each morning we took the long trip by bus, ferry and bus again, Katie, Ann and I. Once in the barracks-like studios, we waited hopefully for calls as extras—we two among perhaps a hundred children, with their mothers. We were always cold. Someone distributed tin cups of hot coffee, and Katie hurried about looking for hot water to dilute it for us. We stood, sometimes for hours, stamping our feet to keep warm, until we were called. Our assignment usually was to mill excitedly about, shouting and waving our arms, while the cameras ground. Sometimes Katie was in the same scene.

"What are you doing. Mommy?" I asked her once.

"I'm earning three dollars, too, today. Now I'll be able to buy you that little muffler you wanted."

One day we waited a long time. We grew blue with cold. Suddenly she exclaimed, "The devil with this! My children aren't going to freeze!" She bundled us up, took us all the way back home, and put us to bed under warm blankets. It was like a party, we told each other: we had never been home so early in the day before. "Babies," she said, "I'm going to heat some nice big rolls for you, with lots of butter and hot cocoa, and I'm going to bring it to you right in bed."

After our treat, she read us the Sunday comics until we fell asleep.

Later Ann and I were rewarded with steady acting jobs. While Ann played Theda Bara as a child on one set, on the other I was an angel in white gauze and lace, waiting to be born. We angels stood perched on a high platform facing a row of dazzling Kleig lights. Just before the action began, a man shouted a warning, "Children, don't look at the lights!"

They flashed on. I blinked, then stared, fascinated. As I watched, they changed shape; the slender incandescent spiral in the center became a winged man, then a glowing giant, growing taller and taller yet remaining the same.

We were homeward bound later, and I was trailing Mother, who was carrying Ann, when my eyes began to smart. I shut them tight, but the pain only increased. "Mommy, where are you!" I screamed. "I can't see you."

She thought I was playing a game. "What are you talking about, Lilly?" she asked over her shoulder. "I'm right in front of you."

"Mommy, I can't find you, I can't see you," I wailed.

She put Ann down and grabbed me up. I felt the pounding of her heart. She began to run, crying hysterically. "Oh, my baby, my baby," and I clung to her, my arms around her neck, my eyes feeling as though a million needles were stuck in them.

The doctor called it "Kleig eyes," and prescribed a rest in bed for me. My father comforted me. "Baby," he said, "you'll get used to those lights and become a great actress. Let's start right now." He taught me, "The Making of Friends," by Edgar A. Guest. I still remember the words, for they were my first dramatic lines.

They began:

If nobody smiled and nobody cheered
And nobody helped us along,
If every each moment looked after itself
And the good things all went to the strong . . .

"What's the use of that?" my mother asked. "She needs ballet, and singing lessons, and so many things—"

"She'll have those, too," said Dad. "But right now I want her to learn this, with all the hand motions, with expression!"

Quite without warning, I had to test my dramatic skill on Dad himself. Katie got word that children were being interviewed for parts in the film, "The Bluebird," and hurried down with me. Several children and their mothers were already eagerly on hand. When the casting director came out to look us over, he pointed at a little girl who sat next to me. She rose and walked over to him. "Everybody else excused," he announced.

Katie and I and the others straggled out disconsolately. I sensed rather than knew that Mother was boiling.

It came like an explosion once we were outside. "Why didn't you get up when he pointed at you!"

"No he didn't, Mommy. He wanted that little Violet Mae sitting next to me."

My mother walked faster. I ran along in the snow, frightened, tripping, trying to keep up with her as she strode along. "He pointed at you and you wouldn't stand up!" Turning suddenly, she slapped me. The blow struck me as I tripped forward toward her: I was knocked off balance into the snow.

She cried out with horror. "Oh, my poor baby! What have I done!" She picked me up, and almost beside herself, began to cuddle and kiss me. My left eye was beginning to puff. "Oh, God, look what I've done!" And then, "Oh my God, what will your father do when he finds out!"

She was rocking me in her arms, both of us crying. I smothered my mother's face with kisses. "Don't worry, Mommy," I managed to get out. "We can tell him I fell against this lamppost, can't we?" I pointed to one conveniently near.

"Oh, he won't believe it," she said miserably.

"Yes, he will. I *could* have slipped . . ."

We memorized our story on the way home. My father was in the kitchen when we arrived. When he saw me he uttered an exclamation. "Come over here, Lillian! Let me look at that eye!"

I walked over slowly, my fingers crossed behind my back so that I could tell a fib without being a bad girl.

"How did this happen?"

284

"I slipped and fell against a lamppost, Daddy. It was very icy—"

My father looked up suspiciously at Katie, then back at me.

"Is that the truth?" he demanded.

"Yes it is, Daddy," I said stoutly. "And I can show you the place, too."

He surely knew then that I could not be telling the truth, but he only grumbled as Katie, maintaining a discreet silence, wrung out a cloth in water and held it tenderly to my eye.

I missed the part in "The Bluebird," but Ann and I played Constance and Norma Talmadge as children; then I was Evelyn Nesbit as a child; then we were cast to play General Pershing's daughters in the film, "Pershing's Crusaders."

Dad's dramatic coaching led only to such bit parts until one January afternoon when a crowd of us children were gathered on an icy Fort Lee hillside. We had been instructed to watch the child stars of the picture kiss each other before they tobogganed down the snowy slope. Wesley Barry, the freckle-faced male star, approached his leading lady to embrace her. But the scenarist hadn't reckoned with feminine modesty. Wesley's leading lady wouldn't kiss him.

Instead, she dissolved in tears and refused to go on.

The director threw out his arms despairingly. "What do we do now?" he demanded.

"I'll do it," I piped up. I was astounded to hear myself say it. The idea of kissing a boy was shocking to me. I could feel the shame burning my face as everyone turned to look at me: if I could have sunk into a snowbank, I would have. But perhaps I was inspired by the disastrous memory of what had happened earlier when I wasn't on my toes. In any case, Mother was beaming, and that was the important thing.

An onlooker called me over after the camera had taken its closeup. "What's your name?" he asked.

"Lillian Roth," I said.

He smiled. "My name's Roth, too." He turned to my mother. "I'm casting a show for the Shuberts and I'd like to see your child tomorrow. I think she's just the type. We're looking for a sad, pensive little girl."

Next day I was in his office. "Honey, can you do a little acting for me?" Mr. Roth asked.

"Oh, yes," I replied. "My daddy taught me 'The Making of Friends,' and I could do that for you." I recited it, with expression. When Katie brought me home, I ran to my father and told him the good news. I had been cast for Wilton Lackaye's little daughter in "The Inner Man," a full-fledged Broadway production.

Daddy was jubilant. "See, Katie, what did I tell you!" He picked

285

me up, threw me into the air, and kissed me. "She's going to be a great dramatic actress. A tragedienne—that's what. Why, she'll be making $1,500 a week in no time!"

I had just turned six.

. . .

Tragedienne or not, I had to go to school, and during the run of "The Inner Man" Katie enrolled me in the Professional Children's School. Classes were held only from 10 A.M. to 2 P.M., but in the four hours you crammed a full day's school work, including diction and French.

After classes Katie took me home, and when we were finished with dinner, made me up for my role as Mr. Lackaye's daughter. I soon discovered there was a great difference between reciting Edgar Guest—even with expression—and performing on the stage. "The Inner Man" called for me to sit on the lap of Mr. Lackaye, who played a criminal finally redeemed by the faith of his little girl. One of my poignant lines was "Daddy, Daddy, won't you PULLEASE come home with me?"

Mr. Lackaye gave me my first professional dramatic lesson.

"A play tells a story and you must pretend it's really happening," he explained. "You must pretend there's nobody in the theater—no audience, no one back stage—just you and me and the other actors. You must pretend I'm your real father. And remember—never, *never* look at the audience."

He said this last so solemnly that my skin crawled. What awful terror lurked out in that vast unknown? After the second day I couldn't hold my curiosity. For a breathless moment I lifted my eyes and looked directly into the forbidden darkness.

I almost screamed. Before me, as far as my eye could reach, was a weird ocean of pale, disembodied heads floating in a gray, ghostly dusk. I buried my face in my stage father's shoulder, and tried to catch my breath. There was something about Mr. Lackaye that was strangely comforting. I snuggled closer: the odor of tweed, the fragrance of talcum, and through it all, the familiar, sweet scent of whiskey—why, I thought, it was just like being on my real daddy's lap!

The Professional Children's School was made to order for those of us already working. If you had rehearsals or matinees, your schedule was arranged accordingly, and there were even correspondence lessons if you went on tour.

As at other schools, the mothers waited outside for classes to let out, but since they were stage mothers, their conversation was studded with Broadway names and punctuated by the rustle of news-paper clippings passed from hand to hand. My classmates' rollcall read like a theatrical *Who's Who* of the future: Ruby Keeler, Patsy Kelly, Milton Berle, Ben Grauer, Helen Chandler, Gene Raymond, Penny Singleton, Helen Mack, Marguerite Churchill, Jerry Mann, and many others.

Sometimes I got out earlier than the other students and overheard the mothers on their favorite subject—the talent of their offspring. For example, Mrs. Grauer: "I really think my Bunny has one of the finest speaking voices I've ever heard."

"Don't I know?" This from Katie. "Didn't I hear him recite 'The Midnight Ride of Paul Revere'? He was wonderful."

Or Sarah Berle, with whom mother often played casino: "Katie, you should have heard Milton at the benefit last night! He tore the house down. When he did Cantor, you'd have sworn it was Cantor. And when he got down on one knee to do Jolson—"

Mother would interrupt: "Shubert came to him and said, 'Get down on both knees, and Jolson goes!' "

They all laughed. They were proud of their children, and if Katie carried no clippings in her purse, it was because, as she once told me, "I didn't have to carry proof, Lilly. Your name was up in lights."

Milton Berle, who was several grades ahead of me but delighted in teasing me, did impressions, and even in those days he was accused of stealing someone else's act. Katie had taught Ann and me to save our acting for on stage: off stage we had to be perfect little ladies, like the little girls on Park Avenue. I couldn't under-stand this, because Milton acted all over school. The moment the teacher left the room, he was running up and down the aisles, clapping his hands a la Eddie Cantor, and sending the rest of us into gales of laughter.

The prettiest of my schoolmates, I thought, was Ruby Keeler. I admired her slim, tapering hands. Mine were stubby, and looked even worse because I bit my nails. I was so self-conscious of my hands that I hid them when I talked; so nobody could see them, I snatched at pencils and books, succeeding only in dropping every-thing so often that I was nicknamed "Butterfingers." Dr. Coué was the rage then, so I pulled hopefully at my fingers and recited, "Every day in every way they're getting more tapering and more tapering, like Ruby's." Critics today, interestingly enough, speak of the way I use my hands to put over a song. I had to learn graceful gestures to draw attention away from my hands.

As I hid my hands, so for a long while I hid my voice. I knew Katie wanted me to be a singer, and I tried. Dad was always singing about the house. I followed suit. One afternoon, I was singing at the top of my voice, "I'm Forever Blowing Bubbles," the current hit, when Katie looked up from her copy of *Variety*. "Oh, Lilly," she said, "that bubble really broke. That last note was way off key." She shook her head. "Just like your father—you can't even carry a tune."

I never forgot her words.

After that I sang in secret, practicing in the bathroom where I turned the taps on full strength in the tub to drown out my voice. The rushing water became my orchestral accompaniment: it became drums, oboes, bass fiddles. I *would* be a singer when I grew up. I would make Katie proud of me.

Katie, to be sure, overlooked few chances for me. After "The Inner Man" closed, a stock company put out a call for a little boy, and I was turned down. Katie hurried me home, dressed me in a velvet Lord Fauntleroy suit borrowed from a neighbor, and rushed me back. "This is my son, Billy," she said. I felt utterly disgraced, but I got the part.

Then Katie got word that Henry W. Savage was casting "Shavings," and had interviewed scores of children for a 50-page part. She had to be with Ann, who was playing in "The Magic Melody" that day, so she dropped me off at the producer's office. She'd learned the play was about a toyshop, and she briefed me. "Now, do your best, baby," she said. "And don't be shy."

Under orders, I approached the "Nothing doing" girl timidly, but with determination. "I would like to see Mr. Henry W. Savage," I announced. She peeked over the desk to find me. "I'm sorry, little girl, but you can only see Mr. Savage by appointment."

"Oh, well," I said. "I have an appointment."

She coughed to hide a smile, disappeared into the next room, and returned a moment later to say Mr. Savage would see me.

I walked into the adjoining room and stopped, transfixed. Behind a desk an enormous man was getting to his feet, rising taller and taller, until when he reached his full six feet four he seemed to tower over me like the giant in *Jack and the Beanstalk*. He was tremendous—massive, broad-shouldered, white-haired—with a voice to match. It boomed out, rattling the ashtrays on his desk. "Good afternoon, young lady. I hear we have an appointment."

I forgot all about my fib. "My mother told me you want a little girl to play a part in a toy shop," I managed to stammer.

He looked down at me from his awful height. Suddenly he said, "How would you ask me, 'Are you the windmill man?'"

All at once it came to me. That's who he looks like—Thor, the God of Wind and Thunder. "Are *you* the *windmill* man?" I asked, in great awe. For all I knew, he was.

Mr. Savage said, "You have the part."

"Shavings" put my name in lights for the first time. Just turned eight, I was billed as "Broadway's Youngest Star." Interviews with me were syndicated throughout the country. Wherever I turned, my face stared back at me, for photographs of Lillian and her one-eyed rag doll Petunia were placarded on subway pillars, telegraph poles and billboards.

Neither my photographs nor the growing scrapbook my parents kept meant much to me. What was exceptional about doing what you were told? Often I felt I'd have more fun with Ann playing Red Cross Nurse, helping the poor Belgian children orphaned by the Germans, a game all the other neighborhood children played. Now and then I stood in the wings and watched the rest of the show, but my eyelids would grow heavy, and Katie would take me into a dressing room, spread my coat over two chairs, and I would nap there until I was due onstage again.

Our home life, what we had of it, held little but indecision—and quarrels. My success, and Ann's during our early years, only stressed our insecurity. We seemed either to be transients, away on tour, or, when we were at home, caught in endless bickering between our parents.

When Dad courted Katie, he was known as the handsomest boy on the block, she as the girl with the most personality. My mother was not beautiful, but she had an enchanting smile, and an immediate, warm sympathy that made her everyone's confidant. Arthur's charm was unmistakeable. Away from home he was merry and fun-loving, immensely popular. He began as a good-time drinker; then it developed into a problem, although liquor never took over his life as completely as it did mine.

Dad had big dreams. He tried his hand at everything, but never succeeded in becoming the man he wanted to be in the eyes of his wife and his children. He sold produce, then greeting cards, then men's clothing; he was a stock and bond salesman; he even operated a waffle shop. One failure followed another. Each time he tried to pass it off lightly. "Well, Katie," he would say, "that wasn't for me, anyway." And he would take a drink to forget it. I am sure, now, that ambitious as he was for us, his ego must have been hurt by the fact that Ann and I earned more than he, and that he was always going from job to job.

In time his drinking made him irritable and suspicious. Once, I remember, he accused Katie of poisoning our minds against him. She snapped, "If you ever saw yourself when you're full of whiskey—how can they love you when you frighten them to death?" I watched, terrified of the blow that might come: once I had seen him strike her. I knew how explosive their tempers were.

As it worked out, however, we were separated from Dad for long stretches from my 9th to my 15th year. For after "Shavings" Ann and I became vaudeville headliners on the Keith Circuit, and Mother travelled with us. This meant three to four months on the road, then back to New York for a brief layoff, and back on the road again. Our act was "Lillian Roth & Co." Ann was the "& Co." until her great sense of comedy caused Katie to change the billing to "The Roth Kids."

I did dramatic impersonations—impressions of Ruth Chatterton in "Daddy Long Legs," and of "Pollyanna," which I abhorred because she was "always glad all over." My greatest thrill came in my impersonation of John and Lionel Barrymore in the duelling scene from "The Jest." Here I could be the extrovert on stage that I could never be in real life. First I was John, taking my duelling stance, rapier in hand, my eyebrows cocked. "Methinks thou art a cur!" Lunge, and back again. "Thou buzzard!" I roared. Jab, and dance away. Then, in an instant, I whirled about and became Lionel, transformed into the wily, cunning cackling-voiced swordsman who parried John's violent thrusts with consummate disdain . . . The audience watched, silent and intent, and I was in raptures. I knew power, I glowed with the magic of the theater. I felt the audience in the palm of my hand.

Then, bathed in perspiration and triumph, I bowed to thunderous applause and turned the stage over to Ann. My sister proceeded to throw herself into a brilliantly hilarious satire of my act. She burlesqued me down to the contemptuous curl of my imaginary mustache. The audience howled, and I suffered. The tragedienne in me was deeply hurt.

We played on bills with such headliners as Georgie Jessel, George Burns and Gracie Allen, Ben Bernie, and the Marx Brothers, and Katie taught us to curtsy to all of them, as was only proper with older persons. Rosie Green of Keno & Green, a comedy song and dance act, carried her baby, Mitzy, around in a little basket, and I often stopped to coo at her as she lay backstage laughing and gurgling.

"See my baby," Rosie once said to me. "She's going to grow up to be a great impersonator, too. Just like you, Lillian."

"Like me? Gosh," I said, flattered. I was all of 10 years old.

Once, in Washington, D. C., Ann and I were told that the President of the United States was in his box that afternoon. After the show the stage manager hurriedly knocked at our dressing room door. "The President wants to see you, kids!" he exclaimed.

Still in our costumes, we rushed out the stage entrance into the back alley, and there they were, President Wilson and the first lady, sitting in a huge open touring car. The President asked us to get in. Ann sat on his lap. I sat shyly between him and Mrs. Wilson.

"What a serious little girl you are, both on and off the stage," the President said to me. "You know, I am going to make a prediction, young lady. Some day you will be a great actress." Then he turned to Ann. "And you, my dear, you were utterly delightful. Mrs. Wilson and I haven't laughed so much in a long time."

I found my voice and thanked him. Ann, busy examining and fingering the interior of the luxurious car, piped up, to my mortification, "Ooh, what a big auto! My daddy has a tin lizzie." The President smiled and turned to Mrs. Wilson. "Shall we take our little guests for a ride around the block?" Away we drove. When we emerged into the street outside, it was jammed with people held back by police on both sides. They waved and applauded as we passed by, and then we were brought back to the stage entrance again.

"Goodbye, little girls, and stay sweet," Mrs. Wilson called back to us as their chauffeur drove them away. I thought, as we went to our dressing room to put on our street clothes, it was just like a beautiful fairy tale—like Cinderella's ride in the pumpkin coach.

Mostly, however, vaudeville on the road was a hard life, made up of lonely train rides (even now a train whistle fills me with haunting sadness), lonely nights in strange hotels, and lonely cities in which we knew no one. "The Roth Kids" in lights in town after town meant little to us. Wistfully Ann and I looked out the train windows, watching the endless procession of backyard gardens flow by, catching a glimpse of little family groups, of children playing with their pets, of mother and father contentedly together on a back porch. We yearned for a home, a garden, a hammock, a sense of belonging.

Like prisoners Mother, Ann and I counted off the days until we got back to New York. "Where do we go next, Mommy?" I would ask. Katie would produce a long slip of green paper. "Hattfield, for three days." "Then where, Mommy?" "Pittsfield, for a split week." And so it was—four days, three days, and week stands, month after month.

But when we returned to New York—and Dad—there were only arguments after the affectionate greetings of the first few hours. For added to Dad's uncontrollable temper was his jealousy.

"Did Mother ever leave you alone between shows," he would ask, taking me aside. "Was she with you all the time?"

I knew Mother went nowhere. Time and again I awakened to see her sitting beside us, reading by the little table light, reluctant to slip into bed with us because of what terrors the night might hold. She feared the darkness, and often in a hotel she saw—or thought she saw —a man peeking over our transom.

Once she was sure of it. She woke us, frantically. "Babies—babies —get up, hurry up, there's a man after us!"

She could hardly dress Ann in her panic. My fingers were all thumbs as I tried to button my clothes. I was sick with the terror on my mother's face. I went into a cold sweat. My heart pounded in my ears. I was sure something monstrous was breathing in the room.

Then we were rushing out and down the stairs into the dimly lit lobby and Mother was screaming at the lone desk clerk—not knowing but that he might have been the man himself. Then we were running through the dark streets, my mother shrieking for help, until we found another place to spend the night. But there was no more sleep.

Once I woke to find her brushing things off us. "What are you doing, Mommy?" I asked sleepily. "Get out of bed," she said excitedly. "It's full of bedbugs!" Minutes later she had us dressed and furiously rushed us out of the hotel.

The streets of the small towns were always deserted late at night when we walked from the theater to our hotel. What might not be lurking behind every tree, every shadow? Sometimes we heard footsteps behind us. We hurried, and the footsteps quickened, and I was limp with fear until we reached the bright lights of the hotel.

Back in New York the arguments grew more bitter. I was in an agony of shame when my father began his accusations, sometimes behind the locked door of their bedroom. I became hot and cold, I tore at my nails. How could I face people who heard them screaming at each other?

Once, a quarrel broke out between them in the kitchen. They began to struggle, and something exploded in me. "Stop it!" I screamed hysterically. "Stop it, I can't stand it!" I grabbed my glass piggy bank and threw it with all my might between them, trying to separate them. It crashed against the wall. My parents, startled, turned to me, and a moment later I was in Katie's arms, and we were both sobbing.

Dad was all remorse. He took a quick drink and then another. "How could I do this to my Katie! To my Lilly!" He began to cry. "They can string me up from a tree if I ever lay a hand on you again, Katie!"

292

My mother could only shake her head. "You and your crocodile tears." She wept, and took me into the bedroom, where Ann slept, undisturbed.

On another occasion, at a gathering, a handsome man engaged Katie in a long, bantering conversation. Dad's face grew pale. He was in an ugly mood when we came home. For a while he drank silently.

Then—"Will you be good enough to tell me—" he began, grinding his teeth as he always did when he was about to explode.

"Arthur. The children . . ."

Praying they would not fight, I tiptoed to bed. But suddenly I heard piercing screams. I leaped out of bed and ran into the kitchen. My mother lay on the floor, blood trickling from the corners of her mouth, her eyes puffed, her face bruised. She was rolling wildly back and forth, screaming uncontrollably, catching her breath, then sobbing and screaming again.

My father, a long red gash on his face, was in his bathrobe, slumped in a chair, his eyes glassy, a bottle beside him. He moaned to himself, "Oh my God, Lillian what did I do?"

He rose, as if to go to my mother, but she shrieked, "Don't come near me—don't touch me!" He fell back into his chair.

I pulled her to a couch and cradled her head in my lap, while my father repeated dully, "Do something, Lillian, do something." I was sick to my stomach with fear and horror, and with a compassion I could not put into words. My mother moaned and wept, and my father slumped in his chair, looking at nothing.

I spent the remainder of the night running between the living room, where my mother lay weeping, and the kitchen, where my father sat staring at the wall, and drinking. Katie fell asleep, but I was in the kitchen every few minutes, tugging at my father's arm, shaking him, imploring him, "Please don't fall asleep, Daddy, please, please!" I did not know what I feared, but I knew he had to remain awake, he *had* to remain awake.

For years afterward there were many nights that I could not fall asleep until daylight came through my bedroom window.

～～～～～～～～～～～～～～～～～～

DISCUSSION AND INQUIRY

Lillian was born into a hopelessly stage-struck family. Her mother was so determined to have her offspring fulfill her own unfulfilled needs to go on the stage that she began her program of

293

*indoctrination while Lillian was in utero by go-
ing to the theater regularly. Is there any evidence that prenatal exposure of this nature has
any tangible effect on an unborn child?*

*Lillian tells of the fear and loneliness she
experienced during her growing years. She com-
plied with her ambitious mother's pressures to
perform because she feared rejection and loss of
love. How do most children cope when rejection
is the tactic used by parents to control behavior?
Consider both how the child behaves and how
he feels under these circumstances. Lillian notes
that she always felt inadequate and lonely. What
far-reaching effects may this have had on her
self-image and on her behavior? Rejection tac-
tics are not only used in families, but are still
used in some schools; for example, a child is
ignored, put in the corner or in the hall, or sent
to the principal's office. Are there manifest behaviors seen in school-age children that could
be attributed to this method of classroom
management? Whose needs are being met when
adults manage children by rejecting them?*

*Five-year-old Lillian found her sexual ex-
perience with the old makeup man both repulsive and incomprehensible. She was certainly
not prepared for it and was unable to share it
with her mother. (See the selection by Lincoln
Steffens for a discussion of a similar problem.)
What are some of the common factors in families
that make it difficult or, in some cases, impossible
to discuss sexual experiences? With the differing expectations among various cultural groups
about sexual experiences and sexual behavior, is
it possible that children in some families feel
quite comfortable discussing their sexual adventures?*

Jean-Paul Sartre

BIOGRAPHICAL SKETCH

Jean-Paul Sartre was born June 5, 1905, in Paris. He received a degree in philosophy and spent several years teaching it. In 1939, he entered the army and, after a year of service, was taken prisoner in Germany. He was released before the end of the war and returned to France, where he taught and was active in the Resistance. In 1945, he gave up teaching and founded the prominent journal, Les Temps Modernes. *A prolific writer, he has produced novels, plays, filmscripts, political essays, and philosophical treatises. In 1964, he was offered the Nobel Prize for literature, which he refused with characteristic intransigence.*

SELECTIONS FROM

THE WORDS

THE death of Jean Baptiste was the big event of my life: it sent my mother back to her chains and gave me freedom.

There is no good father, that's the rule. Don't lay the blame on men but on the bond of paternity, which is rotten. To beget children, nothing better; to *have* them, what iniquity! Had my father lived, he would have lain on me at full length and would have crushed me. As luck had it, he died young. Amidst Aeneas and his fellows who carry their Anchises on their backs, I move from shore to shore, alone and hating those invisible begetters who bestraddle their sons all their life long. I left behind a young man who did not have time to be my father and who could now be my son. Was it a good thing or a bad? I don't know. But I readily subscribe to the verdict of an eminent psychoanalyst: I have no Superego.

Dying isn't everything: one must die in time. Later, I would have felt guilty; a conscious orphan lays the blame on himself: shocked at

295

the sight of him, his parents have gone off to their home in heaven. As for me, I was delighted: my sad situation commanded respect; I counted my bereavement as one of my virtues. My father had been so gallant as to die in the wrong: my grandmother kept repeating that he had shirked his duties; my grandfather, rightly proud of the Schweitzer longevity, would not hear of anyone's disappearing at the age of thirty. In the light of that suspect decease, he began to doubt that his son-in-law had ever existed, and he finally forgot about him. I did not even have to forget; in slipping away, Jean Baptiste had refused me the pleasure of making his acquaintance. Even now I am surprised at how little I know about him. Yet he loved, he wanted to live, he saw himself dying; that is enough to make a whole man. But no one in my family was able to make me curious about that man. For several years, I was able to see above my head a photograph of a frank-looking little officer with a round, baldish head and a thick moustache. The picture disappeared when my mother remarried. I later inherited some books that had belonged to him: a work by Le Dantec on the future of science, another by Weber entitled *Toward Positivism through Absolute Idealism*. He read bad books, like all his contemporaries. In the margins, I came upon indecipherable scribbles, dead signs of a little illumination that had been alive and dancing at about the time of my birth. That defunct was of so little concern to me that I sold the books. I know him by hearsay, like the Man in the Iron Mask and the Chevalier d'Eon; and what I do know about him never has anything to do with me. Nobody remembered whether he loved me, whether he took me in his arms, whether he looked at his son with his limpid eyes, now eaten by worms. Love's labor's lost. That father is not even a shadow, not even a gaze. We trod the same earth for a while, that is all. Rather than the son of a dead man, I was given to understand that I was a child of miracle. That accounts, beyond a doubt, for my incredible levity. I am not a leader, nor do I aspire to become one. Command, obey, it's all one. The bossiest of men commands in the name of another—his father—and transmits the abstract acts of violence which he puts up with. Never in my life have I given an order without laughing, without making others laugh. It is because I am not consumed by the canker of power: I was not taught obedience.

Whom would I obey? I am shown a young giantess, I am told she's my mother. I myself would take her rather for an elder sister. That virgin who is under surveillance, who is obedient to everyone, I can see very well that she's there to serve me. I love her, but how can I respect her if no one else does? There are three bedrooms in our home: my grandfather's, my grandmother's, and the "children's." The "children" are we: both alike are minors and both alike are supported. But all consideration is for me. A young girl's bed has been put into *my* room. The girl sleeps alone and awakens chastely. I am still sleeping when she hurries to the bathroom to take her "tub." She comes back all dressed. How could I have been born of her? She tells me her troubles, and I listen compassionately. Later, I'll marry her to protect her. I promise her I will: I'll take her hand in mine, my youthful importance will serve her. Does anyone think I'm going to obey her? I am so good as to give in to her requests. Besides, she does not give me orders; she outlines in light words a future which she praises me for being so kind as to bring into being: " My little darling will be very nice, very reasonable. He'll sit still so I can put drops into his nose." I let myself be caught in the trap of these coddling prophecies.

There remained the patriarch. He so resembled God the Father that he was often taken for Him. One day he entered a church by way of the vestry. The priest was threatening the infirm of purpose with the lightning of heaven: "God is here! He sees you!" Suddenly the faithful perceived beneath the pulpit a tall, bearded old man who was looking at them. They fled. At other times, my grandfather would say that they had flung themselves at his knees. He developed a taste for apparitions. In September 1914, he appeared in a movie-house in Arcachon: my mother and I were in the balcony when he asked for light; other gentlemen were playing angel around him and crying "Victory! Victory!" God got up on the stage and read the communiqué from the Marne. When his beard had been black, he had been Jehovah, who, I suspect, was indirectly responsible for Emile's death. This God of wrath gorged on his sons' blood. But I appeared at the end of his long life; his beard had turned white, tobacco had yellowed it; and fatherhood no longer amused him. Had he begotten me, however, I think he would have been unable to keep from oppressing me, out of habit. My luck was to belong to a dead man. A dead man had paid out the few drops of sperm that are the usual cost of a child; I was a fief of the sun, my grandfather could enjoy me without possessing me. I was his "wonder" because he wanted to finish his life as a wonderstruck old man. He chose to regard me as a singular favor of fate, as a gratuitous and always revocable gift. What could he have required of me? My mere presence filled him to overflowing. He was the God of Love with the beard of the Father and the Sacred Heart of the Son. There was a laying on of hands, and I could feel the warmth of his palm on my skull. He would call me his "tiny little one" in a voice quavering with tenderness. His cold eyes would dim with tears. Everybody would exclaim: "That scamp has driven him crazy!" He worshipped me, that was manifest. Did he love me? In so public a passion it's hard for me to distinguish sincerity from artifice. I don't think he displayed much affection for his other grandchildren. It's true that he hardly ever saw them and that they had no need of him, whereas I depended on him for everything: what he worshipped in me was his generosity.

The fact is, he slightly overdid the sublime. He was a man of the nineteenth century who took himself for Victor Hugo, as did so many others, including Victor Hugo himself. This handsome man with the flowing beard who was always waiting for the next opportunity to show off, as the alcoholic is always waiting for the next drink, was the victim of two recently discovered techniques: the art of photography and the art of being a grandfather.* He had the good and bad fortune to be photogenic. The house was filled with photos of him. Since snapshots were not practiced, he had acquired a taste for poses and *tableaux vivants*. Everything was a pretext for him to suspend his gestures, to strike an attitude, to turn to stone. He doted upon those brief moments of eternity in which he became his own statue. Given his taste for *tableaux vivants*, I have retained only some stiff lantern-slide images of him: a forest interior, I am sitting on a tree-trunk. I am five years old; Charles Schweitzer is wearing a Panama hat, a cream-colored flannel suit with black stripes, a white piqué vest with a watch-chain strung across it; his pince-nez are hanging from a silk cord; he bends over me, raises a ringed finger, speaks. All is dark, all is damp, except his solar beard: he wears his halo around his chin. I don't know what he's saying. I was too busy listening to hear. I suppose that this old, Empire-bred republican was teaching me my civic duties and relating bourgeois history. There had been kings, emperors; they were very wicked; they had been driven out; everything was happening for the best. In the late afternoon, when we went to wait for him on the road, we would soon recognize him in the crowd of travelers emerging from the funicular by his tall figure and dancing-master's walk. As soon as he saw us, however far away, he would "take his stance" in obedience to the behests of an invisible photographer: beard flowing in the wind, body erect, feet at right angles, chest out, arms wide open. At this signal, I would stop moving, I would lean forward, I was the runner getting set, the little birdy about to spring from the camera. We would remain for a few moments face to face, a pretty chinaware group; then I would dash forward, laden with fruit and flowers, with my grandfather's happiness, I would go hurtling against his knees, pretending to be out of breath. He would lift me from the ground, raise me to the skies, at arm's length, bring me down upon his heart, murmuring: "My precious!" That was the second figure, which the passers-by could not

* *The Art of Being a Grandfather* is the title of a work by Hugo. (Translator's note.)

fail to notice. We would put on a full act with a hundred varied sketches: The flirtation, the quickly dispelled misunderstanding, the good-humored teasing and pretty scolding, the lover's chagrin, the tender pretense of mystery, and the passion; we would imagine our love being thwarted so as to have the joy of triumphing in the end. I was at times imperious, but caprices could not mask my exquisite sensibility. He would display the sublime, artless vanity that befits grandfathers, the blindness, the guilty weaknesses recommended by Hugo. If I had been put on bread and water, he would have brought me jam; but the two terrorized women took care not to put me on such a diet. And besides, I was a good child: I found my role so becoming that I did not step out of it. Actually, my father's early retirement had left me with a most incomplete "Oedipus complex." No Superego, granted. But no aggressiveness either. My mother was mine; no one challenged my peaceful possession of her. I knew nothing of violence and hatred; I was spared the hard apprenticeship of jealousy. Not having been bruised by its sharp angles, I knew reality only by its unsubstantiality. Against whom, against what, would I have rebelled? Never had someone else's whim claimed to be my law.

I nicely allow my mother to put drops into my nose, to put my shoes on my feet, to brush and wash me, to dress and undress me, to rub me down and tidy me up; I know nothing more amusing than to play at being good. I never cry, I hardly laugh, I don't make noise. At the age of four, I was caught salting the jam: out of love of knowledge, I suppose, rather than out of naughtiness; in any case, that is the only crime I can remember. On Sunday, the two ladies sometimes go to Mass, to hear good music, a well-known organist. Neither of them is a practicing Catholic, but the faith of others inclines them to musical ecstasy. They believe in God long enough to enjoy a toccata. Those moments of high spirituality delight me: everyone looks as if he were sleeping, now is the time to show what I can do. Kneeling on the prayer-stool, I change into a statue; I must not even move a toe; I look straight ahead, without blinking, until tears roll down my cheeks. Naturally, I engage in a titanic fight against cramp, but I am sure of winning. I am so conscious of my force that I do not hesitate to arouse within me the most criminal temptations just in order to give myself the pleasure of rejecting them: what if I stood up and yelled "Boom!"? What if I climbed up the column to make peepee in the holy-water basin? These terrible possibilities will make my mother's congratulations after church all the more precious. But I lie to myself; I pretend to be in danger so as to heighten my glory. Not for a moment were the temptations giddying; I am far too afraid of creating a scandal. If I want to astound people, it's by my

virtues. These easy victories convince me that I have a good character;
I have only to give it free play to be showered with praise. Wicked
desires and wicked thoughts, when there are any, come from the outside; no sooner do they enter me than they wilt and fade: I am bad soil
for evil. Virtuous for the fun of it, never do I force or constrain myself:
I invent. I have the lordly freedom of the actor who holds his audience
spellbound and keeps refining his role. I am adored, hence I am ador-
able. What can be more simple, since the world is well made? I am told
that I am good-looking, I believe it. For some time my right eye has
had a white speck that will make me half-blind and wall-eyed, but this
is not yet apparent. Dozens of photos are taken of me, and my mother
retouches them with colored pencils. In one of them which has survived, I am pink and blond, with curls; I am round-cheeked, and my
expression displays a kindly deference toward the established order;
my mouth is puffed with hypocritical arrogance: I know my worth.

It is not enough for my character to be good; it must also be prophetic: truth flows from the mouth of babes and sucklings. Still close
to nature, they are cousins of the wind and the sea: their stammerings
offer broad and vague teachings to him who can hear them. My grandfather had crossed Lake Geneva with Henri Bergson: "I was wild with
enthusiasm," he would say. "I hadn't eyes enough to contemplate the
sparkling crests, to follow the shimmering of the water. But Bergson
sat on his valise and never once looked up." He would conclude from
this incident that poetic meditation was preferable to philosophy. He
meditated on me: sitting in a deck-chair in the garden, a glass of beer
within arm's reach, he would watch me jump and run about; he would
look for wisdom in my jumbled talk, and he would find it. I later
laughed at this folly; I'm sorry I did; it was the working of death.
Charles fought anguish with ecstasy. He admired in me the admirable
fruit of the earth so as to convince himself that all is good, even our
shabby end. He went to seek the nature which was preparing to take
him back; he sought it on the summits, in the waves, amidst the stars,
at the origin of my young life, so as to be able to embrace it in its
entirety and accept all of it, including the grave that was being dug for
him. It was not Truth, but *his* death that spoke to him through my
mouth. It is not surprising that the insipid happiness of my early years
sometimes had a funereal taste. I owed my freedom to a timely death,
my importance to a very expected decease. But what of it! All the
Pythia are dead creatures; everyone knows that. All children are mir-
rors of death.

And besides, my grandfather takes pleasure in being a pain in the
ass to his sons. That terrible father has spent his life crushing them.

They enter on tiptoe and surprise him at a child's knees: enough to break one's heart! In the struggle between generations, children and old people often join forces: the former pronounce the oracles; the latter puzzle them out. Nature speaks, and experience translates: adults have only to keep their traps shut. Failing a child, one can take a poodle: last year, at the dogs' cemetery, I recognized my grandfather's maxims in the trembling discourse that runs from grave to grave: dogs know how to love; they are gentler than human beings, more faithful; they have tact, a flawless instinct that enables them to recognize Good, to distinguish the good from the wicked. "Polonius," said one un-consoled mistress, "you are better than I. You would not have survived me. I survive you." An American friend was with me. With a burst of indignation, he kicked a cement dog and broke its ear. He was right: when one loves children and animals *too much*, one loves them against human beings.

So I'm a promising poodle; I prophesy. I make childish remarks, they are remembered, they are repeated to me. I learn to make others. I make grown-up remarks. I know how to say things "beyond my years" without meaning to. These remarks are poems. The recipe is simple: you must trust to the Devil, to chance, to emptiness, you borrow whole sentences from grown-ups, you string them together and repeat them without understanding them. In short, I pronounce true oracles, and each adult interprets them as he wishes. The Good is born in the depths of my heart, the True in the young darkness of my Understanding. I admire myself on trust: my words and gestures happen to have a quality that escapes me and that is immediately apparent to grown-ups. It doesn't matter! I'll offer them unfailingly the delicate pleasure that is denied me. My clowning dons the cloak of generosity: poor people were grieved at not having a child; moved to pity, I drew myself out of nothingness in a burst of altruism and assumed the disguise of child-hood so as to give them the illusion of having a son. My mother and grandmother often request me to repeat the act of eminent kindness that gave birth to me. They gratify Charles Schweitzer's idiosyncrasies, his fondness for dramatic outbursts. They arrange surprises for him. They hide me behind a piece of furniture. I hold my breath. The women leave the room or pretend to have forgotten about me. I annihilate myself. My grandfather enters the room, weary and gloomy, as he would be if I did not exist. Suddenly I come out from my hiding-place, I do him the favor of being born. He sees me, joins in the game, changes expression, and raises his arms to heaven: I fill him to overflowing with my presence. In a word, I give myself; I give myself always and everywhere; I give everything. I have only to push a door to have—I too—the feeling of appearing on the scene. I place my blocks on top of each other. I turn out my mudpies, I yell. Someone comes and exclaims. I've made one more person happy. Meals, sleep, and precautions against bad weather are the high points and chief obligations of a completely ceremonious life. I eat in public, like a king: if I eat *well*, I am congratulated; my grandmother herself cries out: "What a good boy to be hungry!"

I keep creating myself; I am the giver and the gift. If my father were alive, I would know my rights and my duties. He is dead, and I am unaware of them. I have no rights, since love heaps blessings upon me; I have no duties, since I give out of love. Only one mandate: to please; everything for show. What a riot of generosity in our family! My grandfather supports me and I make him happy; my mother devotes herself to all of us. When I think of it now, only that devotion seems true to me, but we tended to overlook it. No matter: our life is only a succession of ceremonies, and we spend our time showering each other with tribute. I respect the adults on the condition that they idolize me. I am frank, open, gentle as a girl. My thoughts are quite proper. I trust people. Everybody is good since everybody is content. I regard society as a strict hierarchy of merits and powers. Those at the top of the scale give all they possess to those below them. I am careful, however, not to place myself on the highest level: I am not unaware that it is reserved for the severe and well-meaning persons who are responsible for the order that prevails. I remain on a little marginal perch not far from them, and my radiance extends from the top of the scale to the bottom. In short, I make it my business to stand aside from the secular power: neither below nor above, but elsewhere. I, the grandson of a clerk, am likewise a clerk, even in childhood; I have the unction of princes of the Church, a priestly playfulness. I treat inferiors as equals: this is a pious lie which I tell them in order to make them happy and by which it is right and proper that they be taken in, up to a certain point. To my maid, to the postman, to my dog, I speak in a patient and sober voice. There are poor people in this orderly world. There are also freaks of nature, Siamese twins, railway accidents: those anomalies are nobody's fault. The worthy poor do not realize that their function is to exercise our generosity. They are the uncomplaining poor; they hug the walls. I spring forward, I slip a small coin into their hand and, most important, I present them with a fine equalitarian smile. I find they look stupid, and I do not like to touch them, but I force myself to: it is an ordeal; and besides, they *must* love me, that love will beautify their lives. I know that they lack necessities, and I take pleasure in being their superfluity. Besides, whatever their poverty, they will never suffer as much as my grandfather did: when he was little, he would get up before dawn and dress in the dark; in winter, he had to break the ice in the water jug in order to wash. Happily, things have since been put to rights. My grandfather believes in Progress; so do I: Progress, that long, steep path which leads to me.

It was Paradise. Every morning I woke up dazed with joy, astounded at the unheard-of-luck of having been born into the most united family in the finest country in the world. People who were discontented shocked me. What could they complain about? They were rebels. I was extremely worried about my grandmother in particular: it pained me to note that she didn't admire me sufficiently. In point of fact, Louise had seen through me. She openly found fault with me for the hamming with which she dared not reproach her husband: I was a buffoon, a clown, a humbug; she ordered me to stop "smirking and smiling." I was all the more indignant in that I suspected her of belittling my grandfather too: she was "the Spirit that always negates." I would *answer back*; she would demand an apology. Sure of being backed up, I would refuse. My grandfather would seize the opportunity to show his weakness; he would side with me against his wife, who would stand up, outraged, and go lock herself up in her room. My mother, anxiously fearing my grandmother's rancor, would speak in a low voice and humbly lay the blame on my grandfather, who would shrug and withdraw to his study. Finally, she would beg me to go and ask my grandmother to forgive me. I enjoyed my power: I was Saint Michael and I had laid low the Evil Spirit. In the end, I would go and apologize casually. Apart from that, of course, I adored her: *since* she was my grandmother. It had been suggested that I call her Mamie and call the head of the household by his Alsatian name, Karl. Karl and Mamie, that sounded better than Romeo and Juliet, than Philemon and Baucis. My mother would repeat to me a hundred times a day, not without a purpose: "Karlémami are waiting for us; Karlémami will be pleased; Karlémami . . . ," conjuring up, by the intimate union of those four syllables, the perfect harmony of the persons. I was only half taken in, but I managed to seem to be entirely: first of all, to myself. The word cast its shadow on the thing; through Karlémami I could maintain the flawless unity of the family and transfer a good part of Charles' merits to Louise. Suspect and sinful, always on the verge of erring, my grandmother was held back by the arms of angels, by the power of a word.

. . .

I began my life as I shall no doubt end it: amidst books. In my grandfather's study there were books everywhere. It was forbidden to dust

303

them, except once a year, before the beginning of the October term. Though I did not yet know how to read, I already revered those standing stones: upright or leaning over, close together like bricks on the book-shelves or spaced out nobly in lanes of menhirs. I felt that our family's prosperity depended on them. They all looked alike, I disported myself in a tiny sanctuary, surrounded by ancient, heavy-set monuments which had seen me into the world, which would see me out of it, and whose permanence guaranteed me a future as calm as the past. I would touch them secretly to honor my hands with their dust, but I did not quite know what to do with them, and I was a daily witness of ceremonies whose meaning escaped me: my grandfather—who was usually so clumsy that my grandmother buttoned his gloves for him—handled those cultural objects with the dexterity of an officiant. Hundreds of times I saw him get up from his chair with an absent-minded look, walk around his table, cross the room in two strides, take down a volume without hesitating, without giving himself time to choose, leaf through it with a combined movement of his thumb and forefinger as he walked back to his chair, then, as soon as he was seated, open it sharply "to the right page," making it creak like a shoe. At times, I would draw near to observe those boxes which slit open like oysters, and I would see the nudity of their inner organs, pale, fusty leaves, slightly bloated, covered with black veinlets, which drank ink and smelled of mushrooms.

In my grandmother's room, the books lay on their sides. She borrowed them from a circulating library, and I never saw more than two at a time. Those baubles reminded me of New Year goodies because their supple, glistening leaves seemed to have been cut from glossy paper. White, bright, almost new, they served as pretext for mild mysteries. Every Friday, my grandmother would get dressed to go out and would say: "I'm going to return *them*." When she got back, after removing her black hat and her veil, she would take *them* from her muff, and I would wonder, mystified: "Are they the same ones?" She would "cover" them carefully, then, after choosing one of them, would settle down near the window in her easy-chair, put on her spectacles, sigh with bliss and weariness, and lower her eyelids with a subtle, voluptuous smile that I have since seen on the lips of La Gioconda. My mother would remain silent and bid me do likewise. I would think of Mass, death, sleep; I would be filled with a holy stillness. From time to time, Louise would chuckle; she would call over her daughter, point to a line, and the two women would exchange a look of complicity. Nevertheless, I did not care for those too distinguished volumes. They were intruders, and my grandfather did not hide the fact that they were the object of a minor cult, exclusively feminine. On Sundays, having nothing better to do, he would enter his wife's room and stand in front of her without finding anything to say. Everyone would look at him. He would drum on the window-pane, then, not knowing what else to do, would turn to Louise and take her novel from her hands. "Charles!" she would cry furiously, "you're going to lose my place!" He would start reading, with raised eyebrows. Suddenly his forefinger would strike the volume: "I don't get it!" "But how do you expect to?" my grandmother would say. "You open to the middle!" He would end by tossing the book on the table and would leave, shrugging his shoulders.

~~~~~~~~~~~~~~~~~~~~~~~~~~~~~~

DISCUSSION AND INQUIRY

Sartre emphasizes his good fortune of having a father who died when he was a baby. He considers this his fortune because, among other things, he never had to wrestle with the Oedipus complex. Yet, he speaks of marrying his mother to protect her, which certainly has Oedipal overtones. Nevertheless, if no Oedipus complex, then no superego, according to Freud. Sartre admits to having no superego; however, the development of conscience is explained in a variety of ways by theorists who hold differing points of view. How might a behaviorist explain the development of conscience? What does Piaget have to say about conscience development and moral judgment? Is it possible that Sartre really had no conscience?

Sartre further declares that he had no need for power because, as the son of a dead man and the grandson of a benevolent grandfather, he did not identify with a powerful authority figure. Does the need for power typically result from identification with authority figures? Study a few of the authority figures in this book, such as Eisenhower and Nkrumah. (See the selections by Eisenhower and Nkrumah.) Compare their early experiences with authority figures in their families. What similarities and differences do you find?

Sartre speaks somewhat facetiously of the games grown-ups play—the games they play with children. *Grown-ups exclaim approval over beautiful mudpies and clean plates. In your case, it may have been good bowel movements or dry pants. He says he went along with their games to give adults pleasure. In adult-child relationships, who is really being pleased by these games? What role does positive reinforcement play in shaping behavior? Can you think of other reasons for young Sartre's eagerness to please the adults in his world?*

Helen Sekaquaptewa

BIOGRAPHICAL SKETCH

*Born in 1898 in the Hopi indian village of Oraibi
in northeastern Arizona, Helen Sekaquaptewa
has lived a full and happy life. In 1919, she and
Emory Sekaquaptewa were married by civil
license as well as by the traditional Hopi rituals,
and she bore him eight children. She became
active in the Church of Jesus Christ of Latter-
Day Saints, where she met Louise Udall, the
friend who was to record her life story. She and
Mrs. Udall made regular visits to the Maricopa
Reservation as representatives of the church. It
was during these visits that Louise Udall convinced Helen she should write the story of her
life. Mrs. Udall wrote down events as Helen told
them, and published them under the title:* Me
and Mine: The Life Story of Helen Sekaquaptewa.

SELECTIONS FROM

ME AND MINE: THE LIFE STORY OF HELEN SEKAQUAPTEWA

WHEN we were five or six years of age, we, with our parents (Hostiles)
became involved with the school officials, assisted by the Navajo
policemen, in a serious and rather desperate game of hide-and-seek,
where little Hopi boys and girls were the forfeit in the game. Every
day the school principal sent out a truant officer, and many times he
himself went with the officer, going to Hopi homes to take the children to school. The Navajo policemen who assisted in finding hidden
children were dressed in old army uniforms, and they wore regular
cavalry has over their long hair, done up in a knot. This made quite

307

a picture—especially the traditional hair style with a white man's hat. It had not been customary for Indians to wear hats up to that time.

When September came there was no peace for us. Early in the morning, from our houses on the mesa, we could see the principal and the officer start out from the school, walking up the trail to "get" the children. Hostile parents tried every day in different ways to hide us from them, for once you were caught, you had lost the game. You were discovered and listed and you had to go to school and not hide any more. I was finally caught and went to the Oraibi day school one session, when I was about six years old, but not before many times outwitting Mr. Schoolman.

Sometimes, after a very early breakfast, somebody's grandmother would take a lunch and go with a group of eight to twelve little girls and hide them in the cornfields away out from the village. On another day another grandmother would go in the other direction over the hills among the cedars where we would play in a ravine, have our lunch and come back home in the afternoon. Men would be out with little boys playing this game of hide and seek. One day I got left behind and was sent out with a group of boys. I didn't know the man, and the boys' games were not for me, and I cried all day.

A place where one or two small children could be stowed away on short notice was the rabbit blanket. A rabbit blanket is made by cutting dressed rabbit skins in two-inch strips and weaving them into a warp of wool thread. When not in use, in warm weather, this blanket is hung by the four corners from a hook in the rafter beam, to prevent it from being moth-eaten. But once discovered, this hiding place was out. The school officer would feel of the rabbit blanket first thing on coming into the room.

Most houses have a piki storage cupboard in a partition wall. This would be the thickness of the wall and about two by three feet. A cloth covered the front, making a good place to keep the piki supply dry and clean. One day the officers were only two doors away when my mother was aware of their presence. She snatched her young son Henry and put him curled up in the piki cupboard just in time to win the game—that day.

Our houses were two and three stories high. When a lower room became old and unsafe, it was used as a dump place for ashes, peach stones, melon and squash seeds, and bits of discarded corn; anything that could be eaten was preserved in the ashes, and the room was gradually filled. Then in time of famine these bits of food could be dug out and eaten. In the home of my childhood such a room was about three-fourths filled. One September morning my brother and I were hidden there. We lay on our stomachs in the dark, facing a small

308

opening. We saw the feet of the principal and policeman as they walked by, and heard their big voices as they looked about wondering where the children were. They didn't find us that day.

One morning an older man took several boys out to hide. Emory, who later was my husband, was one of these boys. The man took them off the mesa where there was a big fissure in a sheer cliff with a bigger space behind it, away down in the rocks where no horse could go. The grandfather told the boys to stay there and be quiet. He then went a little way away and began hoeing in an orchard. The boys soon wanted to come out and play, but the grandfather said "no." Pretty soon they heard the sound of approaching horses' hoofs and looking up to the top of the cliff saw the Navajo policeman. He rode around out of sight, but pretty soon was seen coming up the valley toward the grandfather. The policeman couldn't get into the crack in the rock but he got off his horse looking for footprints. The boys had been careful to step on rocks and grass and left no footprints. After looking around a while the policeman got on his horse and rode away. After he left and they were sure he would not come back, then the boys came out to play, and later the grandfather brought out the lunch.

Some boys made trouble after they were enrolled in school. At recess they would run away. They could outrun the principal. One principal, in desperation, got himself a .22 rifle with blank bullets. When he shot at the boys they stopped running.

I don't remember for sure just how I came to be "caught." Maybe both my mother and myself got a little tired of getting up early every morning and running off to hide all day. She probably thought to herself, "Oh, let them get her. I am tired of this. It is wearing me down." The hide-and-seek game continued through September, but with October, the colder weather was on the schoolman's side.

So, one morning, I was "caught." Even then, it was the rule among mothers not to let the child go voluntarily. As the policeman reached to take me by the arm, my mother put her arm around me. Tradition required that it appear that I was forced into school. I was escorted down off the mesa to the schoolhouse, along with several other children. First, each was given a bath by one of the Indian women who worked at the school. Baths were given in the kitchen in a round, galvanized tub. Then we were clothed in cotton underwear, cotton dresses, and long black stockings and heavy shoes, furnished by the government. Each week we had a bath and a complete change of clothing. We were permitted to wear the clothes home each day, but my mother took off the clothes of the detested white man as soon as I got home, until it was time to go to school the next day.

Names were given to each child by the school. Mine was "Helen."

Each child had a name card pinned on, for as many days as it took for the teacher to learn and remember the name she had given us. Our teacher was Miss Stanley. She began by teaching us the names of objects about the room. We read a little from big charts on the wall later on, but I don't remember ever using any books.

A feud developed over the years as the people were divided into sides for and against those who came from the outside. These two factions were known as the "Friendlies" (to the government) and the "Hostiles" (to the government), and "they" came to mean anyone who represented an outside influence. Later these groups were known as the "Progressives" and the "Traditionals."

Those who put their children into school voluntarily were given an ax, a hoe, a shovel, or a rake, but stoves and wagons they had to work for. Hostile parents scornfully rejected these tools even though they would have served them better than the implements they made of wood or stone. These overtures were looked upon only as a bait or wedge that would end in no good to them. Hostile parents warned their children, when they were leaving for school, "Don't take the pencil in your hand. If you do, it means you give consent to what they want you to do. Don't do it."

The attitude of the parents carried over to their children, as was shown on the schoolgrounds. The children of the "Friendlies" made fun of us, calling us "Hostiles," and they would not let us join with them in their play, so I was unhappy some of the time. However, I do have pleasant memories of how one of my fourteen-year-old cousins used to carry me on his back down off the mesa to school. Going back up the trail after school was often a skirmish. My older brother would carefully lead his little sister up the trails going home. The "Friendly" children often ran ahead up the trail and gathered rocks and threw them down at us when we came to the bottom of the steep rocky ledge. Sometimes we would try another way up, following little gullies, or going around and coming up on the trail on the opposite side of the mesa—the long way home—to avoid being pelted with rocks.

I liked school. It was pleasant and warm inside. I liked to wear the clothes they gave us at school; but when I learned that the kids were "hostile" to us, I didn't want to go to school. Everyone, even the principal and the teachers and employees, were more or less against us.

The Mennonites had a church in Old Oraibi, but our parents would not let us go even to their Sunday School. We wanted to go, and sometimes we went around the mesa and came to Sunday School by a back path. They would give us a little ticket each time we came, and on

Christmas they gave a big prize to the one who had the most tickets. We did not understand much that they said, but it was nice to be there. I received a few tickets but gave them away. I did not dare to accept a present.

Each little Hopi girl had her family of bone dolls, which she collected and hoarded and treasured, keeping them in a little sack or a baking powder can with a lid, whatever container she could come by. These bones came from the lower parts of the legs of the sheep. A two-inch was the man doll. A smaller one was the woman. The same bones from smaller animals were the children. Chickens were triangular-shaped bones from the horny hoof. When the sheep was slaughtered, the last four inches of the legs were singed, scraped, and cleaned white, and used to flavor a pot of boiled hominy, thus making it rich in glutinous protein. The Hopis knew it was good because it tasted good. As a member of the family ate clean such a bone, it would be given to the little girl, as is done with the wishbone from a chicken or turkey. After the bone was dried in the sun, it was white and pretty like ivory.

Hours could be spent with bone dolls, either alone or in groups. Sometimes the girls brought their dolls to school and would play with them at recess out in the yard. Since I was not included in the play, I liked to stand near enough to listen and watch, but when they discovered what I was doing they would drive me away.

First the girls gathered little flat rocks, then they smoothed the sand and used the rocks to mark off a house, partition the rooms, and make the furniture. One certain bone was the broom. With it the floor was marked, leaving a wafflelike pattern in the sand. A chicken yard was enclosed and the chickens put in their places. An old discolored bone was the grandmother, set surrounded with children or tending the baby.

With the stage all set, the little girl reenacted family life, speaking for the characters, cooking, feeding, training her children, and as the day ended putting them to bed. There would be a quiet time; then, a cock would crow, the chickens would begin to talk, and the mother would get the family started on another day. The girls had boundless imagination as they dramatically portrayed real life.

A little bone doll boy might go outside the village to play and come running back to report, "There is a big giant coming." The giant idea probably came from seeing a big bone. Whereupon the father bone would come out to defend his home. A fight ensued as the two clashed in the hands of the little girl, and the father would put the intruder to flight. Bone women gossiped and discussed their families and neighbors.

. . .

311

Kachinvaki is the first ceremony in which Hopi children participate, being the initiatory step into a society; it is also called "The Whipping." It is in the nature of a baptism—that is, to drive out the "bad." It occurs in the spring of each year in connection with the Bean Dance. All children who have reached the age of seven or eight during the past year take part in Kachinvaki.

Little children are told that the kachinas are magic and come from their home in the San Francisco Peaks to take part in the various ceremonials. Children too young to be initiated are not permitted to go to the night performances, so they don't discover that the kachina is only a man with a costume and a mask. In the daytime part of the dance, little children may watch, but from far off so they won't guess.

When I was the right age my mother chose a woman to be my godmother. My mother gave me a little white cornmeal in my hand and told me to go to a certain woman and ask her to be my godmother and to offer her the cornmeal. I did, and she took the cornmeal; it meant that she would act as my godmother at Kachinvaki and all my life afterward. If she refused it, I was to bring the cornmeal back and try another woman; but she was a kind woman and accepted my offering and was always a good godmother to me. Kachinvaki comes in February, but the godmother is chosen in the summer before to give her time to make a plaque as a gift to her godchild, and for her son or husband to carve a doll kachina to be presented to the child during the rites in February.

When the day came for Kachinvaki, my mother dressed me in freshly washed clothes. First she wrapped an old belt around my waist, next to my skin. It went around two or three times and I wondered at the time why the two belts? In late afternoon, about half an hour before we were to go to the kiva, my godmother came and took me to her house. As we left the house to go to the kiva she gave me an ear of corn which I was to hold in my hand all during the ceremony. My godmother's eldest son went with us to act as my godfather. Each took hold of one of my hands as we left the house.

Everyone in the village was out to watch; the youths were on the housetops watching to see the Kachinas as they came running into the village and to hear the wild shrieks as the whipping got under way.

My godparents still held my hands as we descended the ladder into the kiva; it took us a long time to take the steps. A man was sitting at the foot of the ladder holding a hoop about two and a half feet in diameter, the hoop resting on the floor. Each child in turn stepped into this hoop, and the man lifted it up over the child's body and lowered it four times, ending with the hoop on the floor. There were thirty or more children on this day. The kiva floor has two levels, one-fourth of the area being raised about one foot. My godmother took her place on the upper level with the other godmothers, and my godfather stayed with me on the lower floor. I was so young and scared that I was in a fog, but I thought I could see a sort of cloth tent in one corner of the room and someone in it.

After all the children had come down the ladder and taken their places, a man talked to us for a long time, like a sermon. He is called the "story teller." Talking in a singsong manner, he told us about the kachinas and how they came to be. I could not understand much of what he was saying. Four times during this storytelling, little mudhead kachinas came out from the tent in the corner. They were boys in black kilts with rag masks on their heads with protruding eyes made of balls of cotton wrapped in cloth and painted all over with mud. The upper part of their bodies were painted with pinkish mud. Holding in their hands an ear of corn and some feathers, hands held close together, the mudheads would stop before each child, pass their arms toward the child in a waving motion, and then go back to the tent.

The storyteller told us that the kachinas were coming to initiate us. A man on the roof of the kiva was watching and listening. Another watchman was on a high housetop. The kachinas were watching at the edge of the village. At the proper time, the man on the kiva roof stood up, and this was the signal to the man on the housetop to also stand, and the kachinas knew that it was time to come on the run so as to appear and enter the kiva as the storyteller said, "They are coming, closer. Now they are here." We heard the two whipper kachinas making a lot of noise as they stopped and clanked the turtle shells fastened to their legs. They ran around the kiva four times before coming down the ladder into the kiva. With the whipper kachinas came a mother kachina, carrying in her arms a bundle of fresh yucca to serve as whips. All the children were afraid, and the timid ones were crying already.

Children of the Badger and the Kachina clans are not whipped; neither are the children whose godfathers are from those clans. Their initation is Powamoivaki, not Kachinvaki, and takes place two days earlier. However, they are required to attend Kachinvaki. Even these, who stand with the women, were scared and crying too.

The kachinas came in fast and were fierce-looking things. They stood by the fireplace. The first child in line, if it is a boy, has on only a blanket, which his sponsor removes, and he stands in the nude. The godfather takes hold of the hands of the boy and pulls him over in front of the whippers and lifts the arms of the boy above his head, while he receives four hard lashes. If the godfather sees fit, he may

313

pull the boy away and put out his own leg and take one or two lashes for his godson.

It goes fast, with much crying. When a whip gets limp a new one—four yucca branches—is taken. The whippers take turns with the lash, while the mother whipper urges them on, mostly with the boys, saying, "Whip him hard. He is naughty. Don't be lenient with him." Parents may have told her of some naughty thing that the son has done, which she repeats. There are big welts on the backs of the boys and sometimes they are bleeding.

If a little girl is wearing a shawl, her godfather takes it off, takes hold of her hands and leads her over to get whipped, as he holds her hands above her head. I knew then why my mother put two belts on me. The four lashes were given around the waist and it didn't hurt much. The tips of the yucca did give a little sting.

When all had been whipped my godparents each took me by a hand and we climbed the ladder and out of the kiva and went back to my godmother's house where she gave me a comfortable seat and said she would get me something to eat. I was so upset and scared that I didn't eat much of the nice food that she fixed. Then I went home alone.

At sunup three days later the kachinas came again to the homes and gave presents to the children—the woven plaques and dolls made by the godparents, also gifts from parents and adults of the little initiate. One child might receive as many as ten plaques if she had a lot of aunts. These she could keep or sell, as she chose.

The final event is an all-night dance where the kachinas come and dance; all wear costumes, but some do not wear masks. Other masks are lined up on a shelf, and during the evening all remove their masks so that the children see that it is men and not magic. So now we know. During the dance, all the initiates must sit on a bench with their knees drawn up. They may not hang their feet down at any time. The godmother may step down and get a drink of water for the child, and he is permitted to step outside to relax for a few minutes; otherwise he must stay in that position until the break of day, when the ceremony is finished. At the conclusion, the children are advised that they may now begin to take part in the affairs of the societies; they are admonished not to talk about what they have seen to children who are younger. "If you do tell about this, a lot of kachinas will come and whip you until you are dead."

It was quite an ordeal for me. When I went back to my home I wished I didn't know that a kachina was a man with a costume and a mask, when all the time I had thought they were real magic.

314

∿∿∿∿∿∿∿∿∿∿∿∿∿∿∿∿∿∿∿∿∿∿∿∿∿∿∿

DISCUSSION AND INQUIRY

Hopi children were kept away from school by their families who were hostile to the school and what it represented. Because attitudes are largely shaped and influenced by the family and the society, it is easy to see how the children who were finally dragged to school by the police were seen as outsiders by their peers at school. How does the attitude toward schooling differ in this situation from that in Satchel Paige's case? (See the selection by Satchel Paige.) What is the basis for the difference?

The Hopi children who attended school were not only humiliated by being forced to bathe and wear different clothing, but were given different names as well. Although Helen says she liked wearing the new clothes to school, one wonders what the whole procedure meant to the child in terms of her self-image and her sense of identity. Who am I now that I wear different clothing and have a different name? Why am I bathed when I get to school? When standards of behavior and dress differ between home and school, how might a child react to the conflict and confusion he experiences? Is the difference between home and school as great for the white middle-class child as it is for the black child or the Indian? Why?

Dramatic play with bone dolls was an important aspect of each Hopi girl's play experience. It is interesting to note that children around the world engage in dramatic play in which they adopt familiar adult roles and enjoy emotional release. If you have an opportunity, visit a nursery school and observe the dramatic play in the housekeeping area. What insights do you get into the family life-style of each child? What values and sex roles have already been assimilated?

The ordeal of the Kachinvaki, which is a customary rite of passage among the Hopi, raises the question of parents deceiving children. Hopi children are told that the kachinas, who are

315

really men dressed in unusual costumes, are magic. Can young children deal with the concept of magic? What does magic mean to a young child? How does this change as he matures? What are children likely to learn about being truthful when they discover they have been duped by those who preach honesty? How does this affect the sense of trust the child feels toward the adult? Compare the Santa Claus myth here.

Upton Sinclair

BIOGRAPHICAL SKETCH

Upton Sinclair, the social reformer, was born in 1878 into a poor Virginia family that moved to New York when Upton was 8 years old. At the age of 13 he started to write prose; and at 14, he entered the College of the City of New York. He wrote over eighty books in his lifetime, one significant one being The Jungle, *the book that exposed the meat-packing industry in Chicago. Its impact was expressed by President Teddy Roosevelt when he told Sinclair, partially in jest, to go home so that he could run the country himself. Sinclair died in 1968.*

SELECTIONS FROM

THE AUTOBIOGRAPHY OF UPTON SINCLAIR

MY FIRST recollection of life is one that my mother insisted I could not possibly have, because I was only eighteen months old at the time. Yet there it is in my mind: a room where I have been left in the care of a relative while my parents are taking a trip. I see a little old lady, black-clad, in a curtained room; I know where the bed is located, and the oil-stove on which the cooking is done, and the thrills of exploring a new place. Be sure that children know far more than we give them credit for; I hear fond parents praising their precious darlings, and I wince, noting how the darlings are drinking in every word. Always in my childhood I would think: "How silly these grownups are! And how easy to outwit!"

I was a toddler when one day my mother told me not to throw a piece of rag into a drain. "Paper dissolves, but rag doesn't." I treasured up this wisdom and, visiting my Aunt Florence, remarked with great impressiveness, "It is all right to throw paper into the drain, because it dissolves, but you musn't throw rags in, because they don't dissolve."

317

Wonder, mingled with amusement, appeared on the face of my sweet and gentle relative. My first taste of glory.

Baltimore, Maryland, was the place, and I remember boardinghouse and lodginghouse rooms. We never had but one room at a time, and I slept on a sofa or crossways at the foot of my parents' bed; a custom that caused me no discomfort that I can recall. One adventure recurred; the gaslight would be turned on in the middle of the night, and I would start up, rubbing my eyes, and join in the exciting chase for bedbugs. They came out in the dark and scurried into hiding when they saw the light; so they must be mashed quickly. For thrills like this, wealthy grown-up children travel to the heart of Africa on costly safaris. The more bugs we killed, the fewer there were to bite us the rest of the night, which I suppose is the argument of the lion hunters also. Next morning, the landlady would come, and corpses in the washbasin or impaled on pins would be exhibited to her; the bed would be taken to pieces and "corrosive sublimate" rubbed into the cracks with a chicken feather.

My position in life was a singular one, and only in later years did I understand it. When I went to call on my father's mother, a black-clad, frail little lady, there might be only cold bread and dried herring for Sunday-night supper, but it would be served with exquisite courtesy and overseen by a great oil painting of my grandfather in naval uniform—with that same predatory beak that I have carried through life and have handed on to my son. Grandfather Sinclair had been a captain in the United States Navy and so had his father before him, and ancestors far back had commanded in the British Navy. The family had lived in Virginia, and there had been slaves and estates. But the slaves had been set free, and the homestead burned, and the head of the family drowned at sea in the last year of the Civil War. His descendants, four sons and two daughters, lived in embarrassing poverty, but with the consciousness, at every moment of their lives, that they were persons of great consequence and dignity.

. . .

My father was the youngest son of Captain Arthur Sinclair and was raised in Norfolk. In the days before the war, and after it, all Southern gentlemen "drank." My father became a wholesale whisky salesman, which made it easy and even necessary for him to follow the fashion. Later on he became a "drummer" for straw-hat manufacturers, and then for manufacturers of men's clothing; but he could never get away from drink, for the beginning of every deal was a "treat," and the close of it was another. Whisky in its multiple forms—mint juleps, toddies, hot Scotches, egg-nogs, punch—was the most conspicuous single fact in my boyhood. I saw it and smelled it and heard it everywhere I turned, but I never tasted it.

The reason was my mother, whose whole married life was poisoned by alcohol, and who taught me a daily lesson in horror. It took my good and gentle-souled father thirty or forty years to kill himself, and I watched the process week by week and sometimes hour by hour. It made an indelible impression upon my childish soul, and is the reason why I am a prohibitionist, to the dismay of my "libertarian" friends.

It was not that my father could not earn money, but that he could not keep it. He would come home with some bank notes, and the salvation of his wife and little son would depend upon the capture of this treasure. My mother acquired the habit of going through his pockets at night; and since he never knew how much he had brought home, there would be arguments in the morning, an unending duel of wits. Father would hide the money when he came in late, and then in the morning he would forget where he had hidden it, and there would be searching under mattresses and carpets and inside the lining of clothing—all sorts of unlikely places. If my mother found it first, you may be sure that my father was allowed to go on looking.

When he was not under the influence of the Demon Rum, the little "drummer" dearly loved his family; so the thirty years during which I watched him were one long moral agony. He would make all sorts of pledges, with tears in his eyes; he would invent all sorts of devices to cheat his cruel master. He would not "touch a drop" until six o'clock in the evening; he would drink lemonade or ginger ale when he was treating the customers. But alas, he would change to beer, in order not to "excite comment"; and then after a week or a month of beer, we would smell whisky on his breath again, and the tears and wranglings and naggings would be resumed.

This same thing was going on in most of the homes in Maryland and Virginia of which I had knowledge. My father's older brother died an inebriate in a soldiers' home. My earliest memory of the home of my maternal grandfather is of being awakened by a disturbance downstairs, and looking over the banisters in alarm while my grandfather—a Methodist deacon—was struggling with his grown son to keep him from going out when he was drunk. Dear old Uncle Harry, burly and full of laughter, a sportsman and favorite of all the world—at the age of forty or so he put a bullet through his head in Central Park, New York.

. . .

Human beings are what life makes them, and there is no more fascinating subject of study than the origin of mental and moral qualities.

My father's drinking accounted for other eccentricities of mine besides my belief in prohibition. It caused me to follow my mother in everything, and so to have a great respect for women; thus it came about that I walked in the first suffrage parade in New York, behind the snow-white charger of Inez Milholland. My mother did not drink coffee, nor even tea; and so, when I visited in England, I made all my hostesses unhappy. No lady had ever been known to smoke in Baltimore—only old Negro women with pipes; therefore I did not smoke—except once. When I was eight years old, a big boy on the street gave me a cigarette, and I started it; but another boy told me a policeman would arrest me, so I threw the cigarette away, and ran and hid in an alley, and have never yet recovered from this fear. It has saved me a great deal of money, and some health also, I am sure.

The sordid surroundings in which I was forced to live as a child made me a dreamer. I took to literature, because that was the easiest refuge. I knew practically nothing about music; my mother, with the upbringing of a young lady, could play a few pieces on the piano, but we seldom had a piano, and the music I heard was church hymns, and the plantation melodies that my plump little father hummed while shaving himself with a big razor. My mother had at one time painted pictures; I recall a snow scene in oils, with a kind of tinsel to make sparkles in the snow. But I never learned this wonderful art.

My mother would read books to me, and everything I heard I remembered. I taught myself to read at the age of five, before anyone realized what was happening. I would ask what this letter was, and that, and go away and learn it, and make the sounds, and very soon I was able to take care of myself. I asked my numerous uncles and aunts and cousins to send me only books for Christmas; and now, three quarters of a century later, traces of their gifts are still in my head. Let someone with a taste for research dig into the Christmas books of the early eighties, and find a generous broad volume, with many illustrations, merry rhymes, and a title containing the phrase "a peculiar family." From this book I learned to read, and I would ask my mother if she knew any such "peculiar" persons; for example, the "little boy who was so dreadfully polite, he would not even sneeze unless he asked if he might." He sneezed by accident, and "scared all the company into the middle of next week."

While arguments between my father and my mother were going on, I was with Gulliver in Lilliput, or on the way to the Celestial City with Christian, or in the shop with the little tailor who killed "seven at one blow." I had Grimm and Andersen and *The Story of the Bible*, and Henty and Alger and Captain Mayne Reid. I would be missing at a party and be discovered behind the sofa with a book. At the home of my Uncle Bland there was an encyclopedia, and my kind uncle was greatly impressed to find me absorbed in the article on gunpowder. Of course, I was pleased to have my zeal for learning admired—but also I really did want to know about gunpowder.

Readers of my novels know that I have one favorite theme, the contrast between the social classes; there are characters from both worlds, the rich and the poor, and the plots are contrived to carry you from one to the other. The explanation is that as far back as I can remember, my life was a series of Cinderella transformations; one night I would be sleeping on a vermin-ridden sofa in a lodginghouse, and the next night under silken coverlets in a fashionable home. It all depended on whether my father had the money for that week's board. If he didn't, my mother paid a visit to her father, the railroad official in Baltimore. No Cophetua or Aladdin in fairy lore ever stepped back and forth between the hovel and the palace as frequently as I.

. . .

To return to childhood days: my summers were spent at the country home of the Bland family or with my mother at summer resorts in Virginia. My father would be "on the road," and I remember his letters, from which I learned the names of all the towns in Texas and the merits of the leading hotels. If my father was "drinking," we stayed in some low-priced boardinghouse—in the city in winter and in the country in summer. On the other hand, if my father was keeping his pledges, we stayed at one of the springs hotels. My earliest memory of these hotels is of a fancy-dress ball, for which my mother fixed me up as a baker, with a white coat and long trousers and a round cap. That was all right, except that I was supposed to carry a wooden tray with rolls on it, which interfered with my play. Another story was told to me by one of the victims, whom I happened to meet. I had whooping cough, and the other children were forbidden to play with me; this seemed to me injustice, so I chased them and coughed in their faces, after which I had companions in misery. I should add that this early venture in "direct action" is not in accordance with my present philosophy.

I remember one of the Virginia boardinghouses. I would ask for a second helping of fried chicken, and the little Negro who waited table would come back and report, " 'Tisn' any mo'." No amount of hungry protest could extract any words except, " 'Tisn' any mo', Mista Upton, 'tisn' any mo'." At another place the formula ran, "Will you have ham or an egg?" I went fishing and had good luck, and brought home the fish, thinking I would surely get enough to eat that day; but my fish was cooked and served to the whole boardinghouse. I recall a terrible place known as Jett's, to which we rode all day in a bumpy stagecoach. The members of that household were pale ghosts, and we discovered

321

that they were users of drugs. There was an idiot boy who worked in the yard, and gobbled his food out of a tin plate, like a dog.

My Aunt Lucy was with us that summer, and the young squires of the country came calling on Sunday afternoons, vainly hoping that this Baltimore charmer with the long golden hair might consent to remain in rural Virginia. They hitched their prancing steeds to a rail in the yard, and I, an adventurer of eight or ten years, would unhitch them one by one and try them out. I rode a mare to the creek, her colt following, and let them both drink; then I rode back, and can see at this hou.· the expedition that met me—the owner of the mare, my mother and my aunt, many visitors and guests, and farmhands armed with pitchforks and ropes. There must have been a dozen persons, all looking for a tragedy—the mare being reputed to be extremely dangerous. But I had no fear, and neither had the mare. From this and other experiences I believe that it is safer to go through life without fear. You may get killed suddenly, but meantime it is easier on your nerves.

. . .

When I was eight or nine, my father was employed by a New York firm, so we moved north for the winter, and I joined the tribe of city nomads, a product of the new age, whose formula runs: "Cheaper to move than to pay rent." I remember a dingy lodginghouse on Irving Place, a derelict hotel on East Twelfth Street, housekeeping lodgings over on Second Avenue, a small "flat" on West 65th Street, one on West 92nd Street, one on West 126th Street. Each place in turn was home, each neighborhood full of wonder and excitement. Second Avenue was especially thrilling, because the "gangs" came out from Avenue A and Avenue B like Sioux or Pawnees in war paint, and well-dressed little boys had to fly for their lives.

Our longest stay—several winters, broken by moves to Baltimore— was at a "family hotel" called the Weisiger House, on West 19th Street. The hotel had been made by connecting four brownstone dwellings. The parlor of one was the office. The name sounds like Jerusalem; but it was really Virginia, pronounced Wizziger. Colonel Weisiger was a Civil War veteran and had half the broken-down aristocracy of the Old South as his guests; he must have had a sore time collecting his weekly dues.

I learned much about human nature at the Weisiger House, observing comedies and tragedies, jealousies and greeds and spites. There was the lean Colonel Paul of South Carolina, and the short Colonel Cardoza of Virginia, and the stout Major Waterman of Kentucky. Generals I do not remember, but we had Count Mickiewicz from Poland, a large, expansive gentleman with red beard and booming voice. What has become of little Ralph Mickiewicz, whom I chased up

and down the four flights of stairs of each of those four buildings—
sixteen flights in all, quite a hunting ground! We killed flies on the
bald heads of the colonels and majors, we wheedled teacakes in
the kitchen, we pulled the pigtails of the little girls playing dolls
in the parlor. One of these little girls, with whom I quarreled most of
the time, was destined to grow up and become my first wife; and our
married life resembled our childhood.

Colonel Weisiger was large and ample, with a red nose, like Santa
Claus; he was the judge and ultimate authority in all disputes. His son
was six feet two, quiet and reserved. Mrs. Weisiger was placid and
kindly, and had a sister, Miss Tee, who made the teacakes—this pun is
of God's making, not of mine. Completing the family was Taylor Tibbs,
a large black man, who went to the saloon around the corner twice
every day to fetch the Colonel's pail of beer. In New York parlance this
was known as "rushing the growler," and you will find Taylor Tibbs
and his activities all duly recorded in my novel *The Wet Parade*. Later
in life I would go over to Metro-Goldwyn-Mayer to see him in the
"talkie" they were making of the novel.

. . .

In those days at the Weisiger House I was one of Nature's miracles,
such as she produces by the millions in tenement streets—romping,
shouting, and triumphant, entirely unaware that their lot is a miserable
one. I was a perpetual explosion of energy, and I cannot see how anybody in the place tolerated me; yet they all liked me, all but one or two
who were "mean." I have a photograph of myself, dressed in kilts; and
my mother tells me a story. Some young man, teasing me, said: "You
wear dresses; you are a girl." Said I: "No, I am a boy." "But how do
you know you are a boy?" "Because my mother says so."

My young mother would go to the theater, leaving me snugly tucked
in bed, in care of some old ladies. I would lie still until I heard a whistle,
and then forth I would bound. Clad in a pair of snow-white canton-
flannel nighties, I would slide down the bannisters into the arms of the
young men of the house. What romps I would have, racing on bare
feet, or borne aloft on sturdy shoulders! We never got tired of pranks;
they would set me up in the office and tell me jokes and conundrums,
teach me songs—it was the year of McGinty, hero of hilarity:

> Down went McGinty to the bottom of the sea;
> He must be very wet,
> For they haven't found him yet,
> Dressed in his best suit of clothes.

These young men would take me to see the circus parade, which went
up Broadway on the evening prior to the opening of Barnum and

Bailey's. Young Mr. Lee would hold me on his shoulder a whole evening for the sake of hearing my whoops of delight at the elephants and the gorgeous ladies in spangles and tights. I remember a trick they played on one of these parade evenings. Just after dinner they offered me a quarter if I would keep still for five minutes by the watch, and they sat me on the big table in the office for all the world to witness the test. A couple of minutes passed, and I was still as any mouse; until one of the young men came running in at the front door, crying, "The parade is passing!" I leaped up with a wail of despair.

As a foil to this, let me narrate the most humiliating experience of my entire life. Grown-up people do not realize how intensely children feel, and what enduring impressions are made upon their tender minds. The story I am about to tell is as real to me as if it had happened last night.

My parents had a guest at dinner, and I was moved to another table, being placed with old Major Waterman and two young ladies. The venerable warrior started telling of an incident that had taken place that day. "I was walking along the street and I met Jones. 'Come in and have a drink,' said he, and I replied, 'No, thank you'—"

What was to be the end of that story I shall never know in this world. "Oh, Major Waterman!" I burst out, and there followed an appalled silence. Terror gripped my soul as the old gentleman turned his bleary eyes upon me. "What do you mean, sir? Tell me what you mean."

Now, if this had been a world in which men and women spoke the truth to one another, I could have told exactly what I meant. I would have said, "I mean that your cheeks are inflamed and your nose has purple veins in it, and it is difficult to believe that you ever declined anyone's invitation to drink." But it was not a world in which one could say such words; all I could do was to sit like a hypnotized rabbit, while the old gentleman bored me through. "I wish to have an answer, sir! What did you mean by that remark?" I still have, as one of my weaknesses, the tendency to speak first and think afterwards; but the memory of Major Waterman has helped me on the way to reform.

. . .

I was ten years old before I went to school. The reason was that some doctor told my mother that my mind was outgrowing my body, and I should not be taught anything. When finally I was taken to a public school, I presented the teachers with a peculiar problem; I knew everything but arithmetic. This branch of learning, so essential to a commercial civilization, had shared the fate of alcohol and tobacco, tea and coffee; my mother did not use it, so neither did I.

The teachers put me in the first primary grade, to learn long division;

promising that as soon as I caught up in the subject, I would be moved on. I was humiliated at being in a class with children younger than myself, so I fell to work and got into the grammar school in less than a month, and performed the unusual feat of going through the eight grammar grades in less than two years. Thus at the age of twelve I was ready for the City College—it was called a college, but I hasten to explain that it was in reality only a high school.

Unfortunately the college was not ready for me. No one was admitted younger than fourteen; so there was nothing for me to do but to take the last year of grammar school all over again. I did this at old Number 40, on East 23rd Street; my classmates were the little "toughs" of the East Side tenements. An alarming experience for a fastidious young Southerner, destined for the highest social circles—but I count it a blessing hardly to be exaggerated. That year among the "toughs" helped to save me from the ridiculous snobbery that would otherwise have been my destiny in life. Since then I have been able to meet all kinds of humans and never see much difference; also, I have been able to keep my own ideals and convictions, and "stand the gaff," according to the New York phrase.

To these little East Side "toughs" I was, of course, fully as strange a phenomenon as they were to me. I spoke a language that they associated with Fifth Avenue "dudes" wearing silk hats and kid gloves. The Virginia element in my brogue was entirely beyond their comprehension; the first time I spoke of a "street-cyar," the whole class broke into laughter. They named me Chappie, and initiated me into the secrets of a dreadful game called "hop, skip, and a lepp," which you ended, not on your feet, but on your buttocks; throwing your legs up in the air and coming down with a terrific bang on the hard pavement. The surgeons must now be performing operations for floating kidney upon many who played that game in boyhood.

The teacher of the class was a jolly old Irishman, Mr. Furey; he later became principal of a school, and I would have voted for his promotion without any reservation. He was a disciplinarian with a homemade method; if he observed a boy whispering or idling during class, he would let fly a piece of chalk at the offender's head. The class would roar with laughter; the offender would grin, pick up the chalk, and bring it to the teacher, and get his knuckles smartly cracked as he delivered it, and then go back to his seat and pay attention. From this procedure I learned that pomposity is no part of either brains or achievement, and I have never in my life tried to impress anyone by being anything but what I am.

One feature of our school was the assembly room, into which we marched by classes to the music of a piano, thumped by a large dark lady with a budding mustache. We sang patriotic songs and listened to recitations in the East Side dialect, a fearful and wonderful thing. This dialect tried to break into the White House in the year 1928, and the rest of America heard it for the first time. Graduates of New York public schools who had made millions out of paving and contracting jobs put up the money to pay for radio "hookups," and the voice of Fulton Fish Market came speaking to the farmers of the corn belt and the fundamentalists of the bible belt. "Ladies and genn'lmun, the foist thing I wanna say is that the findin's of this here kimittee proves that we have the woist of kinditions in our kimmunity." I sat in my California study and listened to Al Smith speaking in St. Louis and Denver, and it took me straight back to old Number 40, and the little desperados throwing their buttocks into the air and coming down with a thump on the hard pavement.

As I read the proofs of this book I have returned from a visit to New York after thirty years. The old "El" roads are gone, and many of the slum tenements have been replaced by sixty-story buildings. The "micks" and the "dagos" have been replaced by Negroes and Puerto Ricans, who have taken possession of Harlem.

. . .

Childhood lasted long, and youth came late in my life. I was taught to avoid the subject of sex in every possible way; the teaching being done, for the most part, in Victorian fashion, by deft avoidance and anxious evasion. Apparently my mother taught me even too well; for once when I was being bathed, I persisted in holding a towel in front of myself. Said my mother: "If you don't keep that towel out of the way, I'll give you a spank." Said I: "Mamma, would you rather have me disobedient, or immodest?"

The first time I ever heard of the subject of sex, I was four or five years old, playing on the street with a little white boy and a Negro girl, the child of a janitor. They were whispering about something mysterious and exciting; there were two people living across the street who had just been married, and something they did was a subject of snickers. I, who wanted to know about everything, tried to find out about this; but I am not sure my companions knew what they were whispering about; at any rate, they did not tell me. But I got the powerful impression of something strange.

It was several years later that I found out the essential facts. I spent a summer in the country with a boy cousin a year or two younger than I, and we watched the animals and questioned the farmhands. But never did I get one word of information or advice from either father or mother on this subject; only the motion of shrinking away from something dreadful. I recollect how the signs of puberty began to show themselves in me, to my great bewilderment; my mother and grandmother stood helplessly by, like the hens that hatch ducklings and see them go into the water.

Incredible as it may seem, I had been at least two years in college before I understood about prostitution. So different from my friend Sam De Witt, socialist poet, who told me that he was raised in a tenement containing a house of prostitution, and that at the age of five he and other little boys and girls played brothel as other children play dolls, and quarrelled as to whose turn it was to be the "madam"! I can remember speculating at the age of sixteen whether it could be true that women did actually sell their bodies. I decided in the negative and held to that idea until I summoned the courage to question one of my classmates in college.

The truth, finally made clear, shocked me deeply, and played a great part in the making of my political revolt. Between the ages of sixteen and twenty I explored the situation in New York City, and made discoveries that for me were epoch-making. The saloonkeeper, who had been the villain of my childhood melodrama, was merely a tool and victim of the big liquor interests and politicians and police. The twin bases of the political power of Tammany Hall were saloon graft and the sale of women. So it was that, in my young soul, love for my father and love for my mother were transmuted into political rage, and I sallied forth at the age of twenty, a young reformer armed for battle. It would be a longer battle than I realized, alas!

~~~~~~

DISCUSSION AND INQUIRY

From bedbugs to silken coverlets and back to bedbugs—Upton Sinclair experienced many moves during his early years. He never lived in one place or experienced one life-style for very long. The repeated theme of his novels—namely, the contrast between social classes—came from this early series of "Cinderella transformations." In what ways may these frequent moves have affected young Upton? Where did he get his feelings of security and stability, if, indeed, he had these? Name some of the ways families can help children maintain a sense of security and belonging in spite of frequent moves. This issue takes on greater importance as our society becomes more mobile and future events become more unpredictable.

Upton watched his father drink himself to

327

death; and, he, in turn, became a prohibitionist. Such an outcome is not necessary. Lillian Roth also had firsthand experience with the agonies of a father who was an alcoholic; and, she, in turn, became a drunkard. (See the selection by Lillian Roth.) Can you find an explanation for these differences in outcome?

Upton found himself unable to respect his drunken father, and claims he used his mother as a role model. Consider the effects of this modeling on his emotional development. Is it possible to establish a healthy sex-role identification without a sex-role model? Many boys are reared in fatherless homes. How do they establish a sex-role identification? Can a male teacher in pre-school or primary school serve as a substitute male-role identification figure for these boys?

In an attempt to escape from a life that he found very difficult at times, Upton retreated behind books. Using books as an escape is not unusual; and you may recall times when you retreated into the fantasy world of books. It may be of interest to look at the selection by Gerald Brennan, and then turn to Mark Van Doren or Jean-Paul Sartre in order to draw some comparisons in the ways children use books.

Most children learn to read at about the age of 6, when formal schooling typically begins; but a few, like Upton, are self-taught before that time. What motivates the youngster who learns to read before he receives formal instruction? What motivated Upton? Is there any particular reason for delaying teaching of reading until the age of 6? Can one conclude that a child who reads before 6 is of above-average intelligence?

Lincoln Steffens

SELECTIONS FROM

THE AUTOBIOGRAPHY OF LINCOLN STEFFENS

EARLY in the morning of April 6, 1866, in a small house "over in the Mission" of San Francisco, California, I was born—a remarkable child. This upon the authority of my mother, a remarkable woman, who used to prove her prophetic judgment to all listeners till I was old enough to make my own demonstration. Even then, even though I was there to frown her down, she was ever ready to bring forth her evidence, which opened with the earthquake of 1868. When that shock shook most San Franciscans out of their houses into the streets, she ran upstairs to me and found me pitched out of bed upon the floor but otherwise unmoved. As she said with swimming eyes, I was "not killed, not hurt, and, of course, not crying; I was smiling, as always, good as gold."

My own interpretation of this performance is that it was an exhibit less of goodness than of wisdom. I knew that my mother would not abandon me though the world rocked and the streets yawned. Nor is that remarkable. Every well-born baby is sure he can trust his mother. What strikes me as exceptional and promising in it is that I had already some sense of values; I could take such natural events as earthquakes all in my stride. That, I think, is why I smiled then; that is why I smile now; and that may be why my story is of a happy life—happier and happier. Looking back over it now for review, it seems to me that each chapter of my adventures is happier than the preceding chapters right down to this, the last one: age, which, as it comes, comes a-laughing, the best of all. I have a baby boy of my own now; my first—a remarkable child, who—when he tumbles out of bed—laughs; as good as gold.

. . .

I can recall nothing of my infancy in San Francisco. My memory was born in Sacramento, where it centers around the houses we lived in. Of the first, in Second Street, I can call up only a few incidents, which I think I still can see, but which I may have constructed, in part at least, out of the family's stories of that time. I can see yet my mother with her two hands over her face, and several people gathering anxiously about her. A snowball had struck her in the eyes. It rarely snows in that part of California—once, perhaps, in four or five years—so that a snow fall would have excited those people, all from the east, and they would have rushed out of the house to play in the snow. This I infer from hearsay. But what I see now, and must have seen a bit of then, is my mother standing there in trouble. And the reason I am so sure I recall my own sight of her is that she looks pretty and girlish in this one memory. All my other mental pictures of her are older and—not a girl, not a woman, but just my mother, unchanging, unchangeable, mine as my hand was mine.

I think I see, as from a window, safe and without fear, a wild, long-horned steer, lassoed by three mounted vaqueros who spread out and held him till he was tied to a tree. No one else recollects this scene, but it might well have happened. Sacramento was a center for ranches and mines. Lying in an angle of the Sacramento and the American Rivers, the town was the heart of the life, the trade, and the vice of the great valley of wheat and cattle ranches, of the placer mining of the foothills, of the steamboat traffic with San Francisco and, by the new railroad, with the world beyond. I remember seeing the mule teams ringing into towns, trains of four or five huge, high wagons, hauled by from twelve to twenty and more belled mules and horses driven by one man, who sometimes walked, sometimes rode the saddled near wheel-horse. Cowboys, mostly Mexicans and called vaqueros, used to come shouting on bucking bunches of bronchos into town to mix with the teamsters, miners, and steamboat men in the drinking, gambling, girling, fighting, of those days. My infant mind was snapping wide-eyed shots of these rough scenes and coloring and completing them with pictures painted on my memory by the conversations I overheard. I seem to have known of the gold strikes up in the mountains, of finding silver over the Range in Nevada, of men getting rich, or broke, or shot. I was kept away from this, of course, and I heard and saw it always darkly, under a shadow of disapproval. Other ideas and ideals were held up in the light for me. But secretly I was impatient to grow up and go out into that life, and meanwhile I played I was a teamster, a gun-playing, broncho-busting vaquero, or a hearty steamboat man, or a steamboat. I remember having a leaf from our dining-table on the floor, kneeling on it, and, taking hold of one end, jerking it backward over the carpet, tooting like a steamboat whistle. Three or four big chairs and all the small chairs in the house made me a mountain train of wagons and mules; a clothes line tied to the leader and strung through the other chairs was a rein which I could jerk just as the black-bearded teamsters did. And, of course, any chair is a horse for a boy who is a would-be vaquero.

Horses, real horses, played a leading part in my boyhood; I seem always to have wanted one. A chair would do on a rainy day, but at other times I preferred to escape into the street and ask drivers to "please, mister, gimme a ride." Sometimes they would. I was a pretty boy with lovely long blond curls. This I know well because it kept me from playing with the other fellows of my age. They jeered at my curls and called me a girl or a "sissy boy" and were surprised when I answered with a blow. They were taken off their guard by my attack, but they recovered and charged in mass upon me, sending me home scratched, bleeding, torn, to my mother, to beg her to cut my hair. She would not. My father had to do it. One day when the gang had caught me, thrown me down, and stuffed horse-droppings into my mouth, he privately promised me relief, and the next morning he took me downtown and had his barber cut off my curls, which he wrapped up in a paper as a gift for my mother. How she wept over them! How I rejoiced over them!

No more fighting by day, no more crying by night. The other boys accepted me as a regular fellow, but I got fewer free rides. I have no doubt the drivers liked my angelic locks. Anyway, before they were cut off, drivers used often to take me up in their seats with them and let me hold the reins back of where they held them and so drive real horses. My poor mother suffered so much from these disappearances that the sport was forbidden me: in vain. I went right on driving. I did it with a heavy sense of doing wrong, but I couldn't help going whenever a driver would take me. Once, when I was sitting alone holding the reins to let a team drink at a trough (the driver stood away off at the horses' heads), I saw my father come around the corner after me. I dropped the reins and climbed down off the wagon. My father took my hand and, without a word, led me home. There, at the door, my mother caught me up away from my stern father and, carrying me off into the parlor, laid me across her knees and gave me a spanking, my first. My mother! I had expected punishment, but from my father, not from her; I felt saved when she rescued me from him. And then she did it—hard.

This turned out to be one of the lasting sorrows, not of my life, but of hers. She told it many, many times. She said that my father stood at the door, watching her till she was done with me, and then he asked her why she did it.

"I did it," she said, "to keep you from doing it. You are so hard."

"But," he answered, "I wasn't going to spank him for that. He was having such a good time, he looked so proud up there on that old manure wagon, and when he saw me, he came right down, put his hand in mine, and came straight home, trembling with fear. I couldn't have spanked him. And you—Why did you do it? And why so hard?"

My mother cried more than I did at the time, and she always wept a little when she told it, explaining to the end of her days that she did it so hard just to show that he need not ever spank me, that she could do it quite enough. "And then," she'd break, "to think he wasn't going to do it at all!"

. . .

The world as I knew it in my angelic stage was a small yard, with a small house on one side of it and a wide, muddy street in front. The street was wonderful, the way to heaven. Astonishing things passed there, horses and wagons, for instance. It led in one direction to "the store," my father's place of business, where it was a rare privilege to go and be cheered and jeered at as the boss's boy. Across the street beyond some uninteresting houses was another street, called Front Street, which had houses only on one side. The other side was the reeling, rolling, yellow Sacramento River—a forbidden menace and a fascinating vision. That's where the steamboats plied, the great, big, flat-bottomed cargo and passenger boats, some with side wheels, some with one great stern wheel. I did not know, I did not care, where they went. It was enough that they floated by day and whistled by night safely on that dangerous muddy flood which, if it ever got a boy in its grip, would roll him under, drown him, and then let his body come up all white and still and small, miles and miles away.

But we moved from that Second Street house to a little larger one 'way over on H Street between Sixth and Seventh. A new and greater world. The outstanding features of it were the railroad, the slough, a vacant lot with four big fig trees, and school. The railroad had a switch line on the levee around the slough on Sixth Street, and I used to watch the freight cars shunted in there. I watched and I wondered where they came from. Unlike the steamboats those cars spoke to me of the world, the whole world. In my Second Street mind the steamboats just paddled up and down, as I did on my table-leaf; but those H Street trains of cars came from somewhere and they went somewhere. Where? I could not read, but sometimes those box cars came in covered with fresh snow, and snow was a marvel to me. All my picture books had snow scenes, sledding and skating, houses alight in the dark covered with glistening white. Not for me, any of this. The only snow I ever beheld I saw from my schoolroom window, far, far away on the mountain peaks. The snow-covered cars came, then, from over the mountains, 'way, 'way over, and I wanted to know what was 'way, 'way over. They told me in scraps and I remember sitting by the railroad track, trying to construct the world beyond out of the scraps of information people threw me till I was called sharply to come home, and asked what in the world I was mooning there at those cars for. Grown-ups don't understand a fellow.

And they could not understand the fascination of that "filthy old slough, which ought to be filled up" (as it is now). To me it was a lonely place of mystery and adventure. Sometimes it was high with water, and I could hunt mud-hens with my "slingshot." Sometimes it was almost empty, and—sure it stank, but what of that?—I could play scouts and Indians with the other boys in the brush, dodging along the twisting trails made by the mechanics going to and from the railroad repair shops on the other side of the slough.

The lot with the fig trees was next door to us, and there I built a nest and finally a house up among the branches—my savage stage, which a kid has to claw and club his own way through, all alone, he and his tribe. And there, in our hand-made hut in the monkey-land of those fig trees, there I found out about sex.

Parents seem to have no recollection and no knowledge of how early the sex-life of a child begins. I was about six years old when I built that hut, which was a wigwam to me, a cache; it was a safe place in which to hide from and watch the world below. Small animals, birds, chickens, and sometimes people could be seen from it, and it was fascinating to observe them when they were unaware that I, a spy, an Indian, an army scout, could see all that they did. The trouble was that they never did anything much and I never did anything much. It was becoming a bore when one day a big boy—eight or nine years old —came along under my tree looking for figs. He saw my hut; he spied my two spying eyes.

333

"What ye think you're doing?" he demanded.

"Nothing," I answered.

He climbed up the tree, crept into my hut, looked it over, approving with his nodding head; then he looked at me. I shrank from that look. I didn't know why, but there was something queer in it, something ugly, alarming. He reassured me, and when I was quiet and fascinated, he began there in that dark, tight, hidden little hut to tell me and show me sex. It was perverse, impotent, exciting, dirty—it was horrible, and when we sneaked down into the nice, clean dust of the sunlit ground I ran away home. I felt so dirty and ashamed that I wanted to escape unseen to the bathroom, but my mother was in the living-room I had to pass through, and she smiled and touched me fondly. Horrid!

"Don't, oh don't!" I cried, and I shrank away appalled.

"Why! What is the matter?" she asked, astonished and hurt.

"I dunno," I said, and I ran upstairs. Locking the bathroom door, I answered no calls or knocks. I washed my hands, my face, again and again till my father came home. His command to open I obeyed, but I would not let him touch me; and I would not, could not explain, and he, suspecting or respecting my trouble perhaps, let me off and protected me for a long period during which I could not bear to have my parents, my sisters—I would not let any one I loved touch me: all signs of affection recalled and meant something dirty, but fascinating, too. I could listen when the other boys (and girls) told one another about this dark mystery; I had to. It had the same lure that I felt in the hut that day. And I can remember a certain servant girl who taught me more, and vividly I can still see at times her hungry eyes, her panting, open mouth, and feel her creeping hands.

I do not remember what my first school taught me. Nothing like this, nothing of life. It was, at the beginning, a great adventure, then a duty, work, a bore that interfered with my boy's business. I can "see" now only the adventure. I was led to the schoolhouse by my mother, who must have known how I felt, the anxious confusion of stark dread and eager expectation that muddled me. She took me by the hand to the nearest corner. There I dismissed her; I must appear alone, like the other boys; and alone I trudged across the street up to the gate where I saw millions of boys playing as if nothing were happening. It was awful. Before I dived in I turned and I saw my mother standing, where I had left her, watching me. I don't remember that she made any sign, but I felt she would let me return to her. And I wanted to; how I wanted to! But I didn't. With more fear than I have ever since known, and therefore more courage than I have ever since had to rally, I walked into that Terror, right through that mob of wild, contemptuous, cruel, strange boys—grown-ups don't know how dangerous big boys are—I ran up the stairs and nearly fell, gasping, hot, but saved, into the schoolhouse. I cannot recall anything that happened there, only that we of the infant class were kept (probably to be registered) about an hour and that I came out and walked home with such a sense of victory and pride as I have never known since. I told everybody I met, even strangers, that "I've been to school."

I boasted my great boast all day and it was well received till, in the afternoon, after the "big classes let out," I repeated it to some big boys as a reason for letting me play ball with them.

"Yea," said the leader, "you bin to school, in the ABC class! Naw, ye can't play with us."

I have met that fellow since; everybody has. He is the killjoy that takes the romance out of life; he is the crusher that keeps us down on the flat; he is the superior person, as I well know. I have been that beast myself now and then. What makes us so?

And what makes grown-ups promise things to children and fail them? Charlie Prodger was the only man, except my father and Colonel Carter, who kept his word with me. He was something of a politician, and I was made to feel that there was something bad about a politician. I did not know what it was that was bad, but I did not care in the case of Charlie Prodger. I loved the sight of him coming dapper and handsome, smiling, toward me; and I had, and I have now, a deep, unreasoning respect for him. What grown-ups call good and bad are not what us boys call good and bad. Charlie Prodger was a good man to me then; he promised me a pair of stilts; other boys had them and could walk on them right through mud and water, over low fences and even up steps. Charlie Prodger did not say he would give me a pair; he was more wonderful than that. He said: "You'll get your stilts. Some day you'll find them on your front porch, and you'll never know where they came from." And sure enough, one day soon I found on the front porch the finest pair of stilts that any boy in our neighborhood ever had, and on them I climbed to heaven for a while—and for always to a belief in the word, not of all men, but of "bad" politicians like Charlie Prodger.

But Charlie Prodger never promised me a horse, and it was a horse I wanted, a pony. When he made good with the stilts I asked him to promise me a pony. I was sure that if I could get a promise out of him I'd get my pony. He laughed; he understood, but no, he said he could not give me a pony; so he would not give me the promise of one.

But there is another sort of fellow: the fellow that not only made promises and broke them, but probably never meant to keep them. A driver my father hired sometimes of a Sunday to drive us down Riverside Drive was, I thought, a great man and a good friend of mine. He let me sit up in the driver's seat with him and not only hold the reins behind his hands, but on a straight, safe piece of road he held

335

behind and I held in front. One day he swung his whip at a pigeon, ringing it around the neck with his lash. That made a deep impression on me. He got down, wrung the bird's neck, and brought it to me. Poor pigeon! Yes. But I admired the driver's skill, and he boasted: "Huh, I can do it every time. I was a teamster in the mountains, and I got so I could snap a fly off the ear of my lead mule." No doubt he turned and winked at my fond parents, sitting in adult superiority on the back seat, but I saw nothing. I wanted and I asked my expert friend to catch me a pigeon—alive. He said he could; he said he would, but he didn't. He didn't on that drive, but he promised to on the next. He didn't. For years, I think, I asked that driver every time I saw him for my pigeon, and always he gave me, instead, a promise.

I must have pestered that poor, thoughtless liar, but the men I drove the hardest were those that I asked to give me a horse. And they were many, everybody that had anything to do with horses, and others besides—they all knew that I wanted a pony. My grandfather, Colonel Carter, my father, my father's partners, all received messages and, later, letters, asking for a pony; and most of them did not say they could not or would not give me one; most of them put me off with a promise. I had a stable of promises and I believed those promises. I rode those promises hard, once to a bad fall. One of my father's partners, who was coming from San Francisco on business, wrote that he was going to bring me either a velocipede or a pony—according as I chose the right one. Which did I want? I wrote that I preferred the pony, and when he came, he had nothing.

"You guessed wrong," he said. "I had no pony to give you. If you had chosen a velocipede—"

I stood there staring at him, and he laughed. He did not know the shock, the crushing agony that kept me still. I could not move. My mother had to pick me up and carry me to bed. I might have had a velocipede. I could use a velocipede. I could have made believe it was a horse, or a steamboat, or a locomotive, and it *was* a velocipede. My regret was a brooding sorrow, speechless, tearless, and that liar laughed.

~~~~~~~~~~~~~~~~~~~~~~~~~~~~~~~~~

DISCUSSION AND INQUIRY

Lincoln Steffens assumed that, "Every well-born baby is sure he can trust his Mother." He trusted his adoring mother implicitly, and there were no recalled events from his early life to shake that trust. He was told in many ways that he was loved and appreciated—that he was mar-

velous—that he was good as gold, and he seemingly lived up to that expectation. Do you agree that every well-born baby can trust his mother? How do babies learn to trust the mothering person? At what point in the mother-child relationship does the building of trust (or mistrust) begin?

Young Steffens' blond curls caused him to be the victim of beatings by several boys who took issue with his appearance. His mother was reluctant to have his curls cut. Physical appearance plays an important part in a child's sex-role identification. How can you account for his mother's reluctance to have his curls cut? Considering the relaxed attitudes toward hair styles and dress among the "now" generation, would this have been as much of an issue today? (See the selection by Mark Van Doren for a similar situation.)

Lincoln made some childlike attempts to reconstruct the world beyond his circumscribed life space when he sat beside the railroad track and put bits and pieces of information together. Young children have a very limited concept of space beyond that which is within their immediate experience. Although Lincoln blames adults for giving him only fragmentary information about far-off places, one wonders if his egocentric thinking placed a serious limitation on his ability to assimilate the material he was given. Can children today reconstruct space beyond their house, their neighborhood, their country, their world? Ask them about it. With all the information you have about outer space and space travel, do you really have a clear concept of what it means to travel to the moon or to Mars?

As a 6-year-old, Lincoln had a sexual experience with an older boy. It left an indelible memory of disgust, perversity, and filth. He couldn't talk to anyone about it, and he shrank from the touch of any member of his family because he didn't want to contaminate them. If he really trusted his parents, why couldn't he go to

337

*them with this problem? Sexual experiences with
older children are relatively common, but they
don't necessarily leave the scars of disgust and
guilt experienced by the author. How can
parents help children cope with these experiences? What are some of the ways parents
can deal with the sex information that children
inevitably get from their peers? When dealing
with children, what is the adult's role in facilitat-
ing healthy attitudes toward sex?*

Dylan Thomas

∿∿∿∿∿∿∿∿∿∿∿∿∿∿∿∿∿∿∿∿∿∿

BIOGRAPHICAL SKETCH

At the time of his death at the age of 39, Dylan Thomas was already recognized as a great lyric poet of his generation. Born in 1914 in Wales, he often drew images from his childhood memories in his poetry and essays. His prose books, A Child's Christmas in Wales *and* Quite Early One Morning, *are fast becoming classics in America as well as in Europe.*

∿∿∿∿∿∿∿∿∿∿∿∿∿∿∿∿∿∿∿∿∿∿

SELECTIONS FROM

QUITE EARLY ONE MORNING

I LIKE very much people telling me about their childhood, but they'll have to be quick or else I'll be telling them about mine.

I was born in a large Welsh town at the beginning of the Great War —an ugly, lovely town (or so it was and is to me), crawling, sprawling by a long and splendid curving shore where truant boys and sandfield boys and old men from nowhere, beachcombed, idled and paddled, watched the dock-bound ships or the ships steaming away into wonder and India, magic and China, countries bright with oranges and loud with lions; threw stones into the sea for the barking outcast dogs; made castles and forts and harbors and race tracks in the sand; and on Saturday summer afternoons listened to the brass band, watched the Punch and Judy, or hung about on the fringes of the crowd to hear the fierce religious speakers who shouted at the sea, as though it were wicked and wrong to roll in and out like that, white-horsed and full of fishes.

One man, I remembered, used to take off his hat and set fire to his hair every now and then, but I do not remember what it proved, if it proved anything at all, except that he was a very interesting man.

This sea-town was my world; outside a strange Wales, coal-pitted, mountained, river-run, full, so far as I knew, of choirs and football teams and sheep and storybook tall hats and red flannel petticoats, moved about its business which was none of mine.

Beyond that unknown Wales with its wild names like peals of bells

339

in the darkness, and its mountain men clothed in the skins of animals perhaps and always singing, lay England which was London and the country called the Front, from which many of our neighbors never came back. It was a country to which only young men travelled.

At the beginning, the only "front" I knew was the little lobby before our front door. I could not understand how so many people never returned from there, but later I grew to know more, though still without understanding, and carried a wooden rifle in the park and shot down the invisible unknown enemy like a flock of wild birds. And the park itself was a world within the world of the sea-town. Quite near where I lived, so near that on summer evenings I could listen in my bed to the voices of older children playing ball on the sloping paper-littered bank, the park was full of terrors and treasures. Though it was only a little park, it held within its borders of old tall trees, notched with our names and shabby from our climbing, as many secret places, caverns and forests, prairies and deserts, as a country somewhere at the end of the sea.

And though we would explore it one day, armed and desperate, from end to end, from the robbers' den to the pirates' cabin, the highwayman's inn to the cattle ranch, or the hidden room in the undergrowth, where we held beetle races, and lit the wood fires and roasted potatoes and talked about Africa, and the makes of motor cars, yet still the next day, it remained as unexplored as the Poles—a country just born and always changing.

There were many secret societies but you could belong only to one; and in blood or red ink, and a rusty pocketknife, with, of course, an instrument to remove stones from horses' feet, you signed your name at the foot of a terrible document, swore death to all the other societies, crossed your heart that you would divulge no secret and that if you did, you would consent to torture by a slow fire, and undertook to carry out by yourself a feat of either daring or endurance. You could take your choice: would you climb to the top of the tallest and most dangerous tree, and from there hurl stones and insults at grown-up passers-by, especially postmen, or any other men in uniform? Or would you ring every doorbell in the terrace, not forgetting the doorbell of the man with the red face who kept dogs and ran fast? Or would you swim in the reservoir, which was forbidden and had angry swans, or would you eat a whole old jam jar full of mud?

There were many more alternatives. I chose one of endurance and for half an hour, it may have been longer or shorter, held up off the ground a very heavy broken pram we had found in a bush. I thought my back would break and the half hour felt like a day, but I preferred it to braving the red face and the dogs, or to swallowing tadpoles.

We knew every inhabitant of the park, every regular visitor, every nursemaid, every gardener, every old man. We knew the hour when the alarming retired policeman came in to look at the dahlias and the hour when the old lady arrived in the Bath chair with six Pekinese, and a pale girl to read aloud to her. I think she read the newspaper, but we always said she read the *Wizard*. The face of the old man who sat summer and winter on the bench looking over the reservoir, I can see clearly now and I wrote a poem long long after I'd left the park and the seatown.

. . .

And that park grew up with me; that small world widened as I learned its secrets and boundaries, as I discovered new refuges and ambushes in its woods and jungles; hidden homes and lairs for the multitudes of imagination, for cowboys and Indians, and the tall terrible half-people who rode on nightmares through my bedroom. But it was not the only world—that world of rockery, gravel path, playbank, bowling green, bandstands, reservoir, dahlia garden, where an ancient keeper, known as Smoky, was the whiskered snake in the grass one must keep off. There was another world where with my friends I used to dawdle on half holidays along the bent and Devon-facing seashore, hoping for gold watches or the skull of a sheep or a message in a bottle to be washed up with the tide; and another where we used to wander whistling through the packed streets, stale as station sandwiches, round the impressive gasworks and the slaughter house, past by the blackened monuments and the museum that should have been in a museum. Or we scratched at a kind of cricket on the bald and cindery surface of the recreation ground, or we took a tram that shook like an iron jelly down to the gaunt pier, there to clamber under the pier, hanging perilously on to its skeleton legs or to run along to the end where patient men with the seaward eyes of the dockside unemployed capped and mufflered, dangling from their mouths pipes that had long gone out, angled over the edge for unpleasant tasting fish.

Never was there such a town as ours, I thought, as we fought on the sandhills with rough boys or dared each other to climb up the scaffolding of halfbuilt houses soon to be called Laburnum Beaches. Never was there such a town, I thought, for the smell of fish and chips on Saturday evenings; for the Saturday afternoon cinema matinees where we shouted and hissed our threepences away; for the crowds in the streets with leeks in their hats on international nights; for the park, the inexhaustible and mysterious, bushy red-Indian hiding park where the hunchback sat alone and the groves were blue with sailors. The memories of childhood have no order, and so I remember that never was there such a dame school as ours, so firm and kind and smelling of galoshes, with the sweet and fumbled music of the piano lessons drifting down from upstairs to the lonely schoolroom, where only the sometimes tearful wicked sat over undone sums, or to repeat a little crime—the pulling of a girl's hair during geography, the sly shin kick under the

341

table during English literature. Behind the school was a narrow lane where only the oldest and boldest threw pebbles at windows, scuffled and boasted, fibbed about their relations—

"My father's got a chauffeur."

"What's he want a chauffeur for? He hasn't got a car."

"My father's the richest man in the town."

"My father's the richest man in Wales."

"My father owns the world."

And swapped gob-stoppers for slings, old knives for marbles, kite string for foreign stamps.

The lane was always the place to tell your secrets; if you did not have any, you invented them. Occasionally now I dream that I am turning out of school into the lane of confidences when I say to the boys of my class, "At last, I have a real secret."

"What is it—what is it?"

"I can fly."

And when they do not believe me, I flap my arms and slowly leave the ground only a few inches at first, then gaining air until I fly waving my cap level with the upper windows of the school, peering in until the mistress at the piano screams and the metronome falls to the ground and stops, and there is no more time.

And I fly over the trees and chimneys of my town, over the dock-yards skimming the masts and funnels, over Inkerman Street, Sebasto-pol Street, and the street where all the women wear men's caps, over the trees of the everlasting park, where a brass band shakes the leaves and sends them showering down on to the nurses and the children, the cripples and the idlers, and the gardeners, and the shouting boys: over the yellow seashore, and the stone-chasing dogs, and the old men, and the singing sea.

The memories of childhood have no order, and no end.

~~~~~~

DISCUSSION AND INQUIRY

Imaginative play is much of the essence of child-hood, and Thomas' childhood is no exception. Consider the author's description of the secret societies and the initiation rites. At what age or stage of development do children join clubs or groups such as described by him? In deciding what needs are met by such memberships, one should keep in mind the child's relationship with his family and his need for peer acceptance. Many adults are part of fraternal organizations that have secret handshakes and various other rituals. Are the needs of the adults who belong to such groups the same as those of children who form their own groups?

The initiation rites were in the form of various challenges or dares in an attempt to show one's physical ability or bravery. Very rarely will you come across peer groups where acceptance is based on mental ability. Why is this so? Does this reflect certain values of our society; and are they not in conflict with many of the values we present to children in elementary school?

Reread the selection and find examples of ethnocentrism? What is the relationship between egocentricism and ethnocentrism? Are these "isms" a part of the normal developmental pattern in children, or are they taught by the family and the culture?

Why do children brag about their families, often finding themselves making up unbelievable stories concerning the status and wealth of their fathers? Read the selection by Dick Gregory in which he brags that his family is going to donate more money than anyone to a charity. (See the selections by Dick Gregory and by Gertrude Berg, who as a child tells her friends her father owns a huge country estate.) Does the need to lie or exaggerate have anything to do with the individual's particular need for acceptance? Does society reinforce the child's belief that wealth and status are prerequisites for respect and acceptance?

Mark Van Doren

BIOGRAPHICAL SKETCH

Mark Van Doren, a distinguished poet and teacher, has often been referred to as one of the great names in contemporary American literature. He grew up in rural Illinois, and has many books to his credit. His Collected Poems *won the Pulitzer Prize in 1940. He was a member of the Department of English at Columbia University from 1920 until his death in 1972.*

SELECTIONS FROM

THE AUTOBIOGRAPHY OF MARK VAN DOREN

My FATHER's farm lay a mile west of Hope, Illinois, an all but invisible village halfway between Danville and Urbana. A branch line of the Big Four railroad, and later an electric line which we called "the interurban," connected those two towns and ran through such smaller places as Muncie, Fithian, and Ogden; but Hope, a few miles to their north, was seldom seen by strangers during the six years between 1894 when I was born and 1900 when we moved to Urbana. Nor is it different now. Hope is hard to find in any atlas, though it still exists as Faith and Charity, its sister villages named a century ago, do not.

I was an affectionate child in an affectionate family, so that I have no unhappy memories of that time; or if I do have some, as presently shall appear, they are of such miseries as I soon could even boast about, since they made me the center of attention and in certain cases got built into little stories of which I was the hero. The earliest story of this sort that I remember had in fact two heroes, for it involved my brother Frank, two years older than I and my constant playmate in the long yard, with sheep in it and many trees, which ran down from the big white house to the road. We played here in every season of the year. There were ash and walnut groves behind the house, planted there by a former owner of the farm, and their straight rows fascinated us when-

344

ever we wandered among them; to me those groves are still ideal places, the very type of what all groves should be, and I do not forget my shock at hearing, long after we moved away, that a subsequent owner had cut them down. But perhaps for the very reason that they were mysterious and wonderful we spent less time in them than we spent in the front yard, where our big brothers Carl and Guy, busy in more important ways, knew as little as our parents did of what we might be up to.

The circumstance that dates the tale in question is my inability to talk plain. Not that it does so precisely, because I was slow to speak and stammered till I was twenty. Perhaps I was three, perhaps I was four, when on this day Frank and I decided we would haul coal in our wagon, a red wagon with horses painted on its side. We had got one or two lumps loaded, and were pulling them past the house, when it occurred to us that we were hired men with a real wagon and team. My father was away as he so often was, being the only doctor for miles around, and my mother had gone somewhere too in the buggy which she drove with an expertness I admired. Our grown cousin, Inez Collison, was here from Potomac to take care of us. She was indoors at the moment, so that we thought we were alone as we shouted and swore at our imaginary plugs. At least I swore. "By Dod," I said, "Dod dam"; and more to the same effect. Frank laughed. But Inez, appearing suddenly at an open window above our heads, did not laugh. Instead she shamed us; and worse yet, she announced that when Mother came home that evening she would tell her what we had done. Instantly contrite, we had then to wait upon our punishment: perhaps a switching, perhaps only a scolding, but either was serious. I do not recall how we got through the day. I can still see, however, the buggy as it came up to the barn, with Mother in it counting on us to carry whatever she had brought, or perhaps to help her at the harness. We helped so vigorously, and escorted her into the house so piously, that she may have suspected something even then. I still do not know why nothing happened. For nothing did. Inez either told her or did not; and if she told her, our avenging goddess—who was also a wise and fond parent —may have thought we had sufficiently punished ourselves. The secret of course was ours alone, to be kept alive for months and even years by mutual reminders of a possibility that had never come to pass. We certainly did not tell our mother then; but after more than fifty years I used the incident, with some change of names, in a story called "God Has No Wife."

My mother, passionately devoted to us all, and positive that each of us excelled in something, did nothing to cure my vanity when she asked me, as she often did, "Who is Mama's prettiest boy?" She expected me to say, and invariably I did, "I am." This was because I agreed with her that the long curls she trained to fall about my neck were beautiful beyond compare. The skirts I wore were customary for boys in that generation, but not of course the curls; they were supposed to be unique. There came a time, but this was not until I had started to school, when my being mistaken for a girl, or teased because I dressed like one, no longer gave me pleasure. My mother came home one day and found me hiding under a bed, stricken by what I had done. I had used her scissors to remove, down to my very scalp, the longest of the curls. She wept, and I wept; but then she sensibly removed the rest (and kept them in a shoe box till she died). Years later she admitted that she had wanted me to be a girl in the beginning; now she must have said to herself that having proved myself otherwise I was to be free of further interference. I was not in fact her best-looking child. Carl was, or Guy, or Frank, or in his own time Paul. Nor would she have been happy had she known how often I played up to Frank's admiration for my profanity. I was vain of that too: I loved language, even bad language, and showed off such childish skill in it as I possessed. Doubtless bad talk was one of the ways I took to prove myself a boy.

I was a happy child; I was pleased with myself, and enjoyed almost everything that went on. It was exciting, for example, to become a reader at four. My mother taught me at that age because I was to go to school the next year: earlier than the average, but Frank was to be held back so that we could go together, he at seven and I at five. It was a mile to Hope, and some days the walking would be hard. So both of us were set to learning our letters, and the syllables they composed: a-b, ab, a-c, ac, a-d, ad. I do not remember moving on from this point to words and sentences, but of course I did, and in due time was making my own way through a bound volume of *Our Little Ones*, a children's magazine of which my mother had assembled ten issues for 1890 and 1891, sewing them with strong thread and covering them with heavy oilcloth, the rough side out. The resulting book survives to this day; somehow it descended to me, and it is one of my treasures. We were a reading family; my parents believed in books, and had many in the house; Carl's teacher had given him at nine, the year I was born, no less a prize than Green's *History of the English People* in four volumes; but nothing interested me so much at the moment as this collection of illustrated poems and stories about children who were either good or bad—and if bad, they were sorry. I knew nothing then of Carl's remarkable prize, which had a great deal to do with his becoming what he was when he grew up, a professional reader and writer. I was more interested in hearing my mother laugh as she told how Guy, who was four when the oilcloth book came into being, had mistaken a line in one of the poems. It was supposed to read: " 'Ho-ho!' and 'Ha-ha!' laughed the two little mice." But Guy had said: " 'Ho-ho!' and 'Ha-ha!' laughed the little two mice." And this was a delicious joke, in harmony with the picture above the poem: the brother mouse wore a striped cap, a white shirt, and pants with large buttons; the sister mouse, whose hand he held, had on a sunbonnet and a print dress.

Across the page was an overturned wheelbarrow with two plump legs sticking out behind it. These belonged to a little girl named Helen who had been helping her papa garden, but then had climbed into his wheelbarrow so that she could bark back at a fierce dog that, chained to his kennel, was threatening her over a low stone wall. There was an apple tree in a second picture, and beehives and hollyhocks; and the child, dressed in a long embroidered cloak, had an embroidered cap tied under her chin. I remember the details so well that I scarcely need to look them up. These were my first pictures, as these were my first poems and stories. They went together perfectly in my mind, where they glorified, with just a touch of alien elegance, the reality I relished all about me. I cared less for the fairy-tale themes that occasionally intruded; the angels and the sylphs were unconvincing. No, the stories must be about children and their parents and grandparents; or about animals, which interested me profoundly. There was the horse that punished a boy for tormenting a goat by picking him up with his teeth and throwing him over a hedge. There was Lucy, who when her mother died came to live with her grandmother, and whose father, because he heard she had been brave at the dentist's, sent her a puppy in a Gladstone bag. There was Percy, who went to Egypt and rode on a donkey. There was Gertrude, who lived in Florida and led on a leash a razorback pig whom she expected to eat the snakes in her way. But my favorite stories had to do with cats: the huge white one that left her kitten in Tom's sealskin cap; the minister's, named Deborah, who walked eleven miles through the snow carrying her six kittens in her mouth—five and a half round trips to put them where they ought to be; and best of all the tortoise-shell, old Sally, who saved Baby Winfred's life by running to Grandpa's store with a message for the doctor tied about her neck.

The reality around me was both like and unlike this precious book. I was less pretty and smooth, and yet strict parallels appeared, as when for example, I do not know in what year, a cow chased me across the barnyard and would have had me on her horns had not my father run to close a gate between us. This was like the story of Pollie, to whom exactly the same thing happened; but there was a sequel that would have been out of key with the book. The next day my father shut the cow into a stall and sawed off her horns; I witnessed the operation, and learned for the first time that horns are full of blood. Nor was there any animal in *Our Little Ones* as interesting as Dick, an Indian pony who had been bought for Carl but whom we all seemed to own. Dick was fatter than "Indian" suggests; indeed his back was so broad that several boys could sit on him at once. We adored him in our several ways. Carl was old enough to race him; he was very fast for short distances; but Frank and I preferred to fondle him and poke about at the mule's pace he fancied more. He was lazy, we said, and we liked him so. He was a bay, with beautiful eyes separated by a white band down his forehead and nose. He could be stubborn; my father, who needed him one day and tried to catch him in a five-acre field east of the house, gave up at last and called him "ornery." My father carried a bridle in one hand and an ear of corn in the other; and dozens of times he thought Dick, coaxed by the corn, would either come to him or stand still to be taken; but each time, even though his nostrils were blowing at the grain, he swung his head away and started running at the last possible moment, only to stop in another corner and wait for the farce to be repeated. He was fast enough on these occasions, though with Frank and me he could be slower than sorghum, and sometimes, when he saw no sense in pretending any longer, as stationary as a stump.

I have wondered since how we ever got him to go as far as Potomac, where our maternal grandparents lived. I did not know then that Grandpa Butz had formerly lived in Hope, and in fact had all but created it out of prairie wilderness, or that Grandma Butz was still a legend there for her noble silence and good works. To Frank and me they were simply old people in another town, whither in the spring of 1899 we were driving Dick in a black and red cart with seats along its sides. Nor did we guess why we were going. Paul was about to be born, and it was thought better to have us out of the house. I have no memory of reaching Potomac; the most I can see is the double row of maple trees (Grandpa had set them out) that lined the road north of Hope; we went between those trees, then turned east and north a number of times till we were there. It is difficult to believe now that we were sent by ourselves, or that we could find the way. Perhaps an older person did go with us, though I have no memory of that. But I remember coming home and finding Paul in bed beside my mother. He was the last of us to be born, and even I could henceforth patronize him as "the baby."

. . .

The day came, in September of 1899, when Frank and I went off for our first taste of school. I suppose Carl and Guy walked with us, or it may even be that we were driven to Hope in honor of so special an occasion. But the only moment now surviving in my mind is the moment when Mr. Smith, the teacher, rang his bell and we were expected to rush in. I was busy at the pump in one corner of the yard, doubtless trying in vain to cure the terrible thirst that comes with fear. Frank had filled a cup for me to drink, and now at the sound of the bell he left me with it, supposing I would follow. But I had decided I would never go to school. I had wanted to, the worst way, until this moment. I had talked of it all summer, and I really did want to enter that small white building I had passed so many times. I simply lacked the courage. What I was afraid of I am unable to imagine, nor did I know then, I assume, with any clarity. Certainly it was not Mr. Smith, a benevolent and pleasant man, and a friend of our family. But my terror was genuine, so I held my ground. Then the door opened and Mr. Smith came out to get me. He did not argue or explain. He merely picked me up and carried me in—a sacrifice on his part, for I kicked his shins all the way, and bawled and blubbered so that he must have wondered whether such a disturbance might wreck the day. Frank, he has told me since, felt both sympathy and shame, and there was much talk of the entire business that night at home, when my mother made it clear that she was "mortified." Even so soon, however, I had accepted school; and none of the pupils could have enjoyed more than I did the term that started so unpromisingly. Mr. Smith was a good teacher. I know he was, for I can still see the ruler he sawed into twelve equal parts, each with a number on it, so that we could witness the mysteries of addition and substraction—even multiplication and division—before our very eyes, not to say at the tips of our fingers.

My first year of school was to be our last year in the country, and I am grateful that the two things coincided. The oldest pupils reciting in the same room with the youngest, and to the same person, who meanwhile had of course to keep the others reasonably silent—this was a spectacle I never saw again. It had its merits. Yet I remember too how interesting it was to walk with Frank the mile to Hope and back, along a road that was dusty that fall and again in late spring but for several months in between was either black with mud or white with snow or frozen into iron ruts, and on the very coldest days might be colder still from wind that nipped our cheeks and ears and found its way inside clothes that my mother, a loving seamstress, had made as warm as she could. The lunches we took, packed into a tin box by the same hand, turned out on such days, when we opened them in the coatroom, to be quite suitable for the Eskimos we may have thought we were. The butter and the thick bread both were icy hard, and the boiled eggs, so good with pepper and salt, could have passed until we cracked them for brown rocks.

. . .

I have said that my mother made our clothes, but one of the earliest memories I have of my father concerns a garment that was bought—or rather, two garments, since Frank shared this experience with me as he did every other. Whenever it was, we had of course graduated from wearing skirts; for the garments in question were corduroy pants, short pants, to the knees only. And my father was to buy them at some town, I think Fithian, where he had driven on a professional call. Or perhaps he had ridden, depending on the state of the roads. He owned a spirited big team of grays, Prince and Billy, whom he hitched together when he could; but if the mud was deep, and there was danger of a buggy foundering, he might mount either of these handsome beasts and go off with his medicine case bouncing in one of the two saddle-bags that hung down the side. I have wondered since if this did not account for the particularly powerful smell the case had; occasionally some of the corks must have loosened, and the contents spilled. As soon as he came into a room you knew what he carried; and when he opened the black leather box—ah, the pungent mixture, compounded of chloroform, paregoric, nux vomica, and I know not what else, that had no counterpart elsewhere in the life my senses lived.

But this day, or rather this night, it was my sense of hearing that was most awake. I was lying with Frank in our walnut bed upstairs, a boy's-size bed, with spindles all around it, and both of us were holding our breath lest we miss the first sound of my father at the gate. When we did hear the horse or horses there we jumped out and ran to the window to hear more. But to our sorrow the sound retreated: my father had turned about and gone away again. Unable to understand why this should be, and unable to bear it too, for we had set all our fancy to work upon the figure we would cut in our new trousers, we fell asleep and did not know until morning what had happened. My father, with many other things to think about, for he was both a doctor and a farmer, had forgotten to make the purchase; then at the gate he remembered; and, tired as he surely was, though like Carl I have no distinct memory of his ever looking or sounding tired, he went all the way back so that Frank and I would not be disappointed. I cannot swear to this, but I suspect that our pleasure in the pants was greater next day than our gratitude to him; though for him the one thing might have been identical with the other, and in any case we could scarcely have been expected to realize at such an age that our father was one of the best men in the world. He made no point of his goodness, which we therefore took for granted.

He never punished any of us, my mother used to say, because he was away from home so much, often on calls which kept him overnight, that when he did show up again our being still alive, still there, was more important to him than anything else, and he would no more have thought even of scolding us than he would have confessed that while he was gone his chief thought had been of "you wretched boys," as he preferred to say. He loved to call things by the wrong names—or, it may be, the right ones, fantastically the right ones. Either extreme is poetry, of which he had the secret without knowing that he did. It was natural for him to name two lively rams on the place Belshazzar and Nebuchadnezzar. My mother must not have reckoned on his weakness for language when she determined that none of her sons should ever be nicknamed. She gave them all names of one syllable, supposing that this would settle the matter. But he could not leave it there. Frank became Fritz Augustus—just why, I never inquired—and I was either Marcus Aurelius or Marco Bozzaris. Guy was Guy Bob, and Carl was Carlo. And Paul, when it came time for him to share in the illicit luxuriance, was no other than Wallace P. Poggin—again, I have no faint idea why. My father never discussed his inspirations, any more than he analyzed his spoonerisms, or even admitted that they had fallen from his mouth. He would cough, and appear to apologize by saying: "I have a little throakling in my tit." Of course we liked this, as we liked him, without saying in so many words that he had humor. Other men we knew—uncles, cousins, old men, young men—had reputations for being funny. His reputation was for being kind and wise. Perhaps he never played with syllables except at home. And as for my mother's fear that he would spoil us, there was nothing in that, as I suspect she knew. Pure love never spoiled anybody. If we were spoiled, and I think I may have been, neither of my parents was to blame.

Photographs taken of them soon after they were married tell the story in each case: in my mother's case, of a handsome, proud young woman—and was she not the daughter of Jerry Butz, the patriarch who founded Hope?—with nevertheless a sweetness about the eyes, and a capacity for limitless devotion to the persons she would love; and in my father's case, of a spare, dark, also handsome, also proud young man whose intense gaze communicates to me not only his ambition— to be a good doctor, to have a fine farm, and perhaps to be rich—but, buried somehow within this ambition, a powerful, a subtle, a delicate concern with whatever it is that we mean when we say human life, and a capacity for honoring that life whenever it is most gentle and courageous. The intensity of the gaze is what no one could miss, though someone might remain unaware that it forgave as much as it demanded, and would undertake if necessary to bear what cannot be borne. These two bestowed upon their five sons an equal love in which there was no least hint of favoritism; which may explain, if anything needs to, the lifelong attachment of those five to one another. Carl remarked in his *Three Worlds* that any of his brothers would be his choice for a companion, if he could have but one, on a desert island; the only difficulty, he added, would be in deciding which brother went along. I can say the same thing, even though Carl's death puts him beyond the reach of any such decision. Then I can add that his own example was potent in establishing the affection he described. He himself had it in the abundance that was characteristic of him at every turn. Without this abundance in Carl, nothing might have become what it did become.

My father was angry at the cow that tried to kill me, and sawed off more of her horns than was necessary, but in general he was fond of the animals who lived with us and he saw to it that they were not mistreated. The most he felt against Dick when that little devil would not be caught was frustration: a natural impatience with an adversary who had put him out of breath, but who because he could do that was admirable too. I am glad I can remember some of the horses he had, and can see my father in relation to them. A man and a horse are among other things a pair of wills; we transfer the image when we say of a car that it is stubborn and refuses to start, or that it is lively and responds to our touch, but the two things are not the same. The horse does have a will, as he has good nature (or bad) and can truly take delight in going with us where we go. My father enjoyed his trips with Prince and Billy in all kinds of weather; he considered them great friends, and in later years, after he had sold them, was cast down by the news that their present owner had beaten them about the ears and even about their beautiful eyes (nothing in nature is more beautiful than the eye of a horse). I heard him lament this with my mother, and gathered that he considered it his own fault for ever selling them. But while he had them he made the most of their power and beauty, as I said in "The Little Doctor," written after his death:

> The little doctor with the black
> Ambitious eyes had giant horses;
> High the reins and loud the splash
> Along those muddy country courses.
>
> Black the harness, black the eyes,
> And black the phaeton's new fringes.
> Dappled, though, the necks and flanks,
> And foaming white the fetlocks' plunges. . . .
>
> Yet the straps outsang the wind,
> And yet the hoof-spray drowned the grasses.
> So in that lost, that country time
> The little doctor ever presses.
>
> On and on, a dateless day,
> Down sunken roads where death has prospered,
> Black-eyed breezes still can blow,
> And private glories still be whispered.

I call him "the little doctor" because that is what the neighbors called him when he first came to Hope. I never actually thought of him as little, and during the forty years I knew him I believe nobody else did. But he was of only medium height, and in that early time he was very slender—I seem to have heard that at twenty-one he weighed no more than a hundred pounds, though this scarcely seems possible. His ambition then was the only thing he possessed: the ambition, for example, which drove him as a boy to do the work of three men on his father's farm up north in Illinois so that he could at last walk to Chicago with enough money to pay off the mortgage. His father, William Henry Van Doren, whom I never saw more than once or twice, was a farmer, blacksmith, and preacher combined, and, I gather, not much of a businessman, though he was excellent in his own formidable fashion. My father had gone subsequently to a small medical college in Chicago, and after a year or two of apprenticeship with his half-brother Silas had settled upon Hope as the place where he might find a wife and make his fortune.

I once asked my mother how he found *her*, and was given the modest answer that he enjoyed coming to their house "to hear Pa talk." This would be Grandpa Butz, who was certainly a talker. But the young physician must have listened to Dora, my mother, at least half of the time, and looked at her and loved her. Only, by the code of her generation, she could not tell me so. It was the same code that prohibited her from ever calling him Charlie, or even Charles, in the hearing of any other person, her sons included. He was Papa before us, and Doctor before other people. A child's hunger for signs of affection between his parents is never, I suppose, completely satisfied. There seem to be more arguments than endearments. In my own case I had slowly to understand how hard both my father and my mother worked, how many problems harassed them, and how easily their strong wills could conflict. Also, I had to understand the code. I took on faith the fact of their regard for each other; and learned most about it after he was dead.

My pride in being hailed as "Little Doc" by men I met in Hope was greater than they could have known. To be identified with my father, as it seemed to me I then was, gave me inexpressible pleasure. And I suppose I said to myself that some day I would be a doctor too. But none of us ever followed him into the profession. People remarked about this, saying it was strange, nor can I explain it otherwise than Carl did: my father never hinted that he wanted us to do so. Possibly he did hope that one of us would, but his leniency, which left us so free in little matters, extended to this great matter as well, and no scruple could have been deeper in him than the scruple against urging us to be like him. We are like him anyway, we happily discover now and then.

And for my own part it was enough that he read my early poems, the ones I wrote before he died, and was glad I had written them. He said he found some of them true to his own experience; which was by no means odd, for they were about things he had told me. He learned by heart the short one, "Driver Lost," which represents a horse bringing its driver home after he has fallen asleep over the reins. This time it is not Prince or Billy but a mare without a name; but the thing did happen many nights, and my father used to chuckle as he pointed out that no car would have done it.

> She points an ear at every turn
> Before a hoof arrives.
> What hand is here from which to learn?
> Who is it sits and drives?

~~~~~~

DISCUSSION AND INQUIRY

When the author states he has no unhappy memories about his childhood, the reader can either take him at his word or assume the unpleasant memories have been successfully driven from consciousness. Admittedly, the former and not the latter, will happen to seem more apparent after reading this selection. Why do you, the reader, choose to accept this author's description? Perhaps it has to do with Van Doren's description of his family as loving and affectionate. One cannot imagine too many childhood miseries in the context of such an environment.

The brief swearing episode described early in the selection raises the question of the purpose and meaning of socially unacceptable language in young children. Is its use an imitation of older persons, or rather an identification with older persons? Can it be both? Might it also be used as an attention-getting device? Here, Van Doren says he was proud of his profanity, for he used it to prove his masculinity. The extensive use of profanity in the armed forces can probably be explained for the same reason.

The need for the author's feeling of masculinity as a child might be related to his mother's attempt to keep long curls on his head for as long a period as possible. His mother admitted that she always wanted a girl. What are the possible outcomes of a parent's attitude toward a child where the sex was a disappointment to them? When these attitudes are taken to extremes, can you predict some of the consequences? (See the selection by Lincoln Steffens, who also felt his masculinity was infringed on because of his long curls.)

William Allen White

~~~~~~~~~~~~~~~~~~~~~~~~~~~~~~~~~~~~

BIOGRAPHICAL SKETCH

William Allen White, a newspaperman from Emporia, Kansas, was born in 1868. After various newspaper jobs, he became editor of the Emporia Daily and Weekly Gazette *in 1895. An involved citizen, he received a gold medal for citizenship in 1933. In 1937, he was elected president of the American Society of Newspaper Editors, and he later founded and chaired the committee to Defend America by Aiding the Allies. Besides writing articles for magazines and newspapers, White found time to author several books before his death in 1944.*

~~~~~~~~~~~~~~~~~~~~~~~~~~~~~~~~~~~~

SELECTIONS FROM

THE AUTOBIOGRAPHY OF WILLIAM ALLEN WHITE

I WAS born February 10, 1868, between nine and ten o'clock of a Thursday morning at Emporia, Kansas. I was born "Willie" though named William Allen, a name which did not occur to me nor any of my friends for long years, even decades afterwards. A few days after my birth, this item appeared in the Emporia News, which referred to my father, Dr. Allen White:

There is another man in town they call Pap. He wears a stove pipe hat and carries a cane, and weighs (since the event) eight hundred pounds. He talks of sending the "young man" down on "Warnut" to take charge of the branch store.

I, Willie, was that young man, a baby of whom I know nothing except what has been told: that is that I was husky, always fat, with lusty bawling lungs, and that I was a nursing baby. And for perhaps two years, so far as my memory tells me, I was unconscious. When I was a year old I was taken by my parents to live in Eldorado, a little town in the Walnut Valley, "down on the Warnut," southwest of Emporia, then scarcely as much as a wide place in the road. On the journey I came within an ace of my life. It was spring. The creeks were swollen. We were traveling by spring wagon. We were crossing a stream and missed the ford. The wagon lurched. I was wrapped in a big brown shawl and was thrown into the swiftly moving spring flood. For two or three seconds I floated, and in those seconds I was rescued by the driver of the team and went on my way rejoicing, in my deep infantile sleep. My memory tells me that I waked up when I was nearly two years old. I was in my father's arms. Near me was a large round sheet-iron stove in a rather large living room with a bed in one corner and a door leading to the kitchen-dining-room of a frame house, my home. My father, with his pocketknife, was scraping an apple into pulp and feeding it to me on the point of his knife, and I was gurgling in delight, *a-boo, a-boo, a-boo.* This no one told me. I remember it. And after that I remember many things. For life had begun for me on this planet.

. . .

The first emotional disturbance in my life came when I was about two years old, probably a little older. A baby brother was born. I cannot now remember why I hated him. Of course it was jealousy; but I hated him with a bitter, terrible hate. And this I am sure I can remember: I sneaked around the corner of the house to the east porch where his crib was, of a summer afternoon, and began pounding him with my little fists. They caught me when his screams called them. I had no remorse that I remember. I cannot bring back any pictures of his early death and recall nothing of his funeral.

I was three years old then and had a sense of my environment. For me it remained a strange and lovely world. Two elderly, devoted and adoring persons, whom I called "Pa" and "Ma," guided me and bowed down before me; and I knew it and ruled them ruthlessly. I was spoiled, as what child born of parents in their late thirties and forties, would not be? I could draw a picture today of my home, the old "foundry," with its long kitchen where the dining table stood, its attached woodshed with the trapdoor into the cellar. And between the woodshed and the kitchen, in a covered corridor, they hung my little swing where I would swing for hours, singing a little bee song—a kind of long *ah-h-h-h* of sheer delight. I was a happy child and found a thousand things to please me. The world was made to bring me delight. There was a living room, ruled in fall and winter by a big, round, sheet-iron stove. On our walnut table the tall lamp sat, and here always newspapers were piled and books strewn. A spare bed filled a far corner. Our very best room, the parlor, I rarely entered; for it was dark there by day, and I was afraid of it. My own little bedroom and my parents' larger bedroom adjoined the living-room and the parlor. Of course, I went in and crawled in between them in the morning and seemed to give them much delight. They did not quarrel then, at least not before me. I must have been eight or ten years old before I was conscious of family differences. But in that Elysian childhood where I first opened my conscious eyes to the world about me, I was shielded from pain and sorrow and lived, if ever a human being did live, in a golden age. I must have had an early sense of tune, for one of my childish recollections is that I stood on the grocery scales in my father's store where he had me sing about "the old man who had a wooden leg and had no tobacco; no tobacco could he beg," of which the chorus was:

> Oh, buckle up my shoe, Johnnie,
> Buckle up my shoe.

I also sang a ballad about Barney O'Flynn, who "had no breeches to wear and got him a sheepskin and made him a pair!" The customers enjoyed it. But this I also remember—that my mother came often rushing in and said:

"Now, Doctor, haven't I always told you?"

And she took me in her arms and headed out of the room with me. I did not like this, for I was a born exhibitionist and loved the applause of the multitude. I seemed to turn everything into song. The little bee song of my babyhood became a long cantata which I made up, perhaps —words and tune and all—as I sat, a solitary only child, in the shade of the morning-glories or, best of all, in the barn at the end of our town lot. That barn was my first enchanted palace. Modern childhood has no equivalent to my barn. I don't know how young I was when I invented the story that it was haunted, and scared the daylights out of other children as I pointed to the barn's high rafters, pretending to see faces and fairies which they also pretended to see; and we scared ourselves and wrestled on the hay of the loft and smelled the nice smell of the horses and the cow. Sometimes we sat in the corncrib and watched the pigs beneath, and the chickens. It was all strange and adventurous. The old pig that woofed at us, and that we were sure would eat us if she caught us, made us feel that we were in the presence of a dragon as authentic as that which St. George went forth to slay.

Of Sunday afternoons, Pa and Ma walked with me to the timber between our creek and its junction with the Walnut River. Pa made me hickory whistles and taught me how to tell different trees by their leaves and bark. It was before they had cut out the buckbrush, the wild raspberries, the blackberries, elderberries, and pokeberries. Above this wood's brush were the one-story trees—the papaws, haws, buckeyes, and the redbuds that I loved. Far above these rose the sycamore, the hickory, the elm, the oak, the walnut, the ash, the coffee-bean tree or locust, and the cottonwoods. Walking with Pa and Ma of a Sunday afternoon, I saw squirrels, rabbits, and once in a while Pa would show me a coon at the river's brim, or a hell-diver. Pa had been born in the Ohio woods and loved timber, and he taught me from earliest childhood to know and love the woods. But the thing that gave the woods their glamour for me was that, only a few years before, the Indians had moved out of this timber onto the prairie lands far to the West and the South. I used to play little games by myself in the woods with mythical little Indian boys. And in some way—I never exactly knew how—I imagined or fancied or dreamed it, and I believed that I turned into a little Indian boy and indeed was one. So I believed, or most seriously fancied, that some day soon the Indians would come back and take me with them. I was scared and happy at the fantasy, which hung about me a long time—maybe a week, a month or half a year.

Then, of course, I had the prairies, the wide illimitable stretches of green in their spring and summer verdure, stretching westward from my front door, with not a dozen rivers or important streams, to the Rocky Mountains six hundred miles away. As a child, I did not know how far they went. To me, they were merely illimitable beyond the horizon and nothing could happen to me except the bite of a rattlesnake; and I never heard of a boy being bitten by a rattlesnake in my childhood. So the woods, the little stream, the prairies, and the dusty road by my door were my playgrounds.

And how I loved the velvety highway dust! It was thick and felt good to my skin, especially to my bare feet. I loved to throw it up in the air, make great clouds of it and feel it fall in my face. And I imagine that no small part of the joy was in being hauled out and scolded by my mother. All mothers along all dusty highways, since little Cain and Abel played in the dust on the road past Eden, have had that problem of children turning primitive in the dust—wallowing in it, kicking it up and heaving it into the air. Like all sweet, forbidden sin, it had its penalties. I had to be scrubbed and scolded at the same time. But it was cheap sin at that.

As a little child, before I went to school, I remember the delight of the prairies in the spring and summer when the grass was green and the wild flowers grew everywhere. I used to bring them in little sweaty handfuls to my mother with much delight—foolish little bouquets that I thought were lovely. Two or three hundred yards from our house, where I used to play on these prairies as a child, was a little rock-bottomed creek. In later years they dammed it. But before the dam filled up its channel I was allowed, when I could not have been more than four or five years old, to go down to its banks to play. In the riffle we had a little water wheel which gave me great delight. Here and there, as this brook wormed its way across the prairies, were little pools into which the water ran over the sparkling brown and golden pebbles, and in them silversides, sunfish, and minnows played and could be had with a string and a pinhook. But I caught few. I loved better to watch them, for long minutes, swerving about in tiny schools with tadpoles and sometimes a little turtle, which I brought home and kept in a can or the rain barrel until it got away. I wonder now—I have often wondered—about those little brooks and the courses that they cut in the prairies. For sixty years streets and houses have wiped out those kindly rivulets and springs. In all the prairies across these latitudes, the plow has come and filled the brooks. Even the verdure of the prairies and the pastures is different. The brooks are dry. The land has changed. The white man has come with his presence. The primeval fairyland has gone—fled before the grim reality of man's harrow and his plow, his highway and his house, his horse and his cattle, and all the ugly realities of man's fight to live by the sweat of his brow. The red man, who did not sweat much nor stop to drive away the fairies, knew in some ways how to live more easily in this land than his proud white brother.

As a little child, before they caught and bound me to a school desk, I remember spring, summer, and golden autumn as though I had lived always out of doors. In winter I ranged around the rooms of "the foundry." My mother had pasted copies of the old Emporia News on the kitchen walls to make it warmer there. And while she worked I used to stand and pick out my letters from the advertisements and spell little words and play with my blocks and toys around the big sheet-iron heating stove. The chunks it ate were too big for me to carry, but I cannot remember when I did not have to fill up the woodbox back of the kitchen stove. And there were chips to rake up around the woodpile and bring in for kindling, and cobs to gather. I cannot remember when these duties began, so it must have been early. We called them chores. I am ashamed to admit that the machinations of grown-ups at first concealed from me the fact that they were evil and onerous. I did chores cheerfully in the primitive, savage simplicity of childhood.

. . .

But I was not entirely unsophisticated in those pre-school years. I also had my sly tricks and manners. I knew some way, even then, how to clown, steal a laugh, and avert a crisis. How vividly this picture stands out in my memory! I am sitting by the south window of my bedroom with the sun falling upon me—sitting with my elbows on my knees and my head thrown back, squatting in my little night drawers split down the back, on my little yellow-green striped chamber pot, and I can hear my mother cry:

"Doctor, doctor, come here!"

And both their faces are peering through the door as I lift up my lusty childish treble—I know it was in tune and on key:

360

I 'anta be a nangel and with the angels stand.

Whatever cloud hovered over me, I have forgotten, but the memory that I was beclouded remains. Indeed, the sweet and satisfying knowledge that I had come from under the clouds remains with me still. If life chained me to its duties, I also was wily enough even as I toddled out of infancy to pad the chains with guile.

It was about this time, somewhere late in my third or early in my fourth year, when I made my first public stage appearance. I was always speaking pieces or singing lusty songs for my father at the store. But this time the town went to the courthouse for tableaux, and Leila Heaton and I were dressed to kill—I in a little plug hat with a little black coat and a little high-collared shirt, and she in some long doll dress. We appeared as General and Mrs. Tom Thumb, and I first received the plaudits of the multitude while I first felt the vague sweet pain of love. Leila Heaton, so far as I can remember, was the first object of my adoration. Her mother was a widow and ran the millinery store, and Leila had a big brother—old and very tough, maybe seven or eight years old—of whom I was afraid. And she had lovely gray eyes and dark hair, with corkscrew curls that ranged about her shoulders. I can remember that she called me "Willie" so sweetly that it was a lovely thing to hear. The affair must have been a town scandal. For someone—maybe a big boy or a big girl, it could not within reason have been a grown-up—told me one day that Albert Ewing had taken Leila Heaton into Myer's Candy Store and Ice Cream Saloon. I waited furtively and with the fever of murder pounding in my heart, in the doorway of Ed Ellet's store near by. When the guilty pair appeared, I rushed at them; Albert Ewing fell upon his back, and we rolled together in the board sidewalk dirt—I with the old blood lust of Cain in my heart and he with Abel's fear and amazement in his eyes. The other day Albert and I were talking about it. He insists it was not he, but Theodore Dunlevy, whom I waylaid. I know it was Albert, for I have never quite been able to obliterate the memory of the rage and jealousy with which I pounced upon him—aged four!

My little brother Freddie died when I was still a little fellow. My mother was distraught, and the Ohio family said my father brought her to Ohio to get her away from the lonely home where the baby's little cry in his last illness echoed through the rooms of the old "foundry."

Another thing: I am sure my father went to show me off to his Ohio kin—brothers who were grown-up young men and had soldiered in the Union Army, had reared their families, and heretofore had probably been sniffy with him in his thirties and forties with a wife past the child-bearing age, and with only a hand-me-down, secondhand family.

As a final reason for the trip, my father had a formal authorization as

361

a Solicitor of Aid from the Butler County commissioners (it was, in Kansas, a drought and grasshopper year), and a most elaborate document with a red seal and blue ribbon, signed by Thomas Osborn, Governor of Kansas, authorizing Dr. Allen White to collect money in Ohio. He went at his own expense to solicit aid. He brought back two carloads of clothes and provisions.

Anyway, I had my first railroad ride, and looking down from the heights of the passenger-car window, with my child's eyes all untrained and all undisciplined to perspective, I saw strange things. I have the loveliest memory of the weenty-teenty little men in the fields and the tiny little horses and the little bitsy plows I saw when I rode from Florence down the Cottonwood Valley and presently on across into the great land of Ohio. But here follows the story of "man's duplicity and woman's worse than wickedness": I still cherish a picture deeply etched in my heart: I am sitting on a shady, grassy slope, ranging down to a river from a house much, much larger than "the foundry," which then was the largest house in Eldorado—a beautiful house of two stories, with evergreens around it. I had never seen such evergreens. And there were lovely dandelions. I had never known such gay flowers. Their pollen got on my chin and nose when I smelled them. I was sitting there in the shade on that grassy slope, eating wild strawberries with a lovely little girl with dark hazel eyes, flaxen hair, and pink cheeks. I swear that I know I was flirting, untrue to Leila Heaton. And I liked it! I am sure of this picture because nearly fifty years later in Paris, right after the World War, I met a woman in one of the uniforms American girls and women wore there in the war. And when we fell to talking she said:

"Were you ever in Clyde, Ohio?"

And I said I was there as a little child.

She said: "Do you remember a little girl who lived next door to your Uncle Daniel?"

And I answered: "Did she have light brown eyes and yellow hair?"

The woman nodded.

I said: "Yes."

"Well," she said, "some way, God knows how, she has identified you as a little boy who visited there and played with her."

She was my first philandering conquest, and that before I was five. Lord, how deeply in our hearts God has planted that sweet poison.

They were a stern lot, those Whites—and in particular my Uncle Daniel. I remember he tapped on his glass when I talked too much at the table. He made me eat everything on my plate. His eyes followed me around the room, and I knew he thought I was going to break everything in the house. I wish I had known then what I knew nearly fifty years later, when one of the old cousins, in her doddering eighties, told me that all the family knew that Daniel "kept a woman" in Chicago.

About the time that I was first sipping the stolen waters of love in Ohio, I also learned of death. Of course I had seen death many times, though I do not remember it. Neighbors had died, old and young. But no one's death brought the realization of death to me. I seemed to have reasoned it out. Probably I asked questions. But it came over me with a profound shock that everyone must die, and I too; that we are in this life, and the only escape is death. And I was frightened. It was not the fear of heaven or hell. I cannot remember that hell's terms ever bothered me. My father was a freethinker out of a Congregational background. My mother was a Congregationalist out of a Catholic background. I was put into Sunday school as soon as I could toddle. But all I can remember of my first consciousness of death is lying in my bed in the dark night, amazed and frightened at death as the outward portal of life which may not be escaped. Death was a terror, a change from the animate to the inanimate, something that I could not explain and did not understand, and it set a horror in my heart which probably is deep in the race. Thus mankind first stood, baffled and afraid, before his dead. So much for death generic; now for death specific:

One day there in Ohio, when I was a little fellow, they took me to a neighbor's where an old, old man had died, and I stood with my mother looking at him. She went away for a moment and left me in the room with the body. I stood mute and all atremble in my heart when suddenly, without warning, the old jaw on the dead face unhinged, dropped, and the mouth opened. With an agonized scream I fled from the room, and so as a little child I knew and understood as much as any man has ever known of life's two great mysteries—life and death, joy and sorrow, the way we come and the way we go.

DISCUSSION AND INQUIRY

Conscious memory for William commenced at the age of 2, when he recalls himself happily gurgling as he was being fed in his father's arms. It is noteworthy that this earliest memory was of an oral experience that was accompanied by close physical contact with a significant and caring adult. William also tells of his vivid recollection of the birth of his younger brother and the bitter hate he felt at that time. What is the common denominator of all these earliest recollections? Why might these events be remembered while a myriad of others have fallen from consciousness?

Note that William remembers his brother's

birth, but recalls nothing of his death. He does, however, recall feelings that he had about death as he grew a bit older. He saw death as a terror, as final, and as a mystery. His experience with the dropping jaw of the corpse confirmed his feelings. When do children usually come to grips with the mystery and finality of death? What is the adult's role in helping them handle their feelings?

Young White felt that being born of older parents created a family setting that inevitably led to ...essarily true? Al... ...that childbearing ...in fewer physical ...ies, perhaps older ...own personal de... ...pond more freely ...have been true in ...tors in the White ...William calls his ...the selection by ...scussion on spoil-